Volume XI in the Beyers Naudé Centre Series on Public Theology

THE (IM)POSSIBILITY OF FORGIVENESS?

AN EMPIRICAL INTERCULTURAL BIBLE READING OF MATTHEW 18.15-35

DION FORSTER

Series Editor
Len Hansen

SUN MEDIA

The (im)possibility of forgiveness?
An empirical intercultural Bible reading of Matthew 18:15-35
Published by AFRICAN SUN MeDIA under the SUN MeDIA imprint.

www.africansunmedia.co.za
www.sun-e-shop.co.za
All rights reserved.

Copyright © 2017 Radboud University and AFRICAN SUN MeDIA.

First edition, September 2017

ISBN 978-1-928314-34-9
ISBN 978-1-928314-35-6 (e-book)
DOI: 10.18820/9781928314356

Set in 10/12 Palatino Linotype
Cover photograph by Joana Young
Typesetting by AFRICAN SUN MeDIA

SUN MeDIA is an imprint of AFRICAN SUN MeDIA. Academic and prescribed works are published under this imprint in print and electronic format. This publication May be ordered directly from www.sun-e-shop.co.za.

Printed and bound by AFRICAN SUN MeDIA, Ryneveld Street, Stellenbosch, 7600.

PEER REVIEW CONDUCTED BY

Prof. dr. Eddy van der Borght (Vrije Universiteit, Amsterdam, Netherlands)
Prof. dr. Maaike de Haardt (Radboud University, Nijmegen, Netherlands)
Prof. dr. dr. Kobus Kok (Evangelical Theological Faculty, Leuven, Belgium)
Prof. dr. dr. h.c. Leslie Francis (Warwick University, Coventry, UK)
Prof. dr. Piet Meiring (University of Pretoria, South Africa)

PUBLICATION ACKNOWLEDGEMENT

This book stems from Doctoral research that was conducted by the author at Radboud University under the supervision of Prof dr dr Jan van der Watt and Prof dr Christiaan Hermans. The author wishes to express his gratitude to Radboud University and his supervisors for their investment, guidance and support in the completion of this project. He is grateful for the permission to publish the research in this book. In addition the author wishes to thank the University of South Africa, In Luce Verbi and SAGE Press respectively, for their kind permission to edit and republish some sections of research that has previously appeared as articles or chapters in their respective publications, and are incorporated in this book:

- Forster, D.A. 2006. Validation of individual consciousness in strong artificial intelligence: an African theological contribution. PhD. University of South Africa, pp.164-214.
- Forster, D.A. 2010. African relational ontology, individual identity, and Christian theology An African theological contribution towards an integrated relational ontological identity. Theology. 113(874), pp.243–253.
- Forster, D.A. 2017. A public theological approach to the (im)possibility of forgiveness in Matthew 18:15-35: reading the text through the lens of integral theory. In die Skriflig/In Lux Verbi. 51(3):1–10.

EDITOR'S FOREWORD

According to its website, the Beyers Naudé Centre "focuses on issues in all spheres of society, working in an interdisciplinary way, listening to the voices of both scholarly work and as well as the narratives from so-called grassroots level, adhering to an ecumenical approach, working on an inter-religious basis and drinking in insights of secular voices as well." These foci are also reflected in the Beyers Naudé Series on Public Theology and this edition, the tenth in the series and written by the current director of the Centre, Dion Forster, does so in an exemplary way.

This publication reflects on forgiveness, a difficult and even a contested issue in contemporary South African society. Indeed, this may be the case in many contexts around the world where there is a history of one group of persons abusing another. Moreover, forgiveness is even more complex when race, economic class and religious conviction are added into the mix. Given such a context, Forster sets out to identify the conditions under which forgiveness could be considered possible. Or stated negatively, what might some of the social, political and religious convictions be that could make forgiveness impossible?

In answering the above question Forster engages the complexity of understandings of forgiveness in Matthew 18:15-35 within the context of an intercultural Bible reading process among Black and White South African Christians. He shows that concepts of forgiveness among South African Bible readers are diverse, containing nuanced, even conflicting, expressions and expectations. However, despite this complexity it is suggested that South Africans, and South Africa, could indeed benefit from a rigorous academic engagement with the theologically and culturally diverse understandings of forgiveness that emerge from reading Matthew 18.15-35 in an intercultural Bible reading setting. It is suggested that there are certain conditions under which persons from diverse political histories, cultural identities, racial identities and economic classes, can gain more integral, shared understandings of forgiveness. In this sense, at least, Forster suggests that a possibility for forgiveness may emerge.

As a public theological engagement with the politics of forgiveness in South Africa, this publication fits well in the Beyers Naudé Series on Public Theology. But why is such an interdisciplinary work in Biblical ethics, theological hermeneutics and empirical theology necessary?

First, in the racially, politically and economically divided context of the public of the South African Church, and public of South African society in general, it is helpful to gain academically verifiable insights into how Black (coloured) and White South Africans understand and conceptualise notions and processes of forgiveness. Thus, this book presents the findings of empirical qualitative research in intercultural Biblical hermeneutics. The analysis of the data shows not only what these groups believe, but what informs their beliefs. It is precisely these different theological convictions, which are very different and sometimes even in conflict with one another, that have made some think that forgiveness for the sins of apartheid in South Africa may not be possible.

Second, this book shows that there are certain conditions under which the racial, cultural, political and theological convictions of the two groups can shift from being a hindrance to transformation, to becoming a catalyst for positive change.

Considering the above, this book provides rigorous, textured, and credible theological insight into the complexity of differing understandings of forgiveness in Matthew 18:15-35 from the perspectives of so-called ordinary Bible readers of different cultures, who are members of the same Christian denomination - the Methodist Church of Southern Africa, Helderberg Circuit.

Three theories informed the research that is presented and discussed in this book. First, Ken Wilber's All Quadrants All Levels (AQAL) integral theory is used as a philosophical framework that provides language and structure to "plot" the theological understandings of forgiveness in the text, and in the reading of the text by the participants. Second, intergroup contact theory is used to identify the mechanisms and processes for positive intergroup contact that inform the intercultural Bible reading sessions. Third, the Biblical text is engaged in a scholarly exegetical process so as to avoid collapsing the thought world of the text into the contemporary context. This is a critical aspect of a credible engagement with the Biblical text. This process allows for the construction of a hermeneutic bridge to link aspects of the text to aspects of the interpretive insights of the contemporary readers engaged in this study.

As anticipated, the findings of the research process agreed with some aspects of the research hypotheses and varied from others. The findings of the post intervention research data and analysis shows that to a large extent (except for minor variations which are discussed in the text) the participants of the intercultural Bible reading intervention developed more integral understandings of forgiveness. This means that participants were far more open to accepting understandings of forgiveness that were not held within their in-group, but were more common among members of the out-group.

The primary conclusion Forster comes to is that more integral theological understandings of forgiveness are evidenced among the majority participants in this intercultural Bible reading process, which was conducted under the conditions of positive intergroup contact. Moreover, it is shown that one may give credible empirical content to, and explicate, the theological perspectives, and the hermeneutic informants, of readers of the Biblical text. This helps the Helderberg Circuit of the Methodist Church of Southern Africa where the research was done – and may serve as example for similar interventions by other South African Christian denominations – to understand what some of the barriers to shared understandings of forgiveness may be. Moreover, it allows for the design of intercultural Bible reading interventions under the conditions of positive intergroup contact. It may follow that, in other South African contexts, as the data shows that in this case, the participants in such an intervention may became more open to a more integral theological understanding of forgiveness with the "other".

Finally, this publication makes the following novel contributions to scholarly knowledge and the construction of theory: In New Testament studies the research contributes towards a number of new hermeneutic opportunities that arise from reading the Biblical text from a social identity complexity perspective (informed by Ken Wilber's integral AQAL theory). Moreover, in relation to intercultural Bible reading, the publication provides new insights into how persons who hold different socially informed views of forgiveness may encounter one another constructively under the conditions of positive intergroup contact. In terms of empirical cultural Biblical hermeneutics the book is the first of its kind to provide insights into how Black and White South African Christians understand the concepts and processes of forgiveness in relation to Matthew 18:15-35. The findings show that there is a logic behind the socially informed theological understandings of forgiveness that are expressed by the participants. This holds value not only for Biblical Studies, but also for Systematic Theology in general, and South African Public Theology in particular. Then, from a methodological point of view, the interdisciplinary nature of the theoretical approach that is employed by Forster will hopefully stimulate new avenues for scholarly theological study in relation to problems in practice.

We want to thank Dion Forster for entrusting this manuscript to us. We are delighted to include it in the Beyers Naudé Series as an example of not only rigorous public theological research, but research done in an interdisciplinary fashion and at a grassroots level as we strive to promote. As always we also want to thank Sun Press, the publisher of the series, for an end product we can be proud of.

Len Hansen
Editor: Beyers Naudé Series on Public Theology

DEDICATION

For my children, Courtney and Liam,
and for a more just future shared with all of South Africa's children

ACKNOWLEDGEMENTS

I would like to begin by expressing my sincerest gratitude to Prof Jan van der Watt. He has been a senior colleague and guide in my academic career for more than two decades. He has invested time, energy, and funding in my academic and personal development. His passion for the study of the New Testament is inspiring. I am truly grateful for the opportunity that he afforded me to undertake this study. His efforts to secure funding, to spend time with me at Radboud University in Nijmegen, and his encouragement and trust, have been invaluable in the completion of this project. Similarly, I would like to express my thanks to Prof Christiaan Hermans. He introduced me to Practice Oriented research and the value of qualitative empirical theological inquiry. I have learnt so much from him and value his scholarship and friendship immensely. I am also grateful to Dr Len Hansen, the editor for the Beyers Naudé Centre Series on Public Theology, for his guidance, meticulous care, and input in the publication of this book. It is a great honour and privilege to be able to publish this research with SUN Media as part of the aforementioned series. The Beyers Naudé Centre for Public Theology, and my colleagues in the Centre, do such important work in the various publics of society. Their commitment to justice, service and scholarship is a great motivation for my own work and research.

Radboud University was extremely generous in their support of this project. Over a period of 3 years I spent a number of months living in the Netherlands, reading in the library, and interacting with students and staff. I am truly grateful for this opportunity. I would also like to thank the African Doctoral Academy at Stellenbosch University for their funding that allowed me to be trained in the use of ATLAS. ti. I am deeply indebted to my colleagues and friends in the Faculty of Theology at Stellenbosch University: 'Uncle' Howard Ruiters for his listening ear and help with the manuscript. Mrs Wilma Riekert for her encouragement and practical help. Professors Robert Vosloo, Juliana Claassens, Marius Nel, Louis Jonker, Jeremy Punt, Xolile Simon, Ian Nell, Christo Thesnaar and Dirkie Smit, as well as Doctors Charlene van der Walt, Retief Muller, Len Hansen, Nadia Marais, Ntozake Cezula, Frederick Marais, Leon Venter (the Radboud cohort), and colleagues Helgard Pretorius, Cornelia De Milander and Jaco Botha. They each assisted in different ways (patiently listening, offering guidance, expertise, advice, reading and commenting etc.) I am also indebted to Doctor Carike Noeth, Professor Kurt April, Doctor Katherine Train, Neil Kramm, Marthie Momberg, Barnabé Msabah (ATLAST.ti), and Professor Jacobus (Kobus) Kok (social identity complexity theory).

I am also truly grateful to my family; my wife Megan and our children Courtney and Liam (to whom this work is dedicated). Very few spouses are patient and supportive enough to support someone through a PhD project (let alone two!) I am so grateful for the time, patience, advice, and sacrifice that they have put into this project. In truth, they deserve any credit it may warrant upon completion.

Finally, I am grateful to the Methodist Church of Southern Africa, and particularly the two participating congregations (Church Street Methodist Church and Coronation

Ave Methodist Church). Their courage to approach this challenging topic, and their witness to finding a way to live in forgiveness, is a gift to the Church and our society. I have learnt so much from this journey with them!

Dion A Forster
Beyers Naudé Centre for Public Theology
Department of Systematic Theology and Ecclesiology
Faculty of Theology, University of Stellenbosch

CONTENTS

LIST OF ABBREVIATIONS AND ACRONYMS

AQAL   All Quadrants All Levels
CAQDAS   Computer Assisted Qualitative Data Analysis Software
IJR   Institute for Justice and Reconciliation
LL   Lower Left
LR   Lower Right
MCSA   Methodist Church of Southern Africa
MSS   Manuscript (the actual form of the Greek word in the text)
NIV   New International Version
NRSV   New Revised Standard Version
RIS   Research Information Services
RTF   Rich Text Format
TRC   Truth and Reconciliation Commission
UBS GNT   United Bible Society Greek New Testament
UL   Upper Left
UR   Upper Right

LIST OF FIGURES AND TABLES

FIGURES

TABLES

1.1 Introduction and background to the study

Forgiving another for wrongdoing is a complex and difficult process. Theological understandings of forgiveness vary a great deal among Christians. This is particularly so when persons hold different understandings of the concept based on their readings of the Biblical text. This research will show that social identity, shaped by notions such as race, culture and theological beliefs, play a significant role in understandings of forgiveness.

Moreover, interpersonal socio-political factors such as the nature of the offence, whether reparation has been made (or attempted), the political identities of the parties involved, expectations and conditions for the self and for the other, also play a role in understandings of forgiveness. This research show that forgiveness engages aspects of personal identity, while at the same time operating within a web of social conditions that form varied hermeneutic perspectives. Within the South African social, political, economic and religious context forgiveness of the other (and even the self) is a contested issue. Some suggest that forgiveness is a necessary condition for moving forward to a better future for all South Africans (Thesnaar, 2008: 53–73, 2014: 1–8; Tutu, 2012: 47–48, 74, 218). Yet, some of the entrenched theological, social, racial, economic and political challenges that South Africa faces seem to suggest that forgiveness is almost impossible. The 2015 Institute for Justice and Reconciliation (IJR) report found the following:

> While most South Africans agree that the creation of a united, reconciled nation remains a worthy objective to pursue, the country remains afflicted by its historical divisions. The majority feels that race relations have either stayed the same or deteriorated since the country's political transition in 1994 and the bulk of respondents have noted income inequality as a major source of social division. Most believe that it is impossible to achieve a reconciled society for as long as those who were disadvantaged under apartheid remain poor within the 'new South Africa' (Hofmeyr & Govender, 2015: 1).

Recent events in South Africa, such as the #Feesmustfall protests against economic inequalities and economic injustice in higher education (Baloyi & Isaacs, 2015), the spate of racial slurs on social media (e.g., Penny Sparrow) (Makhulu, 2016: 260; Nhemachena, 2016: 411–416; Surmon, Juan & Reddy, 2016: 1–2), and the re-racialisation of society through identity politics (Mbembe, 2015), seem to support the IJR's findings.

South Africa faces significant challenges with regards to dealing with the 'sins' of its past and the complexity of our present life. How do persons understand forgiveness in such a context? What may forgiveness mean for Black or White South Africans? Is forgiveness in South Africa (im)possible[1]?

This project is predicated upon the notion that complexifying and texturing understandings of how individuals and groups from two racially and culturally diverse Christian communities in South Africa understand forgiveness in Matthew 18.15-35 can garner deeper insights into the theological intersections related to the (im)possibility of forgiveness between these two communities. This interdisciplinary study intersects the fields of Biblical studies and empirical theology by means of a thorough and rigorous public theological consideration[2] of the text as well as the social setting and identities of the participating readers of the text. The understandings of forgiveness in the text are explicated by means of an integral (AQAL) theoretical engagement. The possibility for shifts in theological understandings of forgiveness among the participants are considered in relation to a set of identified mechanisms for positive intergroup contact that are facilitated between the two groups of Biblical readers in an intercultural Bible reading process.

It will be shown in the presentation and analysis of the findings (cf., 6.4.1-6.4.3, 7.2.1) that predictions of the formulated hypothesis could not be falsified. To a large extent, the participants' hermeneutic understandings of forgiveness in the pre-intercultural engagement in-group Bible readings reflected aspects of their primary social identity. That is, the Black participants largely tended to understanding forgiveness to be a social process that required community harmony predicated on identifiable social, economic and relational changes. The White participants largely tended to understand forgiveness as a spiritual activity (between the individual and God) that was not predicated on social or communal processes of tangible change. The post intervention findings largely showed that after intercultural Bible reading sessions between the groups there were theological shifts that can be accounted for as more integral understandings of forgiveness. What this means is that the participants showed evidence of augmenting their hermeneutic views of forgiveness (in their readings of the text) in interaction with the views of the 'others' to some extent.

---

1   The use of (im)possible is deliberate. The notion is predicated on Jacques Derrida's use of im-possible in his lecture, *A Certain Impossible Possibility of Saying the Event* (Derrida, 2007: 441–461), and particularly Richard Kearney's discussion of this concept in relation to forgiveness in *Forgiveness as the limit: Impossible or possible* (Kearney, 2013: 305–320). The concept is discussed in greater detail at a later stage. What is of particular importance is the tension that the phrase creates between what is impossible, and so possible (i.e., the bracketing of the what makes the (im)possible, possible). As shall be shown, the impossibility of forgiveness (the fact that true forgiveness is not possible in an economic or practical sense in South Africa, is what makes true forgiveness, as an act of impossible grace (as seen in Matthew 18.15-35) both possible and necessary). How could one ever attach a price to the violence of apartheid? What possible compensation could truly account for the dehumanizing consequences of this social and political system?

2   An argument is made for an approach to the text that can be identified as a public theological approach by virtue of its ethical nature and interdisciplinary dialogical approach. This argument is present in chapter 4 of this manuscript and also in Forster, D.A. 2017. A public theological approach to the (im) possibility of forgiveness in Matthew 18.15-35: Reading the text through the lens of integral theory. *In die Skriflig/In Luce Verbi.* 51(3):1–10.

There is also some evidence in the findings of instances in which the hypothesis of the research was not upheld (this is discussed in 6.4.3 and 7.2.2). In summary, some participants in both groups did not hold hermeneutic views of forgiveness that were characteristic of their 'in-groups' in the pre-intercultural engagement data. Moreover, there were some participants in both groups who did not make the anticipated theological shifts to more integral views of forgiveness in their readings of the text after the intercultural Bible reading intervention had taken place.

Lastly, this project will show the importance of positive intergroup contact, facilitated through the introduction of the mechanisms that lower intergroup contact anxiety and can facilitate an increase in affective empathy for the other, and cognitive empathy in relation to the ideas of the other (cf., 6.4.5-6.4.6).

1.2 An introduction to the research problem

The research problem for the project is presented and considered in some depth and detail in section 5.2. A thorough engagement with the research problem requires some insight into the Biblical and theoretical aspects that inform the particular understanding of the research problem within the limited scope of this research project, and the research design which is used to engage it. However, at this juncture the context and concerns that give rise to this research project will be outlined in sufficient detail to justify why it is a theological problem that is worth investigating.

South Africa has a very high percentage of self-identified Christians, yet it remains a deeply divided nation. Black and White South African Christians hold very different views on the concepts and processes of forgiveness as the findings in this research project (cf., sections 7.2.1-7.2.3), and the literature show[3]. Vosloo notes that the unfinished business of forgiveness in South Africa reiterates that, "forgiveness and related concepts regarding engagement with the past continue to be influential, albeit also highly contested, in public discourse" (Vosloo, 2015: 363). This is particularly true for the public life and witness of Christian communities and Christian individuals in South Africa.

One significant problem that has been identified, and is evidenced in the findings of this research, is that these un-reconciled persons seldom have contact with each other because legacy of the apartheid system which separated persons racially, according to economic class, and geographically (Hofmeyr & Govender, 2015: 1). The result is that, as intergroup contact theory[4] suggests, each group's own social views and religious beliefs (in-group) become entrenched and the views and beliefs of the 'other' (out-group) are rejected or ignored because they are not understood or engaged across these separating boundaries (Brewer & Kramer, 1985: 219–223; Duncan, 2003: 2, 5; Bornman, 2011: 411–414).

---

3   The following sources offer some insights into the complexity of understandings of forgiveness among Black and White South Africans, (Chapman & Spong, 2003: 169; Villa-Vicencio & du Toit, 2006: 75–87; Byrne, 2007; Thesnaar, 2008, 2013: 1–15; Gobodo-Madikizela & Merwe, 2009: vii–xi; Krog, 2010; Elkington, 2011: 5–35, 135–155; Daye, 2012: 8–18; Tutu, 2012: 10–36, 47–60, 92–124; Vosloo, 2012, 2015: 360–378).

4   Intergroup contact theory is a well-developed and credible academic field. It is one of the two primary theories used in this research. It will be presented and considered in detail in chapter 3 of this manuscript.

In at least one sense this makes forgiveness impossible – not only is it impossible for persons to forgive one another since they have no proximate or authentic social engagement, forgiveness is also a theological impossibility because of deeply held and entrenched faith convictions about the nature and processes of forgiveness (Kearney, 2007: 151–152). In other words, there is both a hermeneutic and a social barrier to forgiveness. Paul Ricoeur suggests that what is needed is an act of translation[5] that can bridge the differences in language and the very nature of the difference between the self and the other (Ricoeur & Brennan, 1995: 7)[6]. Kearney comments on the necessity for such acts of translation and forgiveness that it,

> ... is only when we translate our own wounds in the language of strangers and retranslate the wounds of strangers into our own language that healing and reconciliation can take place. (Ricoeur, 2007: xx)

As this research project shows, it is in the shared encounter of persons in the intercultural Bible reading space, that some persons will share aspects of our language and experience, while others will differ from ours. This shared encounter of persons can help participants to understand further aspects of the journey of forgiveness. While this project focusses primarily on understandings of forgiveness, the findings do offer some possibilities for contributing towards the broader objective. As such de Gruchy notes that the process of forgiveness, and even reconciliation, "is a work in progress, a dynamic set of processes into which we are drawn and in which we participate" (De Gruchy, 2002: 28). The notion of participation in the process of forgiveness, from the perspective of developing broader and deeper understandings of what it may mean through encounter, is thus important. It shows just how much we need one another, the 'self' and the 'other', to discover what may make forgiveness possible. He goes on to say that forgiveness, in this shared relational sense, is more than a mere event or a goal for which we aim. Rather, it is a varied and multifaceted discovery that grows out of our togetherness. In the processes of encounter the opportunity for translation and discovery of new meaning among the participants becomes possible. The shared journey may even lead to the creation of new understandings of forgiveness that unsettle, or transcend, the previously held notions of the participants as they discover a new and possible future.

From the perspective of a public theological engagement of communities with the Biblical text Koopman notes:

> Although the Scriptures do not give blueprints for our societal problems, our ideologies are corrected by the light the biblical principles provide. In South Africa, where the race factor has also determined how people understand the Bible, it is of utmost importance that people listen jointed to the Word to discover God's will for us today. This joint listening to

---

5   "Translation can be understood here in both a specific and a general sense. In the specific sense – the one in common contemporary usage – it signals the work of translating the meanings of one particular language into another. In the more generic sense, it indicates the everyday act of speaking as a way not only of translating oneself (inner to outer, private to public, unconscious to conscious, etc.) but also more explicitly of translating oneself to others." (Ricoeur, 2007: xiv–xv).

6   "The identity of a group, culture, people or nation, is not that of an immutable substance, nor that of a fixed structure, rather, of a recounted story" (Ricoeur & Brennan, 1995: 7).

the Word wills us to develop a common story which belongs to all of us. This common heritage corrects our racial ideologies, but also liberates, encourages and energizes us to work for a new society which reflects something of the biblical ideals. (Koopman, 1998: 165).

Koopman is thus suggesting that there is an interplay between what he calls "biblical ideals" and racially and social informed understandings of the Bible. This would seem to be a hermeneutic circle. The Bible informs identity through its "ideals", and identity informs how the Bible is read and understood. This project aims to engage both 'parties' in the hermeneutic process – the Biblical text, and the readers of the Biblical text.

One of the more interesting parts of this research project is the empirical intercultural Biblical hermeneutic engagement with the Bible readers. The project involves working with two racially and culturally diverse communities to map their understandings of forgiveness in relation to a scholarly an engagement with Matthew's understanding of forgiveness as found in Matthew 18.15-35. The scholarly, exegetical, engagement with the Biblical text is presented in chapter 4 of this manuscript, and the various perspectives of the readers of the text are discussed and analysed in chapter 6.

That being said, it must be noted that the Christian scriptures contain many different perspectives on forgiveness. There is no single concept of forgiveness in the Bible. This study is limited to a New Testament text. Even though forgiveness is presented as an important concept in the New Testament, its presentation and understanding is by no means uniform or singular as recent studies in the field have shown (Nel, 2002; Konstan, 2010; c.f., Hägerland, 2011; Mbabazi, 2013). In the Gospels, in particular, the concept of forgiveness is frequently viewed as both a teaching and a practice. Moreover, there are many texts that deal with the notion of forgiveness from a variety of perspectives (theological, social, restitutional, gracious, developmental) – the most recent and extensive project on forgiveness in the New Testament is *Jesus and the Forgiveness of Sins*, (Hägerland, 2011). Within Matthew studies the most complete recent studies on forgiveness are by Nel and Mbabazi (Nel, 2002; Mbabazi, 2013; Nel, 2013a, 2014a, 2015)[7]. Naturally this study has attempted to focus on the aspects that are more relevant and necessary in relation to the research problem.

Because of such theological, social, and historical complexity, it is argued that in order to best gain a textured insight into forgiveness from a Biblical text, and certain readers' understandings of the text, an integral approach to hermeneutic meaning construction is necessary.

I have previously argued that in the construction of social identity and the construction of concepts of meaning we should guard against falling into the trap of what has become known as "Descartes' error" (cf., Forster, 2006: 119–140; Damasio, 2008: 3–19, 34–51, 245–252). What I mean by this is that we must be careful that we do not make the mistake of inadvertently believing that the mind is "free to engage in its own operations (quite apart from the body and from other minds)", which has

---

7   The topic of forgiveness in the Biblical text is extremely broad and extensive. For a very helpful scholarly overview of this area please see, Gowan, *The Bible on Forgiveness* (Gowan, 2010) and Nel, *Vergifnis en versoening in die evangelie volgens Matteus* (Nel, 2002).

the result of countering a non-negotiable emphasis on embodiment (Green, 2006: 4)[8]. Bodily, social, engagement is crucial for hermeneutic insight into the complexities of forgiveness in the South African context.

Intellect and affect are not separable; neither are mind and behaviour. This concept is particularly important when one is dealing with forgiveness which cannot be narrowed merely as a concept or idea in the mind of individuals, it has inescapable ramifications for social systems, as both the reading of the text in chapter 4 and the findings of the readers' interpretations in chapter 6 will show. Moreover, forgiveness is not a moment, rather it is a process of increasing embodiment over time, even it if is understood as a series of event-inaugurated shifts. Religious experience, and the language by which we articulate and perpetuate it, are embodied in a cognitive and social framework.

The cognitive neuroscientist Joseph Le Doux colloquially states that, "People don't come preassembled, but are glued together by life" (in Green, 2006: 5). His point is that formative events, experiences, moments of learning, understanding and awakening are not merely encoded in the synapses of the central nervous system. Rather, so much of what we know and learn to do is shaped by learning that takes places with others in community. This is both a conscious and an unconscious social process of formation. Throughout our lives our engagement with concepts, persons, and social systems shape who we are, what we believe and what we do.

This has two important consequences (among others):

First, who we are can never be divided into isolated or separated parts. Forgiveness is not merely an aspect of theological knowledge, or personal realisation, it is a process of social transformation that touches on multiple aspects of our individual and collective life. Simply stated, this research shows there can be no transformation that is not fully embodied in both a personal and a social sense.

Second, if the systems that shape how we think, what we feel, believe, and inform and shape how we behave, are constantly being sculpted in the context of our social engagement, then we can only truly speak of forgiveness and transformation in relational terms. As Green says, "Our autobiographical selves are formed within a nest of relationships, a community" (Green, 2006: 7). Jim Grisby and David Stevens further support this view when they write:

> Personality is shaped by the interaction of constitutional processes and the experiences of individuals in unique environments. In other words, we are, at least in part, who we learn to be. As a result of these experiences, learning drives the acquisition and refinement of a wide repertoire of enduring perceptions, attitudes, thoughts, and behaviors. The relative permanence of learning and memory reflects the operation of processes that modify the microscopic structure of the brain, yielding changes in different aspects of functioning over time as a result of the individual's interactions with the world. (Grigsby & Stevens, 2000: 39).

---

8   In summary, knowledge (or emergence into knowing), "is not just epistemic (stemming from observable cultural, or even biological systems in relation to the individual) it is also phenomenological (it is a reflective and descriptive study of such systems or processes as understood by the conscious individual)" (Forster, 2006: 119).

In the light of this proposition, it can be concluded that embodied human life is a cultural phenomenon, a neuro-hermeneutic system, which locates, and makes sense of, current realities by drawing on experiences in the past and shaping the future.

The French philosopher, Paul Ricoeur, seems to concur with this concept in his critical work *Memory, history and forgetting*[9]. His work reminds Christian theologians, including Biblical scholars, to be careful of creating a simplistic soteriological short-circuit between remembering and forgiving. He does so by calling to mind the eschatological horizon of memory (Ricoeur, 2009: x). Ricoeur emphasises the importance of understanding forgiveness as a process, rather than just a moment (or belief), when he writes:

> Forgiveness, if it has a meaning and if it exists, constitutes the joint horizon of memory, history and forgetting. The horizon... puts the stamp of incompleteness on the whole enterprise... what is at stake is to project a sort of eschatology of memory, and as its consequence, of history and forgetting. (Ricoeur, 2009: 593, 595).

Ricoeur connects forgiveness to both a cognitive and a social process that leads to forgiveness being embodied, or realised, in a "eschatology of memory". Perhaps, it could be termed a possibility for forgiveness?

He discusses these stages of the embodied journey of forgiveness under the headings of remembering (memory), forgetting, guilt, being together (*Mitsein*) and historical voilences (Ricoeur, 2009: 6–10).

The important point to recognise for the work of this research is that forgiveness is a complex and nuanced theological and social process and concept. This is a theological problem that requires patience – the patience of uncomfortable presence to history, the patience of uncomfortable engagement between the self and the other, and even the patience of discovering the disconnect between the "biblical ideal" and personal and social reality of an un-reconciled South Africa (Koopman, 1998: 165).

Indeed, to state it differently, the problem necessitates a willingness to try to understand that forgiveness goes beyond mere mental constructs, or the complex, yet social incomplete, and historically distant understanding of the concepts communicated in the text. The problem is more than just what is conceptualised in the mind of the individual, or in the beliefs and values of a community. Rather, as pointed out in the famous debate on the universality of hermeneutics between Gadamer and Habermas (Negru, 2007: 113–119), there will always be a difference between what the individual reader / scholar constructs in his or her mind and what the social world constructs as a form of historical reality.

This is why it is argued that there is a need for drawing on a wider set of tools and approaches to gain varied and diverse perspectives, that will inform our Biblical understanding of the concept and process of forgiveness and forgiving as it is read, and understood, and acted upon, from the Biblical text.

It is into this complex hermeneutic, social and contextual reality that this research enters.

---

9   See, (Ricoeur, 2009). *Memory, History, Forgetting.* (translated by Blamey, K and Pellauer, D). Chicago: University of Chicago Press.

Thus, an aim of this project is to understand the theological and hermeneutic development of concepts of forgiveness in two diverse South African Christian communities. In addition to this, the research will investigate how positive intergroup contact can foster integral changes in understanding concepts and processes of forgiveness between two racially and culturally distinct South African Christian communities.

1.3 Hypothesis and assumptions

The overarching hypothesis that will shape this study is that reading Matthew 18.15-35 with 'the other' under the carefully facilitated conditions of intergroup contact theory allows participants to develop broader and deeper understandings of the concepts and processes of forgiveness (these are characterized as integral understandings of forgiveness).

1.3.1 The Biblical text

In chapter 4.8 of this study we shall see that there are several different, and hermeneutically complex, understandings of forgiveness in Matthew 18.15-35. Amongst others, it is possible to understand that forgiveness has some individual (personal) aspects as well as some collective (social) aspects. Similarly, forgiveness in this text can also be understood in spiritual terms (in relation to God and God's will for persons and communities), but also in social, economic and structural terms (such as justice, restitution, and economic recompense).

The hypothesis that is developed and engaged in this study is that participants from Group A, who are from a predominantly Coloured (Black) middle class Christian community (cf., 5.7.3), would have a hermeneutic understanding of forgiveness in Matthew 18.15-35 that reflected their social and cultural identity. By this it is understood that their hermeneutic perspective on forgiveness in the text would be understood in terms of social and structural harmony within the community (i.e., true forgiveness has tangible elements to it, such as just social systems that are practised and experienced by all members of the community – the rich and the poor). This is generically termed as a political understanding of forgiveness (i.e., the use of 'polis' in this context relates to the Greek term that denotes the structuring of the community). In addition to this it is hypothesised that members of this community would understand that forgiveness is also a communal matter, and not only between the individual and God. Rather, for God to offer forgiveness, the relationships within the community (interpersonal relationships) would need to be restored, or that there should at least be an attempt at such restoration among members of the community.

In addition, it is hypothesised that Group B (cf., 5.7.3), who are from a predominantly White, Westernised, upper middle class Christian community, would have a hermeneutic understanding of forgiveness in this text that is largely reflective of their social and cultural identity – namely, they would view forgiveness in largely individual and spiritual terms. By this is meant, that they would interpret forgiveness in relation to Matthew 18.15-35 to be primarily a matter of spiritual concern (the forgiveness of sin by God). Moreover, forgiveness is largely understood as a matter of individual concern (the individual has a responsibility to be right with God in her or his spiritual relationship).

1.3.2 Intercultural Biblical Hermeneutics

As alluded to in the section above, it is hypothesised that members of the respective communities (Group A and Group B) will approach the Biblical text from a hermeneutic perspective that is consistent with their individual and social identity. Thus, it can be said that the participants will display a culturally informed Biblical hermeneutic. This being the case, the study further postulates that when the participants engage in Biblical interpretation in an intercultural Biblical setting that they will undergo some hermeneutic shifts. The new intercultural setting will lead to a broader intercultural Bible hermeneutic perspective that will alter their theological understandings of forgiveness.

1.3.3 Intergroup contact

The intercultural shift, discussed in the previous section, is facilitated by means of positive intergroup contact (cf., section 3.3). In other words, mere contact between the participants from two different homogenous cultural groups is not sufficient to facilitate a positive integral shift in hermeneutic and theological understandings of forgiveness in Matthew 18.15-35. Negative intergroup contact could lead to an increase in anxiety between the in-group and out-group participants (from both group perspectives). Thus, rather than allowing for a positive, more integrated and culturally diverse Biblical hermeneutic, it could lead to a closed, more entrenched, or more strongly held in-group perspective on the interpretation of forgiveness in the text.

Thus, the hypothesis is that if the intercultural Biblical reading process takes place under conditions in which the mechanisms for positive intergroup contact are introduced with care, the participants will experience a decrease in anxiety and an increase in affective empathy and cognitive empathy, that could facilitate the conditions under which participants are willing re-evaluate their own hermeneutic perspectives of forgiveness in the light of the perspectives of members from the other group that is in conflict with other out-group perspectives.

1.4 Research objectives

The primary reason for conducting this research project was to produce rigorous, textured and credible information on the identified problem of differing understandings (and the hermeneutic reasons behind such understandings), of forgiveness when a Black and a White Methodist community read Matthew 18.15-35. Stated simply, this project aimed to extrapolate and present aspects of the hermeneutic complexity of intercultural Bible reading on forgiveness in this racially divided Church context. Thus, the study sought to:

A. Provide textured theological insights into the hermeneutic complexities, and differences in hermeneutic perspectives, on forgiveness in Matthew 18.15-35 among two racially and culturally diverse groups readers of the text.

B. Gain understanding into the ways in which the social moderators and mediators of positive intergroup contact constructively facilitate the conditions for integral understandings of forgiveness to develop among the intercultural Bible reading participants.

The desired outcome of this project is thus to engage in a research process that would yield theological information for the problem owner (the Methodist Church of Southern Africa, Helderberg Circuit) that could help them to gain a deeper understanding of the complexity of intercultural Biblical hermeneutics in relation to forgiveness in Matthew 18.15-35.

1.5 Research questions

Having introduced the problem that led to this research project, and the objectives that the research aimed to achieve, it is important to consider the primary and secondary questions that shaped the research project.

1. To what extent do theological understandings of forgiveness differ among Christians of different race groups?

2. To what extent have theological understandings of forgiveness among Christians of different race groups changed in a more integrative manner after an intercultural bible reading of Matthew 18.15-35?

3. To what extent is the change in theological understandings of forgiveness among Christians of different races (Group A and Group B) stimulated by the mediators and moderators of the intercultural Bible reading practices?

To do this the research also engaged the following:

1. What theoretical framework can be used to understand and explain the complexity of individual and social identity in relation to concepts of forgiveness in an intercultural Bible reading process?

2. How do the social moderators and mediators of intergroup contact theory help to facilitate positive intergroup contact that may lead to an integral understanding of forgiveness among racially diverse Christian groupings reading Matthew 18.15-35 in an intercultural Bible reading process?

3. What is an integral understanding of forgiveness based on a careful Biblical scholarly AQAL[10] reading of Matthew 18.15-35?

4. How do Christians of different races understand forgiveness when reading Matthew 18.15-35?

5. In what ways does intercultural Bible reading under the facilitated conditions of positive intergroup contact contribute towards a more integral understanding of forgiveness in Matthew 18.15-35?

1.6 Methodology

This research project is designed as a practice oriented research intervention that engages two communities on the subject of empirical intercultural Biblical hermeneutics. The details of each of these aspects, namely practice oriented research design are presented in detail in section 5.6-5.7.

---

10 All Quadrant All Level (AQAL) theory is used to understand the theological content of the participants' understandings of the concepts and processes related to forgiveness. AQAL theory is presented and discussed in detail in chapter 2 of this study.

A practice oriented research method was chosen for this Biblical studies research project since:

A. The research problem is a problem in practice. There is a problem owner for the problem addressed in this research (the Methodist Church of Southern Africa, Helderberg Circuit). So, a research method was selected and adapted that could offer insight and new understandings of the problem and possible ways of engaging the problem that would be useful in both the "public" of the theological academy and to the problem owner, in the "public" of the church[11].

B. The problem identified in this research project can be related to a much broader theological and contextual discourse. However, the particular problem that this research addresses has a limited scope. Hence it is framed as a limited scope practice oriented research project. It involves two communities who have sanction from their authorizing institutions to participate in a process of intercultural Bible reading to gain deeper insights into how such a process impacts hermeneutic understandings of forgiveness in relation to Matthew 18.15-35.

C. In order to achieve the research objectives of the project it was necessary to design a research intervention that would solicit empirical data from the participants that represent the two communities. It was also necessary to establish protocols for the validity of the gathering and analysing of the data, and to facilitate a process in which the data can be used to engage the three primary theoretical informants of the study (namely, the Biblical text – Matthew 18.15-25; Ken Wilber's AQAL integral theory – used to form qualitative descriptions of the theological understandings of forgiveness among participants; Positive intergroup contact theory – which informed the design of the research intervention that took the form of intercultural Bible reading meetings).

After extensive investigation, consultation, and reflection, it was decided that a qualitative study designed as a practice oriented research project would be best suited to engaging the research problem and addressing the objectives of the research. This process can be described as an empirical intercultural Biblical hermeneutic research project. For specific arguments for the choice of each of the constituent elements of the research design, as well as the ways in which they were used in the project, please refer to sections 5.6-5.7.

In addition to the above, some attention must be given to the methodological approaches adopted in relation to the Biblical text in chapter 4. The choice was made to approach the text by focussing especially on the social aspects. The choice for these methods is presented, and argued, in chapter 3. The researcher felt that it was important to pay careful attention to the hermeneutic distance between the Biblical

---

11   Tracy suggests that there are at least three 'publics' in which theologians can, and might, make a contribution. These are the public of the Church, the public of the academy and the public of society in general (Tracy, 1975: 287–291, 2014: 330–334; Forster, 2017: 1–3). It is in this sense that a public theological approach to the Biblical text and readers of the text is inter-disciplinary and even transdisciplinary in approach. It seeks some measure of theological bilingualism – namely, the conducting of credible, rigorous and critical theological engagement (for the public of the theological academy) that can be translated into the public of the Church or the public of society in general.

text with its historical, contextual and social uniqueness, and not to collapse these into the contemporary problem under investigation in this research project. That being said, the text does have a great deal to offer the contemporary concerns of this study, if it is treated in a careful, scholarly, manner. The text itself functioned as a "reflective surface" against which the intercultural Biblical hermeneutics of the participants was extrapolated (cf., Van der Walt, 2010, chaps 3, 7, 2014: 2–3).

1.7 The significance of the study

Forgiveness is a crucial issue in contemporary South Africa. As has been pointed out above, this research project wishes to address a concrete concern in South African society – namely a lack of forgiveness and community harmony within the Church. This is an actual situation that exists between two communities of a single denomination in one town. These communities were separated through racial prejudice – the Church Street Methodist Church and the Coronation Ave Methodist Church (please see 5.7.2 for a more detailed historical narrative of these events). The reality of these two Churches that remain un-reconciled, is a grave indictment on the witness and work of the Christian Church (please see 6.4 for some examples of how the participants experienced this reality in the intercultural Bible reading interaction)[12]. The reality of enmity and un-forgiveness that exists between Christians of diverse racial, social and economic contexts in South Africa (and elsewhere in the world) is not in keeping with the true nature of Christian community, it not only harms the Church's work and witness, it also dishonours God.

South Africa has a complex and painful social and political history that has impacted on just about every aspect of the nation's collective and individual psyche and social structure[13]. The reality is that the result of centuries of racial segregation, economic

---

12   Religious identity is a complicated, and often contested, social, psychological and theological notion. It is more apt to speak of religious identities in relation to how persons hold and express their identity in relation to varied social and theological convictions. However, it is also crucial to keep in mind that the Christian community should bear some characteristics in common (what some may call virtues or values of Christ and the Christian faith). For a very helpful and critical discussion of the complexity of faith and social identity in the Christian faith please see, (van der Borght, 2008, 2010). For a recent discussion on the complexity of the witness of the Church in relation to justice and racial reconciliation in South Africa please also see, *Justice and the Missional Framework Document of the Dutch Reformed Church*, (Botha & Forster, 2017: 1–9).

13   A significant attempt was made to engage this painful complexity in the establishment and processes of the Truth and Reconciliation Commission (TRC). The TRC sought to create a space, and opportunity, for South Africans to tell of the atrocities of apartheid, in a safe environment where victims of apartheid (or their relatives) could engage with the perpetrators of abuse. The intention was to facilitate a measure of reconciliation. For a powerful narrative of the establishment, work, and outcomes of the TRC please see, *Chronicle of the Truth and Reconciliation Commission: A Journey through the Past and Present into the Future of South Africa*. In particular, I found the following narrative of forgiveness between two Christian ministers deeply moving, "[a]t the cross of Christ the impossible became true, two ministers could experience that the things that bound us together were infinitely more than those that kept us apart" (Meiring, 2014: 90). It speaks to the hypothesis of this project, namely, that forgiveness becomes possible when persons encounter one another under safe conditions in which they experience one another's humanity. This is an aspect of grace that should be common among Christians.

subjugation and even religious abuse has led to a fractured and broken Church. South Africans who share a common faith, which is predicated on the concept of unmerited forgiveness, find it very difficult to live with one another in harmony. The South African Church remains largely segregated along racial, ethnic and economic lines (cf., van der Borght, 2009; Hofmeyr & Govender, 2015). This is a problematic situation as van der Borght notes with reference to the findings of the Institute for Justice and Reconciliation (IJR)[14],

> ...what these data and analyses confirm is that race goes far beyond perception and that racial thought is still deeply imbedded in South African society. It continues to influence people's lives, and the struggle to bend racial inequality and exclusion is still long. Indeed, racial reconciliation is unfinished business in South Africa, and it might be for a long time to come. (van der Borght, 2009: 9).

The witness and mission of the Church, as well as its worship and service, are tainted and weakened as a result (Botha & Forster, 2017: 1–9). This study provides a carefully constructed engagement with these communities of faith that can facilitate the a deeper and more nuanced understanding of the complexity of forgiveness, and perhaps even facilitate some possibilities for more integral understandings of forgiveness to emerge.

However, the contribution that this research project aims to make is limited. It is envisioned that this empirical hermeneutic Biblical study will yield knowledge in at least two primary academic fields (with some contribution towards one other field). The two primary fields are that of intercultural Biblical hermeneutics of the New Testament (cf., 5.5.1-5.5.2) and positive intergroup contact theory in relation to cultural identity and understanding of forgiveness (cf., 3.3, 6.4.4). Thus, the research makes the following novel contributions to scholarly knowledge and the construction of theory: In New Testament studies the research contributes towards a number of new hermeneutic opportunities that arise from reading the Biblical text from a social identity complexity perspective (informed by Ken Wilber's integral AQAL theory). Moreover, in relation to intercultural Bible reading, the project provides new insights into how persons who hold different socially informed views of forgiveness may encounter one another constructively under the conditions of positive intergroup contact. In terms of empirical cultural Biblical hermeneutics this study is the first of its kind to provide insights into how Black and White South African Christians understand the concepts and processes of forgiveness in relation to Matthew 18.15-35. The findings show that there is a logic behind the socially informed theological understandings of forgiveness that are expressed by the participants. Hence, this holds value not only for Biblical Studies, but also for Systematic Theology in

---

This project shows that there is work to be done at the local congregational, communal, and individual levels, for forgiveness and reconciliation to be made possible in South Africa. For an academic engagement with the TRC please see, (Meiring, 1999: 241–244, 2002: 719–735).

14 Van der Borght cites the findings of the 2008 IJR report, however, the findings of that report are largely upheld in the 2015 report cited earlier in this chapter. Please refer to van der Borght's address for a detailed and theologically textured analysis of the complexity of racial segregation in the contemporary South African church (c.f., van der Borght, 2009).

general, and South African Public Theology in particular. From a methodological point of view, the interdisciplinarity of the theoretical approach that is employed in this research stimulates new avenues for scholarly theological study in relation to problems in practice.

The findings of the research do show a number of integral shifts in understandings of forgiveness among the participants. However, as will be shown, further research will be necessary to extrapolate those findings and develop them for greater value to both the academy and the church.

1.8 Limitations of the study

While it is suggested that this study has some contribution to offer to the academic discourse and the church as problem owner, it must also be noted that there are some important limitations to this study.

First, this study is limited by the fact that it is a limited scope practice oriented research project on intercultural Biblical hermeneutics. As discussed in 5.6 the limitations of a sampled practice oriented research approach entail that the findings of this study are not normative or conclusive in a context that is broader than the constituent variables of this case. Moreover, as will be seen in presentation and analysis of the findings from the datasets, only illustrative examples from the data are presented for analysis. Naturally it is necessary to make choices about what is chosen to illustrate either support or disapproval of the hypothesis of the study. The full datasets could be worked through in later research to extract different information or reach other conclusions.

Second, because of the interdisciplinary nature of the project, great care was taken to limit the research instruments and analytical tools identified and used in the research design and research process, to the three theoretical informants (AQAL integral as discussed in chapter 2, intergroup contact theory as in chapter 3, and the exegetical engagement with the central Biblical text discussed in chapter 4). Naturally, there are many other possible and equally credible alternatives for engaging this text, and similar social hermeneutic issues, as those considered in this project. This project has a specific design, and it is hoped that the findings are reasonable and justifiable within the parameters of the design. Great care needs to be taken not to overstate the findings or the consequences of the findings as a result.

Third, it is also possible that the study may have been able to offer value in other fields or disciplines related to the project as a whole, or aspects of the project. This study was however, limited to attempting to contribute in two primary areas, namely that of empirical intercultural Biblical hermeneutics, and notions of the 'possibility' of forgiveness particularly as it is related to intergroup contact theory.

In this sense the research offers a modest contribution. It is hoped, that the approach used in the study, and the findings of the research, will offer some opportunities for engagement and future, or other possible, research (these possibilities are considered in the conclusion of the study, cf., 7.4.1-7.4.2).

1.9 Outline of the chapters

The presentation of this study comprises 7 chapters. The study is shaped in such a way that the theory and practice streams of the research are presented in a sequence that gives meaning to the research design and contributes towards the achievement of the objectives of the study.

- **Chapter 1** – Introduction

This chapter introduces the topic of the study. It gives an overview of the topic itself and seeks to offer some initial insights into the research problem. The complexity of intercultural Biblical hermeneutics, within the context of two South African Methodist communities reading Matthew 18.15-35 is thus considered and pertinent aspects that predicate the study are highlighted. A case is presented to explain why this particular topic should be addressed in the manner in which this study engages it. This chapter serves as a conceptual roadmap for the study, showing where it began, pointing towards where it ends, and highlighting some of the steps followed in-between.

- **Chapter 2** – Ken Wilber's Integral AQAL theory

A theoretical framework was sought to give structure and linguistic coherence to the mapping of the theological concepts of forgiveness in the exegesis of Matthew 18.15-35 and in the various group readings, over the period of the research process. The theory that was chosen to fulfil this task is Ken Wilber's integral AQAL theory. Ken Wilber is well regarded as a philosopher of contemporary social identity theory. His work is widely cited and used in this field (Esbjörn-Hargens 2009:33). Naturally, his work has its critics (c.f., Schneider, 1987: 196–216, 1989: 470–481, 2012: 120–123). Notwithstanding such critique, there is a sufficient scholarly acceptance of his contribution to utilise it in the manner proposed within this study. Moreover, the researcher was cognisant that some of the deficiencies of Wilber's model needed to be engaged and supplemented with the insights of other scholars and scholarly contributions. This chapter presents AQAL theory in detail since the framework and language it provides helps to lend logical coherence to the discussion of complex social identity in the chapters that follow. It presents Wilber's model with the design of this study in mind – namely to consider the complex ways in which individual and social identities emerge, and how meaning is constructed in subjective, objective and intersubjective ways. The outcome of this chapter is the provision of a theoretical framework that serves as a structure used in the rest of the project to trace and explain understandings of forgiveness in the Biblical text (Matthew 18.15-35), and in readings of the text by the participants.

- **Chapter 3** – Intergroup contact theory

The next important theoretical component of the study is positive intergroup contact theory. Since this study deals with the complex intersection of social identity (in the Biblical text[15] and among the readers of the text) a theory in social psychology was identified that could facilitate a positive intercultural Bible reading process. This chapter builds on the discussion of chapter 2, in which the complexity of subjective,

---

15   See Kobus (Jacobus) Kok's ground-breaking work in Social Identity Complexity Theory and the Biblical text (Kok, 2012, 2014a,b; Kok & Dunne, 2014; Kok, 2015). This body of research is considered and engaged in sections 3.4.4 and 3.4.5 of this study, as well as 4.8.

objective and intersubjective identity is presented in relation to how persons make meaning of social contexts and texts. One of the challenges with intercultural Bible reading is that participants are frequently unaware of their own hermeneutic biases, and their unengaged prejudices of others and their perspectives. This chapter shows that mere contact between persons of different race groups is not enough to engage such prejudice – what is required is positive intergroup contact (Dixon, Durrheim & Tredoux, 2005: 699–700; Levine & Hogg, 2009: 468–469). The conditions for positive intergroup contact are presented in detail and related to important aspects of this research such as race and religion. These elements informed the overall design of the research intervention, the social identity reading of the text, and the social identity analysis of the intercultural Bible reading meetings. The contribution of this chapter to the study is that it provides a number of positive intergroup contact mechanisms that were introduced in the intercultural Bible reading intervention to lessen anxiety and facilitate the increase of affective empathy and cognitive empathy among the participants.

- **Chapter 4** – An exegetical engagement with Matthew 18.15-35

This is a study in Biblical hermeneutics. Hence, it was imperative that an argument is made for the Biblical text that would be used in the research process – this chosen text is Matthew 18.15-35. Once the case is presented for why this text was suited to a project of this nature (i.e., intercultural Biblical hermeneutics on forgiveness in South Africa), a thorough and technical academic exegesis was undertaken of the text in which particular attention was paid to the social aspects. As this chapter argues, such approaches were suited to the research design since it was necessary to see in what ways the text was intended to function within its cultural and historical and social setting. It is crucial that the conceptual and theological worldview of the Matthean community is not collapsed into the contemporary concerns of Southern African Methodists. Aspects of the previous two theories were used as theoretical lenses to build a hermeneutic bridge between the world and context of the text and the contemporary issues of this research project. The text itself functioned as a "reflective surface" against which the intercultural Biblical hermeneutics of the participants was extrapolated (cf., Van der Walt, 2010, chaps 3, 7, 2014: 2–3). This chapter concludes with an AQAL reading of the text which serves to show the various possible readings of the text by participants in the intercultural Bible reading process.

- **Chapter 5** – Research design and process

Having laid the theoretical groundwork of the study in detail, chapter 5 presents the design aspects of the research project. This chapter offers a complex and thick description of the research design elements that are necessary to provide credible and rich information towards achieving the research objectives. In keeping with the practice oriented research approach, this chapter addresses both the theoretical and the praxis streams of the research project in detail. It explains the way in which the various research protocols were identified and implemented, how data was gathered, validated, and analysed. The chapter also contains a code book with examples of the codes and sample quotations that were used in the computer aided qualitative research process.

- **Chapter 6** – Research findings and analysis

The findings of the research process are presented in three sections, as predicated in the research design. First, the findings of the pre-intercultural engagement Bible reading meetings are presented for Group A and Group B (the groups are introduced in detail, and the demographic data is presented, in 5.6 and 5.7.3.3). Then the post-intercultural engagement findings for the Bible readings by Group A and Group B are presented. The pre-intercultural engagement and post-intercultural engagement findings are then analysed and compared to one another to see whether the proposed changes highlighted in the hypothesis (cf., 1.3.1-1.3.3 and 5.3) are evident or not. The findings of this comparison are then considered in the light of the intercultural Bible reading meetings, to ascertain what role the positive intergroup contact theory design played in influencing the changes, or lack of changes, between the pre-intercultural engagement and post-intercultural engagement Bible reading meetings. Since this is a limited study, the findings in this section are not conclusive or of universal value. Rather they point out specific events that took place in a specific set of contextual and historical variables related to this case.

- **Chapter 7** – Conclusions and discussion

This is the summative chapter of the research study. It revisits the problem that predicated this research project and offers some suggestions for how the research process has engaged the identified research problem. Significant findings and possible future research are highlighted from the previous sections. The limitations of the research are presented and there is a discussion of how the findings of the research will be disseminated among the problem owner, participants and academic communities. Some suggestions are offered for the further development of aspects of the research findings, and areas that the research could not cover because of its limitations.

1.10   *Relevant terms for this study*

Language, and its use, is a complex phenomenon. The author does not presume that the readers of this text will share the same understanding of certain key concepts of words used in the study. Hence, it is necessary to give a brief insight into how some important terms and concepts are used within the parameters of this study. These definitions are not intended as normative definitions, rather, they are intended to show something of the nuance and particularity of their usage in this study. Several of the terms (such as forgiveness and consciousness) will be considered in much greater depth, and related to the academic literature and schools of thought relevant to this study, in later stages of the book.

Forgiveness – The notion of forgiveness is a central concept in this study. Each of the sections of the study engages this concept in some way or another, explicating aspects of its meaning in relation to the various processes and steps of the research. In some instances, forgiveness is considered as deeply spiritual (i.e., a right spiritual relationship between persons and God). In other instances, forgiveness has clear social aspects (i.e., the restoration of relationships and social structures in communities). In chapter 4 the notion of forgiveness is considered in some detail in relation to the framing Biblical text used in this study. In chapter 6 some attention is paid to the social and communal aspects of forgiveness between the two participating communities in this study.

Hermeneutics – This study seeks to engage the notion of hermeneutic understanding in two ways. First, since this is a study of a New Testament text (i.e., Matthew 18.15-35), the usage of the term hermeneutics is used to refer to the complex problem of understanding an ancient text within its own context, and then responsibly and carefully interpreting that text in relation to the current context. Furthermore, hermeneutics in this study refers to the complexity of how persons understand forgiveness in relation to the particular Biblical text used in the study in an intercultural setting. In this sense hermeneutics refers to the approach and content of the readers that inform their understandings of forgiveness in the text (constructive hermeneutics), as well as the ways in which they give expression to their understandings (descriptive hermeneutics). Moreover, in this study the hermeneutic approach is considered as part of a process of intercultural engagement between the readers of the Biblical text as they share their understandings of forgiveness with one another [16]. Each of these two uses of the notion of hermeneutics are pointed out, and expanded upon, in the relevant sections of this study (particularly chapters 4, and 6).

Community (Church) – This study is focussed on participants from two religious communities, members of the Church Street Methodist church (Group A) and members of the Coronation Avenue Methodist Church (Group B) (both of which are Methodist congregations in the town of Somerset West, South Africa). The terms community and Church are used interchangeably within the study, although the author is well aware that this is not always the case in the academic literature. At times the term Church has theological meaning. In other instances, it is used as a term to denote a group of persons who identify as belonging to the same religious grouping. Dirkie Smit[17] suggests that there are six general forms of being "the church", which can be simplified into three broad categories (Smit, 2007a: 61–68). Theologically, the term Church may refer to a local congregation, or community, of persons who identify as members or adherents of a worshipping community (e.g., Church Street Methodist church). This usage of the word Church often conveys a measure of theological homogeneity (shared beliefs), and in the South African context, there are often cultural, economic and racial commonalities among the members (Philander, 2011: 177). The second use of the word Church refers primarily to the organisational or institutional structure of a religious community. Philander notes that often this expression of church is what people would point to as an expression of the collective denominational or confessional identity (e.g., Methodist, Protestant) (Philander,

---

16 For a detailed discussion of the complexity of building a bridge of meaning (hermeneutic bridge) between the world and intention of the original Biblical author and the contemporary reader please see (Lategan, 2015). Smit writes about this hermeneutic bridge saying, "'The continuity of our actions with the biblical documents does not lie in words, but – with reference to Jüngel – in the quality of our *Verhalten*, our presence, our attitude,' in other words, in our life together, as integral part of our interpretation." (Smit in Lategan, 2015: 9–10).

17 Dirk Smit presents a nuanced theological perspective on the theology of the Church sighting six variations, or forms, (termed "gestaltes" in Afrikaans) (Smit, 1996: 119–129). Please also see (Forster & Oostenbrink, 2015: 4–8) for a detailed discussion of how the author understands and uses the term "Church" in his writing.

2011: 177). Smit notes that this is the third way in which people think of the church, as individual believers who are salt and light in the world, each involved in living out their faith on a daily basis in their own particular ways (Smit, 2007a: 68). The research has discussed these concepts in detail elsewhere, and so they will not be treated in great detail in this study (cf., Forster, 2015a: 1–10; Forster & Oostenbrink, 2015: 4–8).

Consciousness (meaning making and identity) – the notion of consciousness is a complex and contested phenomenon in philosophy and theology. This concept is engaged and explicated in some detail in chapter two. Within the confines of this study the notion of consciousness refers to the complex set realities that contribute towards the construction of meaning and identity in the individual person and in communities of persons.

Ordinary reader – An aspect of this study is built around the academic study of what De Wit calls "ordinary readers" (De Wit, 2012: 7). The "ordinary reader" is a non-technical reader who does not have any formal training in Biblical exegesis, or does not have the specific intent of reading the Biblical text for academic purposes. The academic interest in the views of "ordinary readers" is a relatively recent development in Biblical scholarship. It can be argued that there is a hermeneutic relationship between the "privileged position of power" of formal academic readers of the text, and their interpretations of the text from that position of power. Naturally, the same is true for "ordinary readers", whose unique engagement with the text outside of the categories of academic Biblical scholarship will influence their readings of the text (Van der Walt, 2014: 4). Hence, this study deliberately chose to bring these two sets of readers into conversation with one another. The hermeneutic views of the "formal readers" are mainly discussed and considered in chapter 4, while the hermeneutic perspectives of the "ordinary readers" are mainly discussed and considered in chapter 6. It is correct to assume that such a distinction (between formal and ordinary readers) is a theoretical construction. Yet, it is regarded as a credible approach in South African Biblical scholarship. See for example Van der Walt's use of "ordinary women" readers in *Towards a communal reading of 2 Samuel 13*, (Van der Walt, 2014: 4–5), and West who employs a similar approach in his work. See, for example, *Contending for Dignity in the Bible and the Post-Apartheid South African Public Realm* (West, 2015: 78–98).

Race – The term race is not to be understood in an essentialist manner in this study. Hammet points out that race identity remains fluid, with both the "reification or erasure of racial identities" continuing to take place among population groups and social and political structures in South Africa (Hammett, 2010: 247–248). The notion of race identification remains contested and complex in South Africa (van Wyngaard, 2014: 157–170; Boesak, Fitchue, Fitchue, Fluker, Harris, Koopman, Mingo, Nel, Pilusa, Senokoane, Vaden, Vellem & van Wyngaard, 2015). In reality there is no racial category that could adequately contain the complexity of human identities (Hammett, 2010: 247). The terms that are used in this study are informed by the literature, and are terms used by the participants in identifying their own race identities. The three dominant self-descriptors are Coloured, Black and White. Some of the participants described themselves as White. Some participants described themselves as both Black and Coloured. The research shows that Black and Coloured identity is based on an understanding that is relational in some contexts and political in others. At times race is identified and described in relation to a community of reference. For example in relation to family and friends a person may self-identify as Coloured, while in a political setting the same persons may self-identify as Black persons so as not to be excluded from the political solidarity of redressing the racial legacies of apartheid (Adhikari, 2005: 98–130, 162–188; Hammett, 2010: 247–260; Goldin, 2014: 156–181).

Methodist – The terms Methodist, Methodists, or Methodism, are employed in two primary ways in this study. First, they may refer to members of the Christian denomination known as the Methodist Church. In this instance the two participating communities are members of the Methodist Church of Southern Africa. The second usage of the term may refer to a loosely held set of common theological beliefs among theologians and members of the Methodist Churches. Where necessary such theological convictions are identified and explained.

Mechanisms – Within the context of this study mechanisms are the social "mediators" and "moderators" of positive intergroup contact (discussed in 3.3.6). These "mechanisms" are identified in the literature as social specifications from intergroup contact theory that can be introduced, and facilitated, in intergroup contact to facilitate a decrease in anxiety and an increase in empathy among in-group and out-group participants (Paolini, Hewstone, Cairns & Voci, 2004: 770–786; Paolini, Hewstone, Voci, Harwood & Cairns, 2006).

The literature shows that intergroup contact mediators (or social conditions / mechanisms) need to be facilitated in an intergroup contact setting in order to positively change the social moderators (i.e., to decrease anxiety and increase empathy among participants). These mechanisms are discussed in detail in section 3.3.6 and analysed in the data in section 6.4.4.

1.11   Concluding remarks

This chapter offered an introduction to the research problem and the foundations of the study. It sought to introduce the problem of understandings of forgiveness among Black and White South African Christians. In order to effectively engage this complex problem, the primary and secondary research questions were identified. A basic introduction was given to the research approach (since the research design is discussed in greater detail in chapter 5). Next, an overview of the book was presented and some key terms for the study were considered.

Having presented these foundational thoughts, we can move on to the next steps of the research process, and ultimately the research findings and conclusions, in the chapters that follow.

An integral (AQAL) theory for complex individual and social identity
mapping of theological understandings of forgiveness

2.1 Introduction

As the previous chapter stated, this project is primarily interested in understanding
in what ways an intercultural Bible reading process under carefully facilitated
conditions can shift understandings of forgiveness among two diverse groups of
Christians reading Matthew 18.15-35.

This is a qualitative empirical[18] study by design – as shall be seen in 5.6-5.7. This
means that at various stages in the intercultural Bible reading process it will be
necessary to chart the understandings of forgiveness evidenced by the participants.
This data will then be comparatively analysed in order to see if anything has
changed over the process of the research intervention. If it has changed, attention
will be given to what the extent of the change is, and what may have contributed to
the changes. Of course, the converse may also apply. If an anticipated change does
not take place, or a change takes place in an unanticipated manner, one would also
need some theoretical framework that can be credibly employed in order to give an
account of the unanticipated result.

In order to manage this complex set of variables, and the related processes, the project
employs two theories. The first theory will be discussed in this chapter. Its specific
contribution and relevance to the project will also be highlighted and extrapolated.
The second theory will be discussed in chapter 3 with a similar intention.

2.2 The need for a conceptual framework to plot understandings of forgiveness

In conceptualising this project it was understood that a theoretical basis would
need to be presented that helps the researcher, and the reader, to place the complex
and varied understandings of forgiveness that emerge from an engagement with
Matthew 18.15-35 within a nuanced and credible framework of meaning. In this
chapter, it will be argued that Ken Wilber's AQAL integral theory can serve this
function. In the next chapter such a case will be stated for intergroup contact theory.

At this stage it need simply be noted that the second of the two theories upon which
this study is predicated, namely intergroup contact theory, and particularly the
mechanisms of positive intergroup contact, offer some insights into the possible
ways in which conditions can be facilitated among diverse Christian groups that
could facilitate the capacity for theological shifts that possibilise the seemingly
impossible notions of differing, and even conflicting, understandings of forgiveness.

---

18   The choice for a qualitative empirical study was considered apt since it allows for the
      analysis and comparison of data that was sourced at different stages in the practice
      oriented research process. For a discussion of qualitative empirical research study
      approaches please see Blatter's description on p.70 of the following resource (Blatter,
      2008: 68–70).

The purpose of presenting the theoretical frameworks is to show how that they can be used in the research design of the project for the development of identifiable theological concepts, as well as processes and mechanisms that are expressed in 3.3, and 5.9 as explanatory and descriptive codes.[19] These codes serve to engage, explain, and offer some understanding of the complex processes of intercultural Bible reading and the possibilities of identifying and developing different understandings of forgiveness among the Bible readers under carefully facilitated intergroup conditions.

This chapter begins with a presentation of the salient elements of Ken Wilber's integrative AQAL theory[20]. The methodological imperatives of this study, as shaped by the research questions and the hermeneutic approach, inform what is included in the discussion of this theory. It would not be possible, or necessary, to present every aspect of this theory in totality for the purposes of this study. However, this theory will be critically presented in some detail. It is necessary to do so since it deals with the complex philosophical notion of intersectional identity. The density of this theory stems from the fact that it touches on individual and social dimensions of identity. These are crucial for the purposes of this project where individual identity is an informant of, and informed by, social identity. It is further complicated by the intersection of the subjective and objective (and even intersubjective and interobjective) notions of identity. Hence, there is a need for a more detailed presentation of the salient aspects of this theory, as well as some discussion of the relevance of the theory for the purposes of this present study.

One could ask why Wilber's theory was chosen for a study of this nature in the South African context – was there no Southern African, or African, theory of meaning construction and identity that could have served this purpose? The researcher took this challenge very seriously and did an extensive and comprehensive literature review before settling on Wilber's AQAL integral theory.

The answer to the earlier question is that after an exhaustive survey there was no single theory of consciousness that engaged the notions of meaning construction and identity from within the South African (or African) context that could adequately address the theoretical complexity of this study. This does not mean that African

---

19 Saldaña explains the process of using qualitative data sets, such as those gathered in this research process, to develop descriptive codes that describe primary topics, and then moving on to a second (and further) phases of data analysis that produce more complex and textured codes to identify and explain subtler understandings of concepts, events, and meanings in the data (Saldaña, 2013: 4–6). Please see Friese's NCT approach (Noticing things, Collecting things, Thinking about things) that is also used in this research to engage the empirical data in a qualitative analytical process (Friese, 2014: 12–14). These processes are discussed in detail in the research design section of this book in chapter 5.

20 It is worth noting that Wilber's work is not without its critics. In particular the work of Kirk Schneider has pointed out some deficiencies and weakness in Wilber's integral theory over the last two decades. Other scholars have also engaged his work in both appreciative and critical review (c.f., Schneider, 1987: 196–216, 1989: 470–481, 2012: 120–123; Rich, 2001; Paulson, 2008; Meyerhoff, 2010; Brys & Bokor, 2013). Some of these aspects will be addressed in the sections that follow. However, such critique not withstanding there is sufficiently credible acceptance of Wilber's work for it to be used in the manner in which it is employed in this project.

sources will be ignored – on the contrary, this project sought to bring aspects of African scholarship on identity, theology hermeneutics, and social psychology to bear on the argument at every relevant point.

For example, the work of Gobodo-Madikizela, Thesnaar, de Gruchy, Vosloo and Tutu formed an important component of the shaping of the complex understandings of forgiveness and identity among South African Christians[21]. In terms of Southern African approaches to individual and social and religious identity the work of Biko, Boesak, Cezula, Shutte, Balcomb, Muller, Setiloane, Forster, and du Toit were consulted[22]. In particular the relevant contribution of Kok was a helpful contemporary source to aggregate Wilber's notions of identity, and the discussions of social identity complexity theory in chapter 3 (Kok, 2012: 227–246, 2014a, b: 1–9, 2015: 1–12). With regards to Southern African identity intercultural Biblical hermeneutics the work of Jonker, van der Walt, Claassens, van der Watt, Cezula, Dube, West, Nadar, Mtshiselwa were most helpful[23].

Thus, the researcher has sought to remain deeply contextual, drawing on important and relevant contributions to the complex understandings of identity and meaning construction from within the Southern African theological and philosophical context. Yet, the value of a single integrative theory of consciousness was considered a helpful framework, although aggregated, by contextual African and South African resources.

It is worth noting that some aspects of the theoretical introductions that will be provided in this chapter and the next are philosophically and theologically dense and technical. Such rigour will prove both important and valuable when the theories are employed to understand notions of forgiveness within the selected Biblical text, as well as understandings of forgiveness among the various participants. There will be a sufficiently detailed general introduction to each theory, with specific attention being paid to the necessary elements of each of the theories that help to bring greater understanding and depth for the express purposes of this research as outlined in chapter 1.

Once the AQAL theory has been presented, and it has been shown and substantiated how it adds value to the research objectives, there will be some concluding remarks that show how and where the theory is applied within the scope of the research process.

---

21 Please see the following resources that informed this section of the discussion, (cf., Gobodo-Madikizela, 1997: 271–272, 2002: 7–32, 2003a, b: 51–60, 2008a: 169–188, b: 57–75, c: 331–350, 2011: 541–551, 2012; Cochrane, De Gruchy & Martin, 1999; De Gruchy, 2002; Thesnaar, 2008: 53–73, 2013: 1–15, 2014: 1–8; Tutu, 2012; Vosloo, 2012, 2015: 360–378; Van der Riet, 2014).

22 The following resources were consultedin this regard, (cf., Balcomb, 1993, 1996: 12–20, Shutte, 1993, 2001, 2009: 85–99; Setiloane, 1998; Biko, 2002; Du Toit, 2004; Forster, 2006, 2007: 245–289, 2010a: 1–12, b: 243–253; South African Science and Religion Forum, 2007; Boesak, 2008: 636–664; cf., hybridity in Muller, 2008: 819–820; Du Toit & Doxtader, 2010; DeYoung & Boesak, 2012; Cezula, 2013, 2015: 131–151).

23 Please see the following resources for further information, (cf., West & Dube, 1996: 7–17; Masenya, Phiri & Nadar, 2005: 47–59; Nadar, 2006: 339–351; Van der Walt, 2010; Mtshiselwa, 2011: 668–689; Phiri & Nadar, 2012; Van der Walt, 2012: 110–118; Cezula, 2013; Mtshiselwa, 2014: 205–230; Van der Walt, 2014; West, 2014b: 1–10; Cezula, 2015: 131–153; Claassens & Birch, 2015; Jonker, 2015; West, 2015: 79–98).

We now move on to a discussion of Ken Wilber's integrative AQAL theory.

2.3 An introduction Ken Wilber's integral AQAL theory

Ken Wilber is a native of North America, born in 1949. He initially sought to train as a medical Doctor by enrolling for studies at Duke University in North Carolina (1968)[24]. However, he soon became disillusioned with what western science had to offer in relation to human wholeness. He went on to complete a Bachelor's degree in chemistry and biology. However, he was already much more interested in developing his understanding of Eastern philosophy and Western psychology at this point.

At present Ken Wilber is regarded as "the world's foremost integral philosopher" (Palmer in Wilber, 2004: ix). In particular, it is Wilber's thoroughgoing scholarship and enormous body of work on the 'integral approach' to individual and social identity that has led to him receiving this recognition. His AQAL theory is of particular interest to this research project, since it presents a comprehensive and thoroughgoing conceptualisation of non-dual integrated identity that considers the complex and nuanced nature of individual and social identity. Of course, no model is conclusive. However, as will be shown, Wilber's model offers sufficient theoretical insight to shape the conceptual aspects of articulating and plotting understandings of identity and forgiveness as required in this study.

The section that follows will present an introduction Ken Wilber's integral AQAL theory drawing links to notions of individual and social identity, and particularly the concepts of constructing meaning out of individual or social experiences, or individually or collectively shared beliefs. Each of the following sections will introduce and discuss different aspects of Wilber's theory AQAL theory[25].

2.3.1 Ken Wilber's Integral Philosophy in relation to the construction of meaning and identity

Wilber's Integral philosophy, on which AQAL theory is based, stems from an integral psychological model referred to as the "psychological spectrum of consciousness" (Wilber, 1975, 1993; Snyman, 2002: 71; Wilber, 2003: 22–49, 2011a). This model aims to provide a philosophical framework that illustrates how consciousness in the human person can be related to aspects of human identity and the construction of meaning within the complex interrelationship of the self and the rest of reality.

Forster's research on identity, meaning construction, and consciousness showed that studies in this field traditionally tended towards one of two models of reality

---

24   Parts of this section of the manuscript are adapted, in edited form, from my previous research cf., Forster, D.A. 2006. *Validation of individual consciousness in strong artificial intelligence: an African theological contribution.* PhD. University of South Africa. (Forster, 2006: 156–217).

25   Naturally it would not be possible to cover every aspect of Wilber's corpus of thought that could form an entire study on its own. Only those aspects that help us to understand the core concepts of AQAL integral theory, and allow us to see the value of this theory for the current study, will be presented and discussed. For a very helpful overview of Wilber's broader contribution to integrative discourses please see (Snyman, 2002; Howard, 2005; Forster, 2006; Ferreira, 2010; Visser, 2012; Brys & Bokor, 2013).

and meaning-making. On the one hand, there are those models that seek to locate identity within an empirical study of the functioning of the human brain (namely empirical and scientific studies). On the other hand there are those approaches that conduct a phenomenological investigation into the philosophical, or theological, aspects of mind and self (Forster, 2006: 111–154, 2010a: 2–4). Wilber's model seeks to deal with both the objective and the subjective states of identity, and the construction of meaning – namely, the brain and the mind, in order to avoid dualism and reductionism in the development of a truly integral theory of identity and meaning construction. Wilber calls this state consciousness[26]. Snyman writes that Wilber's objective in this regard is to

> … impart a clear and precise understanding of the way consciousness develops and interrelates with other aspects of the universe, which includes all the vast depths of not only the physical, but also the psychological, spiritual, cultural and sociological "Kosmos."[27] (Snyman, 2002: 71).

Thus, Wilber's aim was to provide a philosophical framework, and some language, that could help us to understand how we view ourselves (identity) and relate to the rest of the world (construct meaning) through engagement with the varied and complex sources of our conscious existence. To construct this integrative model Wilber conducted extensive research on developmental and evolutionary theories of consciousness. At present his integral approach is regarded as one of the most comprehensive and synthesised models of the twelve most influential areas of consciousness studies (cf., Forster, 2006: 104–111).

In order to understand Wilber's integral philosophy, it is necessary to investigate his findings concerning identity in three research areas. Firstly, it will be necessary to see what Wilber gleans from the perennial philosophy. Secondly, it will be important to present and discuss Wilber's mapping of meaning construction and identity (consciousness), which he derives from his explorative research into the world's consciousness philosophies and religious traditions. Lastly, this discussion will present Wilber's view of meaning construction and identity in relation to the four ontological and existential quadrants of existence (AQAL). These quadrants are the objectivist, sociological, cultural and spiritual realms.

2.3.2 Ken Wilber's understanding of the construction of meaning and identity from the perennial philosophy: A neo-perennial philosophy

There is wide consensus among scholars that until the sixteenth century there was a universal philosophy throughout the world that was known as the perennial

---

26 In the sections that follow it will be show that Wilber uses the term "consciousness" (cf., Wilber, 2003: 22–49) to express his understanding of the complex manner in which human persons, and even the "Kosmos" (Snyman, 2002: 71), formulate, or awaken to, the complexity of self-identity and construct meaning of the self and others in relation to a multifaceted engagement with different aspects of reality (including self-awareness, other persons, and creation).

27 According to Snyman, Wilber chooses to use the word Kosmos to describe the non-dual universe, rather than the "anaemic, depth-denying and surface bound 'cosmos' of modern science that has not allowed room for spirit and consciousness in its deliberations" (Snyman, 2002: 71).

philosophy (Wildman, 2010: 49). The perennial philosophy is regarded as a 'strand' of shared truth that can be identified in most of the world's ancient and living religions according to Leibniz (cf., Schmitt, 1966: 505–532). The term was popularized by Aldous Huxley in his book, *The Perennial Philosophy* (Huxley, 1945).

Wilber's research expanded on these notions of shared experience and truth within certain religions and philosophies (Wilber, 2000a: 1, 2001a: 115–118). According to Griffiths this universal wisdom prevailed from about 500 AD until about 1500 AD (Griffiths, 1990: 11).

The perennial philosophy was based on a belief that all of the Kosmos was pervaded by, and could find its explanation in, a transcendent reality. Gradually however, as a mechanistic and materialistic view of reality began to take over it diminished the prominence of the perennial philosophy (Griffiths, 1990: 11). This change took place mainly in the West. To a large extent, the perennial philosophy was maintained in the cultures and religions of the East.

The psychologist, Stanislav Grof, suggests that the reason for the survival of this philosophy in the east is that the eastern mind-set is far more open to a cosmic consciousness and creative intelligence as primary attributes of existence (Grof & Valier, 1984: 4). The value of this view of reality is notable. For instance, whereas the materialistic view of reality sees humans as highly developed animals, or thinking biological machines, the perennialists see humans as one with the whole universe and its transcendent creator; humans are regarded in relation to all of creation and the divine (Grof & Valier, 1984: 4). Materialistic science is reductionist, seeking to alleviate human suffering by sociological and psychopharmacological means. The perennial philosophy, on the other hand, is far more spiritual, seeking to liberate the spirit as part of the liberation of the whole person. Some contemporary perennialists thinkers, such as Bede Griffiths, affirm that while western science and a materialistic world view have done much to alleviate physical suffering, they have often neglected genuine spiritual and emotional fulfilment (Griffiths, 1990: 279). Griffiths remarks, in turn, that cultures such as those of the East, that have maintained the perennial philosophy, have had a much stronger emphasis on spiritual liberation (Griffiths, 1990: 279). However, their struggle was that they often failed to offer practical solutions for the problems of everyday existence. What is necessary is an approach to life that combines the positive aspects of the perennial philosophy with the positive aspects of western science in order to offer a holistic approach to existence, meeting the needs of body, mind and spirit. It should also care for individual needs, community needs and do so in relationship with all of creation (Griffiths, 1990: 281). As will be shown, such an integrative approach to reality is important to understand the complexity of individual and social forgiveness, as well as the interaction between interior (spiritual) and exterior (physical) concepts of forgiveness.

One of Wilber's greatest achievements has been the articulation of what he calls a "neo-perennialist" philosophy (Forster, 2006: 167–168; Paulson, 2008: 366, 370–371; Ferreira, 2010: 1). Wilber concurred with Huxley's notion that an enduring philosophical system existed which viewed all reality as fitting into a "Great Chain of Being" (Wilber, 2000b: 69, 85; Lovejoy, 2011: xii). This view maintained that all reality could be understood as interconnected. It was made up of multiple levels that range from the most basic, (dense), forms of reality to the highest levels which are much more subtle (Wilber, 2000a: 1; Forster, 2006: 169). Within the Great Chain of Being, Spirit is that un-nameable, transcendent, aspect of reality at the subtlest, or highest, end of the chain. On the other end of the chain, on the lower levels, one finds matter. Snyman, however, notes that in Wilber's neo-perennial philosophy, this

> … spirit is, paradoxically, also said to be the all-pervading Ground of all the previous, less integrated, levels. Spirit is no further from matter than from its own inner reality. Put in terms that echo Christian Trinitarian thinking, God is within his own inner relational reality, equidistant to all that exists. (Snyman, 2002: 72).

Wilber refers to the different levels of the Great Chain of Being using three terms interchangeably – structures, levels, and waves – as descriptors of these developmental, or cosmic evolutionary milestones. *Structure* indicates that each stage has a holistic pattern that blends all of its elements into a structured whole. *Level* denotes that these patterns tend to unfold in a relational sequence, "with each senior wave transcending but including its juniors" (just as cells transcend but include molecules, which transcend but include atoms, which transcend but include quarks) (Wilber, 2000a: 1). In this regard one can notice a distinct similarity, and the direct influence, of Teilhard de Chardin's understanding evolutionary cosmology as a movement of increasing complexity (Forster, 2005: 29–44; De Chardin, 2008: 52–55, 181, 213). Lastly, the term *wave* indicates that these levels are fluid and flowing. Wilber writes that,

> … the senior dimensions do not sit on top of the junior dimensions like rungs in a ladder, but rather embrace and enfold them (just like cells embrace molecules which embrace atoms). These developmental stages appear to be concentric spheres of increasing embrace, inclusion, and holistic capacity. (Wilber, 2000a: 1).

Within the ambit of psychological identity Wilber understands these aspects of being to be "levels of consciousness" that span the entire spectrum from subconscious to self-conscious to superconscious (Murphy, 1992; Wade, 1996: 239, 269–277; Wilber & Wilber, 2000: 237–238, 268). This is an important consideration for the subtle and complex nature of social identity within the ambit of this project.

Wilber relates his understanding, as discussed above, directly to the notion of the "Great Chain of Being" (cf., Huxley, 1945; Lovejoy, 2011). However, his neo-perennial philosophy suggests that the aforementioned name is something of a misnomer. Since it is not a linear chain, but rather a series of enfolded spheres. He writes:

> It is said that spirit transcends but includes soul, which transcends but includes mind, which transcends but includes body, which transcends but includes matter. Accordingly, this is more accurately called "the Great Nest of Being." (Wilber, 2000a: 1).

The diagram below gives a visual illustration of Wilber's understanding of this evolutionary and developmental concept where each successive stage includes the former.

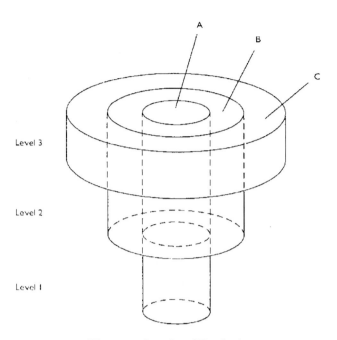

Figure 1: Levels of Evolution

The diagram above (from Wilber, 2001a: 115) represents three levels of evolution or development, each being a progression on the next, yet whilst progressing beyond the preceding level each successive level enfolds the previous ones. In this diagram (A) represents the noosphere, (B) the biosphere and (C) the physiosphere (Wilber, 2001a: 115–118).

In relation to the construction of meaning, identity, and the human psyche Wilber most often refers to nine or ten basic levels (or waves) of consciousness. His divisions are variations on the traditional divisions in the Chain of Being, namely: simple matter, body, mind, soul, and spirit. For a detailed breakdown of Wilber's research in this regard see *The Atman project* (Wilber, 2014). Wilber commonly divides the spectrum into the following major levels: sensorimotor, phantasmic-emotional, representational, rule/role, formal, vision-logic, psychic, subtle, causal, and non-dual. The categorizations will be revisited in chapter 6 when we analyse the data from the intercultural Bible reading process.

Wilber suggests that this perennial world-view, which was under-valued, and even largely destroyed, by Western reductionist and materialist thought, is re-emerging. In particular, the 'new sciences' such a quantum theory are finding a great affinity to this interconnected evolutionary model. Snyman points to a quote by Ludwig von Bertalanffy, the founder of General Systems Theory, who says:

> Reality, in modern conception, appears as a tremendous hierarchical order of organised entities, leading, in a superimposition of many levels, from physical and chemical to biological and sociological systems. Such hierarchical structure and combination into systems of ever higher order, is characteristic of reality as a whole and of fundamental

importance especially in biology, psychology and sociology. (Snyman, 2002: 73; cf., Wilber, 2011b: 49).

Snyman further notes that many other prominent theorists from varying scientific disciplines concur with this notion, i.e.,

> Rupert Sheldrake speaks of a "nested hierarchy of morphogenetic fields", Karl Popper of a "hierarchy of emergent qualities", Jürgen Habermas of a "hierarchy of communicative competence". If there is anything at all resembling a unifying paradigm in modern and postmodern thought, it is precisely this understanding of evolutionary hierarchy. (Snyman, 2002: 73).

Thus, Wilber employs this concept to express his fundamental belief that reality, in its varying forms, can be represented by a notion of an ever complexifying hierarchical chain of being in which each successive level is more complex and subtle, including the preceding levels. In relation to Kosmic consciousness, to use Wilber's understanding of the term, the lower levels are less dense and conscious, and the higher levels are most conscious and subtle – thus having a more complex and nuanced approach to the construction of meaning and identity. A further important aspect of this evolutionary understanding of reality is that it is an attempt at representing something of the mystery of being, and is not a truth within itself. Snyman notes that truth is ultimately beyond names and forms and limited to no single expression (Snyman, 2002: 74). David Bohm, the quantum theorist, noted that one could no more have a symphony that so encompassed all music that no further music would be necessary (Keepin, 1993: 4; Bohm, 2002: 62–63). Each symphony presents the truth of the beauty of music in part, but it could never encapsulate all of the subtleties and beauty of all that is music. Bohm says, "there can no more be an ultimate form of such thought that there could be an ultimate poem (that would make all further poems unnecessary)" (cf., Bohm, 1993, 2002: 63). Similarly, Wilber comments on this expression of reality:

> We cannot make a statement about the *whole* of reality, because any conceivable statement is itself merely a part of that Reality, and thus the perennial philosophy, as a direct insight-union with that Reality itself, could never be adequately captured in any set of doctrines or ideas…. Radical Truth can be *shown* (in contemplative awareness) but never exhaustively *said* (in discursive language) all of which are partial. (Wilber, 2011b: 59).

Thus, in summary, for Wilber the perennial philosophy is not a fixed all-encompassing truth, since the complexity and evolution of reality is still in process. All statements regarding truth are approximations. They are expressions that refer to an ever-complexifying reality. Hence, both the expression of reality, and the reality itself are evolving. At each stage of evolution, the previous statements and understandings are transcended and included into new forms, new concepts, new symbols, grounded in the one single being of Spirit. What is important for this research, is that Wilber's neo-perennial philosophy points to the fact that there is a link between all aspects of being, the personal and the corporate, the interior and the exterior, matter and spirit. Moreover, the notion that identities (and truths) are interrelated and transcended, rather than discarded and moved beyond, will prove to be valuable in understanding the complex interaction between personal and social identities in the intergroup engagements.

This approach is not a wholeness theory which seeks to unify or link separated aspects of reality, rather it is 'holarchical' in nature. Consciousness permeates every aspect of the Kosmos since all lower, denser, forms of reality are transcended and included in the higher forms of reality. Consequently, one could say that there is a common consciousness at the highest levels, a non-dualistic, cosmic consciousness expressed in many varying, less complete, less complex, individual expressions at other levels below.

Wilber's neo-perennial philosophy offers an insight into reality that has its roots in ancient wisdom and its expression in modern thought and research. It is an integral approach that does not devalue past understandings, or previous levels, of reality in the process of evolution to further states of consciousness or experience – the construction of meaning and development of identity is integral, and thus inclusive. It recognises that each developmental stage is adequate, yet as Snyman points out, "each successor is more adequate" (2002:75). It is constructive of reality, rather than destructive.

In the context of this research project an integral approach is important since it breaks down the hierarchical and dualistic views of experienced truth in relation to the truth claims of the in-group social identity and the out-group social identity. It shows that truth can be deepened and given textured, benefiting from the complexity of intersubjective and interobjective engagement between persons and ideas. Moreover, this theory allows for the development of descriptive categories that will be employed to explicate implicate meaning, both within the thought world and communicative intent of Matthew 18.15-35, and in the shared space of the intercultural Bible readers.

The section that follows will discuss the framework, or model, into which Wilber places this integral philosophy.

2.3.3 Towards a mapping of the construction of meaning and identity: Ken Wilber's holarchic approach

The discussion up to this point has shown that in the perennial philosophy there is an understanding that all identity and construction of meaning can be related to different levels (what Wilber refers to variously as structures, levels and waves). Moreover, the understanding that results from this view is that there is a goal associated with these different, all-encompassing, levels; that is, an evolution towards the higher levels of Spirit. Thus, as this research suggests, the goal of all reality is to progress from the lower levels of identity (matter, characterised by a lack of complexity, a low level of consciousness and gross forms of constructing meaning etc.) to the higher, subtler, levels of identity (what some have called Supra-mental, transpersonal, perfection etc.).

Nonetheless, such a notion or hierarchy tends to destroy, or at least work against, the very characteristic nature of the higher levels, i.e. non-duality, equal value, and interconnectedness. It can easily be observed, in many spheres of investigation, that hierarchies tend to encourage ranking and domination that either disregard or marginalise lower levels in the hierarchy. Snyman suggests that as a result many scholars have opted for a model of "heterarchy" that is more egalitarian and plural in nature, in which all components have equal value (Snyman, 2002: 76). The struggle with such views is that they often present a phenomenological interpretation (frequently closely linked to postmodernist and deconstructionist approaches to language) of concepts and symbols used to express the reality being dealt with. An example of such an approach is that of Fritjof Capra who refers to the Kosmos as a "web of life", employing the linguistic symbolism of a living, interdependent, co-equal, organism (in which one part is not more or less important than any other since all parts are essential for survival). He does this in order to counter the Newtonian view that represents reality as a complex law-bound machine, such as a clock, wherein certain parts are more essential to the functioning of the machine than others and each part can be seen in isolation from the whole (Capra, 1996: 20, 26, 67, 157–160). The struggle is that scientific empirical studies, which underpin the hermeneutics of such discussions, suggest that hierarchy is an inherent aspect of reality (they do not necessarily support the mechanistic world-view, but there is a clear understanding of hierarchy, evolution and development) (cf., Bohm, 2002: 149–152 as an illustrative example). Hence a simple avoidance of such hierarchies could lead to inaccurate, and even false, conclusions.

Wilber's aim is to seek to address both of these areas of concern. Snyman writes that Wilber

> ... maintains there is some confusion over the actual meaning of hierarchy, and that [it] is critical to distinguish not only between normal and pathological hierarchies, but also normal and pathological heterarchies. (Snyman, 2002: 76).

The way in which he seeks to address these concerns is through a conceptual model and accompanying theory of Holons and Holarchy. This brings us another step closer to Wilber's AQAL integral theory.

Wilber traces the etymology of the word holarchy from the Latin *hiero*, meaning sacred or holy, and *arch* which means governance or rule (Wilber, 2001a: 17). The notion of hierarchies, in theology, was most notably articulated by the sixth century Christian mystic Dionysius the Areopagite who used the term to refer to nine celestial orders, with Seraphim and Cherubim at the top and archangels and angels at the bottom (Coakley & Stang, 2011: 79). In this scheme, the notion of hierarchy was intended to refer to higher levels of virtue and illumination that could be accessible through contemplative awareness. As philosophy and theology influenced politics and science in subsequent years this notion of hierarchies became common in a multitude of disciplines. Wilber sums up the contemporary understanding and use of the term:

> As used in modern psychology, evolutionary theory, and systems theory, a hierarchy is simply a ranking of orders of events *according to their holistic capacity*. In any developmental sequence, what is whole at one stage becomes a part of a larger whole at the next stage. A letter is part of a whole word, which is part of a whole sentence, which is part of a whole paragraph, and so on. (Wilber, 2001a: 17 italics in the original).

This notion applies not only to linguistic, or representative forms (such as writing or script), it is also widely accepted in empirical disciplines, such as biology and physics, that deal with the forms themselves. Howard Gardner gives the following example of such an approach in biology:

> Any change in an organism will affect all the parts; no aspect of a structure can be altered without affecting the entire structure; each whole contains part and is itself part of a larger whole. (in Wilber, 2001a: 17).

Essentially, that which is a whole in one context, yet at the same time is a part of another context, is called a 'holon'.

Within the context of this study in intergroup contact theory, this is an important conception since it allows for an understanding of identity that is both individual and collective in nature. In one instance a person may hold certain views to be true, yet when engaged in a different context an entirely different set of ideas may be held as true by the same person (Allport, 1954: 28; c.f., Duncan, 2003: 138–141; Ypma, 2014: 11–12). This does not mean that the former ideas are no longer valid, but simply that the depth of identity and complexity of understanding has been altered through the bridging of various contexts of meaning.

Wilber says that reality,

> ... is not composed of things or processes; it is not composed of atoms or quarks; it is not composed of wholes nor does it have any parts. Rather, it is composed of whole / parts, or holons. This is true of atoms, cells, symbols, ideas. They can be understood neither as things nor processes, neither as wholes nor parts, but only as simultaneous whole / parts, so that standard "atomistic" and "wholistic" attempts are both way off the mark. There is nothing that isn't a holon.... Before an atom is an atom, it is a holon. Before a cell is a cell, it is a holon. Before an idea is an idea, it is a holon. All of them are wholes that exist in other wholes, and thus they are all whole / parts, or holons, first (long before any particular characteristics are singled out by us). (Wilber, 2001a: 33–34).

Contained in Wilber's understanding of holons are two underlying conceptual frameworks. Firstly, the notion of inclusion in which each holon is at the same time a part that is simultaneously a whole. Secondly, such a view necessitates some concept of hierarchy, where parts are included into and superseded by a greater whole. Whereas the first concept mentioned above is understood as a 'holon', the second concept of a hierarchy of such holons is understood to be a 'Holarchy'. Snyman sums up Wilber's conceptual Holarchic framework as follows:

> The whole is always more than the sum of the parts precisely because it provides the means by which the parts are held together. Without this principle, one would be left with isolated parts, or only "heaps" instead of "wholes". (Snyman, 2002: 77).

Thus, in large part, this framework engages the notion that hierarchies are simplistic linear systems. The essence of such notions often centre around abuses associated with ranking things, and so empowering higher orders whilst disempowering lower orders. This is a common form of abuse in intergroup prejudice. Value laden judgements frequently seek to rank persons, groups, or ideas using a false hierarchical value set.

Wilber's notion of holarchies stresses the fundamental interdependence of the elements in both ascending and descending order. Higher orders are fundamentally dependent upon the inclusion of lower orders. The value of a higher order is found in the value of the lower orders. For example, one cannot have a moving poem without sentences, and sentences themselves require words, and one cannot have words without the letters of the alphabet. The sequencing of lower orders to higher orders is an indispensable aspect of the Holarchy. Each holon is both part and whole at the same time. The poem, as a whole, cannot exist without the words. Yet, the words cannot convey the meaning of the poem without being included into its poetic and expressive structure.

Thus, the development of holons (or part / wholes) has to occur in stages, and these stages occur sequentially from lesser to greater wholes. However, this growth does not devalue or dissempower any higher or lower stage of the Holarchy.

The examples cited above are very simple, linear, examples of the formation of one form of holon (e.g. letters, to word, to sentence, to poem). Holons, however, are seldom brought about in such simple formations. More often the holon (and its composite Holarchy) are complex interactions between vastly connected interdependent elements. I will extrapolate on the metaphor used above to illustrate this point. The whole outcome may be a desire for reconciliation and forgiveness between two communities. A possible part / whole (or holon) of this outcome, amongst many other interventions (such as political alliances, negotiations etc.), might be that two prominent political families, one from each community, are joined together in a common interest. One possible holon that could facilitate this (among many others) is the marriage of two persons (one from each community). Their happiness is facilitated by the fulfilment of certain emotional expectations (e.g. attraction and love). A poem might be one small contributor to the success of this venture. Well-structured sentences, composed with carefully chosen words, made up of recognisable letters would be a further necessary element in fulfilling this aspect of the outcome.

Hence, if one simply looks at one single letter of the alphabet (which is the reductionist, mechanistic approach to understanding reality by breaking it down to its smallest parts (cf., Bohm, 2002: 219–226)) one can understand very little of this complex inter-community encounter. However, in a complex system, holistic patterns tend to appear later in the development of the holons, since they await the emergence of various parts that will eventually unify to offer a greater meaning and holarchic perspective. It is only once the two persons relate the importance of the poem in facilitating the engagement that made their love possible that one can appreciate the importance of the words (and letters) in the poem that created the opportunity for their discovery of one another. The poem now not only conveys romantic meaning, but also (at the same time) operates as a location for mutual discovery, in the broader context it is both one thing (a poem) and another (a space for mutual discovery of the other).

It is important to understand that both the lower levels (words and letters) and upper levels (the space and opportunity for engagement out of which love emerges) have their own form of value. In fact, as Roger Sperry points out, the lower levels (which simply means the less holistic levels) have the power to influence the higher levels (the more holistic levels) through a process of "upward causation" (in Wilber, 2001a: 20). In reference to the example above, if the poem were written in a language that had an alphabet which was not understood by the recipient, it may not have had the intended impact and so may well have jeopardized the desired love between the two individual persons and the eventual peace between the two communities. However, if the poem is well crafted, and clearly understood, it may evoke the necessary emotion in the recipient that opens the way to a far greater possibility of love. This in turn could lead to the desired peace between the communities from which each of the lovers comes. However, such an understanding necessitates a restoration of the balance of power by affirming that higher levels must also have some power to influence or control lower levels. This is what Sperry calls "downward causation" (Wilber, 2001a: 20).

Let's return to our example to draw some links to the purpose and intent of this current research project. If one family is English and the other Afrikaans, it would mean that the poem (from the English son of one family to the Afrikaans daughter of the other family) needs to be written in Afrikaans. Thus, at the lower level, the symbolism, linguistic structure, and even the alphabet, (such as the use of Afrikaans diacritics) are affected by a factor on a higher level of complexity. That level relates to the engagement between two persons who come from communities that speak different languages. This is an example of an instance of downward causation.

Such complex causalities need to be accounted for within this study where individual identities are formed in relation to group identities. Moreover, the respective group identities have a view of themselves (an in-group identity) and a view of the other group (an out-group identity). Neither of the groups is likely to hold the same view of themselves as the other group holds of them. This is a complex set of social identifiers that influence prejudice and positive intergroup encounter. The identification and explication of these identities, and the consequences of their engagements with one another require both a structure and a language for their adequate expression.

Moreover, within a given level of such a hierarchical pattern the constituent elements also operate according to a heterarchy. Simply stated, no one element on that level is more important than any other since each contributes more or less equally to the health of that level of the system. Neither of the two children who have to fall in love is more or less important (on that level) than the other. Both need to fall in love and accept the prospect of marriage. However, a higher order whole, of which this lower order whole is a part, can exert an overriding influence on each of its components. The two fathers decide that their children are suitable for marrying each other. They instruct them to marry for the sake of uniting the two families. The patriarchs then use this unity to lead their two communities towards peace, this is a higher order exerting influence over a lower order. Conversely, if two young people from two combatant communities simply decide to marry causal direction is not the same. Their decision to marry will not necessarily result in peace between those two communities – the tail cannot decide to wag the dog.

Thus, a systems approach to this conceptual framework would suggest that *within* each level there is *heterarchy*. However, *between* levels there is *hierarchy*.

Thus, Wilber sums up that in any developmental growth sequence,

> ... as a more encompassing stage or holon emerges, it *includes* the capacities and patterns and functions of the previous stage (i.e., of the previous holons), and then adds its own unique (and more encompassing) capacities.... Thus, whatever the important value of the previous stage, the new stage has that enfolded in its own makeup, plus something extra (more integrative capacity, for example), and that "something extra" means "extra value" *relative* to the previous (and less encompassing) stage. (Wilber, 2001a: 20–21).

Wilber's contention is that in its truest form a non-pathological heterarchy and hierarchy[28] is actually a Holarchy. An overemphasis on heterarchy results, as is said above, in differentiation without showing their interdependence leaving one with "heaps" rather than "wholes" (since each is equal and so cannot be included 'into' another, i.e., which of two equals has the right to subsume another equal?) Whilst an overemphasis on the notion of hierarchy (in which greater, or more important levels subsume lower levels) leads to a domination paradigm which again divides the whole into separate non-dependent parts (cf. Wilber 1995:24). It is not surprising that many systems theorists from varying disciplines (political science, sociology, psychology, economics) have sought to move away from any hierarchical system that tends to rank persons or systems, and so inadvertently introduce domination hierarchies based on domination and compliance. The response has been the postmodernist shift towards heterarchy in an attempt to embrace radical pluralism, "which, in emphasising equal values, is perceived to be more egalitarian, more compassionate" (Snyman, 2002: 80).

The difficulty with this shift is that an acceptance of heterarchy as better than hierarchy establishes an actualisation hierarchy, while trying to maintain that all views are equal. Stated in this way, one can see that such an approach is self-negating and illogical, it destroys the very notion it proposes by making the proposal. Charles Taylor, in his book *Sources of the self: The making of modern identity* (Taylor, 1992), has traced the development of value judgements that deny that they are value judgements. He points out that it is unavoidable for persons to make "qualitative distinctions" since we constantly operate in various contextual frameworks and settings, and these contexts are within ever complexifying contexts (holons within holons) (Taylor, 1992: 30, 81–83; Wilber, 2001a: 26). Each context, by the very nature of it being contextual, or a context, constitutes "various values and meanings that are embedded in (every) situation" (Wilber, 2001a: 26). In terms of the topic of this research project, those who either elevate the importance of one form of meaning construction and identity over the other (e.g. individual identity over social identity, or spiritual identity over material identity, or vice versa), or seek to break down all distinction and inherent value in each of the forms of identity, are engaged in a

---

28 A pathological hierarchy is one which seeks to divide, exclude and dominate, resulting in abusive power imbalances between the levels. Whereas a non-pathological hierarchy recognises the mutual interdependence of lower and higher levels, thus resulting in a shared power approach based on mutual interdependence between the levels.

self-negating process. Often such positions are necessitated by the perceived need to opt for a hierarchical understanding of meaning making and identity i.e., this form of identity is of more value than that form. This is a common explication of prejudice in in-group and out-group intergroup contact. As will be shown in the next chapter, certain mediating conditions can engage such behaviour and aid in the deconstruction of the unconsidered prejudice.

An alternative to the above binary a wholesale application of a heterarchical understanding of identity could be forced i.e., while there are different forms of identity none is more valuable than any other. Such a process is not helpful either. It forces theorists into an "ethics of suppression" according to Taylor (Taylor, 1992: 19–20). This is because one has to suppress one's own value judgements (the informants of the decision) that a certain form of identity is either completely equal or unequal value to another. In short, this incoherent process requires one to judge that no judgement has taken place. It is as a result of this that any view that favours a wholesale acceptance of either hierarchy or heterarchy is fundamentally flawed. Within the context of intergroup contact one could reason that it is neither an honest engagement, nor productive for honest social engagement.

Holarchy is thus a more sensible alternative to both hierarchy or heterarchy since it affirms distinction and value. It differentiates without separating (i.e. it maintains wholes in heterarchy). It also values without setting up a domination paradigm (i.e., each part / whole, or holon, has both intrinsic value as a whole in itself and relational value as a part of a greater whole).

With regards to this research project, the notion of Holarchy is of seminal importance. Holarchy allows for the recognition of the value of individual meaning construction and identity in all its forms. Yet at the same time, without devaluing it, it emphasises the necessity of locating that approach to constructing meaning and identity within the Holarchy of a wider universal social consciousness. Individual consciousness and identity can thus be discussed as a holon (part of a whole, and at the same time a whole in itself) of this greater Holarchy of consciousness and social identity.

In summary then, Wilber's neo-perennial philosophy acknowledges its hierarchical nature and accepts that qualitative statements within the hierarchy are unavoidable. Yet, the right to make such qualitative statements is based upon a holistic view that posits the value statements within the framework of value that is carried from lower levels to higher levels (and the dependence of higher levels for some part of their value on the inclusion of uniquely valuable lower levels), and higher levels to lower levels (and their dependence of valuable lower levels being included into higher levels so adding value to these higher levels).

2.4 Holistic identity and the construction of meaning in relation to Ken Wilber's four quadrants of reality

An important aspect of this research is the understanding that individual and social identity are complex interrelated realities. While it is possible to know some things about a person or community only by accessing or studying one aspect of their identity, it is certain that a richer and more textured picture will emerge if one is able to do a multifaceted study of their identity that takes the complexity of multiple quadrants and levels of reality into account. This section will discuss such

THE (IM)POSSIBILITY OF FORGIVENESS?

an approach to identity with particular reference to Ken Wilber's four quadrants of reality.

We shall begin the discussion on holistic identity from the vantage point of the evolution of consciousness and the Kosmos. Teilhard de Chardin, the Catholic theologian, wrote the following concerning evolutionary theories of the Kosmos, which has a bearing a Holistic understanding of human identity:

> Things have their within. I am convinced that the points of view require to be brought into union, and they soon will unite in a kind of phenomenology or generalised physic in which the internal aspect of things as well as the external aspect of the world be taken into account. Otherwise, so it seems to me, it is impossible to cover the totality of the cosmic phenomenon by one coherent explanation (De Chardin, 2008: 52).

One of the weaknesses of much evolutionary theory is that it has tended to focus exclusively on the empirical aspects of the Kosmos, i.e., that which is observable and measurable, such as physical and biological development. For example, there are very many valuable studies of the physical and biological development of the brain, tracing its increasing complexity and neurological capacity over time. Similarly, there are many valuable studies on the development of social and technological development as expressions of social order. However, there is much less research on the 'interior' aspect of these holons. Such research would be considered phenomenological in nature[29]. It can be said that an understanding of the emergence of the complex triune brain, its neural connections and bio-chemical operations, cannot fully account for the development of its interior processes e.g., the move from producing concepts to producing multifaceted concepts and meta-conceptual frameworks, all the way to the complexity of the kinds of conceptual tasks that my brain is engaged in at the moment of writing this text. Frequently when the 'interior' elements of this holon (the Holarchic development of the conscious brain) were investigated they were dealt with using the same empirical and analytical tools that were applied to the holon's exterior. Snyman notes that "the sciences" have a marked tendency to reduce, or collapse, the interior into the exterior (Snyman, 2002: 84). This has the result of devaluing and misunderstanding the importance of the interior in the overall development of this holon (i.e., the conscious brain).

Wilber suggests that scholars have tended to follow two approaches in the study of the construction of meaning and identity, broadly labelled as the objectivist and the subjectivist approaches (Wilber, 2001a: 118 ff.). The objectivists, as the designation implies, deal with objects, external or material facts in order to give an account of subtle or unseen 'interior' realities. A good example of this approach in current thought can be found in Barrow and Tipler's book *The anthropic principle* (Barrow & Tipler, 1988). Snyman lists Thomas Aquinas' famous argument for the existence

---

29 Within the context of this research the phenomenological method is based upon the philosophy of Edmund Husserl who pointed to this method of enquiry on the basis that reality consists of events and objects that are perceived and understood in human consciousness. They are thus not separate from human consciousness. See *Husserlian Phenomenology in a New Key: Intersubjectivity, Ethos, Societal Sphere, Human Encounter, the Pathos*, for a superb introduction to Husserl's phenomenology (Tymieniecka, 1991).

of God within the objectivist approach (2002:85). In this regard, a large portion of Christian theology, particularly those elements that rely on natural theology, fit into this approach. There is little doubt that such approaches have value for theology. One of the clearest examples of this can be found in the writings of the apostle Paul who understood that God clearly revealed something of the interior mystery of God's self and God's will for creation in the physical, material, world (cf. Romans 1:18-20). The difficulty with an overemphasis on the objective approach to reality is that it relegates subtler forms of being (such as psyche, spirit, and God) to the realm of unknowable and inexpressible mystery.

As we shall see in a later section of this research, a purely objective approach to identity can lead to an inadequate engagement with the complex and subtle concept of forgiveness in intercultural encounter. It is precisely the mistake of making judgements about a person in entirety, or their whole community, based on observation of the external that fosters and supports intergroup prejudice (Pettigrew, 1998: 66–70; Duncan, 2003: 139–141; Bornman, 2011: 729–730; Ypma, 2014: 12).

The other general approach to identity and reality is described as the subjectivist approach. "Subjectivist theorists and theologians begin not with quantifiable observations, but with the immediacy of consciousness itself" (Snyman 2002:85). Thus, those elements of consciousness that are experienced and lived in one's primary awareness – such as an experience of God, or the revelation of a spiritual truth, or a moment of enlightenment – form the basis of one's approach to understanding reality.

Such an approach to reality finds expression in the philosophy of the Greeks (e.g. Plotinus sees God as "not external to anyone, but present with all things") (in Pelikan & Fadiman, 1990: 529). The Christian mystics are another example of this approach in Theology. Meister Eckhart, Julian of Norwich, Dionysius the Areopagite, St John of the Cross, and Catherine of Siena, are just a few Christians throughout history who have sought to understand and express the mystical experience of God based on their inner encounter with God and God's revelation to humanity (Pelikan & Fadiman, 1990: 531).[30]

Once more, it will be shown in the research findings that an exclusively subjective approach to identity is inadequate to fully capture the complexity of understandings of forgiveness within the context of intercultural encounter.

In some senses, there is a clear dualism between the approaches of the objectivists and the subjectivists, between the primacy of identity as located within the interior world, or as located in the exterior world. Such dualism can even be identified within particular population groups, and even individual persons. For example, the Western world has made practical distinctions between essence and form, mind and body, morality and nature, transcendence and immanence, the sacred and the profane (Snyman, 2002: 86).

In philosophy, the divide between the objectivists and subjectivists seemed, to a large extent, to manifest itself in the differences between the Anglo-Saxon and

---

30   For an en excellent discussion of the complexity of theology, mystery, the brain and physical reality see De Gruchy's *Led into mystery: Faith seeking answers in life and death* (De Gruchy, 2013: 23–56).

Continental philosophers. The Anglo-Saxon philosophers[31] tended to apply the analytical, empirical, approach, in which knowledge of the world was immediate. The five senses were seen as the primary building blocks of our understanding of the world. Sensory data was impressed upon the blank slate of the mind to build up an understanding of all reality.

The Continental philosophers[32] declared that knowledge was mediated, not so much through the senses as, through innate *a priori* structures. These structures included elements of human makeup that could be understood through a study (or deconstruction) of the contexts and backgrounds that govern what a person is able to experience in the first place (thus sociological, psychological and anthropological studies were an important element in wrestling with knowledge). For example, the place where a person lived, their background, race, education etc., determined the kinds of questions that they asked. The type of question in turn determined to some extent the kind of answer possibilities that will be received.

Such theoretical approaches are evidenced beyond philosophy. In psychology, a field closely related to much conventional research in relation to meaning making and identity, the objectivist approach resulted in behavioural studies, while the subjectivist approach led to the development of psychological schools such as the psychoanalytical, Gestalt and Jungian psychological approaches. Within the context of social psychology – an important aspect of this study – both subjectivist and objectivist approaches are considered valuable and necessary. Hence the choice for Wilber's integral philosophy that seeks to derive hermeneutic value from holding both approaches in a dialectic tension.

Wilber suggests that a non-dualistic structure be employed for attempting such a task (Wilber, 2011b: 84 ff.). Having discussed Wilber's approach to the dealing with exterior and interior structures through the application of a non-dualistic approach in broad terms, it is necessary to deepen the discussion of identity in relation to his AQAL approach in order to show its applicability for this study.

2.4.1 "A view from within": Interiority, meaning and identity

"A view from within"[33] – as has been noted above, Wilber contends that a holistic understanding of identity has to take cognisance of exterior and interior aspects of being, the parts and the whole, the lower and the higher levels. Much of the research into meaning making and identity (such as the widely known work of Zohar, 1991; D'Aquili & Newberg, 1999; Rausch Albright, 2000) has tended to focus almost exclusively on an objectivist understanding of the construction of meaning and

---

31 Examples of such approaches can be found in the works of Francis Bacon, John Locke, George Berkeley, David Hume (which was later refined by GE Moore) Bertrand Russell and Wittgenstein (Snyman, 2002: 85–86).

32 Most notable here is Immanuel Kant, whose *Critiques* followed the reasoning of Descartes. Then, there were others such as Schelling, Spinoza, Liebniz, Hegel, Heidegger, Foucault and the contemporary Derrida (Snyman, 2002: 85–86).

33 This title is take from Chapter 4 of Wilber's book *Sex, ecology, spirituality: The spirit of evolution* (Wilber, 2001a).

identity. At times, such approaches have dealt only with the exterior and the lower levels, at the exclusion of the interior subtler levels[34].

Because of such "flatland"[35] approaches to the study of identity and meaning; feelings, symbols, ideas, and experiences, are subjected to the same empirical analysis used for the holon's exterior. Some theorists, who purport to be holistic, even go so far as ignoring consciousness[36] altogether which leads to their discussions being little more than an investigation of the exterior which seeks to make some tenable links to the interior (Wilber, 2001a: 110). A second mistake is to seek to explain the whole Holarchy of meaning construction and complex identity by only dealing with one particular level, or holon, at the exclusion of higher or lower levels. The integrative approach, affirms that parts are always whole (in themselves). Thus, in a Holarchy one cannot seek to understand the parts without attempting to understand the whole. This is particularly valuable in the context of the reciprocal relationship of identity formation in intergroup interactions. Individual identity informs group identity, and at the same time group identity informs individual identity.

Thus, while it is contended that all holons have certain basic characteristics[37] in common, it would be improbable to arrive at a full perspective of a holon by only studying a part of it. Moreover, according to Wilber any dualistic approach, which seeks to study only the interior, or exterior for that matter, will be an incomplete approach. The twenty tenets Wilber suggests (cf., Wilber, 2007; Dea, 2010: 136) help us to understand that a holistic approach to all aspects of a Holarchy are essential for a fuller understanding of its complexity in terms of both fundamental and subtle, or significant, elements or levels. Snyman says the following on Wilber's tenets:

> These tenets are fundamental to all holons, including the least developed. However, since they are the most *fundamental*, they are also the least *significant*. Holons emerge, which means that on each new and deeper level, something is added to the whole on that level, something that is new and unexpected. This is the holon's characteristic of creative

---

34 As an alternative, the development of therapeutic techniques such as narrative therapy has allowed for the expression of the individual subjective account of reality. Naturally, if one studies enough of these individual subjective narratives one should be able to discern the development or presence of a common paradigm or 'master narrative' that is common to all humanity. A popular example of this is to be found in the individual subjective narrative of the young girl, Anne Frank, that has proven to resonate with the 'master narrative' common to all humanity. What makes studies of such narratives valuable is not only the individual subjective narrative, or the objective sociological master narrative, but paying attention to both and relating one to the other.

35 The notion of collapsing a holon to one level, or one quadrant, which will be discussed in detail in the next section, is a common mistake made by researchers of consciousness. For a detailed discussion of this see (Wilber, 2001a: 129–133).

36 See Wilber's discussion of (Jantsch, 1980; Laszlo, 1987) in (Wilber, 2001a: 108 ff.). Whilst Wilber does not doubt the brilliance of these studies from an empirical perspective, he does offer significant critique of their method to apply the insights gained wholeheartedly to the 'interior'. As will be discussed, Wilber believes that such approaches fall prey to "subtle reductionism" unless a different hermeneutic approach is not applied (Wilber, 2001a: 129–133).

37 Wilber suggests approximately 20 common characteristics, what he calls the 20 tenets, of all holons. These characteristics are common to all holons and form Wilber's model of manifest reality (cf., Wilber, 2001a, 2007: 35–78).

emergence, self-transcendence, differentiation or increasing complexity that bequest to that holon significance. (Snyman, 2002: 88–89 italics from the original).

Thus, there is an important distinction between what is fundamental and what is significant. Here is an example of the difference between the fundamental and the significant that illustrates why it is necessary to seek to understand and study both. When life is injected into a holon, enabling it to do things that were not previously possible, such as reproduce, it is an important evolutionary shift. The holon is now more capable of survival and living because of the new evolutionary level it has attained. In the same way when consciousness is injected into a holon it is enabled to do things that its predecessors knew nothing about, e.g. to think critically, to do mathematics, to enjoy art, or even to pray. Such new capacities give life (in Holarchic terms) a new, deeper, *significance*. These significant elements are evolutionary, they will cause an incorporation of earlier levels and a rise to a higher level, yet they are not fundamental. If they did not arise, or if in such higher orders significant aspects were destroyed (e.g. a person who sustains brain damage in an accident), life would continue, albeit at a lower Holarchic level. Breathing, eating food, and drinking water are *fundamental* to life. Without such activities life would cease. However, in their basic forms they are not significant. Snyman gives the following good example: "Wildebeest eat grass and drink water in the veld, but they do not pray to God: more fundamental, less significant" (Snyman, 2002: 89).

The notion is that a holistic understanding of the holon of human identity would need to take cognisance of both of these elements, the fundamental and the significant.

With regards to the topic of this research, it is essential to understand that a mere objective approach to the construction of meaning and identity may be able to point to some of the fundamental aspects of individual human consciousness and their identity (such as brain function, or describable behaviour). However, human meaning construction and identity has many more complex and subtle elements that have to do with significance, such as memory, emotion, choice, experience, reason and belief. These aspects are particularly important when it comes to intergroup contact and engagement – biological brain function or observable individual behaviour is much less significant (in the context of this study) than the thoughts, beliefs and values that inform action and reaction, and arise out of interaction.

An understanding of the construction of meaning and identity at the centauric level will be much more integral and holistic than one at the mythic rational level, as we shall see (Wilber, 2014: 167). However, in order to garner as full an understanding as possible of meaning construction and identity at the centauric level one cannot skip the mythic relational level since it is more fundamental (Wilber, 2014: 27, 177). In essence it is important to note that an integral view of identity does not operate in binary categories or radical dualism, but rather it seeks to approach the notions of the construction of meaning and identity from the perspective of nuance and textured complexity.

Snyman summarises Wilber's understanding of the subtleties of meaning making and identity in relation to approaches that investigate the interior and exterior, the subjective and the objective as follows:

> They key issue for Wilber is that consciousness itself is not merely tagged on to the end of a developmental sequence: matter – body – consciousness, like a step-ladder to higher levels. It is rather that each of these aspects develops within their own separate, yet interrelated domain. Each stage of development has its corollary within the other realms, but each is not reducible…[entirely] to another realm. (Snyman, 2002: 89).

In summary, some of the mistakes that are made in the study of meaning construction and identity are either to completely ignore the 'within' of the human person and simply assume that the 'within' is directly reducible to what can be observed and deduced externally (e.g. neural oscillations, chemical inhibitors, stimuli, language, intelligence, emotional reactions, body movement, etc.). This is most often a mistake made by purely empirical, objectivist, approaches to human meaning construction and identity. A subtler mistake is to assume that consciousness is only present in the higher levels of a Holarchy. This is a fairly common mistake among those who adopt a subjective approach to the study of meaning construction and identity. It is true that a fuller picture of consciousness will come from a better understanding of the observable and measurable aspects of the brain, body and context of an individual. This is important for a detailed and nuanced study of identity and the construction of meaning. Accordingly, one will gain a fuller perspective from a deeper understanding of the subtler, significant, elements of the interior experience of the construction of meaning and identity as one progresses to higher levels of the Holarchy.

Such an integral approach would naturally seek to address itself to every aspect of reality in relation to the construction of meaning and identity of the individual being engaged (interior, exterior, individual and collective). Wilber has constructed a model that can aid one in this complex task. The section that follows will first discuss the four existential realms that Wilber identifies as part of his model for engaging and understanding of meaning construction and identity. Thereafter it will go on to discuss these realms in relation to his theory of the Four Quadrants.

2.4.2 The Four existential realms

Thus far we have been somewhat critical of the philosophy of Rene Descartes. Such critique needs a measure of balance. Descartes' central philosophical claim, *cogito ergo sum* (I think, therefore I am) (Descartes & Cress, 1993: 17–19), is valuable and important in that it recognises an essential truth. Namely, that the starting point for an investigation of consciousness is to be found in the individual. Wilber's theory, of course, would speak of consciousness not only in terms of the individual mind but of the holon i.e., the part / whole. Naturally, the earlier critique needs to be held in tension with this statement. An overemphasis on the individual mind to the exclusion of the Kosmos can be counterproductive to truth and present with dualistic, or only partial, results.

In Wilber's book *Up from Eden* (Wilber, 1996a) he makes a significant investigation of individual consciousness building on the work of Jean Gebser (c.f., Gebser, 1985) and Jean Piaget (c.f., Piaget, 1976). Using the important work of these authors Wilber maps out the four epochs of the structural evolution of individual consciousness (as a form of constructing meaning and developing identity). One can clearly see evidence of Gebser's influence in Wilber's use of the terms archaic, magic, mythic and mental. He employs these, together with some others, to describe the stages in which holons develop as they evolve along the different (complexifying) levels of meaning construction and identity.

However, it is essential to remember that holons do not only express or embody consciousness (as an all-encompassing element of the interior reality). Each holon, as was shown above, has both an interior and exterior reality, an individual and a social aspect. The individual aspect of a holon generates its own particular and unique sense of space-time, law, morality, cognitive style, self-identity, drives and motivations, types of religious experience, and of course also pathologies. The social aspect of each holon also has evidence of development in such complexifying levels of social identity. The structural levels in the social aspect of the holon correspond to those in the individual aspect. Thus, the social world-views, which are generated in each stage, correspond with the individual consciousness of the holon at each stage. The social structures include the archaic, magic, mythic and mental world-views. Magic corresponds to preoperational thought, mythic to concrete operational thought and mental with formal thought (c.f., Wilber, 2001a: 111–114; Snyman, 2002: 90 for a more detailed explanation of these categories). The elements of the holon's interior identity can be found in both individual and social states (e.g. 'I think' as a correlate to 'we think', or, 'I am' as a correlate to 'we are').

The development of a holon's individual exterior form is relatively easily identifiable, it ranges from atoms to molecules, cells to organisms and ends in the triune-brained neural organism. As is shown above, the development of a holon's social exterior can also be identified in such exterior structures as families and groups to villages, nations to planets and even larger exterior structures such as planetary systems.

The interior of the individual organism develops from sensation and impulse to concept, then to concrete and formal operational thought to higher and further stages of meaning construction and identity. In human evolution the correlation between the interior and exterior evolution sees the social growth of deeper and more encompassing world-views; magic, mythic, rational, and higher.

Wilber provides the following simple guide of correlations between the development of the interior and exterior of a holon (2001:113, also see figure 2).

Table 1: Interior and Exterior holon correlations

Exterior	Interior
Atoms	Prehension (forms of rudimentary consciousness)
Cells (genetic)	Irritability
Metabolic organisms (e.g., plants)	Rudimentary sensation
Proto-neuronal organisms (e.g., coelenterata)	Sensation
Neuronal organisms (e.g., annelids)	Perception
Neural cord (fish / amphibians)	Perception / impulse
Brain stem (reptiles)	Impulse / emotion
Limbic system (paleomammals)	Emotion / image
Neocortex (primates)	Symbols
Complex neocortex (humans)	Concepts

In keeping with the concept of holons and Holarchy it is important to note that each emergent interior, or exterior development, transcends and includes (i.e., operates upon) the information or structure presented by lower level holons and this fashions something novel in the interior consciousness stream or the exterior developmental, or evolutionary, structure. It is also worth noting that as the exterior structure evolves the interior structure deepens, much along the lines of what was discussed above in relation to Teilhard de Chardin's notion of the law of increasing complexity and deepening consciousness (Forster, 2005: 31–33). Wilber sums it up by saying: "Since... evolution tends in the direction of greater complexity it amounts to the same thing to say that it tends in the direction of greater consciousness (again, depth = consciousness)" (2001:113).

Thus, Wilber's model suggests that there are four primary existential realms: the interior, the exterior, the individual and the social, (also labelled Intentional, Behavioural, Cultural and Social) (Wilber, 1997: 72). The following diagram (adapted from Wilber's image, 1995: 122) gives a pictorial representation of this view.

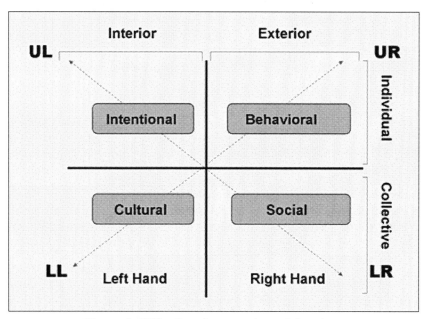

Figure 2: Wilber's primary existential realms

This leads to the next area of discussion that is pertinent to this research, namely, Ken Wilber's notion of the Four Quadrants.

2.4.3 Ken Wilber's Four Quadrants

Based upon his earlier work (particulalry Wilber, 1996a), Wilber developed a model that extrapolates the four existential realms of reality. It also shows the interdependence and interrelationship between holons in the Holarchy at each level and in each existential sphere of the four existential realms. This theory is most clearly articulated in his work *Sex, ecology and spirituality* (Wilber, 2001a).

Wilber developed his schematic of the "four quadrants of existence" through examining,

... over two hundred developmental sequences recognized by various branches of human knowledge – ranging from stellar physics to molecular biology, from anthropology to linguistics, from developmental psychology to ethical orientations, from cultural hermeneutics to contemplative endeavours – taken from Eastern and Western disciplines, and including premodern, modern and postmodern sources.... I noticed that these various developmental sequences all fell into one of four major classes – the four quadrants – and further, that within those four quadrants there was substantial agreement as to the various stages or levels in each... [my theory] thus represents an *a posteriori* conclusion, not *a priori* assumption. (Wilber, 2012: 4).

The diagram below from (Wilber, 2012: 4) offers a visual representation of Wilber's four quadrant theory. It will be helpful in the discussion that follows.

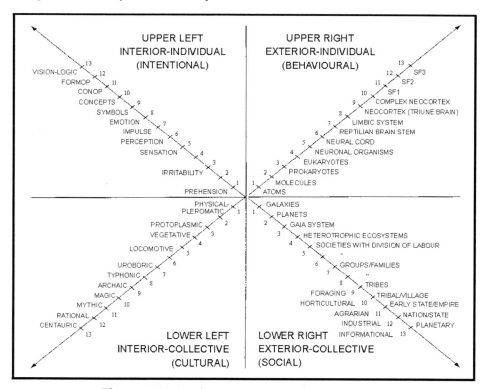

Figure 3: A visual representation of AQAL theory

It is worth noting, before the detailed discussion ensues, that Wilber regards this, and other such, diagrams of the AQAL model as analogous in nature. In particular Wilber is keen to impress that this view is not all encompassing. Furthermore, while it is necessary to represent the developmental aspect of this schema through the use of linear projection, he feels that the development of the quadrants might be more accurately described as a "branching tree". "Each quadrant includes both hierarchies (or clear gradations) and heterarchies (or pluralistic and equivalent unfoldings within a given grade)" (Wilber, 2012: 4–5).

Returning to the diagram above, the upper half of the diagram refers to the development of individual holons (in their interior and exterior correlation), while the lower half of the diagram represents the development of social holons (in their interior and exterior correlations). The whole left hand side of the diagram (both individual – top left, and social – bottom left) represents how the holon looks from within, whereas the whole right side of the diagram (both individual – top right, and social – bottom right) represents how the holon looks from the outside. This schematic gives four quadrants: The Upper Left (UL), Upper Right (UR), Lower Left (LL) and Lower Right (LR).

The UR quadrant will show itself to be most familiar once it is described. It is the standard hierarchy which is commonly presented by modern evolutionary science. It begins with the inception of reality (often referred to as the 'Big Bang'), to atoms and molecules, to cells and organism etc., each of which transcends and includes its predecessor in an irreversible fashion. Cells include molecules, but not vice versa, molecules contain atoms, but not vice versa. The "not vice versa" constitutes the irreversible hierarchy of time's evolutionary arrow. Thus, to repeat what was discussed earlier, each of these individual units is what Wilber calls a holon, a *whole* that is simultaneously a *part* of some other whole (a whole atom is part of a whole molecule, a whole molecule is part of a whole cell, and so on) (Wilber, 1997: 76, 2001a: 17ff). The UR quadrant is thus simply a representation of commonly accepted research on the evolution of individual holons. With regards to an objective study of human beings, this quadrant represents behaviourism (Wilber, 2001a: 121). In other words, it represents that study of behaviour that can be seen by others or the self. Wilber points out that since it can be empirically observed it has tended to occupy the focus of most empirical science (e.g., the study of the *behaviour* of atoms, of gas, of fish, the *behaviour* of humans) (Wilber, 2001a: 121). Such investigations seldom venture into the murky and uncertain depths of the interior, which correlate to the Upper Left (UL) quadrant. This quadrant will be discussed in some detail at a later stage.

Returning to the UR and LR quadrants (i.e. the correlation to the exterior aspects of reality), it is worth noting that every individual holon always exists in communities of similar holons, in fact the very existence of individual holons often depends on the community of holons that, if nothing else, provide the background fields in which holons can exist (Wilber, 1997: 76). In the next chapter this relationship of individual identity and social identity will be clearly explicated as a form of identified in-group and out-group identity.

Erich Jantsch, in his ground-breaking book *The self-organizing universe* (Jantsch, 1980) pointed out that every micro event, or individual holon in Wilber's language, exists embedded in a macro event, a community or collective of similarly structured holons to employ Wilber's terminology. Wilber cites Jantsch's example, noting that when atoms were the most complex individual holons in existence, galaxies were the most complex collective (or social) structures; with molecules it was planets; with prokaryotes it was the Gaia system; and with limbic systems it is groups and families (c.f., Jantsch, 1980; Wilber, 1997: 76). Jantsch makes a further fascinating observation that while individual holons (UR) generally get bigger as they evolve (because they transcend and include their predecessors e.g., molecules are bigger than the atoms they contain) the collective holons (LR) generally get smaller (planets are smaller than galaxies, families are smaller than planets etc.) – the reason being that as an individual social holon gets more complex and possesses more depth, the number of holons that can reach that depth become fewer and fewer, and thus the collective becomes smaller and smaller. For example, there will always be fewer families than individual human persons, and fewer nation states than families. Wilber deals with the implications of this trend in some considerable detail in *Sex, ecology and spirituality* (Wilber, 2001a).

The discussion above has thus presented the two Right Hand columns, namely the individual exterior and the social exterior. What they have in common is that they are empirical phenomena which are located and exist within the sensorimotor worldspace i.e., they can be seen or heard, felt, tasted, smelled (they can be experienced through the senses or their extensions). The holons of these two quadrants are thus objective and inter-objective realities, what holons look like individually or socially, from the 'outside' of life, identity and reality. For example, whilst the UR would include such disciplines as anatomy (the study of the structure of the human body), the LR would deal with sociology (the observed behaviours of human persons).

However, as has already been pointed out, there is a vast body of evidence that points to the belief that every exterior has a related interior. In the context of this research, for example, social identity can be related to external intersectional realities such as gender, race, class and geographic location.

At this stage I will not discuss the Quadrant interrelations in great depth, since that will be done later on. However, it would be fitting to give a similarly brief introduction to the two Left Hand columns of Wilber's schema of reality, namely, the Upper Left (UL) and the Lower Left (LL).

Wilber's research points to various types of evidence that suggests that every external also has an internal (Wilber, 1997: 77, 2001a: 122–125). While there is not a great deal of contention about such correlations, there is endless debate about how 'deeply' these levels of interrelation between exterior and interior can stretch. The contention is particularly in relation to the quality of depth of consciousness, subtlety of meaning construction, and complexity of identity, at successive deepening levels i.e., how "far down" one can push such prehension (forms of rudimentary consciousness) (Wilber, 1997: 77). Wilber comments on this saying that Whitehead,

> … pushes it all the way down, to the atoms of existence (actual occasions), while most scientists find this a bit much. My own sense is that, since holons are 'bottomless, how much 'consciousness' each of them possesses is an entirely relative affair… the whole point of the hierarchy of evolutionary emergents of apprehension is that consciousness is almost infinitely graded, with each emergent holon possessing a little more depth and thus a bit more apprehension. However much 'consciousness' or 'awareness' or 'sensitivity' or 'responsiveness' a tree might have, a cow has more; an ape has more than that and so on. (Wilber, 1997: 77).

In this reasoning the UL quadrant represents the interior of *individual* holons. This quadrant is the interior form of the individual with each level corresponding with successive points on the right-hand side of the schema (UR). With reference to human beings the UL quadrant would contain all of the interior individual sciences such as psychoanalysis, phenomenology, mathematical theory and spirituality. Yet as always, every individual holon exists in *communal relationships* with other holons of a similar depth, which is represented in the LL quadrant. The LL deals not with individual behavioural patterns, but rather with interior social systems. These may include such sciences as sociology, politics, cultural studies and cultural and religious formulation. For example, in relation to the construction of meaning and identity, it is most often suggested that humans possess not only a subjective space (UL) but also certain *intersubjective* space (LL). The two scholars who are most notable for carefully investigating this particular area of consciousness (i.e. the relation between the evolution of human consciousness (UL) and the emergence of cultural world-views (LL)) are Michel Foucault and Jürgen Habermas. Wilber outlines their research in his book *Up from Eden* (Wilber, 1996a).

Thus, in summary of the schema of holons: The Upper half of the schema representing the Upper Left and Upper Right, refer to individual holons. The Lower half of the schema, representing the Lower Left and Lower Right, refer to the collective forms. The Right half refers to the exterior and objective aspects of holons, and the Left half refers to their interior and subjective forms.

Having sketched, in outline, the functioning of the four quadrants it is necessary to move on to discuss the interrelations between the four quadrants[38].

2.4.4 The interrelations among the Four Quadrants

Wilber illustrates the interrelations between the different quadrants, often referring to them as "domains", by using the example of a single thought, namely, that of going to a grocery store (Wilber, 2011b: 11 ff).

When the actual thought takes place, there are certain empirically measurable changes in the physiology and chemistry of the brain (increased dopamine, changed beta wave patterns etc.). This correlates to the UR domain. One's interior apprehension (that is the UL domain) of the thought takes the form of experience and association of images and symbols that give the thought meaning personal meaning and agency. Most current research gets stuck here. Because one can measure and perceive changes in the physical aspects of the brain (UR), some have sought simply to reduce meaning (UL) into measurability (i.e. the experience itself is simply collapsed into a chemical and bioelectrical change). The problem is that the thought itself (UL) cannot be reduced entirely into the UR quadrant without remainder. The thought of going to the grocery store is a thought, and not merely an experience of dopamine. Further adding to the holistic nature of the thought is the individual thinker's relating of the images and symbols of the thought to their social and cultural background (this occurs in the LL quadrant). Snyman notes that for the San Bushman, the need to find food would be expressed more appropriately in the need to track and hunt a wild animal, as opposed to the modern urbanite who may associate it with finding an elusive parking spot outside of the local McDonalds (Snyman, 2002: 93).

---

38   For a more detailed discussion of my own attribution and explication of the four quadrants theory in great detail please see (Forster, 2007, 2010a,b).

The vast networks and contexts of one's cultural community serves as the intrinsic background in which the thought arises, and shapes thought itself, in the life and upbringing of the thinker. (Snyman, 2002: 93).

Furthermore, it has to be borne in mind that culture itself has material components, just as thoughts have material components (e.g., the individual thought (UL) is related to the individual brain (UR)). For the original thought, itself to be possible certain social, external, realities need to present (e.g. not only the culture of fast food dining (social inward – LL), but also the technology and structures that make such thoughts possible, such as transport, roads, restaurants, menus, etc. These are all LR expressions of the holon since they are social, external, necessities). Wilber refers to these LR elements as the "social action system" and "concrete material components" which are necessary for the actual world-view within which the thought arises to exist. Snyman gives the following very clear example.

Thus, I might be among Bushmen hunters, watching their interaction during the hunt. While I may well be physically in their society (LR), even listening to their language, unless I have learned the dialect I will not understand what is meant by the speech and symbols used, thus I am not within their culture (LL). (Snyman, 2002: 94).

Wilber's concludes his own example of the operation of the four quadrants in saying,

... my supposedly 'individual thought' is actually a phenomenon that intrinsically has (at least) these four aspects to it – intentional, behavioural, cultural, and social... the social system will have a strong influence on the cultural worldview, which will set limits to the individual thoughts that I can have, which will register in the brain physiology.... They are all mutually determining. They all cause, and are caused by, the others, in concentric spheres or contexts within contexts indefinitely. (Wilber 1998:12)

The importance of this interrelated understanding of consciousness cannot be emphasised strongly enough in relation to the topic of this research project. As will be shown at a later stage, it simply is not possible to seek to 'collapse' all elements of human meaning construction and identity into a simplistic model of consciousness that only attends to the observation of the external identity, such as gender, race, age of individuals, or the observation of collective external identity, social group dynamics, geographical location etc. Such modelling deals, at best, with the right-hand elements of the domain, at worst it deals only with a collapse of the Upper Left (thought) into the Upper Right (supposedly observed traits) – this is at the root of prejudice.

2.4.5 Meaning and validity claims in relation to Wilber's Four Quadrants

Understanding how one makes claims of what is valid is an essential step towards the construction of a model that can plot the complexity of individual and social intergroup identity. Previously it was suggested that there were two basic approaches to truth, the subjective and objective approaches. Most of philosophy, science, and even theology, has operated from one of these two approaches (i.e., the empirical or the phenomenological). However, Wilber's theory suggests that there are at least four fundamental areas from which validity claims can be made, each accumulating and validating data from within its own domain. Stated differently, each domain has its own epistemologies, ways of knowing, and kinds of truth. Please refer to figure 4 below for a diagrammatic representation of Wilber's four domains of validity claims, from (Snyman, 2002: 95; c.f., Wilber, 2011b: 13 ff.)

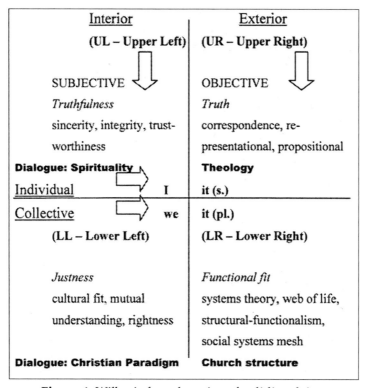

Figure 4: Wilber's four domains of validity claims

We start with the quadrant that is most often the departure point for validity claims, the Upper Right quadrant. Wilber observes that this domain, with its emphasis on the individual exterior of holons most often looks at truth that is *representational*, *propositional*, or *corresponds to*. In this regards something is said to be true if it matches observable facts, or if it is an accurate representation of that which is studied, or closely corresponds to it.

The Upper Left quadrant deals not so much with what is observable (i.e. the facts) but with the truthfulness of the one who is making the claim or statement. Snyman notes that "the only way it is at all possible to understand the interior states of another is through dialogue and interpretation" (Snyman, 2002: 96). Thus, one is not only interested in the observable behaviour, but in unobservable aspects as well i.e., feelings, state of mind, desires, joy and fear. Thus, validity claims within this quadrant rely very much on *trustworthiness* and *sincerity*. With regard to the topic of this research it is worth noting a comment that Snyman records about validity claims in this quadrant.

Of course, there is always the possibility that the other may be lying to themselves, or otherwise misinterpreting their subjective condition. This brings one into the entire field of depth psychology. (Snyman 2002:96).

Hence, a thorough understanding of the sincerity and truthfulness, as well as the meaning and complexity of an individual's interior state offers some significant insight into his or her validity claims about truths from this quadrant. Thus, the validity claims in the upper quadrants have to do with the individual holon. Statements of truth may begin with "I see…" (Upper Right – individual exterior), or, "I feel…" (Upper Left – individual interior). This perspective forms an important aspect of the empirical research design, data gathering, and data analysis aspects of this project (presented and discussed in chapters 5 and 6).

The Lower Right quadrant deals with the social exterior. This is a communal objective position. It locates the truth claim of an individual within a much larger, intermeshing system. Truth in this quadrant is related to a *functional fit* (i.e. does what this individual claims as true relate to general observable truth as seen and experienced in the broader community?) The validation of truth is done in relation to elements such as systems theory, web of life, structural-functionalism, social systems mesh etc. This is the interrelationship between individual identity and action and in-group identity and action.

The Lower Left quadrant (interior social i.e., cultural) does not attempt to show how holons function together as an observable functional whole, but attempts to understand and express how subjects fit together in "acts of mutual understanding" which in turn creates the "intersubjective space of commonly shared background contexts and worldviews" (Snyman, 2002: 96; c.f., Wilber, 2011b: 16–17). Snyman uses the following example: not only does a Christian share the same physical space with other Christians (Lower Right), there is also a sharing of the same intersubjective space of mutual recognition that is shared with other Christian believers (Lower Left). "Within the intersubjective space, ways have to be found to fit not only bodies, but minds together, recognizing and dealing creatively with the differences in culture, theology, ethics and morality" (Snyman, 2002: 96). This realisation shapes the careful design and facilitation of the intercultural Bible reading process using positive intergroup contact theory.

Thus, as can be seen from the above discussion that each quadrant has its own type of evidence and data to verify whether something is true or not true. This is what Wilber refers to as each quadrant's "fallibilist criteria" (Wilber 1998:18). Within such a holistic schema there are at least three necessary factors for making judgements in relation to an understanding of the truth. These are the 'instrumental injunction', the 'intuitive apprehension', and the 'communal confirmation'. Thus, before anything can be understood and judged as valid or not valid, some things need to be done. If one truly wants to understand and judge the teachings of Christ's teaching on social harmony and forgiveness in Matthew 18.15-35, one would first need to learn to read the relevant text from Matthew's Gospel (hence this is done in extensive detail in chapter 4, and particularly 4.8). This is the fulfilling of the necessary injunction. Having read the text some realization of the meaning of the sayings of Jesus can begin to dawn (intuitive apprehension) (this is done using AQAL theory and intergroup contact theory in section 4.8). However, one's interpretation and understanding needs to be tested as valid or invalid by a community that is regarded as adequate, or the authority, in this field. This is the purpose of the process of empirical intercultural Bible reading.

The empirical scientific method which concentrates almost exclusively on the Upper and Lower Right quadrants has, in the West particularly, been regarded as the most valid and useful element of knowledge. There is some strength in the understanding that knowledge should have a sound grounding in experiential and quantifiable evidence. However, it cannot be denied, as Schrödinger's Cat Paradox pointed out (Greenstein & Zajonc, 2006: 185–186; Schrödinger, 2012: 128–134), that the individual is always part of the experiment.

The moment I observe something I have already altered the outcome of the data. In some sense, it is argued that there is no such thing as truly objective research. The introduction of test conditions, equipment, and even the desired outcome of the investigator are all an impression of the interior on the exterior. The challenge of such utilitarian science is highlighted as a risk, to be kept in mind in intergroup contact research, by Zuma (Zuma, 2014: 53–54).

The second factor of knowledge accumulation, that is, intuitive apprehension of data that is immediately available to the researcher, is of equal importance. Thomas Kuhn's much misunderstood notion of paradigms emphasises this (Kuhn, 2012: 1–9, 52–65). A paradigm is not merely a concept. It is in fact an actual practice or series of practices that acts as a means of gaining new, or different, data (in Wilber, 2011b: 86). Snyman summarises that the "questions, quite simply, determine the very possibilities of the answers" (2002: 97).

The third factor of knowledge referred to above is that aspect of being able confirm or reject something as true or not true. Karl Popper emphasized the importance of the notion of falsifiability (Popper, 2002: 261–271; Wilber, 2011b: 87). This is necessary in order to prevent the representation of individual dogma as truth without verification within the wider social context. Unfortunately, though Popper and Kuhn insisted that these factors were limited only to the sensible realm (i.e. that which could be clearly observed, quantified, and understood). They gave little credence to the fact that in addition to sensory experience there are also intuitive mental experiences, and particularly, spiritual experiences which are hugely defining in terms of validity claims.

Thus, the process of injunction, illumination and confirmation (falsifiability) applies not only to the sensible, empirical, scientific realm (i.e. that truth most often associated with the Upper and Lower Right quadrants), but also to the *intelligibila* and *trancedelia*[39]. Wilber insists that we cannot solve the,

> … absolute / relative problem empirically, using the eye of the flesh and its sensibillia; nor can we solve it rationally using the eye of the mind and its intelligibilia. The solution rather, involves the direct apprehension of transendelia, which are disclosed only by the eye of contemplation

---

39 These are terms that Wilber uses to denote the mode of "knowing" within the realm of spirituality as opposed to *sensibilia* and *intelligibilia* (referred to as the eye of the flesh and the eye of the mind) in the empirical realms (Wilber, 2001b, 2011b).

and are most definitely verifiable or falsifiable in that domain, using what are in fact quite *public* procedures – public, that is, to all who have completed the injunction and disclosed the illumination. (Wilber, 2001b: 80)

This is an important aspect for the research design and analysis of this project. It illustrates the importance of facilitating a process that allows for engagement, contemplation, reflection and articulation. It is for this reason that the research design, data capture, coding and data analysis has incorporated these critical elements of experience and identity within and among the participants.

2.4.6 Common Reductionist pitfalls in relation to the four quadrants

Reductionism is a common mistake among theorists who seek to make statements concerning a whole aspect of reality by only investigating a certain part. Wilber identifies two basic forms of reductionism (Wilber, 2001a: 141, 409 ff., 2011b: 20 ff.).

Firstly, there is what he classifies as gross reductionism. This approach is subjective, seeking to explain reality in terms of its physical parts (UR) and the metaphysical laws and rules that regulate these physical parts (LR). Secondly, Wilber points to a far subtler, yet pervasive, form of reductionism. This subtle reductionism, Snyman notes, seeks to reduce everything "in both left hand Quadrants to their empirical correlates in the right hand Quadrants" (Snyman, 2002: 99). Mind becomes brain, praxis becomes technology, and so on. He further notes that it is precisely because holons have an exterior, a physical, quantifiable, reality that subtle reductionism can be so convincing. Even in the disciplines that seek to encapsulate a larger scope of reality this subtle reductionism is evident. One need only look at the language used in speaking of reality, very often the neuter is applied in the form of a non-personal pronoun i.e., the word 'it'. There is very little discussion of beauty, depth, spirit and emotion. Thus, Snyman notes, many of the holistic, systems orientated, sciences are simply a subtle reductionism giving a "flatland of interwoven 'its'" (Snyman, 2002: 99).

The consequence is that if any quadrant is ignored in a system, the disregarded truths often reappear as plain contradictions. Wilber names these subtle reductionisms that plague theorists as:

- *Scientism* – it refuses to concede the interdependent reality of both left and right hand quadrants. Thus, everything that cannot be detected with the senses is simply ignored[40].

- *Cultural constructivism* – which attempts to deny any form of objective truth at all. Here all truth is reduced to the lower left quadrant, suggesting that all truth is culturally and linguistically relative, thus there can be no universal truth. However, if there are no universal truths how can this statement itself be true? This is simply a performative contradiction. Wilber writes that aspects of knowledge are indeed "intersubjectively constructed, but those constructions are set in networks of subjective, objective and interobjective realities that

---

40   However, as Thomas Kuhn pointed out, all scientific facts are embedded within cultural and social paradigms (Kuhn, 2012: 43–51, 66–76). The very assertion that truth is empirical is an intersubjective assertion.

constrain construction" (Wilber, 2011b: 25). It has to be conceded that culture itself is to some extent constructed upon a-priori sensory inputs and possibilities that prevent purely arbitrary assertions. For example, one cannot say that the statement "people grow younger" is an arbitrary statement that has no validity in relation to the truth of the experience of age and reason. It is clearly not arbitrary, it is false.

- *Aesthetic reductionism* – this is a set of theories that is loosely associated with hedonism. It considers that whatever the individual considers to be worthiest, most beautiful, or likeable, is the truth. This collapses all the quadrants into the Upper Left where one's own subjective inclinations become the final truth.

Wilber suggests that one of the greatest achievements of the Enlightenment was the differentiation of the three realms of being as I (Upper Left), We (Lower Left) and It (where 'It' includes both right hand columns of the four quadrants) (Wilber, 2011b: 24 ff.). As a result of this Wilber sees the task of post-modernity, in relation to modernity, not simply as replacing atomism with holism, but to integrate the "it of flatland holism with the depth of I and the community of we" (1998:145). This task is urgent since there is a great deal of subtle reductionism in the dualistic world-views of both modern atomism and postmodern holism. Wilber's Holarchic approach, of the four quadrants, aims to include truth that is derived from each of the four quadrants, the empirical (right hand), constructivist (Lower Left) and aesthetic (Upper Left) by "situating them in a truly inclusive embrace" (Snyman, 2002: 101).

It was for this reason that Ken Wilber's AQAL integral theory was chosen for this project. A theory was sought that would be complex, robust, and rigorous enough to deal with the complexity of forms of individual and social identity in relationship. Moreover, not only would these forms of identity be brought into relationship with one another, but also with the Biblical text and the hermeneutic complexities of building bridges from the text to the contemporary identity and experience of the current readers.

2.5 AQAL theory and empirical intercultural Bible reading

From the discussion in this chapter one can already begin to see the importance of avoid flatland reductionism of identity and belief to the Upper Left quadrant, or prejudice as on ly in the Upper Right and Lower Right quadrants. Subtle and complex formulations of meaning construction and identity need to be located in a far more encompassing approach to reality. Identity and the construction of meaning are never only an inward reality; neither are they only a matter of individual experience.

What Wilber's Holarchic model shows is that true identity requires more than just a subjective reflection on individual interior experience – such reflection can serve to enforce prejudice of the out-group strengthen the un-questioned values of the in-group. Moreover, it is also not sufficient to simply apply an objective observation of individual or collective behaviour to validate truth claims about the 'other'. The exterior has correlates in the interior of both the observer and the actor.

Any attempt to grapple with the complexity of holistic identity requires a far more rigorous and interactive engagement with the conscious being (not just a passive observation and reflection on static knowledge gained from the person's actions).

It requires engagement with the individual's subjective experience and the group's beliefs, social structure and values.

For the topic at hand, namely engaging Matthew 18.15-35 in order to gain a fuller understanding of Christian forgiveness, the value of the AQAL integral approach is clear. Engaging the text in an integral manner allows the Biblical scholar to gain a variety of valuable insights. In terms of text reception and hermeneutics it allows one to do some mapping of perception and action in order to understand how the reader, and various communities of readers, understand the content of the text and respond to their understanding.

For the purpose of this project the AQAL hermeneutic approach will be brought into conversation with the text to illustrate the textured variety of interpretive opportunities that emerge from such a scheme (c.f., section 4.8).

Within the context of the larger study, the AQAL approach makes it possible to identify reader responses to the text that may locate them largely in one or more quadrants of the AQAL integrative theoretical framework. For example, if a person had a legalistic reading of the text that sought only to follow the process set out in vv.15-20 (UR, individual confrontation of the sinner, and LR, collective and community confrontation of the sinner), yet they did not understand the intention of the process was the re-establishment of holistic harmony in the community (i.e., restoration of the individual relationship, UL; restoration of proximate relationship between the sinner and the sinned against, UR; the deepening of shared values of forgiveness and reconciliation, LL; and the creation and deepening of the benefits of social cohesion, LR), the individual could miss the entire intention of the process, namely to mimic the merciful King and restore true individual and communal harmony by forgiving the brother or sister from one's heart (v.35).

This understanding frames the value of using Matthew 18.15-35 in the intercultural group readings. It is highly unlikely that any one individual would have a completely integrated understanding of the text (locating meaning in each of the four quadrants and understanding the importance of the interaction between these categories of meaning). However, when a variety of readers engage the text in a safe space, without judgement or competition[41] (c.f., Gobodo-Madikizela, 2008a: 169–188), it is possible that the various perspectives of the readers could enrich and deepen each other's understanding of both the text, and the communicative intention of the text.

In addition to this, the theme of forgiveness makes for a very helpful concept that can be extrapolated from the Biblical text in order use the AQAL approach to engaging the Biblical text and its intercultural readers. There are a number of reasons why this is so. In part, it is because this theme has both religious (UL and LL) as well as social (UR and LR) implications. Moreover, the concept of forgiveness touches on individual (UL and UR) and communal (LL and LR) aspects of being and identity. In summary, the concept itself deals with thoughts and emotions (UL) and values (LL) which have an impact on actions (UR) and social structure (LR).

---

41   The mediators of positive intergroup contact will be discussed in detail in sections 3.3.1 and 3.3.4, also please see (Swart, Hewstone, Christ & Voci, 2010: 309–333; Cakal, Hewstone, Schwär & Heath, 2011: 606–627; Goosen, 2011; Swart, Hewstone, Christ & Voci, 2011: 1221–1238).

In choosing the theme of forgiveness as a point of consideration and study in Matthew 18.21-35 one is able to draw upon a variety of insights from a number of different methods and exegetical approaches to the Bible. It will be shown how each of the various approaches leans towards a particular understanding of the text in each of the four quadrants, and that when these understandings are brought together they add layers of texture and complexity to the understanding of the text.

2.6 Concluding remarks

This chapter presented a detailed and critical discussion of the Ken Wilber's AQAL integral theory. This theory forms and important component for the current project in empirical intercultural Bible reading on forgiveness.

AQAL theory provides the language and philosophical framework that was used to understand and explain the complexity of theological perspectives on forgiveness in Matthew 18.15-35 in chapter 4 (see 4.8 in particular, and also Forster, 2017). Moreover, the theory provided a sound basis for understanding the complexity of individual and social identity in the intercultural Bible reading process. The AQAL theory informed the research design of this project by helping to facilitate the manner in which different forms of knowledge are explicated from the research intervention process. These forms of knowledge relate to the four quadrants of Wilber's integral theory. These are the intentional (UL), behavioural (UR), cultural (LL) and social (LR). This will be evidenced in research design and intervention design cycle of the intercultural Bible reading process (see chapter 5 for the research design, and chapter 6 for the discussion of the findings from the research intervention).

At certain points in the research process data points will necessarily be extracted: The AQAL reading of Matthew 18.15-35 in section 4.8 is important. A pre-intercultural engagement separate in-group Bible reading with each of the two groups is important. Then there are the two intercultural Bible readings with the combined in-group and out-group dynamics, and a post-intercultural engagement separate in-group Bible reading with each of the two groups. This data will be analysed and meaning identified and extrapolated from the perspective of the AQAL theory to plot individual and group understandings of forgiveness from the reading of Matthew 18.15-35. In particular it is important to have comparative data sets of the two groups from the pre-intercultural engagement readings of the text and the post-intercultural engagement readings of the text. This allowed us to see whether the positive intergroup contact intervention (theoretically presented in chapter 3, and discussed in the research design in chapter 5) had the intended effects on the intercultural Bible readers.

Thus, Ken Wilber's theory provides a sound theoretical framework for understanding complex cross-sectional theological data about the participants' concepts of forgiveness in Matthew 18.15-35 (i.e., allowing for a schema to map their understandings at certain stages in the intervention). Moreover, it allows for an engagement where correlational data analysis is conducted between the pre-intercultural engagement and post-intercultural engagement readings of the text.

In the following chapter, we will present the second foundational theory of this research – namely intergroup contact theory.

3.1 Introduction

In this chapter, we shall discuss the second important theoretical framework that shaped this study – namely intergroup contact theory.

The previous chapter presented AQAL integral theory (c.f., chapter 2). That theoretical framework allowed for the expression of language and a structure of thought to extrapolate a complex set of identity locators around which a variety of theological positions from both the Biblical text and the intercultural readers of the text could be considered. This chapter, however, discusses the second theoretical framework that was employed within the intercultural Bible reading process. Intergroup contact theory informed the structuring of the intercultural Bible reading encounters in an attempt to lessen anxiety and increase the possibility for empathy among the participants that would lead to the possibility of more integral understandings of forgiveness.

The stated intention of this study was to chart the progressive understanding of concepts of forgiveness in relation to the 'other' between two distinct groups of readers engaged in a process of intercultural Bible reading. Hence, it was necessary to have both a theory to plot the theological understanding of the participants at various points in the process (AQAL theory), and a theoretical framework around which to structure the intercultural Bible reading encounters themselves (intergroup contact theory).

The structuring of the intercultural Bible reading encounters was informed by the contact hypothesis (Allport, 1954). Allport's contact theory proposes that positive intergroup contact reduces prejudice by dealing with the affective mediators of contact between 'in groups' and 'out groups'. The two most commonly researched affective mediators in contact literature are "anxiety and empathy" (Swart, Hewstone, Christ & Voci, 2010: 311–312). These concepts will be considered in detail below. However, at this point it can simply be noted that intergroup contact anxiety can lead to contact avoidance, reserved intergroup engagement, insincerity in engagement, or conflict. Whereas "affective empathetic responses have been associated with numerous positive outcomes including an increased tolerance for other groups and an increased concern for the well-being of others" (c.f., Batson, Polycarpou, Harmon-Jones, Imhoff, Mitchener, Bednar, Klein & Highberger, 1997: 105–118; Batson, Chang, Orr & Rowland, 2002: 1656–1666; Swart, Hewstone, *et al.*, 2010: 311). Recent research has shown a strong link concerning positive intergroup contact between conflicted groups and the possibility of facilitating the conditions in which forgiveness operates (Swart, Turner, Hewstone & Voci, 2011; Swart & Hewstone, 2012).

It was for these reasons that intergroup contact theory was chosen to inform the practices and mechanisms of the intercultural Bible reading process. Naturally other approaches were considered and evaluated for the design of this process. In the end the researcher concluded that because of the wealth of research in this field, and particularly the links between intergroup contact theory and religion, and intergroup contact theory and social identity in South Africa, that this theory was well suited to the study.

We shall now move on to presenting the necessary and salient aspects of intergroup contact theory that were employed in this study. We shall begin with some background to the development of the theory. Next, we will discuss the generally accepted dimensions (or mechanisms) of positive intergroup contact. We shall also offer some insight into the affective mediators of contact – namely anxiety and empathy. Some attention will also be given to secondary aspects of intergroup contact and its distributed effects, namely, religion, cross group friendships, quantity and quality of intergroup contact, and direct and extended contact. Finally, we shall contextualise this theoretical framework within the South African context.

3.2 Intergroup contact theory and the contact hypothesis

The notion that positive intergroup contact could be used to facilitate the conditions under which better intergroup relations are developed and prejudice of the other is reduced was first put forward by Robin Williams in *The reduction of intergroup tensions* (Williams Jr, 1947). However, it was the social psychologist Gordon Allport whose work established the notions of contact theory and intergroup contact theory within the broader academy (c.f., Allport, 1954). While Allport only anticipated the positive effects of direct intergroup contact in his early work, it has since been shown that indirect contact (or secondary contact) also has positive effects on intergroup relations.

At the heart of Allport's contact hypothesis was the notion that bringing persons together in "face-to-face" encounters under certain conditions could reduce intergroup prejudice and conflict The conditions that Allport identified, "…involved equal status among the participants, cooperation on common goals between groups, and institutional support" (Hewstone & Swart, 2011a: 375). These, as well as some further contributions, will be considered in detail later in this chapter.

In subsequent decades Allport's contact hypothesis has been shown to be largely valid. The most convincing evidence is to be found in Pettigrew and Tropp's meta-analysis of 515 research studies on intergroup contact. They clearly substantiated the view that positive intergroup contact significantly reduced prejudice (mean $r = -.22$, $p < .001$), and that it was even more effective when the intergroup contact was facilitated under Allport's conditions (Pettigrew & Tropp, 2006: 751–755). As Swart notes,

> The evidence is encouraging in that it suggests that intergroup contact… is capable of simultaneously reducing the negative factors associated with outgroup prejudice and augmenting the positive factors associated with more positive intergroup relations. (Swart, Turner, *et al.*, 2011: 181).

Swart's perspective is particularly helpful in that it shows two possible orientations for intergroup contact theory research that are of value to this study. First, the traditional emphasis on mediating the negative aspects of intergroup contact and even intergroup conflict. Second, the possibilities of facilitating or fostering positive intergroup relations. While the former is descriptive and explicative, the latter tends to be constructive. Naturally these orientations are not entirely separate from each other, but show the possibilities of a wide variety of contributions to both theory and practice. Within the context of this research it was important to employ a sound and credible theoretical framework that could allow for a rigorous and careful explanation of the notions of identity and their interactions in the intergroup settings. At the same time, it was important to have a credible set of theoretical mechanisms that could shape the ongoing process of engagement, and even change, hypothesized through the intercultural Bible reading process.

Thus, intergroup contact theory is widely regarded theoretical approach to intergroup contact. It has a proven track record in research that gives credence to the contact hypothesis – namely that positive intergroup contact not only reduces prejudice but can contribute to better intergroup relations[42].

Having established this, we can delve a little deeper, going into more detail in the next section where we discuss Allport's key dimensions of positive intergroup contact.

3.3 Key dimensions of positive intergroup contact

It has already been mentioned that intergroup contact theory research could take a descriptive approach. In other words, some researchers have sought to do cross sectional studies of intergroup engagements to describe and understand the character, nature and content of such encounters. This is very valuable information since it helps us to understand notions of identity and identity formation in relation to other persons and other contexts. However, there is also the second aspect of intergroup contact theory research. This is what I have termed the constructive approach. This approach involves the testing of the dimensions, or mechanisms,

---

42   It is important to note that intergroup contact theory is not without its critics. Some researchers have rightly pointed out that while positive intergroup contact does facilitate better intergroup relations it may be negative in its avoidance, or suppression, of honest and necessary conflict. It has also been suggested that the interventionist nature of intergroup contact could have significant consequences for social engineering – e.g., bringing about engagement among persons or communities in processes without actually engaging the ideological underpinnings of prejudice. There are also some critics who question whether facilitated intergroup contact does not inadvertently strengthen strong groups and further weaken the position of weaker minorities. It remains a challenge of intergroup contact research to be conscious of these, and other, critiques and not to inadvertently invalidate real and necessary concerns among groups or individuals, or subtly protect the majority at the expense of minority views and subversive movements. This research has sought to be conscious of these challenges, and others, in the design and implementation of the research processes and instruments. For some discussion of the critique of intergroup contact theory please see (Parkin & Forbes, 1999; Wright, 2003: 409–430; Dixon, Durrheim & Tredoux, 2005: 697–711; Prestwich, Kenworthy, Wilson & Kwan-Tat, 2008: 575–588; Wright & Lubensky, 2009: 291–310; Hewstone & Swart, 2011a: 379–380)

of positive intergroup contact that have been identified as contributing towards the reduction of prejudice and the facilitation of positive intergroup relations.

Intergroup theory gained prominence in academic research within a particular socio-historical context. After the end of the Second World War soldiers were returning home from situations of conflict and needed to reintegrate into diverse social settings. Moreover, as Dixon notes, the political climate in America was one of structural discrimination (Dixon *et al.*, 2005: 698). America was at the cusp of the civil rights movement and the social, political, and moral dominance of the White majority was being challenged. Within this group there was a profound distrust of the "value of desegregation… many people believed that legal systems of racial segregation were necessary for the maintenance of social stability and harmony" (Dixon *et al.*, 2005: 698). These social struggles and conflicts that were present in society needed to be understood and engaged in a constructive and scientifically verifiable manner.

Allport's "contact hypothesis" proved to be the most influential contribution in the development of this positive intergroup contact theory. His hypothesis, contained in his 1954 book *The nature of prejudice*, identified and presented a number of situational criteria for diminishing prejudice through facilitated intergroup contact (cf., Allport, 1954).

3.3.1 The moderators and mediators of prejudice reduction and positive intergroup contact

Swart and Hewstone identify these aspects as the "moderators" and "mediators" of contact (Hewstone & Swart, 2011a: 375–376). Moderating factors indicate *when* contact is most likely to have a positive effect, whereas mediating factors indicate *how* contact can be positive effected. Allport's work was most influential in identifying the moderators of positive intergroup contact, this view was further developed by Pettigrew and Tropp (Allport, 1954; Pettigrew, 1998: 65–85; Pettigrew & Tropp, 2006: 751–755). Importantly Swart and Hewstone note, "A major development since Allport's (1954) pioneering work is that researchers have moved from merely demonstrating that contact works to showing *how* it works" (Hewstone & Swart, 2011a: 376). Thus, what we have come to understand is that it is not just merely contact between in-groups and out-groups that reduces prejudice, but particular types of contact – what has become known as positive intergroup contact. That stands to reason – certain types of contact that fuel distrust, enforce stereotypes about the other, or that are deemed to be physically or psychologically damaging, will not be considered positive intergroup contact events or processes. These can be categorized as "negative affective mediators" of contact (Swart, Hewstone, *et al.*, 2010: 313). The research has shown that, to a large measure, the mediation of affect contributes towards positive intergroup contact. Hewstone and Swart write of such positively mediated contact that it,

> … exerts its effect on prejudice reduction both by reducing negative affect (e.g., intergroup anxiety) and by inducing positive affective processes (e.g., empathy and perspective taking). (Hewstone & Swart, 2011a: 376).

Zuma rightly points out that the current emphasis on intergroup contact theory masks the fact that this theory has its basis in the study of prejudice (Zuma, 2014: 40). The notion of understanding and engaging prejudice is the foundation upon which subsequent studies on intergroup relations are based. At the heart of Allport's hypothesis was the notion that prejudice is the is the source of intergroup conflict and strife. Allport's "least effort principle" suggests that the human brain tends to opt for efficiency in making sense of the world (Allport, 1954: 21). As such we tend to relate to other persons, and social structures, based on learned or received stereotypes about them – these are our prejudices. In general individuals and communities find it difficult to honest engage such overgeneralised categories, since this takes mental effort, and as Allport states, "effort… is disagreeable" to the brains efficiency system (Allport, 1954: 21). Allport did, however, suggest that persons and social groups are willing to engage and amend their prejudices, moving stereotypes to more nuanced perspectives when they are motivated to do so by some form of psychological energy (e.g., interest in a person or culture, friendship, fascination etc.) In such cases, we frequently come to understand that the larger whole, of which we have a prejudice, has subcategories (e.g., not all men are the same). However, at its very core, his theory engaged prejudice between in-group identity and out-group identity (Dovidio, Glick & Rudman, 2008: 40).

It is the expression of prejudice, or the experience of prejudice, that increases anxiety and limits the capacity for empathy. It was Allport's intention to address this aspect of social identity that formed his hypothesis on contact theory:

> Prejudice (unless deeply rooted in the character structure of the individual) may be reduced by equal status contact between majority and minority groups in the pursuit of common goals. The effect is greatly enhanced if this contact is sanctioned by institutional support (i.e., by law, custom or local atmosphere), and provided it is of a sort that leads to the perception of common interests and a common humanity between members of the two groups. (Allport, 1954: 281).

3.3.2 Individual identity and social identity: in-groups and out-groups

From the previous quote one can see that there is some correlation to the notions of individual identity (UL) and social identity (LL) as discussed in the previous chapter. The identity of the self (UL), or the in-group (LL) frequently finds articulation and expression in relation to the perceived identity of the other individual (UR) or out-group (LR). In an encounter with the other, "all sorts of psychological elaboration" takes place which leads one to "easily exaggerate the degree of difference between groups, and readily misunderstand the grounds for it" (Allport, 1954: 19). The result is, according to Dovidio et al. that uncontested out-group homogeneity forms (UR / LR), i.e., "they are all alike", and in-group attributions are highlighted and strengthened (UL / LL) "we are intrinsically good" (Dovidio *et al.*, 2008: 40). Hence we tend to see out-groups as less variable than our in-group and in-groups as more variable than average (Tajfel, 1970: 96–103). So, these social stereotypes, with their latent psychological strength are a great challenge to open and honest intergroup engagement. What makes it even more difficult is the brain's reliance on memory – the psychological mechanism is particularly "stubborn and resists change" (Allport, 1954: 23).

Our individual identity (UL) requires a measure of affirmation, strengthening and support that comes from a shared set of beliefs and values in the in-group (LL). The survival and strengthening of our individual and collective in-group identity is undertaken by "setting it apart from other groups that have different and therefore competing goals" (Dovidio *et al.*, 2008: 42). One of the primary psychological orientations in the encounter with others is to place them as either a friend (part of the in-group) or a foe (part of the out-group). Second to this, according to Dovidio, is the question around ability or inability – is the person or group able or unable to support and strengthen in group goals and identity? Or, if the person or group is part of an out-group, are they able or unable to threaten in-group goals and identity? Interestingly the research has shown that in general these categorisations serve to create emotional distance in four broad ways: High warmth, low competence (e.g., older persons, disabled persons for whom there is a paternalistic regard with little threat); low warmth, high competence (e.g., rich and powerful persons, or successful persons for whom there is low regard with a high measure of threat). The first group is distanced through idealised paternalism or pity, while the second group is distanced through distrust. The remaining two categorizations are: Low warmth, low competence (e.g., poor persons, persons on welfare who distance through disgust and contempt); high warmth, high competence (e.g., persons who share our values, are our allies and are successful within our social group). The first of these two groupings are at times actively harmed (through attack) or passively harmed (through neglect), while the second grouping are admired and regarded as aspirational (Dovidio *et al.*, 2008: 42–43).

So, the result is that in-group identity is often exaggerated and idealised, while out-group identity is simplified and prejudged according to social and historical prejudices. This could be disastrous in complex and diverse social environments leading to misrepresentations, misunderstandings, conflict and abuse between in-groups and out-groups. In large measure Allport's contact theory sought to understand the relationship between prejudice as antipathy (the low warmth, low competence – an out-group) and prejudicial love (high warmth, high competence – the in-group). It was within this social framework that Allport moved from understanding aspects of prejudice to finding ways to bring persons together for honest and constructive intergroup contact. The result of which was that he developed and highlighted a number of important contact mediators between in-groups and out-groups.

3.3.3 Cognitive and affective mediators of intergroup prejudice

Before we discuss Allport's prejudice engaging contact mediators, below – it is worth mentioning however, that his favoured mediator ("knowledge of the out-group" (Allport, 1954: xvii), which is a cognitive mediator) has not proven to be as effective in the research findings as he initially anticipated (Levine & Hogg, 2009: 471; Hewstone & Swart, 2011a: 376). Allport had anticipated that cognitive mediators (knowledge about the out-group, their customs etc.) would be the primary contributor to the decreasing of out-group prejudice. Of course knowledge of the 'other' does play some role. But simply knowing things about another person or group (UR or LR) does not necessarily translate to a change of judgement or values in relation to them (UL or LL).

Thus, the research has found that affective mediators have proven much more important than cognitive mediators in addressing in-group, out-group, prejudice (Levine & Hogg, 2009: 471–472). The affective mediators fall into two broad categories – namely the emotion of anxiety and the emotion of empathy. The research has shown that there is a physiological change in the anxiety levels of group participants through frequent positive intergroup contact. Thus, if certain mediating conditions are met in the intergroup contact (which shall be discussed below) the levels of anxiety in the participants decreases which allows for a positive experience of the contact, and for constructive contact itself. This has shown to lead to a decrease in prejudice against the out-group (Levine & Hogg, 2009: 471). Moreover, the research shows that positive intergroup contact also enhances empathetic emotion among the participants. This creates not only an emotional openness to the other, but also a willingness to take on aspects of their views and perspectives, since there is a measure of shared experience (Levine & Hogg, 2009: 471).

In light of this it is reasonable to see how the possibility of cross group friendship may contribute towards positive intergroup contact. Friendship has shown to lessen anxiety and increase empathy in a more natural and sustained manner between in-group and out-group participants (Paolini *et al.*, 2004: 770–786; Barlow, Louis & Hewstone, 2009: 389–405; Levine & Hogg, 2009; Swart, Hewstone, *et al.*, 2010: 309–333; Goosen, 2011; Lewis, 2014: 471).

3.3.4 From contact hypothesis to contact theory

Lastly, it is worth noting that when Allport first presented his work he was clear to identify it as a hypothesis rather than a theory. He was not entirely sure that all of the mediators would function (or function as he supposed) in all settings. This seems to be both a sensible and academically reasonable approach. His work did however spark a long line of subsequent research that has shown much more clearly and carefully how the various mediators of prejudice operate in relation to in-group and out-group contact (Levine & Hogg, 2009: 468–470). Thus, Hewstone has suggested that the contact hypothesis has evolved from a speculative proposition to a more textured and verifiable theory (Hewstone, 2009; Hewstone & Swart, 2011a: 380).

Among others, the work of Pettigrew and Tropp, as well as the extensive work of Hewstone, have allowed this hypothesis to develop from a speculative supposition to the verifiable, nuanced and technical, "contact theory" that we work with at present (Hewstone, 1996, 2009; Pettigrew, 1998; Pettigrew & Tropp, 2005, 2006, 2011; Hewstone & Swart, 2011b). In its most succinct form this theory "is concerned with when (situational specifications)… and (psychological processes) intergroup contact leads to effects that ultimately reduce prejudice" (Zuma, 2014: 45).

3.3.5 From intergroup contact to positive intergroup contact

Another important component to intergroup contact theory is that the quality of the contact is essential. While prejudice is frequently as a result of a lack of contact with the out-group, some forms of prejudice are fuelled by unmediated or poorly conceived instances of intergroup contact (Dixon *et al.*, 2005: 698). As Dixon suggests, "Allport wanted to highlight the importance of contextual prerequisites in promoting meaningful change" (Dixon *et al.*, 2005: 698). Theoretically, Allport suggested, frequent superficial contacts could "strengthen the adverse associations we have" of the out-group (Allport, 1954: 264). Thus, Allport developed the "situational specifications" that would allow social psychologists to distinguish between favourable (positive) intergroup contact, and unfavourable (negative) intergroup contact[43]. The intention was to understand the subtleties of both the frequency and quality of intergroup contact in order to identify and understand the "optimal contact strategy", and to "elucidate the conditions under which contact works most effectively to reduce prejudice and, by implication, to increase the possibility of social harmony" (Dixon *et al.*, 2005: 699).

3.3.6 Intergroup contact moderators: Some situational specifications / mechanisms for positive intergroup contact

Allport's hypothesis suggested that at least four "situational specifications" (what I am calling mechanism within the research design of this project) need to be present for a positive intergroup contact to take place. In other words, these mechanisms need to be present and operable in the intergroup contact situation in order to mediate a change in the affective moderators of intergroup contact (psychological processes) (Levine & Hogg, 2009: 468–469). Allport's situational specifications, mentioned below, have since been extensively tested and researched and, as we shall see, there have been some developments since his initial contact hypothesis was presented. What is noteworthy is that these overarching mechanisms (moderators) have proven to be effective in reducing prejudice through mediating anxiety and heightening intergroup empathy (Pettigrew & Tropp, 2006). They are:

- *Equal status within the situation:* Allport stressed the importance of facilitating equal status among the participants within the situation of the intergroup contact. Pettigrew points out that there is wide spread consensus on the importance of equal status among the participants in an intergroup contact session to reduce anxiety and increase empathy (Pettigrew, 1998: 66). If participants in the process feel that there is an imbalance of personal or institutional power between the in-group and out-group, they are less likely to trust either the process or the participants who hold power over them. Thus, it is critical to structure the groups, and the intergroup contacts, in a manner where power is largely equal and shared. This will include such aspects as age, gender, class, language, education and a variety of other variable within the representative groups. Moreover, there are some researchers who emphasise the importance of equal status going into the session (in other words, the expectation of equality is as important as the experience of equality in the intergroup contact session) (Brewer & Kramer, 1985: 235–236). As such it will be shown that the selection of the participants for

---

43 It is not directly germanie to this study, however, it must be noted that Allport's contact theory has sparked a variety of different fields of research within the academy. Conceptually, some scholars have an interest in how, when and why certain situational variable "maximize prejudice reduction". Methodologically, a sub field has developed that has a particular interest in the empirical testing of the association between intergroup prejudice and more ideal forms of intergroup contact. Then there are scholars working in the applied sciences who are "attempting the translation of theory into practice" (Dixon *et al.*, 2005: 698). Also, please see the work of Scheepers for insights into the complexity of social identity and political identities in relation to free choice and social pressure (Van Der Meer, Te Grotenhuis & Scheepers, 2009: 227–241; Gesthuizen, Scheepers & Savelkoul, 2011: 1091–1107).

this process, as well as the communication of the identity of the groups and the shared tasks, place of meeting and manner of operation of the groups was done in such a manner as to minimise power hierarchies.

- *Common goals:* The reduction of prejudice in contact among groups requires a common focal point (Pettigrew, 1998: 66). Inter-racial sports teams serve as a good illustration of this point. In striving to win a sporting game inter-racial sporting teams show a need for one another, a respect of talents and abilities, and create opportunities for flourishing in order to achieve the common goal of winning the match or season. This mechanism in intergroup contact has become known as "instrumental contact" (Wilcox, 2011: 33). Instrumental intergroup contact occurs when members feel that in-group and out-group contact can work towards the achievement of a shared and valued goal. However, the converse is also true. If the groups perceive that their contact with the other is counterproductive to an important goal they will seek to sever the contact or diminish its effects on the in-group. The famous "Robbers Cave" illustrates how subordinate goals serve to reduce intergroup prejudice (c.f., Relations & Sherif, 1961; Wilcox, 2011: 33).

- *Intergroup cooperation:* Allport pointed out that where persons from in-groups and out-groups cooperate in the achievement of shared tasks without competition prejudice was lessened. What Pettigrew suggests with this point is that intergroup cooperation, without unhealthy competition, is required to lessen anxiety and increase empathy in order to create the opportunity for positive engagement within the intergroup contact (Pettigrew, 1998: 67). Aronson's "jigsaw classroom" has frequently been cited as an example of a mechanism or process in which such conditions for positive-intergroup encounter are facilitated (c.f., Aronson, 1978; Wilcox, 2011: 33–34). In such a setting students are assigned to learning groups where each group learns a different part of the new material, after this the students are re-assigned to heterogeneous learning groups. In each of these new groups, one person from each of the previous learning groups has the responsibility to teach the others what they know about the subject. This creates an openness to learning from others and a reliance upon their knowledge and expertise in learning.

- *Support of authorities, law or custom:* Allport identified that positive intergroup contact functions best when the participants know that they have the support of authorities, laws or customs in engaging the out-group positively. It would stand to reason that with explicit social sanction from figures or institutions of respected authority an intergroup contact has a better chance of achieving a positive effect. If persons participate in intergroup contact knowing that they will face shame, ridicule or persecution from authorities in their in-group they are less likely to have the kind of engagement in which the affective mediators are constructively engaged. In such unsanctioned settings anxiety is likely to remain high and there will be little opportunity for vulnerability in the encounter with the other that can lead to increased empathy (Pettigrew, 1998: 65–85). This is particularly challenging in contacts with significant social consequences for disobedience to figures of authority or community rules – such as religious settings (Parker, 1968; Zuma, 2014). A person may fear the consequences of shifting their primary in-group identity to a position that is conflict with that of the primary group of belonging, identity and care. As a result, it will be shown in the design, selection and conduct of this research project how important it was to gain the official sanction of the 'problem owner', the Methodist Church of Southern Africa. The selection, sanction, and communication of authority support was an important part of the process in setting up the representative groups for the intergroup contact sessions.

Dixon *et al.*'s (2005: 699) review of the literature over the last 50 years, since Allport's first work, has led to the construction of the following more textured and detailed list of situational specifications for positive intergroup contact:

- Contact should be regular and frequent
- Contact should involve a balanced ratio of in-group to out-group members
- Contact should have genuine "acquaintance potential"
- Contact should occur across a variety of social settings and situations
- Contact should be free from competition
- Contact should be evaluated as "important" to the participants involved
- Contact should occur between individuals who share equality of status
- Contact should involve interaction with a counter stereotypic member of another group
- Contact should be organized around cooperation toward the achievement of a superordinate goal
- Contact should be normatively and institutionally sanctioned
- Contact should be free from anxiety or other negative emotions
- Contact should be personalized and involve genuine friendship formation
- Contact should be with a person who is deemed a typical or representative member of another group

A careful consideration of this list of specifications will show that to a great or lesser extent each of these specifications is a complexification of one of Allport's broader initial categories. Naturally the corpus of research on intergroup contact theory over the last half a century has yielded a wide and varied taxonomy of conditions for positive intergroup contact. In particular, the research has sought to understand the complex set of related variables that lead to the reduction of prejudice and a positive engagement with the affective moderators (anxiety and empathy). Hence, such a detailed sub-categorization of the overarching general categories is valuable for rigorous and credible scientific research.

The list of situational specifications presented above informed the design of the research and intervention cycle of this current study. This is evidenced in chapter 5 where one can see how aspects of these specifications were introduced and considered in both the design of the research instruments, and the facilitation of the intercultural Bible reading processes. However, Dixon *et al.*, warn against an overly complex set of situational specifications, and interrelations between them in contemporary research. They have noted that contemporary work in the field has sought to return the use of the more substantial overarching situational specifications to allow both for applicability and coherence (Dixon *et al.*, 2005: 699–700).

As a result, the current research focused primarily on the following situational specifications and intergroup contact mechanisms (c.f., Levine & Hogg, 2009: 468–469):

- Equal status in the situation (equality among participants and groupings)
- Common goals (shared goals)
- Intergroup cooperation
- Sanction from formal authorities.

Please refer to chapter 4 to see how these theoretical aspects were considered and employed in the research design and implementation.

3.3.7 Indirect and extended contact effects

A further point of interest for this current project is the reporting in the research field that positive intergroup contact has wider positive effects on prejudice reduction than just between the in-group and out-group participants. Levine and Hogg's findings suggest that,

> [s]tudies in Germany, Northern Ireland, and the United States demonstrate that simply having ingroup friends who have outgroup friends relates to diminished prejudice (Levine & Hogg, 2009: 471–472)

Technically this is known as the "balance theory" – if my friend has a friend in the out-group the balance of trust is placed in the judgement of the known entity (my friend) and the benefit of the doubt is given to the person in the out-group. Witnessing or experiencing a trusted person having contact with an unknown, or prejudged, out-group person helps to make the contact normatively acceptable. For the purposes of this research, it will be shown, that while the facilitated intercultural Bible reading process could only directly involve a limited number of participants, the indirect or extended contact effects hold possibilities and further reaching consequences for prejudice reduction, and even the possibility for integrally developed understandings of forgiveness, in the broader community.

While this is the case, the research also demonstrates that the effects of indirect, or extended, intergroup contact are affective to some point, the attitudes produced by this means are less strongly held, and the degree of certainty in prejudice reduction is more easily changed (Paolini *et al.*, 2004: 770–786; Paolini, Hewstone & Cairns, 2007; Levine & Hogg, 2009: 472; Dovidio, Eller & Hewstone, 2011: 147–160; Vezzali, Hewstone, Capozza, Giovannini & Wölfer, 2014: 314–389).

3.3.8 Intergroup contact theory and forgiveness

As has been shown above, positive intergroup contact has been directly associated with reducing the negative effects of out-group prejudice and facilitating the positive effects of intergroup social relations (Pettigrew, 1998: 65–85; Swart, Turner, *et al.*, 2011: 181). The focus of this present study is to ascertain whether facilitated positive intergroup contact, in the form of intercultural Bible reading, can positively engage the moderating factors of intergroup contact (namely the lessening of anxiety and the increasing of empathy) which in turn allows for a greater willingness to understand, or even adopt, the perspective of the outgroup in relation to forgiveness. Swart *et al.* (2011) have done significant and extensive research on the notion of forgiveness in post conflict societies. In particular their study engaged communities in social strife in Northern Ireland and South Africa where the out-group attitude is general prejudiced and negative (Bornman, 2011: 729; Swart, Turner, *et al.*, 2011: 182; Adams, Van de Vijver & De Bruin, 2012: 377–388). In particular the studies show that positive and sustained intergroup contact can lead to an increase in affective empathy among in-group and out-group participants – this is particularly powerful in settings where cross group friendships are formed (Goosen, 2011; Swart, Hewstone, Christ & Voci, 2011: 1221; Swart, Turner, *et al.*, 2011: 184–185; Lewis, 2014). In summary, the affect of empathy is the "ability to engage in the cognitive process of adopting another's psychological point of view, and the capacity to experience affective reactions to the observed experience of others" (Davis, 1994: 45). Swart identifies the two previously mentioned aspects as "perspective taking" and "affective empathy" (Swart, Turner, *et al.*, 2011: 188). Perspective taking involves the ability to see and understand (to some measure at least) the world from the perspective of the other, i.e., to frame reality in their terms and not just your own. Affective empathy involves the ability to experience reality vicariously from the perspective of the other, i.e., to connect emotionally with the affective psychological experience of the other person or group. It is noted that these two powerful psychological states have been strongly associated with positive social interpersonal relationships. They allow for balanced evaluative judgements of others (rather than mere prejudice). They have shown to increase concern for the wellbeing of the other, increased desire to engage in sacrificial and altruistic behaviour, a strong sense of shared anger to injustice and discrimination, an understanding of a shared humanity, the breakdown of unconsidered stereotyping, and of course the reduction of prejudice (Davis, 1994; Batson *et al.*, 1997: 105–118, 2002: 1656–1666; Finlay & Stephan, 2000: 1720–1737; Swart, Turner, *et al.*, 2011: 188).

This array of affective and cognitive psychological states is particularly important in engaging past memory and present conflict – which are both significant inhibitors of forgiveness. Cycles of aggression frequently recur in settings where there is a lack of forgiveness and intergroup conflict fuelled by prejudice. In large measure this can be attributed to the memory and experience of victimization between the in-group and the out-group that limits the willingness for victims (and perpetrators) to freely engage and understand both the reality and the experience of past wrongs (Swart, Turner, *et al.*, 2011: 190–191). Victims of abuse justifiably feel a sense of having suffered wrong (in-group) at the hands of their perpetrators (out-group). Perpetrators of wrong doing (in-group) frequently cannot share the perspective of their victims (in-group) in a cognitive or affective manner.

In the psychological literature conceptualizations of forgiveness are most commonly associated with the release of anger and the giving up of the right to perpetrate violence in the form of revenge (Cloke, 1994; Boleyn-Fitzgerald, 2002: 483–498; Swart, Turner, *et al.*, 2011: 189–190). Positive intergroup contact research is showing significant results in facilitating such intergroup experiences that allow for these conditions to operate (Cairns & Hewstone, 2002; Hewstone, Cairns, Voci, McLernon, Niens & Noor, 2004; Hewstone, Kenworthy, Cairns, Tausch, Hughes, Tam, Voci, Von Hecker & Pinder, 2008; Cairns, Hewstone & Tam, 2006; Swart, Turner, *et al.*, 2011; Swart & Hewstone, 2012). This present study has drawn upon this body of research in taking the necessary step from positive intergroup contact (and the reduction of prejudice) – which is effectively a neutral social state – to forgiveness, which is a further step in the intergroup engagement process.

3.3.9 Intergroup contact theory and race

One of the critical elements of specificity that is necessary to consider for this present study is the importance of race and race identity in positive intergroup contact. In South Africa race identity is an contested, historically painful and complex issue (van Wyngaard, 2014: 157–170; Boesak *et al.*, 2015). The description of race identity in this study is not intended to be essentialist in any form. In fact, as will be seen in the research findings (chapter 6) some participants identified themselves as Coloured in relation to their primary group of social reference, yet as Black in terms of their political identity. This is not uncommon in South Africa (Goldin, 2014: 156–181). Similarly, those who identify themselves as White were also subject to complex descriptions of their racial and social identity, particularly in relation to notions of the attached notions of class associated with whiteness (Steyn, 2001: 85–103; Steyn & Foster, 2008: 25–51; van Wyngaard, 2014: 157–170).

This is important since race is not incidental in the present study since it engages participants who identify themselves from two different race groups in South Africa. As Duncan rightly notes, race identity in South Africa "a significant symbolic marker of social, political and economic entitlement and organization" (Duncan, 2003: 139). The South African apartheid system categorized persons by race and stratified them socially, politically and economically according to those lines. Some 20 years after the end of political apartheid the race categories still operate between the dominant in-group (economically this is the White minority and politically the Black majority) and the out-groups. Sadly these race categories continue to "divide people into discrete reified social categories so as to justify extant patterns of domination, exclusion and entitlement" (Duncan, 2003: 139). These categories form both in-group social identities and prejudiced out-group social identities. Moreover, since these categories are still operable, not only psychologically, but economically and geographically, they are a particularly significant hindrance to positive intergroup contact. However, as has already been shown, there is wide ranging consensus within the literature that intergroup contact theory is primarily about engaging prejudice (Pettigrew & Tropp, 2005: 951–957; Paolini *et al.*, 2007; Zuma, 2014: 40–57). Zuma has questioned the sustainable efficacy of intergroup contact theory in dealing with deeply entrenched and strongly held racial prejudices on the basis of facilitated intergroup contact being utilitarian in nature (Zuma, 2014: 53–54). It becomes particularly complex when there is no social solidarity with the cause of prejudice engagement and reduction (or even direct social, political and economic opposition to such a position). However, even in these contexts the contact mediators and moderators have proven effective in deconstructing prejudice between in-groups and out-groups in carefully constructed and facilitated intergroup contact events (Swart, Hewstone, *et al.*, 2010: 309–333; Cakal, Hewstone, Schwär & Heath, 2011: 606–627; Goosen, 2011; Swart, Hewstone, *et al.*, 2011: 1221–1238). The central point seems to be that racial identity is a socially constructed and mediated psychological and cognitive concept. While in group identity and out-group prejudice is particularly strongly held when under threat or scrutiny, it is nonetheless possible to create environments in which the cognitive and affective moderators are engaged through social mediators (such as those conditions or mechanisms mentioned by Allport's contact hypothesis and subsequent intergroup contact theory, above). This complex intersection was thus taken seriously and careful considered in the design and implementation of the current research project. The research design and findings show to what extent positive direct and indirect intergroup contact was possible.

3.3.10 Intergroup contact and religion

There is little doubt that religion and religious conviction can lead to the development and strengthening of out-group prejudice. There is a well-documented, and widely accepted, body of literature that shows how ill-conceived religious convictions can form prejudiced views of out-groups such as persons who hold different religious convictions (Cairns & Hewstone, 2002: 217–218; Cairns *et al.*, 2006), a different ethnicity or race (Swart, Hewstone, *et al.*, 2011; Swart, Turner, *et al.*, 2011), or sexual orientation (Collier, Bos & Sandfort, 2012: 899–907), to cite just a few examples. However, it is also entirely reasonable to say that,

> ...religious communities will tend to reduce prejudice between groups if they encourage social contact between them, particularly under certain facilitating conditions (e.g., equality of status between the groups, successful cooperation, affirmation of positive distinct identities, etc.) (Burch-Brown & Baker, 2016: 1).

Again, as with the previous discussion on race and ethnicity, in-group religious identity is a social identity construct. The religious views that persons hold, and that groups espouse, are based on shared values and beliefs in the in-group and expressed prejudices directed towards the out-group. Burch-Brown *et al.*, rightly point out that one of the challenges with this particular field of research is that it has focused on aspects other than social psychology (which is the locus of social identity) (2016: 1-2). Most engagements in religious prejudice have inadvertently made the same mistake that Allport made in his early contact hypothesis – namely, thinking that mere understanding of the out-group will reduce prejudice. As such, religious prejudice studies have tended to focus on matters of theological conviction (the content of religious reasoning), whereas intergroup contact theory research has shown conclusively that prejudice is most prominently addressed by attending to both cognitive and affective psychological mediators. Yes, knowledge and theology are important in engaging prejudice towards the out-group, but positive intergroup contact is far more effective (Pettigrew, 1997: 173–185; Barlow *et al.*, 2009: 389–405; Hewstone & Swart, 2011a: 374–386; Christ, Schmid, Lolliot, Swart, Stolle, Tausch, Al Ramiah, Wagner, Vertovec & Hewstone, 2014: 3996–4000).

As has already been argued in this research, South Africa is a deeply religious society. Yet, the religious convictions of South Africans have contributed towards the fuelling and sustaining of out-group prejudice. In particular, this in-group identity has formed a hermeneutic position on the Biblical text that makes forgiveness very difficult to achieve without carefully mediated and facilitated positive intergroup contact. It is this very premise that formed this project as a whole – namely that what is required is a theology of mind and body to effectively facilitate positive intergroup contact – we cannot only deal with theological ideas. We must also engage the persons who hold the ideas, the histories that have shaped and sustained them, and most of all, deconstruct the unquestioned emotions and memories that hinder progress towards a shared life.

Burch-Brown *et al.*, have suggested that the following conditions are necessary in religious communities and settings to foster positive intergroup contact (2016: 2-4):

- *A move from essentialism to contextual understandings of human and religious differences*: One of the challenges with religious conviction is that it tends to appeal to transcendent or ontological characteristics in formulating its notions and beliefs. Religious communities will best be able to address prejudice when they approach intergroup contact with the intention of explaining "important differences in the social world by pointing to differences in circumstances, instead of by reference to innate or essential group characteristics" (2016: 2). Much of the difference that fuels prejudice is based on custom (LR), culture (LL) and appearance (UR) which can all be engaged and transformed through positive intergroup contacts that lessen anxiety and reframe prejudicial views of the out-group through empathy. The encounter with persons, rather than concepts, and the capacity to vicariously experience the worldview and perspective of the other allows for significant and important changes to intergroup dynamics (Davis, 1994; Batson *et al.*, 1997: 105–118, 2002: 1656–1666; Finlay & Stephan, 2000: 1720–1737; Swart, Turner, *et al.*, 2011: 188).

- *The promotion of inclusive and pluralistic theological perspectives*: When a religious community, or tradition, is open to the possibility of truth existing in different forms and expressions to their own convictions, there is a possibility for the reduction of prejudice. The capacity to engage the views of others, without feeling threatened or diminished, is an important social and theological principle. Many of the world's religions present themselves as peaceable, operating for the common good, just, with a shared and widely translatable set of virtues and values for humanity. Such views are known as pluralistic religious views. They are constructive rather than destructive. David Ford identifies such a view as a "theology of correlation" since it "brings traditional Christian faith and understanding into dialogue with modernity, and tries to correlate the two in a wide variety of ways" (Ford, 2005: 2). The contextual framing of doctrine within the social, historical, and religious contexts is a significant contributor towards the deconstructing of religious prejudice.

- *An opposition to prejudice promoting ideologies and beliefs*: When religious groups operate from a position of shared concern for humanity, and act in the interests of the common good of all, they should clearly and unequivocally engage any ideology or belief that promotes prejudice. Naturally this is an exceedingly complex thing to do in a situation where there is a clash of values between the religious community concerned (the in-group) and a prejudiced grouping (e.g., persons with a particular sexual orientation, or members of another faith tradition). However, there is great precedence within the Christian tradition to show that the just, fair, and loving treatment of the supposed other is a primary value orientation. Moreover, that the destruction, humiliation, or denigration of another, even where there is significant theological difference, is not in keeping with the values and beliefs of the Christian faith (Critchley, Kearney, Dooley & Hughes, 2001; c.f., Rieger, 2001; Smith, 2007; Jones, 2008; Young, 2011; Kearney & Zimmermann, 2015).

- *Model ways of categorizing the social world that have been shown to reduce prejudice*: There is a wide body of research that shows that while there are important distinctives among religious groupings, there are also many points on which there is coherence or even agreement between major faith traditions (Benner & Crabb, 2004; Kim & Kim, 2008; Hewstone, 2009: 242–300; c.f., Heilbron, 2012; Nkurunziza, 2014; Burch-Brown & Baker, 2016: 2). One of the ways in which religious groups can address out-group prejudice is by affirming and celebrating similarities with out-group religious traditions. It is also important to recognize in-group differences (i.e., that not all in-group members may feel the same way, or agree, on certain beliefs) since this creates the possibility of some tolerance towards out-group members who hold differing beliefs.

- *Encourage intergroup contact, cooperation and friendship*: Opportunities to bring together persons from the in-group and out-group to work together on a common project or goal, if carefully facilitated, will be beneficial to addressing and deconstructing stereotypes. As has already be argued, positive intergroup contact, and particularly cross group friendship, is a very effective means of overcoming stereotypes and creating a natural environment in which prejudice is reduced and the affective mediators are positively changed (Paolini *et al.*, 2004: 770–786; Barlow *et al.*, 2009: 389–405; Swart, Hewstone, *et al.*, 2010: 309–333). Since many religious communities are engaged in projects of charity and care, frequently with limited resources, cooperation is frequently a positive form of intergroup contact (Swart, Rocher & Erasmus, 2010; Swart, Gouws, Pettersson, Erasmus & Bosman, 2012; Swart & De Beer, 2014).

The basic supposition, which we shall return to when considering the research findings and analysis, is that engagement between persons is critical to religious communities engaging stereotypes and prejudice. Theology may change as a result of such positive intergroup contacts. However, it is unlikely to occur in the opposite order, where the engagement forms around doctrines or ideas (Burch-Brown & Baker, 2016: 16).

3.4 Conceptual framework and terminology

A number of concepts, and some important terminology, requires some further explanation and consideration since these inform both the research design and its implementation. These concepts stem from intergroup contact theory as presented in the previous sections.

3.4.1 In-groups

All humans are initiated into social structures from birth to death. In fact all of us belong to multiple groups of identity and belonging, for example gender groups, age groups, language and dialect, cultural groupings, groups of preference etc. these groups of belonging shape our norms, values and view of the world (Tajfel, Billig, Bundy & Flament, 1971: 151). Within the context of this research a group is described as that social structure in which persons share a set of relationships and interactions that form their way of life and view of the world (cf., Verkuyten, 2010: 35). When we claim the characteristics of a group as our own, or are claimed by the group, we become a part of the in-group and adopt aspects of social identity into our individual identity.

Individuals normally function according to a system of social and psychological roles within such a group. As Ypma points out, "Hiermee bieden groepen de mogelijkheid tot beloning in de vorm van inkomen, liefde, status of respect" (Also see, Eagly, Baron, Hamilton & Kelman, 2004: 50; Ypma, 2014: 11). These positive psychological mediators of belonging are important in the formation of a strong personal identity.

Another important aspect of groups, and particularly in-groups, is that they tend to be transient in role, yet remain secure as a structure of identity and belonging. As our social, geographical or relational context shifts our role within the group, or sense of identity with the group can shift significantly. For example, Allport uses the illustration of the family (one of the primary in-groups in society) to illustrate this dialectic between changing role and contingent identity. Even though our role may change within the family group (from dependence as an infant, to care giver as an adult child of ageing parents) something of the group's identity remains significant; for example, "…race, stock, family tradition, religion, caste, and occupational status" (Allport, 1954: 31).

In summary, an in-group is a social structure of belonging. We identify ourselves with the group and its values and world-view, or even external markers such as race, geographic location or possessions (Ypma, 2014: 11). Ypma points out that there are times where we are identified with a group because of observable or identifiable traits (race, gender, age, social status etc.), however we would rather be identified or see ourselves as part of another group. For example, a young person may wish to identify with an older group, or a person of a certain race group would see themselves as having more in common with another race. This group of self-identification then becomes our group of reference, or reference group (Also see, Duncan, 2003: 138–141; Ypma, 2014: 11–12).

3.4.2 Reference group

Ypma sums up the difference between an in-group and a reference group succinctly when she writes, "In-groups zijn de groepen waartoe wij behoren, en reference groepen zijn de groepen waartoe wij onszelf rekenen of waartoe wij willen behoren" (Ypma, 2014: 11). In some situations, an individual's in-group and reference group could be same (for example family group and religious group). However, this is not necessarily always the case. For example, a person may identify him or herself with a certain economic group in society as a result of financial achievement, whereas society at large may identify them more strongly with a particular race group. The person in question may even succumb to such an identification by the 'other' if that judgment comes from a majority group in society and there is pressure to confirm to the judgment in order to function (Allport, 1954: 38). As an example, this is commonly seen among gay men and women in Christian communities who may self-identify themselves as gay, yet will confirm to social and gender stereotypes attributed to heterosexual persons of their gender in order to function within the Christian group identity.

Within this study it is important to differentiate between an in-group identity and a reference group identity. As will be shown in the research findings, some of the expected or hypothesised outcomes of the intergroup contact engagements did not achieve the anticipated outcomes fully, or in part. The data show that to some measure, at least, this can be attributed to reference group identity informants.

3.4.3 Out-group

In the context of this research the out-group is the 'other' that forms part of the intergroup engagement process. The out-group is a group with which we do not identify based on classifications or preference. This be social, religious, political or prejudicial in nature (Brewer & Kramer, 1985: 224–226; Duncan, 2003: 139–141). Prejudice plays a significant role in how we view out-groups. Ypma and Duncan both suggest that we tend not to see out-groups based on the individuals in the groups, or the individual identities and characteristics of each individual in an out-group. Rather, we view them as a homogenous group with certain shared and clearly identifiable common traits (Duncan, 2003: 139–141; Also see, Bornman, 2011: 729–730; Ypma, 2014: 12). These identified traits often stem from prejudice rather than contact. The net result is that we tend to be quick to form opinions and prejudge the out-group and its members rather than paying attention to the personalities and character traits of the individuals concerned. Sanderson suggests that this could be because we have less trust in the out-group and its motives (Sanderson, 2010: 334). As such, they pose a threat to our identity, goals and security. Brewer and Kramer further suggest that there may even be neurological support for such cognitive bias toward the in-group and against the out-group. This is a consequence of memory – our brains respond to years of social input, stimuli, rewards and punishments that cause us to favour the identity and social context we have chosen as 'better' than that of the out-group (Allport, 1954: 23; Brewer & Kramer, 1985: 222–223; Swart, Turner, *et al.*, 2011: 190–191). The most recent neuroscientific research at the Donders Institute, Radboud University, seems to support this notion of memory informed cognitive bias (van Kesteren, Rijpkema, Ruiter, Morris & Fernández, 2014). This research shows that it is far easier to add knowledge to a pre-existent schema than it is to develop new knowledge or perspectives that have no relation to an existing schema, or that is in conflict with the existing schema (see, van Kesteren *et al.*, 2014: 4–5, 11). However, research does show that with carefully mediated engagement in intergroup contact there is the possibility for the development of new attitudes, perspectives and behaviours towards the out-group (Pettigrew & Tropp, 2005, 2006, 2011; Bornman, 2011; Kuchenbrandt, Seidel & Eyssel, 2013).

3.4.4 Intersectional / fluid identity

The next important concept, that is related to the previous one, is that of intersectional or fluid identity. This is an aspect of the relationship between AQAL theory and intergroup contact theory. Namely, that all persons have multiple identies which emerge or dominate within differing social situations (Snyman, 2002: 71; Wilber, 2003: 22–49; Forster, 2006: 165–166; Verkuyten, 2010: 29, 89). This is particularly evident where persons accentuate or present different aspects of their self as social identifiers in differing contexts to show adherence to an in-group, or differentiation from an out-group'. Buitelar expresses this concept of the dialogical self. He writes:

> Thus viewed, identity is the temporary outcome of our responses to the
> various ways in which we are addressed on the basis of our positions

in the power relations in and between the different social and cultural fields in which we participate. (Buitelaar, 2006: 261)

As a result, individuals may express their identity in terms of the group (or groups) to which they relate in different ways at different times. For example, these could include the adoption of certain religious practices in certain situations, or overt forms of masculinity or femininity, or leaning towards certain cultural stereotypes. In this way, we seek to express different aspects of our shared identity (LL) in relation to our cultural values, social standing (LR), or individual traits (UR). Within the world of work a person may adopt a very different form of identity determination than what she or he represents within the home (Verkuyten, 2010: 30). Verkuyten goes on to say that one's age, race and gender are primary categories of dialogical identity since they are visible to others (UR). One often faces either privilege or prejudice as a result of the social norms associated with certain desirable or undesirable social identity traits (Verkuyten, 2010: 29–33; Ypma, 2014: 13). In this regard Ypma writes,

> Als mens veel waarde hecht aan het lidmaatschap van een groep is mens doorgaans meer geneigd om de groepsidentiteit in te zetten als leidraad voor het eigen doen en laten. (Ypma, 2014: 13).

This is confirmed as an operative social phenomenon in intergroup theory, since individuals seek to identify visually, but also culturally, with the 'in group' (Tajfel *et al.*, 1971: 151; Pettigrew, 1998: 66, 70; Bornman, 1999: 412; Duncan, 2003: 140). It is another reason why dominant groupings tend to respond more easily to intergroup contact mediators and address prejudice from their position of power and security (Hewstone & Swart, 2011b: 379).

Within the context of this research it was important to identify such markers of fluid identity and recognize that under certain carefully facilitated conditions the dividing walls between in-groups and out-groups can be shifted, or done away with, to form a possibility for a shared identity. Pettigrew notes that mechanisms that can facilitate such shifts are learning about the out-group, changing perceptions of behaviour in the out-group, generating affective ties (friendship, concern etc.), and engaging in a reappraisal of the values and identity of the in-group (Pettigrew, 1998: 70–73).

These mechanisms were carefully built into the intergroup contact interventions of this research through the structure of the meetings, the social nature of the Bible reading project and the frequent reframing of the primary authority of the Biblical text as a shared identity space.

3.4.5 Social identity complexity theory

Social construction is a complex phenomenon. Individuals and communities construct meaning and identity through "higher-order cognitive functions" such as reflection on the self, the other, and the relationships that may or may not exist between the perceptions of the self and the other (Harré, 2002: 611). These constructions often find expression and form through in-group and out-group social identity representations. As discussed in 3.4.1-3.4.5, persons, and communities, form their identity through shared forms of meaning (in-groups) or differentiating themselves from persons or groups who do not share their primary identity or construction of meaning (out-groups). This is the basis of social identity theory (Allport, 1954: 6, 20; Verkuyten,

2010: 35; Ypma, 2014: 13). However, there is an increasing awareness in the scholarly discourse that persons "can belong to several different groups at the same time; people could hold multiple social identities" (Kok, 2014b: 2). Kok's important work in this regard has related this research to contemporary understandings of complex social identity, as well as the complex social identities of represented groups and persons in the Biblical text (c.f., Kok, 2014a, b: 1–9; Kok & Dunne, 2014; Kok, 2015: 1–12). His basic contention is that "people *represent* their multiple social identities in different ways" (Kok, 2014b: 2). By this Kok means that the complexity of social identity stems precisely from the representation of multiple social identities with a shared social space. For example,

> … there might be people who simultaneously belong to particular groups each of a different nature (intimacy groups, loose associations, religious groups, and so forth), but in their own mind, and in a particular context, they might view a certain group (and loyalty to that group) as being more important than another group. (Kok, 2014b: 2).

As the different social settings intersect a hierarchy of value and meaning is actualized in relation to aspects of social identity. For example, while a person may have a male gender identity, in a family setting they may have a greater affinity with their female sibling than their male sibling. In this intersectional social setting the familial identity bond is given prominence over general gender identity. What makes these forms of social identity even more complex in seemingly homogenous communities (such as the two groups that participated in this study) is that each participant engages in the social interaction not only with different social identities, but also with different priorities for the various social identities that they hold.

Within this study the researcher attempted to keep Kok's social identity complexity theory in mind in working with the participants in this project, the data sourced from the empirical intercultural Biblical hermeneutic engagements, and also in dealing with social identity in the interpretation of the Biblical text. The intention in doing so was to avoid "reducing the subjective inclusiveness of in-groups in a simplified manner" and so to strive for a more complex and textured understanding of the complexity of social identity (Kok, 2014b: 2). As Roccas and Brewer point out, when one engages social identity with an awareness of complexity, it allows for opportunities to express textured, inclusive and nuanced expressions of meaning and social identity both in interaction between in-groups and out-groups and in social identity construction (Roccas & Brewer, 2002: 89–92). It is unlikely that any study, whether subject, objective, or intersubjective in approach would ever be able to adequately account for the true depth and complexity of social identity. However, when approached with humility and care it is possible to learn and gain aspects of understanding of the hermeneutic process and its consequences for social engagement in order to provide a "thick description" of social identity in the Biblical text and in contemporary social engagement (Kok, 2014b: 8).

3.4.6 Judgment / theological position

As has already been shown, intergroup contact theory suggests that one of the reasons why we find it difficult to bridge the gap between the in-group and the out-group is that we pre-judge the out-group based on uninformed, or under-informed prejudices about the nature of the other and their identity (Allport, 1954: 6, 20; Verkuyten, 2010: 35; Ypma, 2014: 13). Essentially what happens is that we build up a set of value judgments about the 'other' based on knowledge acquired from experience, social constructs that come from our moral and intellectual formation in our in-group, and through placing persons, their actions and choices in certain categories of judgment (Allport, 1954: 17–23; Burch-Brown & Baker, 2016: 14–16). We treat members of the in-group with much more grace, and judge their actions and identity with fare greater nuance, since we feel that we understand who they are and why they behave or act as they do. This is evidenced particularly when members of the in-group deviate from standard beliefs or social conventions, yet are accommodated because of a nuanced understanding of their identity. Such behaviour stems from an intimate and longstanding contact with members of the in-group (Allport, 1954: 23; Ypma, 2014: 14–15). For example, we may still think that an elderly member of our family is a good person, even though they hold outdated and irrational views of race identity or class relations. This textured view of the identity of the in-group, i.e., that one can have gradations of goodness or badness in aspects of one's life, without being entirely bad (which correlates to Ken Wilber's pluridimensional understanding of levels of identity within the identity 'holon' (Wilber, 1996b: 99; Snyman, 2002: 71; Forster, 2006: 24, 233–234)), is as a result of intersubjective engagement (LL). It is for this reason that prolonged positive social engagement, within a carefully facilitated process that causes the in-group and out-group to engage one another personally is so valuable in facilitating social and theological shifts. As has been argued previously, beliefs and theological convictions are socially mediated and constructed concepts. They are textured through social formation (reward and punishment, promise and curse), and as such they can be positively engaged by being placed within a broader social and religious context (Ford, 2005: 1–6; Kim, Kollontai & Hoyland, 2008; Burch-Brown & Baker, 2016: 15–16).

The structure of the intercultural Bible reading interventions carefully created the conditions under which persons encountered persons, rather than persons engaging race groups, or genders, or stereotypes, or the doctrines of 'the other'. What such engagement facilitates is the possibility of empathetic engagement, in other words moving beyond concepts of the other, to a discovery of the person of the other as a primary engagement, and then reframing their perspectives of the world view and beliefs of the other.

3.4.7 Anxiety

Another important reason why differing groups seldom have fruitful engagements with 'the other' is because of anxiety that stems from having to deal with the unknown (Ypma, 2014: 15). Such anxiety can take on varying levels, from nervousness, to stress and even debilitating anxiety in the presence of the other

> By contrast, intergroup anxiety often has a basis in reality. People sometimes do make embarrassing mistakes, are taken advantage of, and are rejected by in-group or out-group members in intergroup interactions. Intergroup anxiety differs from shyness and social anxiety in two ways: (1) it is specific to members of certain out-groups and may not apply to in-group members, and (2) it has a range of consequences

broader that a simple reluctance to engage in conversation. (Stephan & Stephan, 1985: 160)

Clearly such anxiety, in its varying levels, did have a negative effect on the level to which participants in the research project were willing to share their own ideas, make themselves vulnerable within the group, and even take on the ideas of others. As such the research design tried to structure the intergroup contact interventions in a safe, neutral space, in which all persons were equal, all ideas and inputs were respected and equally valued and there were opportunities for the expression of fears and concerns without judgement or reprimand.

3.4.8 Empathy

As has already been discussed, in intergroup contact theory, anxiety and empathy go hand in hand in the facilitation of prejudice reduction. Where anxiety can be lessened, and open, vulnerable and safe contact can be facilitated between in-group and out-group participants, the capacity for empathetic engagement increases (Batson *et al.*, 2002: 1656–1666; Turner, Hewstone & Voci, 2007: 369; Swart, Turner, *et al.*, 2011: 187–189). In certain conditions participants will exhibit empathy as "perspective taking", i.e., where they can see a certain situation from the perspective of the other. In other situations the empathetic episode may present as a form of "affective empathy", i.e., the ability to feel, or imagine, the emotional experience of the other (Swart, Turner, *et al.*, 2011: 187). In some instances, both forms of empathy are evidenced to varying degrees. Batson *et al.*, have identified three steps in the empathetic process (Batson *et al.*, 1997: 105–118). The first step emerges after the self-disclosure of a member of the out-group under safe and trusted conditions. The self-disclosure elicits an empathetic response of perspective taking as the in-group participant begins to see a situation from the perspective of the other. Often this new perspective will elicit an affective empathetic response in the in-group participant.

In the second step, this new emotional state, supported by new information, will frequently create a sense of increased concern for the well-being of the other – a condition that is termed as the self-other overlap (i.e., I imagine how I, or my group, my feel in this situation and it evokes concern which is transferred onto the out-group member) (Swart, Turner, *et al.*, 2011: 188–189). As a result of the affective empathetic experience a number of personal categories and attributes (UL and LL) used to describe the self are attached with the member or members of the out-group (UR and LR). This in turn leads to an increasingly textured and nuanced view of the out-group member, no longer simply seeing him or her as a monolithic stereotypical representative of a group, but rather identifying him or her as a specific person with a multifaceted and complex identity.

The third step in the empathetic intergroup shift is when the affective and cognitive empathy that is associated with the individual is shifted to the out-group as a whole. Suddenly the in-group individual is able to see the textured, complex and multifaceted identity of members of the out-group. This experience of awakening to the individual significance of the others could lead to increased concern for their well-being, or the varied and differing natures of their experiences of the situation. The result is that the in-group participant can no longer easily employ stereotypes for processing group-related information (Swart, Turner, *et al.*, 2011: 189). In the context of this project, Swart states:

> As the outgroup is viewed, and understood, in more empathetic, human terms, it should generate a greater willingness among the ingroup to forgive the outgroup for wrongs of the past. (Swart, Turner, *et al.*, 2011: 189).

These aspects were important to identify and explicate for the purposes of this research project. They were considered and integrated into the research design and implementation, and are also discussed and considered in the research findings.

Having presented an overview of the contingent theoretical elements of positive intergroup contact theory that relate to this study, we shall now move on to consider more concretely the explicit relationship between this theory and the present study.

3.5 Intergroup contact theory and intercultural Bible reading on forgiveness

There are a multitude of theories that could be used to understand the dynamics that exist between the two representative groups. For the purposes of this research we shall be using intergroup contact theory for the reasons that shall be shown below (c.f., Bornman, 2011; Pettigrew & Tropp, 2011; Adams *et al.*, 2012; Amodio & Hamilton, 2012; Brown, 2012; cf., Cakal, 2012).

There are two primary reasons for this choice:

First, intergroup contact theory is a widely accepted and highly regarded social identity theory that is applied in the academy for understanding how groups form, and operate from, with respect to their primary individual and social identities (Bornman, 2011; cf., Pettigrew & Tropp, 2011; Amodio & Hamilton, 2012; Brown, 2012). Hence, the social mediators of intergroup contact theory are relatable to the AQAL theory of Ken Wilber. Moreover, this theory also shows how identity formation affects the possibility of engagement with the 'other', i.e., how in-groups and out-groups engage one another (Bornman, 2011; Amodio & Hamilton, 2012; cf., Brown, 2012; Kuchenbrandt *et al.*, 2013). Again, this allowed for the design of a process that could be carefully considered and evaluated within this study.

Second, recent research has shown that carefully structured intergroup engagements are not only helpful in gathering data about the self-understanding of groups and their perceptions of others, but also that such engagements can facilitate the possibility for positive change in intergroup relationships (Islam & Hewstone, 1993; Pettigrew, 1998; Miller, 2002; Pettigrew & Tropp, 2005; Turner, Hewstone, Voci, Paolini & Christ, 2007; Swart, Hewstone, *et al.*, 2010; cf., Kuchenbrandt *et al.*, 2013; Ypma, 2014: 21).

As a result, it was decided to employ intergroup contact theory in this study since it is hypothesised that this approach will allow for the development and implementation of necessary mechanisms that lessen anxiety and increase empathy among 'in-groups' and 'out-groups'.

The application of intergroup contact theory within the intercultural Bible reading interventions has the intention of facilitating a positive space of encounter with 'the other' that could allow for the possibility of theological shifts in the understanding of forgiveness to take place among the participants (c.f., Cairns *et al.*, 2006; Swart, Turner, *et al.*, 2011). As has already been shown, intergroup contact theory suggests that change is possible between in-groups and out-groups when a number of requisite conditions are facilitated (Allport, 1954; Pettigrew, 1998; Pettigrew & Tropp, 2011). These include at least the following, "…equal group status within the situation, common goals, intergroup cooperation and authority support" (Pettigrew, 1998: 65).

The focus group interventions, referred to as intercultural Bible readings, that were developed in this research process allowed for the creation of a shared task, equality of status (namely the interpretation of a Biblical text by non-technical, 'ordinary', Bible readers[44]), a common goal (seeking to understand what forgiveness means from a shared reading of Matthew 18.15-35), participation with the permission of authorities (the nomination of the participants by their pastors) (Brewer & Kramer, 1985; Pettigrew, 1998; Pettigrew & Tropp, 2011; Amodio & Hamilton, 2012). In particular, the interpretation of a text by 'ordinary' readers is a perfect tool to facilitate these conditions and this process (Van der Walt, 2014: 52–54). The manner in which this theory informed the design and implementation of the research project and the intercultural Bible reading engagements, is discussed in detail in the research design (chapter 5) and research findings (chapter 6) of this book.

3.6 Concluding remarks

This chapter introduced the second important theory upon which this research project is predicated – namely intergroup contact theory. It was shown that this theory holds great possibility for understanding, designing and implementing positive intergroup engagements among diverse religious communities. The critical concepts of positive intergroup contact were explained – showing that not all intergroup contact is positive. Rather, certain intergroup contact mediators (or social conditions / mechanisms) need to be in place in order to positively address the social moderators (i.e., the decreasing of anxiety and the increasing of empathy). The mediators and moderators of positive intergroup contact where explained in some detail and located within a critical reflection on intergroup contact research. Three important differentiators, that have a particular bearing on this project, where presented – namely indirect contact, intergroup contact and forgiveness, and the complexity of positive intergroup contact in a religious setting.

The conclusion of this section of the research is that intergroup contact theory is a valuable and important theoretical informant for the design and implementation of an intercultural Bible reading process on forgiveness that can foster the conditions for a more integral understanding of forgiveness among diverse Christian groups. The findings of this chapter will be evidenced in the research design and data analysis chapters of this manuscript, as well as in the conclusions.

---

44   The 'Dwelling in the word' process was used since it encourages active listening to the other. This means that the participant does not need to impress the group with his or her expertise, but rather that active and careful listening to the perspective of the other is encouraged (Ellison & Keifert, 2011; Nel, 2013b). Please refer to section 5.7.3 for a presentation and discussion of this approach in the intercultural Bible reading engagement.

4   AN EXEGETICAL READING OF MATTHEW 18.15-35

The Biblical text as reflective surface

4.1 Introduction

We now come to introducing the core foundation upon which this study is predicated – namely forgiveness in Matthew 18.15-35. This is a study in intercultural Bible reading on forgiveness between two racially and socially different communities. As such, this chapter introduces text and concepts that the readers engaged during the research process.

In this chapter a case will be made for the importance of the Biblical text in shaping the beliefs, values and actions of South Africans. Next, we shall consider why this particular text was suitable and important for this project. After that has been established we will do a careful scholarly reading of the text to understand the intricacies of this passage within the Matthean worldview and context. The choice was made to approach the text by focussing primarily on the social aspects (cf., Elliott, 1993: 7; Venter, 1994: 35). We shall also see whether it is possible, and responsible, to make any theological and social links between the worldview and context that Matthew addressed in this text, and some of the contemporary issues that the communities who are reading the text today face. This is a critically important exercise, since our aim is to treat the Biblical text with respect, seeking to find plausible coherence, and not merely to simplistically collapse the text into a number of contemporary concerns.

As was mentioned in chapter 1, a very important aspect of the structure and coherence of this study is a sound Biblical hermeneutics. Thus, we not only want a careful and scholarly reading of the text, we also want to do some further theological work by building a hermeneutic bridge between the text and the concerns of contemporary readers. As a result, this chapter will also consider some coherent links to the notions of intergroup contact within the Matthean community and lay a foundation for theological engagements between that reading and the readings of the research participants. Lastly, we shall relate the AQAL theory (chapter 2) to Matthew 18.15-35 in order to see if there is anything that we could learn from such a reading of the text that can help us to shape and inform the research design and research implementation process for an empirical intercultural Bible reading process.

Before discussing Matthew 18.15-35 in some detail it is necessary to give attention to the importance of the Biblical text in South African Christian faith. South Africa's Christian population are predominantly members of the protestant and independent churches[45] which view the Bible as having a central place in the shaping of faith

---

45   Forster, D, *God's mission in our context – critical questions, healing and transforming responses.* in 'Methodism in Southern Africa. A celebration of Wesleyan Mission'. Forster, D & Bentley, W, Kempton Park. AcadSA Publishers (Forster, 2008a: 70–99). Also see the *2005/6 Christian handbook*, WITS University Library, Johannesburg. 2005. These statistics are also available online http://www.statssa.gov.za/census01/html/default.asp accessed

life, developing of doctrine, the guideline for moral and ethical concerns, and also the deepening and sustaining of Christian spirituality (Migliore, 2004: 49–52; Kok, 2016: 21–22). Philip Jenkins, a highly regarded missiologists in the contemporary academy, points out that a clear characteristic of Christianity in the global South is that it has "a much greater respect for the authority of Scripture... Even a cursory acquaintance with African or Asian Christianity reveals the pervasive importance it gives to the Bible" (Jenkins, 2006: 68). West and Dube (2001: 29-39), Dube (2013: 1-4), Kok (2016: 21-22), Punt (2006), Jonker (2006: 24-25), and van der Walt (2014: 52-54) who are all South African theologians and Biblical Scholars, agree that the Bible plays a critical role in the development, shaping and sustaining of the Christian faith in South Africa.

Of course the level at which the text is engaged, and the manner in which that is done differs substantially (West & Dube, 2001: 29–31, 36–39; Migliore, 2004: 47–49, 52–62; Forster, 2008b: 25–29; Dube, 2013: 1–4). This research project discusses and considers the complexity of this phenomenon. It can be said with relative certainty that the Biblical text is critical to shaping both the belief and the behaviour of South African Christians.

Thus, it is the contention of this study that Biblical text is a very important tool for shaping belief and practice – the Biblical text thus functions a normative source of theological and ethical formation. Jonker notes, that the Bible

> ... is a powerful tool that crosses boundaries... People from all cultures, ethnic groups, genders and sexual orientations belong to the Christian part of the South African society. The Bible is a common denominator for them, as it is regarded as authoritative in their religious practice. The Bible is determinative in the values and norms pursued by this part of society. 'Bible reading' is therefore an activity that cuts across cultural, racial and gender boundaries in South Africa. (Jonker, 2006: 24–25).

The importance of the Biblical text in forming theological concepts and values, and the importance of the process of Bible reading for South Africans, was affirmed in the empirical data gained in focus group intercultural Bible readings conducted with the study participants (cf., 6.2, 6.3, 7.2.1).

In addition to the above it was argued that the use of an inter-cultural group reading of a Biblical text contributes towards the ideal conditions required to test the theoretical hypothesis of intergroup contact process (cf., 4.2, 5.5.1-5.5.2, 5.7). In the empirical study the reading of the text formed a carefully constructed 'reflective space' within which the researcher gathered important theological and sociological data on the group participants. In particular, the reading of a Biblical text allowed for the gathering of information on their theological understanding of the concept of forgiveness, and also ascertained to what extent an intergroup contact encounter allows for the development of a more textured and nuanced understanding of

---

10 July 2007, 22h09. A theological critique of this data is available in Hendriks, J & Erasmus, J. Religion in South Africa: 2001 population census data. *Journal of Theology for Southern Africa*, Vol 121. (Hendriks & Erasmus, 2005: 88–111). For a presentation of the most recent statistical data on religion from the 2013 South African household survey see (Forster & Oostenbrink, 2015: 2).

the complex phenomenon of forgiveness between Black and White South African Christians.

The aim of this chapter is, however, to treat the text that was used in the inter-cultural Bible reading process in a careful scholarly and technical manner. This is important, since as Jonker further notes, "we should certainly be aware of the 'danger' of biblical interpretation. The interpretation of the Bible does not escape the influence of pervasive ideologies" (Jonker, 2006: 24). Kok argues that to responsibly engage the Biblical text, the contemporary reader needs to have a clear and sober understanding of the world of the text and the contemporary world – building a "suspension bridge" between "then" and "now" through the use of theological metaphor (Kok, 2016: 20). Kok builds on Burridge's idea that credible Biblical scholarship must be "deeply rooted in the world of the text and in our own world to bring the two of them together" (Burridge, 2007: 356).

Indeed, the Biblical text is not only a tool for theological understanding, it is more important than that. The original author of the text had an intended purpose for the original readers. Moreover, the hermeneutic distance between that original Matthean community and its context, and the current reading community and our context needs to be carefully understood and considered. Failing to do so may lead not only to shallow and simplistic theological and social correlations, it may even contribute towards causal errors in interpretation and uses of the text in the current situation.

Hence this section of the study will present a careful exegetical reading of Matthew 18.15-35. The purpose of this reading is to establish a normative baseline for possibilities of understanding a variety of perspectives on Christian forgiveness that emerge from reading the text through an All Quadrants All Levels (AQAL) lens[46]. This is important since this baseline reading will be the "reflective surface"[47] upon which the results of the focus group engagements with the members of the two communities will be considered and discussed.

It is thus essential to have a broad and thorough understanding of both the exegetical and hermeneutic aspects of the text. Moreover, it is important to approach the text from a clearly articulated theoretical perspective that can be applied in the study to engage the theological insights of members of the focus groups. In this instance the theoretical approach that was selected was an AQAL approach since it allows for a

---

46   Please see chapter 2 of this research for an introduction to Ken Wilber's All Quadrants All Levels integral theory that is being used as a hermeneutic lens within this study. Please also see (Forster, 2017).

47   For a detailed and helpful discussion on the use of the Biblical text as a reflective surface in empirical theological research please see (Van der Walt, 2010, chaps 3, 7, 2014: 2–3). She writes, "Within the process of contextual Bible reading, complex Biblical narratives are often used as a so-called reflective surface. The text becomes the point of reference in a conversation where the singular reader as constructed in the traditional bipolar model of biblical interpretation is replaced by a more realistic diversity of readers around the biblical text in a multipolar model" (Van der Walt, 2014: 2). She links this to Rainer Kessler who coined the phraseology "from Bipolar to Multipolar" understandings of the Biblical text (Kessler, 2004: 452–459). Please see van der Walt's discussion of Kessler's theory, and the application of his theory as it relates to an understanding of the Biblical text as a reflective surface in the following locations (Van der Walt, 2014: 6, 52–54, 65).

textured and detailed understanding of collective, individual, interior and exterior aspects of forgiveness that can be explicated in Matthew 18.15-35.

This text is a cornerstone component of the overall research project. It is through the reading of Matthew 18.15-35 that the theological and hermeneutic development of concepts and actions of forgiveness in, and between, two diverse South African Christian communities can be explicated, considered and analysed. The Biblical text forms the basis from which understandings of forgiveness will be extrapolated and developed in the communities. The AQAL approach will be used to chart and interpret the understandings of forgiveness that arise from a reading of the text and from interaction with, and between, the participating communities.

4.2 Why Matthew 18.15-35?

Matthew 18.15-35 forms the centre of this project. As will be seen in the sections that follow, this text is comprised of a set of three narratives that approach the complex topic of forgiveness from different perspectives. Of interest in this study was the importance of forgiveness as a spiritual and theological concept (i.e., forgiveness as a process that restores relationships with God) (UL / LL), and of equal importance is the text's emphasis on forgiveness as a social concept (i.e., the restoration of relationships within a broken community) (UR / LR). The interplay between the intent of the original author and the originally intended reader's context, and the contemporary readers, allows for a fascinating study. In particular, when this text, with its multifaceted approach to forgiveness, is read in the context of a racially divided South African Church it creates wonderful opportunities to explicate both the theology and ethics of contemporary readers of the text. It must be said at this point, that it was certainly not assumed that the social context, and struggles, of the Matthean community were the same as those of the participating communities in this research project. Kok rightly warns that such an oversimplification is a grave mistake and will deny the social complexity of the text, as well as the social complexity of the contemporary in-group, out-group identities of the participants (Kok, 2014b). However, while there is no direct correlation between the theological or social issues in this text and those of the participants, it does not mean that Matthew 18 has nothing to offer. On the contrary, Kok points out that a social identity complexity approach to the Biblical text holds significant hermeneutic value as a heuristic tool (Kok, 2014b: 9).

Furthermore, Van der Walt notes that, employing a text of this type in a study of this nature allows the text to function "simultaneously as a conversation starter for intercultural conversation and as a reflective surface" that allows the participants to "reflect on their own contemporary and contextual experiences" (Van der Walt, 2014: 2). Thus, of the many texts on forgiveness in the New Testament it was decided that the narrative structure, social and cultural setting of the Matthean community, and the theological content of Matthew 18.15-35 best fits the criteria that the AQAL processes of engagement. Reading this text in an AQAL framework allows for a holistic and multifaceted engagement around the issues of forgiveness and reconciliation between two groups of South African Christians.

Within the corpus of Christian Scripture there are many texts that deal with the Christian notion of forgiveness from a wide variety of perspectives (theological, social, restitutional, gracious, developmental). The most recent and extensive project on forgiveness in the New Testament is *Jesus and the Forgiveness of Sins*, (Hägerland, 2011). However, within Matthew studies the most complete recent studies on forgiveness are by Nel and Mbabazi (Nel, 2002; Mbabazi, 2013; Nel, 2013a, 2014a, 2015)[48]. What makes Matthew 18 suitable for the intended purpose of this research is that it finds its place within the *community discourse* of Matthew's Gospel (Senior, 1987: 403–407; Weren, 2006: 171–200).

Since this research aims at facilitating a process of engagement between two divided Christian communities this particular text is very valuable. A central focus of Matthew 18 is a discourse on community ethics[49]. This particular section (18.15-35) deals with the concepts of alienation and forgiveness with a strong emphasis on power relationships within the community (for a detailed discussion of community ethics in Matthew please see, Van der Watt & Malan, 2006: 23–45). As such it will be of direct benefit to the process of explicating notions of spiritual and psychological forgiveness (UL and LL), the cost of forgiveness, and the social implications of forgiveness (UR and LR), within the Christian communities that are engaged in this study.

The conceptual thrust of harmony in the Christian community, as expressed in Matthew 18, is triggered by the question that is asked in Matthew 18.1 "Who is the greatest in the kingdom of heaven?"[50] (Ἐν ἐκείνῃ τῇ ὥρᾳ προσῆλθον οἱ μαθηταὶ τῷ Ἰησοῦ λέγοντες· τίς ἄρα μείζων ἐστὶν ἐν τῇ βασιλείᾳ τῶν οὐρανῶν)[51]. Peter's question in v.21 returns the focus to this theme, "Then Peter came and said to him, 'Lord, if another member of the Church (family) sins against me, how often should I forgive? As many as seven times?'" (Τότε προσελθὼν [αὐτῷ ὁ Πέτρος εἶπεν] · Κύριε, ποσάκις ἁμαρτήσει εἰς ἐμὲ ὁ ἀδελφός μου καὶ ἀφήσω αὐτῷ; ἕως ἑπτάκις). The whole of chapter 18 presents Jesus' formulated reply to these questions in various parables and accumulated sayings.

---

48   The topic of forgiveness in the Biblical text is extremely broad and extensive. It will not be possible to engage that entire discourse in this study. This work will be confined to specific theological and philosophical texts of relevance to this study (particularly those on forgiveness in the Gospel according to Matthew as referenced above). For a very helpful scholarly overview of this area please see, Donald E Gowan, *The Bible on Forgiveness* (Eugene, Or.: Pickwick Publications, 2010); Please also see, Marius Johannes Nel, *Vergifnis en versoening in die evangelie volgens Matteus* (Thesis DTh – University of Stellenbosch, 2002).

49   There are numerous excellent studies of the structure of Matthew's Gospel (literary, narrative, geography, topical, conceptual etc.) please see the following book for a good overview, (Bauer, 1989) From my research there seems to be a general acceptance of the fact that Matthew 18 stands as a discourse on community (with some variation on the structuring of the contents of the chapter). Please also see the excellent discussion of ethics and ethos in Matthew's Gospel in 'Identity, Ethics and Ethos in the New Testament, Volume 141' (Van der Watt & Malan, 2006: 27–27, 40–45).

50   Unless otherwise stated all references to the Bible will come from the New Revised Standard Version of (*The Holy Bible*, 1989).

51   Unless otherwise stated all references to the Greek text will come from: Aland, Barbara; Aland, Kurt; Black, Matthew; Martini, Carlo M.; Metzger, Bruce M.; Wikgren, Allen: *The Greek New Testament*. 4th ed. Federal Republic of Germany: United Bible Societies, 1993, c1979, S. 49.

When Jesus places the child in the middle of the group and tells the disciples that they will not enter the Kingdom of heaven unless they are like a child (18.3) he destabilises the accepted social order and so introduces a new approach to the structuring of the community that is based on Kingdom principles rather than social standing or cultural rights (Senior, 1987: 403; Duling, 1999: 6).

It is the notions of community and forgiveness in Chapter 18 (particularly as they are expressed in Matthew 18.15-20, 21-22, and 23-35) that are the focus of this research. Of course these sections cannot be read in isolation from the rest of the Gospel, or the rest of the chapter, however, the focuses on forgiveness and harmony in the community are a key theme, and a necessary delineator for the purposes of this research project. It was for this particular reason that this passage was chosen.

In summary chapter 18 has been widely identified as a discourse for the Church or a discourse for the community of disciples. The sections on forgiveness, dealing with sin, and parable of the unforgiving servant tie together a number of important themes that run through the chapter. These include, but are not limited to, the characteristic values that members of the community should extol, which will be discussed in greater detail below (humility vv.1-7, restraint and discipline vv.8-9, mercy and grace vv. 21-35). In addition, there are a number of theological insights that build throughout the chapter towards the final parable (eschatological expectation of salvation or judgement vv. 3, 8, 9, 35, the relationship between actions in this life and God's eternal Kingdom vv.1, 10, 14, 18-20, 23, 35).

The overt theme of Matthew 18.21-35 appears to focus on the forgiveness and the wellbeing of the community, (cancellation of a debt, setting a person free – ἀφήσω (v.21), ἀφῆκεν (v.27), ἀφῆτε (v.35)). However, this overt theme is part of the larger aim of the whole chapter, namely the facilitation of healthy relationships in the community of disciples.

So, to summarise, why was Matthew 18.15-35 chosen as the cornerstone text in this study? Taking the preceding discussion into account it can be summarised that this text was chosen for the following primary reasons:

4.2.1 The topic of the text.

First, this text was chosen since it has the overt theme of forgiveness in various forms running through its narrative. Particularly, as numerous Biblical commentators point out, this is a passage that deals with issues of interpersonal relationships, discipline in the Church, and community forgiveness (Hagner, 1995: 515–516, 528–529, 534–537; Mounce, 1995: 173–174; Overman, 1996: 262–276; Carter, 2005: 361–376; Viviano, 2007: 211–219; Zimmermann & Dormeyer, 2007: 448–453; Eubank, 2012: 19–25). The thematic and theological content of this text is both necessary as a theological informant for the development of a necessary understanding of Christian forgiveness, as well as functioning as a helpful framework within which to structure the focus group engagements around forgiveness. Thus, it functions both as an aid to theory development (theology) and as a pragmatic device for structuring the conversation and parsing the theological data recorded from the conversations.

4.2.2 The layered understanding of forgiveness in the text.

The next reason why this text was chosen is because it offers a layered understanding of forgiveness that touches on the four general areas of human experience and reality; namely individual, collective, spiritual and physical. This will be discussed in greater detail below. However, at this point it can simply be said that this text presents a nuanced understanding of the complexity of forgiveness that is in keeping with theoretical and theological perspective of the research. Ken Wilber's AQAL theory shows the importance of diverse and layered understandings of reality and social understanding that cover all four aspects of human identity and being (Paulson, 2008). This text allows for the consideration of the complexity of forgiveness in such a multifaceted approach. Moreover, we understand that forgiveness is a complex process of shifting from one set of realities and experiences to another through various phases of social interaction and inner change (Hannoum, 2005; Kaplan, 2008; Duffy, 2009; Ricoeur, 2009; Vosloo, 2015). Lastly, this text has sufficiently detailed social information for the reasonable correlation with concepts in social identity and social dynamics that explicate the complexity of intergroup social identity (Tucker & Baker, 2014: 147–173) and intergroup contact (Brewer & Kramer, 1985; Pettigrew, 1998; Pettigrew & Tropp, 2011).

4.3 A close reading of the text

The exegetical strategy that is followed below engages the chosen passage, Matthew 18.15-35 within its literary and social context.

The reader will see that the exegetical and text critical apparatus, and approaches, that were adopted in this study were the following: First, a consideration of the narrative structure of the text will be considered in order to give a coherent, substantiated and developed understanding of the thematic foci of Matthew's Gospel, and how these find expression in this particular part of the narrative. This allows for the building of a hermeneutic bridge that relates this section of Matthew's gospel to focus of this study. In large measure the narrative critical approach shapes the overarching understanding of the text and its intent (c.f., Eubank, 2012: 19–25). Second, a great deal of consideration was given to a historical critical engagement with the text. However, that being said, a purely historical critical approach tends to be "incommensurate with the intention of the texts" (Herzog, 1992: 760). Hence this approach is aggregated by a socio-historical and socio-scientific analysis of the text within its social, political, and historical context. As Elliot explains,

> Social-scientific criticism of the Bible is that phase of the exegetical task which analyzes the cultural and social dimensions of the text and of its environmental context through the utilization of the perspectives, theory, models and research of the social sciences. (Elliott, 1993: 7).

This aggregated approach allowed for a richer, more grounded, understanding of the complexity of social interaction, social ethics, and social expectation in the Matthean community. Such an approach guards against collapsing the thought world and social structure of the Matthean community into the contemporary worldview and context. Yet at the same time it explicates the social complexity of the text within its own setting. Third, there is also an emphasis on the grammatical structure, communicative linguistic texture and intricacy of meaning within the text. As will be seen, the choices of words and the structure of sentences give a great deal of insight into the complexity of forgiveness, and the nuance of different concepts of forgiveness, in the Matthean communal setting.

The result of this process is a rich and textured understanding of the text and possible understandings of its communicative intent. Naturally this required translating, structuring and commenting on pertinent aspects of the text. Some important aspects related to the topic of this study, that are of socio-cultural and socio-historical significance, are considered in the text. Finally, the text is considered from the AQAL perspective.

4.3.1 Literary context and sources

There is wide ranging debate on the structure of Matthew's Gospel. What is certain is that there is little consensus among the scholars. Among the more notable contributions are the chiastic outlines (Lohr, 1961: 427–431; Bauer, 1989: 36–40)[52], theories related to *inclusio*[53], however, I have found the perspectives presented by narratological approaches that analyse the plot and structure of the Gospel most helpful in to the task at hand (Combrink, 1982: 1–20; Matera, 1987: 233–253; Kingsbury, 1989: 1–24; Carter, 1992: 463–481; Powell, 1992: 341–346; Allison, 2005, chap. 7; Luz, 2005, chap. 11). BW Bacon (1930: 145-261)[54], with which many contemporary scholars such as Gundry (1994: 136ff.) and Allen (2013: 1-24), proposed that the Gospel of Matthew can be organised into 5 books which each consist of a narrative and a discourse. Of course this theory, as any theory, has its critics and detractors. However, it does provide a sensible schema for understanding the overall narrative of the Gospel as a whole. Weren explains that Bacon's theory is based on two phenomena that are present in the text (Weren, 2006: 171–200). First, Jesus concludes each of his five discourses with a formula: Καὶ ἐγένετο ὅτε ἐτέλεσεν (when Jesus had finished his teaching or sayings) in 7.28; 11.1; 13.53; 19.1; 26.1). Second, Bacon points out that each discourse (D) is introduced and preceded by a narrative (N). This occurs five times in the text, hence the five sections of Matthew (Bacon, 1930: 145–261).

- Preamble 1.1–2.23
  - o Book 1 3.1–4.25 (N) and 5.1–7.27 (D – sermon on the mount); formula: 7.28-29

---

52   For a survey on the Chiastic outlines see David R. Bauer, *The Structure of Matthew's Gospel: A Study in Literary Design* (JSNT Supplement #31; Sheffield: Almond Press, 1989), pp. 36-40. Also see Charles Lohr, "Oral techniques in the Gospel of Matthew," *CBQ* (1961), pp. 403-435, esp. pp. 427-431.

53   Leithard writes: "For instance: The name 'Mary', used twelve times in the gospel, appears only once (13:55) between chapters 2 and 27. The gift of a rich tomb recalls the gifts of the magi at Jesus' birth. Herod's efforts to eliminate Jesus as a rival king are matched by Pilate's willingness to impede the spread of the message of resurrection, and the death of the innocents at the beginning of the book finds a striking analogy in the death of innocent Jesus. Many have noted the contrasting parallelism between the 'blessings' of the Beatitudes and the 'woes' of Matthew 23" (Leithart, 2012)

54   See especially Bacon, (1930: 145-261) for an exposition of his theory, and also the more recent work of Allen, (Allen, 2013: 1–24).

- ○ Book 2 8.1–9.35 (N) and 9.36–10.42 (D – missionary discourse); formula: 11.1
- ○ Book 3 11.2–12.50 (N) and 13.1-52 (D – parabolic discourse); formula: 13.53
- ○ Book 4 13.54–17.20 (N) and 17.22–18.35 (D – community discourse); formula: 19.1a
- ○ Book 5 19.1b–22.46 (N) and 23.1–25.46 (D – eschatological discourse); formula: 26.1
- Epilogue 26.3–28.20

In this schema Matthew 18.15-35 would form part of the discourse of the fourth book in Matthew. Matthew 18 is most frequently described as a community rule, or guidelines for dealing with conflict in the Christian community (Duling, 1999: 6–7). Jesus begins the chapter by emphasising that his disciples will need to have a childlike faith and humility (18.1-3). He then goes on to issue warnings about causing others who are less mature in the community to stumble (18.5-14). In the following section Jesus gives his disciples the procedures that must be used in dealing with sin among the 'brothers' of the community (18.15-20). Next Jesus illustrates the spirit of grace and forgiveness that is required in the community by telling a parable (18.21-35).

This section of the Gospel signals a break in the chapter. As in 18.1, 18.21 begins with a question by one of the disciples (Peter in this case). This signals a shift in the narrative direction of the ensuing passage. That notwithstanding, some theological links remain between 18.21-35 and 18.15-20. First, in both passages there is the matter of a member sinning (18.15, 21). A second link stems from the fact that the lengthy discourse on forgiveness that is the subject of 18.23-35 flows naturally from the discussion on discipline in the community that is the subject of 18.15-20 (Brown, 2002: 74–76).

Matthew 18 has two predominant narrative thrusts, vv.1-14 (with the subsections of 18.1-5, 6-9, 10-14) that is concerned with care for the "children" and the "little ones" (the less powerful, the humble) ending with the strong warning of God's judgement in v.14 "So it is not the will of your Father in heaven that one of these little ones should be lost". The second narrative section is to be found in vv.15-35 (with the subsections of 18.15-20, 21-22, 23-35) that is a further explication of the Father's judgement on anyone who does not forgive from the heart (Senior, 1987: 403; Duling, 1999: 6). Below is a more detailed breakdown of the narrative sections in Matthew 18.

Chapter 18 of Matthew's Gospel can be divided into following thematic subsections. Each section contains a key term, or set of terms, and a key theme.

1. The little children and true greatness (18.1-5)
2. Sin and temptation, and warnings against temptations that can destroy the community (18.6-9)
3. The parable of the lost sheep (18.10-14)
4. Dealing with sin in the community (18.15-20)
5. The unlimited forgiveness of sins (18.21-22)
6. The parable of the unforgiving servant (18.23-35)

In the sections that fall within the scope of this research (4, 5 and 6) the key term is brother (ἀδελφός) (vv.15, 21) (Davies & Allison, 1988: 750–751; Morris, 1992: 456–477; Hagner, 1995: 514–515; Talbert, 2010: 215–218), and the common theme is conflict and the resolution of conflict among the 'brotherhood' – which Duling calls the "fictive kin" (Duling, 1999: 4–6). Elsewhere Duling argued that the "brotherhood" is in fact the *ekklesia* that Matthew 16.18 refers to (Duling, 2002).

4.3.1.1 A brief discursus on intertextuality.

It is necessary to spend some time considering the relevance and importance of intertextuality at this point in the discussion on the literary sources and context of Matthew 18. The most common text critical approach that is used to engage with sources is intertextual criticism.

Within the ambit of Biblical studies intertextual criticism can be approached from two directions. First, one can engage in intertextual criticism from the perspective of placing the textual elements of our chosen section, Matthew 18.15-35, more carefully within their broader source textual framework and context. Luz notes that such an approach to textual analysis is important in understanding the historical development of theological and historical concepts within the communicative intent of the author. In such an approach, one seeks to identify the development if ideas, concepts and notions in the text in relation to other historical texts in time, (whether these be direct uses of sections of another text, or thought fragments from another text, within the specific text being studied in order to gain a deeper and more meaningful understanding of construction and intention of the text, and by virtue of this, the author's communicative intent) (Luz, 2004: 120)[55]. Watts notes in this regard that "ancient grammars were based on imitation, the practice of imitating previous texts to shape the Greco-Roman student" (Watts, 2013: 1). In this regard we can see how Matthew's style, grammar and symbolism can be related to other similar texts of its time to understand more clearly what he intended for his original readers to receive through his narrative. In particular, we shall look at the parts of our chosen text that relate to passages in the synoptic Gospels and other ancient near eastern texts that convey social, historical and ethical content.

Second, within the narrative of Matthew 18 itself the author has employed vivid mimetic language, which is itself an echo of intertextuality. In identifying these thought constructions, social practices and accepted forms of reasoning or speech in the text, we can relate our text to other similar Biblical and extra-Biblical texts. Luz suggests that such an approach to textual analysis, where one can identify, explicate and place "memories" of other texts or contexts within the specific text being studied helps us to gain a deeper and more meaningful understanding of words and concepts in the text. This will be done a little later in this chapter when we discuss mimesis and reciprocity as social practices in the ancient near east and relate them to mimetic strategies and the concept of reciprocity in Matthew 18.

---

55   In recent years there have been a number of fascinating developments in Speech Act Theory, and some applications of this theory in Biblical Studies. Please see the following sources in particular for a discussion of communicative intent and Speech Act Theory in the Biblical text, (Vanhoozer, 1990, 1998: 209, 245, 2005; Kim, 2014: 89). For a superb general introduction to the philosophy of communicative intent and Speech Act Theory as it relates to linguistic theory please see, (Searle, 1969, 1975, 1976, 1985; Austin, 1975).

Thus, we can employ an approach to mimetic theory as a socio-cultural and historical concept that was common the ancient near east and is traceable and understandable through a study of a variety of preceding texts and texts that are contemporary to Matthew 18. Luz indicates that in this approach the intention is to find another credible way to reconstruct the sense of the authorial intent that is contained in the text (Luz, 2004: 121). Mimetic theory and intertextual criticism are applied as tools that clarify the affinities and intentions of the author in a descriptive manner, seeking to identify and highlight not only the linguistic strategy, but more importantly the communicative intent, the intended meaning, for the reader that is embedded in the text and its intertexts. Scholars frequently identify this process as an uncovering the "rhetorical strategy" of a text (Luz, 2004: 122).

See for example, Matthew 18.19, and most specifically the parable of the unforgiving servant in vv.23-35. This narrative concludes with the understanding that unless the reader behaves in the same way as the forgiving King behaves (imitation or mimesis), she or he will bear the dire consequences that come from having an un-forgiving heart (v.35 οὕτως καὶ ὁ πατήρ μου ὁ οὐράνιος ποιήσει ὑμῖν, ἐὰν μὴ ἀφῆτε ἕκαστος τῷ ἀδελφῷ αὐτοῦ ἀπὸ τῶν καρδιῶν ὑμῶν). When one frames the narratives that precede v.35 within a mimetic lens, one can begin to ask questions about the educational intent of the narrative itself and the selection of normative examples to achieve this intention (such as sayings, deeds and religious teaching). This task allows us to gain a deeper insight into Matthew's authorial intent and his theological reasoning (Watts, 2013: 1). This strategy makes it possible to go beyond a reliance on secondary socio-cultural and socio-historical understandings of concepts that are explicitly listed in the text, such as forgiveness and community (which are important concepts in Matthew 18) in the ancient near east, to deeper and less obvious concepts and processes that formed part of the thought world of the original author and the worldview of the original reader.

One of the challenges in Biblical scholarship is that if the text is treated like an island it can be mistakenly assumed that it has no connection or relationship to other texts contemporary to its writing (Luz, 2004: 120–122). Watts comments, that if "we are to treat the New Testament honestly, then we must not remove it from its historical Greco-Roman-Judean setting" (Watts, 2013: 3). Luz further comments, that mimesis and intertextuality are,

> ...nothing less than the textual shape of how culture, history, and society engraved texts. This concept transcends a text-immanent structuralism and show how texts are mirrors or echoes of the world. (Luz, 2004: 120).

A further challenge to consider is that each of the sections of the Biblical text (and in this instance the New Testament, and Gospels in particular) did not start out as a single text unit. Of course we do need to do intertextual studies within the canon of scripture itself[56], however, it is equally wise to remember that before Matthew's Gospel became a Gospel of the Christian Bible, it had a particular intent that is quite different from that for which it is used in contemporary Christianity and Christian scholarship. Before we attempt to explicate a theology from the collective texts of the Bible, we must remember that it was theology that brought them together – before Barth and Calvin and Luther, in fact before the Canon forming Synod of Hippo

---

56   See three topical examples of this in (Viljoen, 2006; Huizenga, 2009; Sim, 2009).

Regius (AD 393) and the Councils of Carthage (AD 397 and 419), each of the texts in our Canon were written with particular intentions and reasons. This does not mean that we should not do careful theological work with these texts as text units, but we should first recognise their original identity and intention. Watts comments, "[t]he Gospels are literary compositions similar to forms existing in the late first century milieus of Roman and Judean schools of rhetoric and religion" (Watts, 2013: 5). As a result it is important to place our text within the historical and contextual framework of classical antiquity to better understand its meaning and intention, both for the original reader and contemporary readers. As Roland Barnes comments:

> Every text is an intertext; other texts are present in it, on different levels, in more or less recognizable forms: the texts of the earlier culture and those of the surrounding culture. Each text is a new tissue of past quotations... a general field of anonymous formulas, whose origin is only rarely detectable; of unconscious or automatic quotations, reproduced without quotation marks. (Barthes, 1990: 372; Barthes, translated in Luz, 2004: 120).

Luz notes that as a Biblical scholar there are three important motivations for engaging in this approach to the text (Luz, 2004: 122): First, as an exegete it helps one to gain an author oriented view of the text. Second, as an exegete and historian, it allows one to be attentive to the connection between the text and its historical context. Third, as a hermeneut, it enables one to gain a more widely connected reader-oriented perspective on the understanding and interpretation of the text for its original readers (i.e., text reception history).

Having laid the groundwork of the importance of this approach we shall move on to a consideration of the source structure of Matthew 18. As part of the diachronic engagement with Matthew 18.15-35 we shall also consider the socio-cultural and socio-historical concepts of mimesis and reciprocity. This task will be undertaken in the section of this chapter where we consider other important socio-cultural and socio-historical concepts such as forgiveness and community in the text.

4.3.1.2 *A proposed source structure for Matthew 18*

As can be expected there is a great deal of scholarly debate on the sources of Matthew 18[57]. One of the most commonly accepted starting points is to relate Matthew's Gospel (as a whole) to the Gospel of Mark and the Sayings Source (Q) (Köster, 1990: 319; Luz, 2004: 124–125). While this field of scholarship is lively with debate and disagreement about the smaller technical differences, there is general consensus that Matthew would have made use of these intertexts to varying extents (depending on which discourse one follows) in structuring the Gospel (Farmer, 1976: 201; Neville, 1994: 85–103; Riches, Telford & Tuckett, 2001: 24; Lybaek, 2002: 225–229; Thomas, 2002: 340–352; Goodacre, 2004: 16; Sanders, 2006: 184–189; Christopher, 2010: x–xxii; Powers, 2010: 344; Kloppenborg, 2014: 127)[58]. Moreover, some scholars have argued that neither Matthew nor Luke derived anything from Q, and some that Matthew derived his source material from a "special M" (referred as M S in the table below)

---

57 Please see the following article for an excellent survey of this debate, (Catchpole, 1983)
58 The use of the term "Gospel" is itself a contested topic. For a discussion of its usage in history and the Biblical text please see (Köster, 1990: 9–14). I cannot enter into a detailed discussion on this topic, since it is not necessary for this study.

to, Matthew 18.6, 15 and 21-22 have an identical sequence to Luke 17.1-2, 3 and 4 (Köster, 1990: 324). As such Duling and Catchpole (Catchpole, 1983; Duling, 1999) seem to agree that except for the quotations of scripture in 18.16b, Matthew derived verses 15-17 and 21 from Q, while 23-35 don't feature in either Luke or Mark. There are two variations on this approach. The first is that Matthew took over 18.15-17 from a secondary version of Q, while Luke retained the use of the original (or earlier) version of Q (Duling, 1999: 6). The other option is that vv.16-20 formed part of what is referred to as Q, (i.e., vv.16-17, 18 and 19-20 between 18.15 is from Q 17.3 and vv.18.21-22 is from Q 17.4) – Duling favours this last option since it most suits his argument concerning "fictive kin" associations in 18.15-17 (Duling, 1999: 6–7).

Considering all of the above, the following source structure is proposed for Matthew chapter 18.

Table 2: A proposed structure for Matthew 18

Pericope	Matthew	Mark	Luke	M S[59]
The little children and true greatness	18.1-5	9.33-37	9.49-50	
Warnings concerning temptations	18.6-9	9.42-50	17.1-2	
The parable of the lost sheep	18.10-14	-	15.3-7	vv.12-14, Q15:3-7
Dealing with sin in the community	18.15-18	-	17.3	v.15, Q17.3 vv.16-17, M S v.18, M S
"Where two or three are gathered together"	18.19-20	-	-	v.19, M S v.20, M S[60]
On Reconciliation and the unlimited forgiveness of sins	18.21-22	-	17.4	vv.21-22, Q17.4
The parable of the unforgiving servant	18.23-35	-	-	vv.23-35, M S
Conclusion of the 4th Discourse	19:1-2	10:1	-	

I favour the approach tabled above since it shows that the author of Matthew included particular material related to both the concepts of harmony in the early community with a spiritual connotation (vv.19-20), and the necessity of forgiveness in a very particular sense (vv.15-17, 21-22, 23-35), in order to build a strong rhetorical argument for the intended readers. If the community wished to have the authority of God (v.19) and the presence of Christ (v.20), then unmerited and unlimited grace would need to operate within the 'brotherhood' (vv.21-22) and a just social order that stems from the heart (v.35) would need to be established in the community that reflects the gracious mercy of God (vv.23-34).

---

59   The abbreviation M S refers to "Matthew's special source", please see the following reference for a detailed discussion of this source and its inclusion in Matthew 18 (Köster, 1990: 324–325).

60   A parallel saying to Matthew 18.20 can be found in the *Gospel of Thomas*, 30 (Köster, 1990: 325).

4.3.2 A translation and exegetical analysis of Matthew 18.15-35

Table 3: Translation and exegetical analysis of Matthew 18.15-35

Verse	Greek[61]	Translation
v.15	Ἐὰν δὲ ἁμαρτήσῃ [εἰς σὲ] ὁ ἀδελφός σου, ὕπαγε ἔλεγξον αὐτὸν μεταξὺ σοῦ καὶ αὐτοῦ μόνου. ἐάν σου ἀκούσῃ, ἐκέρδησας τὸν ἀδελφόν σου·	"An if your brother or sister[62] sins [against you][63], go and rebuke him [or her] just between the two of you. If she or he listens, you have gained your sister or brother.
v.16	ἐὰν δὲ μὴ ἀκούσῃ, παράλαβε μετὰ σοῦ ἔτι ἕνα ἢ δύο, ἵνα ἐπὶ στόματος δύο μαρτύρων ἢ τριῶν σταθῇ πᾶν ῥῆμα·	But if he or she does not listen, take with you one or two others, in order that 'Every matter may be established by the mouth of two or three witnesses'[64].
v.17	ἐὰν δὲ παρακούσῃ αὐτῶν, εἰπὲ τῇ ἐκκλησίᾳ· ἐὰν δὲ καὶ τῆς ἐκκλησίας παρακούσῃ, ἔστω σοι ὥσπερ ὁ ἐθνικὸς καὶ ὁ τελώνης.	But if he or she does not listen to them, tell it to the church. And if he or she does not listen to the church, let that person be to you as a Gentile and a tax collector.
v.18	Ἀμὴν λέγω ὑμῖν· ὅσα ἐὰν δήσητε ἐπὶ τῆς γῆς ἔσται δεδεμένα ἐν οὐρανῷ, καὶ ὅσα ἐὰν λύσητε ἐπὶ τῆς γῆς ἔσται λελυμένα ἐν οὐρανῷ.	Truly I say to you: Whatever you bind on earth shall have been bound in heaven[65] whatever you loose on earth shall have been loosed in heaven[66].
v.19	Πάλιν [ἀμὴν] λέγω ὑμῖν ὅτι ἐὰν δύο συμφωνήσωσιν ἐξ ὑμῶν ἐπὶ τῆς γῆς περὶ παντὸς πράγματος οὗ ἐὰν αἰτήσωνται, γενήσεται αὐτοῖς παρὰ τοῦ πατρός μου τοῦ ἐν οὐρανοῖς.	Again, [truly][67] I say to you that if two of you agree concerning any matter about which you ask, it will be done for them by my Father who is in heaven.
v.20	οὗ γάρ εἰσιν δύο ἢ τρεῖς συνηγμένοι εἰς τὸ ἐμὸν ὄνομα, ἐκεῖ εἰμι ἐν μέσῳ αὐτῶν.	For where two or three are[68] gathered together in my name, there am I in their midst."
v.21	Τότε προσελθὼν ὁ Πέτρος εἶπεν αὐτῷ· κύριε, ποσάκις ἁμαρτήσει εἰς ἐμὲ ὁ ἀδελφός μου καὶ ἀφήσω αὐτῷ; ἕως ἑπτάκις;	Then Peter came and said to him[69], "Lord, how many times will my brother or sister sin against me, and I must forgive that person? As many as seven?"
v.22	λέγει αὐτῷ ὁ Ἰησοῦς· οὐ λέγω σοι ἕως ἑπτάκις ἀλλὰ ἕως ἑβδομηκοντάκις ἑπτά.	Jesus said to him: "I tell you not as many as seven, but as many as seventy times seven[70]

---

61   The Greek version of the text is taken from (Aland, Aland, Universität Münster, Institut für Neutestamentliche Textforschung & Deutsche Bibelgesellschaft, 2005)
62   "Brother or sister" and "he or she" are used in the interest of inclusive language even though the text uses masculine nouns and pronouns.
63   For a thorough discussion on the inclusion of "against you" please see 4.3.2.1 of this research. Please also see (Mbabazi, 2013: 66–68)
64   The order of the last four words in this sentence varies in the MSS. This translation, however, seems most consistent with the rest of the text. See also (Hagner, 1995: 529).
65   ἐν οὐρανῷ "in heaven" some manuscripts have adopted the plural, influenced by 16.9 and add the definite article.
66   Please refer to the previous footnote for a discussion of "in heaven".
67   Some sources omit ἀμὴν and have δὲ instead. Because there is a division of opinion on this the words are put in brackets in the Greek text.
68   Some manuscripts have a double negative, "For where there are not (two or three) with them (I am) not."
69   Some manuscripts move αὐτῷ "to him" to after the earlier participle, προσελθὼν which leads to the translation "having come". The UBSGNT committee accepts the latter position as the original.

v.23	Διὰ τοῦτο ὡμοιώθη ἡ βασιλεία τῶν οὐρανῶν ἀνθρώπῳ βασιλεῖ, ὃς ἠθέλησεν συνᾶραι λόγον μετὰ τῶν δούλων αὐτοῦ.	"Because of this, the kingdom of heaven is like the situation of[71] a king who desired to settle accounts with his servants.
v.24	ἀρξαμένου δὲ αὐτοῦ συναίρειν προσηνέχθη αὐτῷ εἷς ὀφειλέτης μυρίων ταλάντων.	As he began to do this[72] a man was brought to him who owed him ten thousand[73] talents.
v.25	μὴ ἔχοντος δὲ αὐτοῦ ἀποδοῦναι ἐκέλευσεν αὐτὸν ὁ κύριος πραθῆναι καὶ τὴν γυναῖκα καὶ τὰ τέκνα καὶ πάντα ὅσα ἔχει, καὶ ἀποδοθῆναι.	But when he was unable to pay it back, the sovereign[74] commanded him to be sold, together with his wife and children and everything he had, in order that the debt might be paid.
v.26	πεσὼν οὖν ὁ δοῦλος προσεκύνει αὐτῷ λέγων· μακροθύμησον ἐπ᾽ ἐμοί, καὶ πάντα ἀποδώσω σοι.	The servant, therefore, falling down, prostrated himself before him, saying: 'Be patient toward me, and I will repay everything to you'.
v.27	σπλαγχνισθεὶς δὲ ὁ κύριος τοῦ δούλου ἐκείνου ἀπέλυσεν αὐτὸν καὶ τὸ δάνειον ἀφῆκεν αὐτῷ.	And the sovereign of that servant was moved with compassion, released him, and cancelled the debt.
v.28	ἐξελθὼν δὲ ὁ δοῦλος ἐκεῖνος εὗρεν ἕνα τῶν συνδούλων αὐτοῦ, ὃς ὤφειλεν αὐτῷ ἑκατὸν δηνάρια, καὶ κρατήσας αὐτὸν ἔπνιγεν λέγων· ἀπόδος εἴ τι ὀφείλεις.	But that servant came out and found one of his fellow servants, who owed him a hundred denarii, seized him and began to[75] choke him saying: 'Pay me what you owe.'
v.29	πεσὼν οὖν ὁ σύνδουλος αὐτοῦ παρεκάλει αὐτὸν λέγων· μακροθύμησον ἐπ᾽ ἐμοί, καὶ ἀποδώσω σοι.	His fellow servant, therefore, fell down and pleaded with him saying: 'Be patient toward me, and I will repay you.'
v.30	ὁ δὲ οὐκ ἤθελεν ἀλλὰ ἀπελθὼν ἔβαλεν αὐτὸν εἰς φυλακὴν ἕως ἀποδῷ τὸ ὀφειλόμενον.	And he would not listen[76] but departed and had him thrown[77] into prison until he paid what he owed.
v.31	ἰδόντες οὖν οἱ σύνδουλοι αὐτοῦ τὰ γενόμενα ἐλυπήθησαν σφόδρα καὶ ἐλθόντες διεσάφησαν τῷ κυρίῳ ἑαυτῶν πάντα τὰ γενόμενα.	When his fellow servants, therefore, saw the things that had happened, they were greatly distressed, and they went and related to their sovereign everything that had happened.

---

70   ἑβδομηκοντάκις ἑπτά can also mean "seventy-seven". Most translators opt for the larger number since it seems to be in keeping with the effect of hyperbole, effectively pointing to the implication of an unlimited number of times (Mbabazi, 2013: 189–191).

71   Hagner suggests that "situation of" be added in the translation for clarity to the English reader (Hagner, 1995: 535).

72   Literally "to reckon", συναίρειν is the same verb as used in the previous verse.

73   This serves to highten the hyperbole, μυρίων "ten thousand". This was an extreme and unimaginable amount. For this reason it makes sense that this translation be adopted rather than a softer "many talents", or as some translators have said "one hundred talents" (Davies & Allison, 1988: 795, 798; De Boer, 1988; Hultgren, 2002: 24–25)

74   ὁ κύριος, literally "the Lord" is translated as the sovereign throughout the parable for consistency with v.23 which refers to the King.

75   "Began to" interprets the verb as an inceptive imperfect.

76   "Listen" is added to the translation in order to complement οὐκ ἤθελεν, "he would not".

77   ἔβαλεν, literally "he cast (him)", denotes the departure of the master (the forgiven servant) and the action of others who cast the man into prison at the command of the departed master.

v.32	τότε προσκαλεσάμενος αὐτὸν ὁ κύριος αὐτοῦ λέγει αὐτῷ· δοῦλε πονηρέ, πᾶσαν τὴν ὀφειλὴν ἐκείνην ἀφῆκά σοι, ἐπεὶ παρεκάλεσάς με·	Then the sovereign called him and said to him: 'Evil servant, I cancelled all that debt for you when you pleaded with me.
v.33	οὐκ ἔδει καὶ σὲ ἐλεῆσαι τὸν σύνδουλόν σου, ὡς κἀγὼ σὲ ἠλέησα;	Ought you not also to have been merciful to your fellow servant as I was merciful to you?'
v.34	καὶ ὀργισθεὶς ὁ κύριος αὐτοῦ παρέδωκεν αὐτὸν τοῖς βασανισταῖς ἕως οὗ ἀποδῷ πᾶν τὸ ὀφειλόμενον.	And his sovereign was angry and handed him over to the torturers until he should render to him all that was owed[78].
v.35	οὕτως καὶ ὁ πατήρ μου ὁ οὐράνιος ποιήσει ὑμῖν, ἐὰν μὴ ἀφῆτε ἕκαστος τῷ ἀδελφῷ αὐτοῦ ἀπὸ τῶν καρδιῶν ὑμῶν.[79]	This also my heavenly Father will do to you, unless each one of you forgives your brother or sister from your heart.

4.3.2.1 *An Exegetical Outline of Matthew 18.15-35*

Matthew's fourth discourse is often described as a discourse on community order or church discipline because of the content of the central pericope vv.15-20 (Morris, 1992: 456–458, 466–471; Hagner, 1995: 514; Overman, 1996: 267–276; Carter, 2005: 361–361). This pericope gives specific instructions to the community about how they should deal with a member of the community who has sinned. Of course the there is a great deal more that one could say about this discourse. Matthew appears to have drawn on a variety of sources to put together the whole of this discourse. Hagner suggests that it may be said that, "the discourse concerns relations between members of the community, dealing in turn with such particular matters as humility, the avoidance of causing others to stumble, and the importance of forgiveness" (Hagner, 1995: 514). What is clear is that Matthew intended that this discourse be a clear and practical guide to living together as a Christian community. This is of central importance to the current research project. The structure of the chapter, and the choice of vv.15-35, are discussed elsewhere in this chapter (cf., 4.3). Now, however, we shall turn to more detailed exegetical outline of the chosen passage.

Handling matters of discipline in the community and brotherly accountability (18.15-20)

Paraphrase

v.15. If your sister or brother (i.e., someone from within the family, or community / Church) sins against you (commits wrong towards you), you should go to that person and explain how they have hurt you. However, make sure that you do it in private, or at least on your own, so that you don't inflict hurt or embarrassment on them (the motive is not reciprocity, but truthful encounter); if the person really listens to you (hears your words), then you have re-gained your brother again (in the sense of a flow diagram, the intervention ends us, the person is re-gained, you have been heard, so the matter is settled and you are reconciled).

---

78 Many MSS add αὐτῷ, "to him". The UBSGNT committee prefers the shorter translation of the verse which has a wider textual representation.

79 Nestle, E., Nestle, E., Aland, B., Aland, K., Karavidopoulos, J., Martini, C. M., & Metzger, B. M. (1993). *The Greek New Testament* (27th ed.) (50–51). Stuttgart: Deutsche Bibelgesellschaft.

v.16. But if your brother (the close member from your family, church or community) does not hear you (or does not respond to the truth of the situation), take one or two members from the family or the community along with you, so that these members who are close to you and your brother can act as witnesses to the words spoken (the truth) and can confirm the case of wrongdoing you are presenting.

v.17. If the words still are not heard as they should be (i.e., as if you are speaking to a deaf person, or someone who will not listen), go to the church body; if the brother is still not, even to those trust members of the church, then you should act towards that person as if they have identified themselves with the values and morals of another community, like that of the tax collectors, or even that of the Gentiles.

v.18. The principle here (i.e., the matter of truth), is that which you hold onto on earth (your way of acting, your mind-set, your way of dealing with people and what is right and wrong) will also be the way it is for you in heaven; similarly that which you let go of on earth will also be released or set free in heaven.

v.19. Again (emphasising the earlier point of v.17), that which two or three agree upon now (on earth), particularly as it can be related to anything that they may ask (agreeing upon the rightness of what they are asking for), their Father in heaven will be sure to do for them.

v.20. Wherever there is a true gathering (or harmony) of community, even if it is only two or three, there I shall be also.

Matthew 18.15-18:

v.15　　Ἐὰν δὲ ἁμαρτήσῃ [εἰς σὲ] ὁ ἀδελφός σου, ὕπαγε ἔλεγξον αὐτὸν μεταξὺ σοῦ καὶ αὐτοῦ μόνου.

ἐάν σου ἀκούσῃ, ἐκέρδησας τὸν ἀδελφόν σου·

v.15 If another member of the church sins against you, go and point out the fault when the two of you are alone. If the member listens to you, you have regained that one.

v.16　　ἐὰν δὲ μὴ ἀκούσῃ, παράλαβε μετὰ σοῦ ἔτι ἕνα ἢ δύο, ἵνα ἐπὶ στόματος δύο μαρτύρων ἢ τριῶν σταθῇ πᾶν ῥῆμα·

v.16 But if you are not listened to, take one or two others along with you, so that every word may be confirmed by the evidence of two or three witnesses.

v.17　　ἐὰν δὲ παρακούσῃ αὐτῶν, εἰπὲ τῇ ἐκκλησίᾳ· ἐὰν δὲ καὶ τῆς ἐκκλησίας παρακούσῃ, ἔστω σοι ὥσπερ ὁ ἐθνικὸς καὶ ὁ τελώνης.

v.17 If the member refuses to listen to them, tell it to the church; and if the offender refuses to listen even to the church, let such a one be to you as a Gentile and a tax collector.

v.18　　Ἀμὴν λέγω ὑμῖν· ὅσα ἐὰν δήσητε ἐπὶ τῆς γῆς ἔσται δεδεμένα ἐν οὐρανῷ, καὶ ὅσα ἐὰν λύσητε ἐπὶ τῆς γῆς ἔσται λελυμένα ἐν οὐρανῷ.

v.18 Truly I tell you, whatever you bind on earth will be bound in heaven, and whatever you loose on earth will be loosed in heaven.

Matthew 18.19-20:

v.19 Πάλιν [ἀμὴν] λέγω ὑμῖν ὅτι
    ἐὰν δύο συμφωνήσωσιν ἐξ ὑμῶν
        ἐπὶ τῆς γῆς
        περὶ παντὸς πράγματος
            οὗ ἐὰν αἰτήσωνται,

    γενήσεται αὐτοῖς παρὰ τοῦ πατρός μου τοῦ ἐν οὐρανοῖς.

v.19 Again, truly I tell you, if two of you agree on earth about anything you ask, it will be done for you by my Father in heaven.

v.20 οὐ γάρ εἰσιν δύο ἢ τρεῖς συνηγμένοι
        εἰς τὸ ἐμὸν ὄνομα,
    ἐκεῖ εἰμι ἐν μέσῳ αὐτῶν.

v.20 For where two or three are gathered in my name, I am there among them.

An outline of vv.15-20 based on: (Hagner, 1995: 530; Overman, 1996: 267–274; Carter & Heil, 1998: 116–122; Talbert, 2010: 221–227; Mbabazi, 2013: 149–151).

I.   **Protocol for the offence (v.15a)**

    A. One on one (v.15 b-d)

    B. Small group (v.16)

    C. Church Body (v.17)

II.   **Authority (v.18)**

III.   **Answer to Prayers (v.19)**

IV.   **The presence of Jesus (v.20)**

In this pericope we see a pragmatic example of community discipline at work in the early Church. As with many aspects of Matthew's Gospel this example of forgiveness is grounded in Old Testament precedent (Overman, 1996: 268–270; Mbabazi, 2013: 191–192), according authority to those who are in leadership in the community and promising the abiding presence of Jesus in his gathered community (Morris, 1992: 466; Hagner, 1995: 530).

This pericope is intended to share specific regulations for dealing with a member of the community who sins against another member. Nel sums it up as follows, saying that the emphasis was upon "...die verantwoordelikheid van die kerk as geloofsgemeenskap om onderlinge dissipline en orde te handhaaf in die nastreef van versoening" (Nel, 2002: 236). It goes as far as dealing with extreme cases of sin that could lead to a member being ostracized, or excluded, from the community. The entire process is given an authoritative basis witnessed to by the promise of prayers that will be answered and Jesus' own presence in the faithful community. As the syntactical sentence diagram (above) and pericope outline show, I have favoured the following structure (Nel, 2002: 235–236; Mbabazi, 2013: 148–151):

1.   The hypothetical ("if") introduction of a procedure to follow in cases of a specific offence (v.15a). This is divided into,

    a. A private meeting and discussion with the offending party (v.15b – d)

    b. A meeting that includes two or three others as witnesses based on the Old Testament stipulation (cf. Dt 17.6 and 19.15) (v.16)

    c. Public exposure and ostracising (v.17)

2.   The statement of the authority behind the discipline (v.18)

3. The answer to prayer in such matters (v.19)

4. The presence of Jesus in such circumstances (v.20)

The most striking structural parallelism is found in the repetition ἐὰν, "if" which opens the clauses at the start of vv.15, 16, 17, 17b and 19. Each of these clauses introduces a potential situation and is followed in the "apodosis" by the appropriate action that should be followed if there is no repentance (Hagner, 1995: 531). In addition to this the appended logion of v.18 has two identically symmetrical halves (this is also evident in 16.19b-c). When one views the structure of the Greek text it is clear that its form would have made it memorable, which may reflect its preparation for transmission in the oral tradition.

Commentary vv.15-20:

v.15. The reference to ὁ ἀδελφός σου, "your brother", shows the reader that they are to read the narrative that follows within the framework of the 'in-group', i.e., the family of the Church or the community of disciples. The use of the imprecise ἁμαρτήσῃ [εἰς σὲ], "should sin [against you]", is most likely deliberate in nature so that it can leave the possibility for a variety of interpretations of the offence or sin. However, as Hagner and Mounce point out the sin in question in this passage was probably more serious and of a communal nature, rather than just trivial or personal (Hagner, 1995: 531; Mounce, 1995: 176). When a member of the community is sinned against they are to go to the person in private and rebuke (ἔλεγξον; this verb occurs only in this instance in Matthew) them. This is not meant to be scolding or verbal abuse for their conduct (i.e., retribution or vengeance in words), but rather to bring the matter to their attention in the hope that they will recognise what they have done and repent in order to be restored into the community. This verb also occurs in the LXX of Lev 19.17 and is also seen elsewhere in the New Testament in the practice of the church (e.g., 1 Tim 5.20, 2 Tim 4.2, Titus 2.15, Gal 6.1, Titus 3.10) (cf., Davies & Jr, 2004: 783). The first stage is intended to bring the sin to light but also to protect the sinner from public shame at this point μεταξὺ σοῦ καὶ αὐτοῦ μόνου, literally "between you and him / her alone" (cf., Prov 25.9). The hope is that the person will hear (listen, ἀκούσῃ) and so repent and be restored to the community, or regained as a brother (ἐκέρδησας τὸν ἀδελφόν σου). Some have suggested that this last cause may be a formal antithesis of excommunication, i.e., some type of ritual of restoration into the community (as opposed to v.17b) (Hagner, 1995: 531; Mounce, 1995: 176). The sinner is thus like the stray sheep in the preceding passage (vv.10-14) who must be sought out and brought back into the fold. Elsewhere in the New Testament we also read that this is necessary for the community to remain intact (cf., Jas 5.19-20).

v.16. This verse represents the next step in process of the social flow diagram. If the person has not heard and remains unrepentant the procedure is to be repeated by now in the presence of two or three witnesses from within the community. This step is patterned explicitly on the stipulation of Deut 19.15 (cf., Deut 17.6 for the Rabbinic background, which Matthew quotes: ἵνα ἐπὶ στόματος δύο μαρτύρων ἢ τριῶν σταθῇ πᾶν ῥῆμα, "so that every word may be confirmed by the evidence of two or three witnesses"). The parallel is not exact, since in the Old Testament the witnesses were witnesses to the deed itself, whereas in this instance they bear testimony to the reproof and appeal for repentance, and if the sinner does not repent, to his or her non-cooperation. This Old Testament formula is also found in 26.60, John 8.17,

Hebrews 6.18 and Revelation 11.3. The course of action that is prescribed to this group is the same as that set out in v.15, however the significant difference is that this step (the inclusion of witnesses) gives the action legal status (cf., 2 Corinthians 13.1, 1 Timothy 5.19). This lays the foundation for a move to the third stage of reproof, and even excommunication if required.

v.17. When the person "disregards" (παρακούσῃ, used twice in this verse, meaning not to listen), the group of two or three, the matter should be brought to the attention of the "whole community", τῇ ἐκκλησίᾳ (literally, "the [local] church"). This is a very significant literary feature, since this word is only used here and in 16.18 in all of the four Gospels. When the matter is brought to the whole community it has an opportunity to make its plea to the offender for him or her to repent. This is the final opportunity in the social process – enough chance has been afforded for the individual to repent, and if the person fails to respond appropriately the only sensible course of action is excommunication from the community, ἔστω σοι ὥσπερ ὁ ἐθνικὸς καὶ ὁ τελώνης ("let such a one be to you as a Gentile and a tax collector"). The derogatory use of ἐθνικὸς by Matthew reflects an in-group, out-group dynamic of social identification. Matthew (and his community) define their in-group identity as Jewish-Christians (Hagner, 1995: 532; Mounce, 1995: 468–469; Carter, 2005: 368) over against those who do not share their social and religious worldview and heritage. Mounce suggests that this is an expression of Matthew and Jesus would not have been as derogatory towards 'outsiders' (Mounce, 1995: 468–469). Carter agrees with this sentiment, pointing out that Jesus frequented with tax collectors and 'heathens' (9.9, 10-13, 11.19), and that he saw such persons as the object of mission, "people to be won over to the community of disciples" (Carter, 2005: 368). Morris says that these are terms that Jewish persons of the time would use in reference to persons of Palestinian origin, and not necessarily the words of the Church Matthew was writing to (Morris, 1992: 469). Regardless, the phrase "let such a one be to you" (ἔστω σοι) indicates that in the end the believer must accept the reality of the situation – the sinner cannot be won back. Everything has been done to win him or her back, and none of it has worked. As such the person is to be regarded as someone who stands outside of the community of the people of God. His decision to exclude himself must be respected. He has been excommunicated. Morris argues that the clause, σοι ὥσπερ, "to you" is personal and so does not mean to imply a formal process, but rather a personal one (Morris, 1992: 469). However, it seems most likely that in the context of the community focus of the discourse, the person is regarded as an outsider by the whole of the community, not just the person who was sinned against. The Pauline admonitions of 1 Corinthians 5.9-13, 2 Thessalonians 3.14-15 have a similar effect.

v.18. Some commentators regard this verse as the conclusion of the preceding narrative with a solemn saying, or lesson to be learnt (Morris, 1992: 468). This is particularly because of the use of ἀμὴν ("truthfully", or "it is so"). This statement is nearly verbatim of 16.19. However in 16.19 Peter is addressed, whereas this statement is addressed at the hearer / reader of the preceding narrative. Moreover, in this instance the verbs are in the plural, which means that the other disciples and leaders of the community are also given the authority to "bind and loose". The binding and loosing is most likely to be understood as the authority to declare what is permitted and forbidden in the community (Morris, 1992: 469; Hagner, 1995: 532).

However, in 16.19 they refer to matters of general conduct, whereas this instance has particular reference to church discipline. What is common is that both instances deal with inclusion and exclusion from the community. Hagner suggests that v.18 could be likened to the admonition that we read in John 20.23 "If you forgive the sins of any, they are forgiven; if you retain the sins of any, they are retained" – loosing is the equivalent of forgiving, binding is the equivalent of retaining (Hagner, 1995: 469). The authority of the leadership of the Church is asserted and strengthened. Certainly, when all other avenues have been followed and a member remains unrepentant of their sin, the Church as a whole has the final responsibility of saying whether what the person has done is permitted or not permitted for a Christian. The verb is future perfect "shall have been bound" (ἔσται δεδεμένα b ἐν οὐρανῷ) and "shall have been loosed" (ἔσται λελυμένα c ἐν οὐρανῷ). Thus, the community is to decide, under the guidance of the Holy Spirit, what God deems as acceptable, and make decisions in accordance with the presence and guidance of Christ in their midst (refer to vv.19-20).

v.19. Once again we encounter the emphatic ἀμὴν ("truly", "it is so"). We also see a link to the continued engagement of Jesus in this matter by the use of Πάλιν, "again", as well as παντὸς πράγματος "every matter". As mentioned in v.18, there are clear links between judgement and discernment – the community can decide on what to bind and loose, but it must do so in the presence of Christ and as true members of the community. While the previous section dealt with community discipline (UR and LR), this section deals with prayer (UL and LL). When it comes to matters of discipline, the leaders of the community can "ask" (αἰτήσωνται), and where two are "agreed" (συμφωνήσωσιν this verb only occurs again in 20.2, 13) they can be assured of God's wisdom and guidance for their decisions. The fact that the father is referred to as "my" (μου) rather than "your" hints at the involvement of Jesus in what is taking place in the community.

v.20. This verse adds a promise to the preceding statement. In the conduct and administration of community life, and in this context, specifically when it comes to matters of unity and discipline, wherever two or three gather in Jesus' name (τὸ ἐμὸν ὄνομα), he will be among them. Hagner notes that "in my name" is another way of saying "under my rule" (Hagner, 1993: 533). The name stands for the person; it is not simply naming the person, but to submit to who and what they are, to worship him and his ways. This statement is closely paralleled to the rabbinic saying that where two or three persons gather to study Torah, the Shekinah glory is present with them (Abot 3.2; 3.6). While there are similarities in gathering and presence, there is a significant difference emphasised here – namely that Matthew's community is to gather in the name of Jesus, and he himself will be among them. This is a strong statement on the Christological presence in the community, not only does it sanction the discernment and discipline of the community about its affairs and discipline, it defines the community's ultimate identity.

What is interesting to note at this juncture in the discourse is how the AQAL lens unlocks religious, social and political meaning in the text. First, the offence is seen as an individual moral or spiritual matter (UL) – a person has been offended by another person. Jesus instructs that it must be moved from the interior to the exterior – from personal to interpersonal (go to the person on your own – UL to UR). If the person does not hear the call to repentance it invokes the collective dignity and coherence of the whole community (first in the two or three witnesses, and then in the Church as a whole). If the person still does not hear and repent there are very definite social and political consequences, "the unrepentant offender is not simply put out of the community but categorized as among the word sort of persons" (Hagner, 1995: 532). This is certain to have social, economic and religious consequences for the excluded member and his family (LL and LR).

For the in-group (the Matthean community) vv.19-20 are particularly important in shaping their identity as the people of Jesus (among whom he dwells), and whom he guides in moving forward as a community of faith. Under his guidance, and with his wisdom, their unity will allow them to know what to bind and loose on earth, and this will be bound and loosed in heaven.

The importance of interpersonal relationships in the community are very important. Just as it is important not to cause any of the "little ones" to stumble (see vv.1-14), so it is important not to sin against one another. However, where someone does sin against you, Jesus provides a process for trying to win the brother or sister back in order to restore harmony in the community. In contemporary Christianity we do not understand the strong social bonds of the ancient near east. Contemporary Christians find their social identity (LL and LR) from careers, social and sporting achievements, possessions etc. This was not the case in Matthew's world. The community was a powerful shaper of social identity through shared values (LL) and shared practises (LR). Exclusion from the community would have dire consequences for one's faith, self-image and psychological state (UL), as well as one's physical wellbeing, health, and perhaps even survival (UR).

What one can see thus far is an intensifying identification with the in-group (Matthew's community, those who have Jesus in their midst) and the exclusion of the out-group in all four quadrants. There is a deepening of religious identity through attachment with belief (individual (UL) and collective (LL)) as well as individual engagement (UR) and collective social engagement (LR). The community establishes itself as being true since Jesus is in their midst (UL and LL), and this presence guides their faith moral life (UR) and their social life (LR). Those who do not fit the pattern of Jesus are excluded, by degrees of engagement, from the true community (UR and LR) and presence of Christ (UL and LL).

The unlimited forgiveness of sins – the depth of forgiveness (18.21-22)

Paraphrase

v.21. Peter asks Jesus, "Lord, what is the proper number of times for forgiving someone from the community or Church who sins against me? Would seven times, as required in the law, be enough?"

v.22. Jesus replied to Peter, "Seven times is not enough, you need to do more than that. It should rather be seventy times seven (or seventy seven times)".

Matthew 18.21-22:

v.21   Τότε προσελθὼν
ὁ Πέτρος εἶπεν αὐτῷ·
    κύριε, ποσάκις ἁμαρτήσει
      εἰς ἐμὲ ὁ ἀδελφός μου
    καὶ ἀφήσω αὐτῷ;
    ἕως ἑπτάκις;

v.22   λέγει αὐτῷ ὁ Ἰησοῦς·
    οὐ λέγω σοι
    ἕως ἑπτάκις
    ἀλλὰ ἕως ἑβδομηκοντάκις ἑπτά.

v.21 Then Peter came and said to him, "Lord, if another member of the church sins against me, how often should I forgive? As many as seven times?"

v.22 Jesus said to him, "Not seven times, but, I tell you, seventy- seven times".

An outline of vv.21-22 based on: (Hagner, 1995: 536–537; Overman, 1996: 267–274; Carter & Heil, 1998: 116–122; Talbert, 2010: 221–227; Mbabazi, 2013: 149–151)

vv.21-22 are independent from the parable that follows, however the subject is related. Matthew uses this interlude to end his previous discourse and create a bridge to the parable that follows. This dialogue also links the preceding and following sections to the rest of the fourth discourse by means of presenting a question to Jesus, which he then answers in narrative form (as in v.1). It would be sensible to conclude that the parable that follows (vv.23-35) follows directly from the question (cf., Διὰ τοῦτο, "Therefore…" in v.23). The use of εἰς ἐμὲ, "against me" (v.21), echoes the use of εἰς σὲ, "against you" in v.15, linking these two passages together, with one difference. In this instance the sinner is assumed to repent, and so is welcomed back into the community, whereupon he or she sins again and the process of engagement must be initiated once more.

The structure of the dialogue is simply (Nel, 2002: 246–248; Mbabazi, 2013: 158–160):

I.   **Peter's question (v.21)**

II.   **Jesus' answer (v.22)**

Commentary vv.21-22:

v.21. This verse introduces the narrative on forgiveness that runs from vv.21-35. It forms part of the fourth discourse with its emphasis on community and is linked to the preceding section with the use of the literary device, ἁμαρτήσει and ἀδελφός (cf., vv.15) Here Peter is presented as a representative leader who respectfully approaches Jesus as "Lord" with a question about forgiveness. This is the second time in this discourse that Jesus is prompted to teach, or speak, in response to a direct question (cf., v.1). In the previous discourse (vv.15-20) there was a well-structured flow diagram of decision making and action, prompted on each occasion with a conditional clause of ἐὰν, "If" (cf., vv.15, 16, 17). If there is repentance, then the person is restored and the action against him ceases. However, if there is no repentance move on to another action with greater social consequences – the most severe being excommunication from the community (v.17) and even separation from God in heaven (v.18 and the presence of Jesus in His community on earth (vv.19-20). No doubt this process is both painful and disruptive for the individuals concerned and for the whole community. In light of this Peter wants to determine what the limit is for the number of times that forgiveness should be extended to a member of the community (v.21).

Knowing the generous nature of Jesus' teaching Peter probably regarded "seven times" (ἑπτάκις), the traditional number of fullness, as both generous and legally sufficient for the believer. As mentioned above, the difference between forgiveness in this passage (v.21-22) and the previous passage (vv.15-20) is that the person in this instance is assumed to have repented of their sin. As such they are readmitted to the community only to transgress again – the result is that the process of forgiveness must be re-engaged multiple times. The Rabbi's had considered three instances of forgiveness sufficient to satisfy justice and righteousness in the law (cf., Yoma 86b-87a). Jesus responds with an outrageously generous answer - ἑβδομηκοντάκις, "seventy-seven" as in Gen 4.24 where the LXX uses exactly the same Greek words. Or, "seventy times seven" which serves to accentuate the hyperbole in the discourse. Thus, not just a finite or realistic number (77), but an unimaginable number (490)[80]. This would certainly be in keeping with the parallel passage in Luke 17.4 in which Jesus' answer is "seven times in a day". The unlimited frequency of forgiveness (ἑβδομηκοντάκις v.22) is linked with the unlimited scope of what is forgiven (ἁμαρτήσῃ v.15, the verb is general in order to include a wide variety of possible "sins"). There is no conjunction between vv.21-22, the asyndeton adds force to Jesus' abrupt reply. Morris suggests that this was to show that Jesus was not concerned with petty forgiveness that tries to "calculate how many offences can be disregarded before retaliation becomes acceptable" (Morris, 1992: 471).

In this section one can once again find some rich insights when applying the AQAL integrative lens. Peter's question is both individual (UL – if someone sins against me εἰς ἐμὲ), but is intended to solicit an answer that is connected to harmony in the group (LL εἰς σὲ). Peter seems to want to collapse the problem into the physical world (UR, LR) by enquiring about the feasibility of re-entering the social process of engagement, confrontation, repentance and reacceptance spelled out in vv.15-20. Jesus answer, however, pulls the conversation back from the pragmatic to the spiritual, his answer is not entirely practical (ἑβδομηκοντάκις v.22) and so should be understood as having a clear spiritual intention (UL, LL), namely to continue to seek the salvation of the 'other', always allowing the opportunity for their repentance to bring them back into fellowship with the community (v.18-19) and relationship with God in Christ (v.20). This section of the discourse brings together all of the quadrants, the individual and the communal, the spiritual and the physical. True community means true forgiveness which engages the individual (v.21) and the community (v.15), their faith (v.20) and their social actions (vv.18-19).

---

80   This concept is known as *gematria*. Bridge describes it as a literary communicative literary device that "blends literature with math" . It stems from the Hebrew and Roman alphabets that used letters for numbers (for example in the Roman alphabet where 1 = I and 5 = V). Ancient authors sometimes used this to weave textured meaning into their narratives – for example, the Hebrew word *vanity* has a numerical value of 37 (h+b+l = 5+2+30 = 37) and in the book of Ecclesiastes it appears 37 times. Another example (although in reverse) is in Revelation 13.18 where the number 666, which is assigned to the beast, corresponds to the sum of the Hebraic form of the Emperor Nero. We know that Matthew employed this device in his writings (cf., for example the genealogy of Matthew 1 where David (daleth+vav+daleth = 4+6+4 = 14) appears in 14th position) (Brown, 1986: 74–81; Bridge, 2004; Nolland, 2005a: 86–87).

The necessity of forgiveness: The parable of the unforgiving servant (18.23-35)

Paraphrase

v.23. So let me give you an illustration (based on the previous discussion on forgiveness), the way in which the Kingdom of heaven operates can be compared to a king who wanted to settle the accounts he had with his servants.

v.24. When the process of settling the accounts began a particular servant who owed the king a massive amount of money (10,000 talents, or an almost incalculable sum) was brought before the king.

v.25. Since the man could not repay what he owed the King, the accepted practice of the time was followed. The king commanded he should be sold as a debt slave, and that his family should also be sold to settle the debt (or pay towards the debt).

v.26. The servant humbled himself and fell to the ground before the king begging, "Please take mercy on me, don't follow this custom! Exercise patience with me and I will make sure that I pay everything that I owe you!"

v.27. The master of that slave, saw him begging, he heard him and felt compassion for him and so he let him go and cancelled the entire debt.

v.28. However that same servant went out and found one of his fellow servants (someone of the same status) that owed him only 100 denarii (a proportionally much smaller amount); he violently grabbed him (by the throat) and said, "You must pay me what you owe me."

v.29. His fellow servant humbled himself and fell to the ground begging (as he had done before the king), "Be patient with me and I wil be sure to repay you."

v.30. But he chose not to be patient, and so he threw the servant in prison because he couldn't settle his debt right away.

v.31. When the rest of the servants heard about this, they felt very troubled and so they decided to go to the king, and they told him what had happened.

v.32. The king called the servant (the unforgiving servant) and said, "You are an ungrateful and unjust man! I cancelled your debt because you humbled yourself and begged me, you know I could have kept you (and your family) in prison for the rest of your life!

v.33. Yet when fellow servant pleaded for mercy in the same way that you pleased when I granted mercy to you, don't you think that it would have been fair and just to show mercy to him in the same way that I showed mercy to you?"

v.34. In his anger the king had the man tortured in prison until he would be able to settle his entire debt of 10,000 talents.

v.35. You will be dealt with in the same way unless you forgive the sins of your brother or sister against whom you hold something, and you must truly forgive them with your whole heart.

Matthew 18.23-35:

v.23 Διὰ τοῦτο
ὡμοιώθη ἡ βασιλεία τῶν οὐρανῶν
ἀνθρώπῳ βασιλεῖ,
ὃς ἠθέλησεν συνᾶραι λόγον
μετὰ τῶν δούλων αὐτοῦ.

v. 23 "For this reason the kingdom of heaven may be compared to a king who wished to settle accounts with his slaves.

v.24 ἀρξαμένου δὲ αὐτοῦ συναίρειν
προσηνέχθη αὐτῷ
εἷς ὀφειλέτης μυρίων ταλάντων.

v.24 When he began the reckoning, one who owed him ten thousand talents was brought to him.

v.25 μὴ ἔχοντος δὲ αὐτοῦ ἀποδοῦναι
ἐκέλευσεν αὐτὸν ὁ κύριος πραθῆναι
καὶ τὴν γυναῖκα
καὶ τὰ τέκνα
καὶ πάντα
ὅσα ἔχει,
καὶ ἀποδοθῆναι.

v.25 and, as he could not pay, his lord ordered him to be sold, together with his wife and children and all his possessions, and payment to be made.

v.26 πεσὼν οὖν ὁ δοῦλος
προσεκύνει αὐτῷ
λέγων·
μακροθύμησον ἐπ᾽ ἐμοί,
καὶ πάντα ἀποδώσω σοι.

v.26 So the slave fell on his knees before him, saying, 'Have patience with me, and I will pay you everything.'

v.27 σπλαγχνισθεὶς δὲ
ὁ κύριος
τοῦ δούλου ἐκείνου
ἀπέλυσεν αὐτὸν
καὶ τὸ δάνειον ἀφῆκεν αὐτῷ.

v.27 And out of pity for him, the lord of that slave released him and forgave him the debt.

v.28 ἐξελθὼν δὲ
ὁ δοῦλος ἐκεῖνος
εὗρεν
ἕνα τῶν συνδούλων αὐτοῦ,
ὃς ὤφειλεν αὐτῷ ἑκατὸν δηνάρια,
καὶ κρατήσας αὐτὸν
ἔπνιγεν
λέγων·
ἀπόδος εἴ τι ὀφείλεις.

v.28 But that same slave, as he went out, came upon one of his fellow slaves who owed him a hundred denarii; and seizing him by the throat, he said, 'Pay what you owe.'

v.29 πεσὼν οὖν
ὁ σύνδουλος αὐτοῦ παρεκάλει αὐτὸν
λέγων·
μακροθύμησον ἐπ᾽ ἐμοί,
καὶ ἀποδώσω σοι.

v.29 Then his fellow slave fell down and pleaded with him, 'Have patience with me, and I will pay you.'

v.30 ὁ δὲ οὐκ ἤθελεν
ἀλλὰ ἀπελθὼν
ἔβαλεν αὐτὸν
εἰς φυλακὴν
ἕως ἀποδῷ
τὸ ὀφειλόμενον.

v.30 But he refused; then he went and threw him into prison until he would pay the debt.

v.31 ἰδόντες οὖν οἱ σύνδουλοι αὐτοῦ
τὰ γενόμενα
ἐλυπήθησαν σφόδρα

καὶ ἐλθόντες
διεσάφησαν τῷ κυρίῳ ἑαυτῶν
πάντα τὰ γενόμενα.

v.31 When his fellow slaves saw what had happened, they were greatly distressed, and they went and reported to their lord all that had taken place.

v.32 τότε προσκαλεσάμενος αὐτὸν ὁ κύριος αὐτοῦ λέγει αὐτῷ· δοῦλε πονηρέ, πᾶσαν τὴν ὀφειλὴν ἐκείνην ἀφῆκά σοι, ἐπεὶ παρεκάλεσάς με·	v.32 Then his lord summoned him and said to him, 'You wicked slave! I forgave you all that debt because you pleaded with me.
v.33 οὐκ ἔδει καὶ σὲ ἐλεῆσαι τὸν σύνδουλόν σου, ὡς κἀγὼ σὲ ἠλέησα;	v.33 Should you not have had mercy on your fellow slave, as I had mercy on you?'
v.34 καὶ ὀργισθεὶς ὁ κύριος αὐτοῦ παρέδωκεν αὐτὸν τοῖς βασανισταῖς ἕως οὗ ἀποδῷ πᾶν τὸ ὀφειλόμενον.	v.34 And in anger his lord handed him over to be tortured until he would pay his entire debt.
v.35 οὕτως καὶ ὁ πατήρ μου ὁ οὐράνιος ποιήσει ὑμῖν, ἐὰν μὴ ἀφῆτε ἕκαστος τῷ ἀδελφῷ αὐτοῦ ἀπὸ τῶν καρδιῶν ὑμῶν.[81]	v.35 So my heavenly Father will also do to every one of you, if you do not forgive your brother or sister from your heart."

An outline of vv.23-35 based on: (Hagner, 1995: 536–537; Carter & Heil, 1998: 116–122; Nel, 2002: 248–253; Mbabazi, 2013: 163–189).

I.   **The King and His subjects (v.v. 23-27)**

  A. The King's decision to settle his accounts (v.23)

  B. The servant with the impossible Debt (v. 24)

  C. The decision to force repayment (v. 25)

  D. Cry for Mercy (v. 26)

  E. The cancelling of the debt (v. 27)

II.   **The servant and the fellow servants (v.v. 28-31)**

III.   The servant forces his fellow servant to repay a small debt (v. 28)

IV.   A cry for Mercy (v. 29)

V.   Mercy Denied (v. 30)

VI.   The report of the other servants to the sovereign (v. 31)

VII.   **The King's Reply (v.v. 32-34)**

  A. Confrontation and Rebuke from the King (v. 32-33)

  B. Reinstatement of the original Debt (v. 34)

VIII. **Application and implications of the parable by Jesus (v. 35)**

Sections I and II are remarkably similar in several aspects, but especially in the demand for the payment of debts (vv.25, 29) and the plea for mercy (vv.26, 30). There is also some similarity between the treatment of the fellow servant (cf., the final clause of v.30) and the eventual treatment of the unforgiving servant in III (cf., final clause of v.34). Another important point to note is that while the parable is explicitly dealing with financial indebtedness, the underlying principle is broader than that. We see that v.33 speaks of showing mercy (ἐλεῆσαι), while v.35 (which pulls the

---

81   Nestle, E., Nestle, E., Aland, B., Aland, K., Karavidopoulos, J., Martini, C. M., & Metzger, B. M. (1993). *The Greek New Testament* (27th ed.) (50–51). Stuttgart: Deutsche Bibelgesellschaft.

whole discourse together) speaks of forgiveness (ἀφῆτε – this is the language used to refer to the cancellation of debt in vv.27, 32 and of course has a direct thematic link to the conjunctive narrative on forgiveness in vv.21-22). The phrase Διὰ τοῦτο, "Therefore", or "Because of this" links the parable that follows closely with the preceding verses. This parable, like in chapter 13 of this Gospel, concerns ἡ βασιλεία τῶν οὐρανῶν, "the Kingdom of heaven". This phrase in v.23 also serves to link this section back to the theme with which the discourse began (cf., vv.1, 3-4). The phrase, ὡμοιώθη ἡ βασιλεία τῶν οὐρανῶν ἀνθρώπῳ βασιλεῖ (v.23) is identical to introduction of the parable of the marriage feast in Matthew 22.2.

Commentary vv.23-35:

v.23. As is mentioned above, this verse links the parable that follows with the preceding narrative on forgiveness, but also with the fourth discourse about the Kingdom of Heaven as a whole. Jesus makes use of a simile to introduce the parable, the Kingdom of heaven, and by association life, for the members of the Matthean community, "is like" (ὡμοιώθη) the situation that will be explicated in the story that follows this verse. This word occurs 8 times in Matthew (out of a total of 15 times in the New Testament), it is thus a common literary device employed by Matthew to create links between the teaching of Jesus and real life. Matthew employs the literary device ὡμοιώθη ἡ βασιλεία τῶν οὐρανῶν ἀνθρώπῳ βασιλεῖ to introduce the parable (as he does in 22.2), literally, "the kingdom of heaven is like a man, a king". The word "king" is not mentioned again in the parable and is replaced by ὁ κύριος ("the Lord", which is translated as "the sovereign" in keeping with the theme of this parable). Hagner suggests that the word king is not essential to the parable and was probably inserted to facilitate as a linking analogy with God in v.35 (Hagner, 1995: 538).

v.24. It is likely that the servant was a governor or some form of senior official for the sovereign. As the settling of accounts begins he is brought before the sovereign with an unimaginably high debt. The fact that he is brought may indicate that he did not appear willingly (Morris, 1992: 472). Regardless, we are told that he owes the master, μυρίων ταλάντων, most frequently translated as "ten thousand talents". The use of μυρίων, meaning "myriad" or "ten thousand" is a deliberate hyperbole pointing to a debt that was so high that it was practically incalculable. By comparison, Josephus speaks of the entire taxes from Palestine as amounting to 8000 talents (Ant. 12.175), whereas Antipas received 200 talents in taxes from Perea and Galilee combined (Ant. 17.318-320), and only 600 talents in taxes were collected from all Judea, Idumea and Samaria in 4 B.C (Ant. 17.11.4). This gives some idea of the magnitude of the debt. By today's standards it would be a debt amounting to billions of dollars. It was clear that the servant would never be able to repay it. As a result, the sovereign ordered that he and his family be sold into debt slavery (v.25) (for the Old Testament background to this form of slavery see, 2 Kings 4.1, Nehemiah 5.3-5; Amos 2.6; Isaiah 50.1). While this punishment could never have repaid the debt, it may have been enforced for two reasons, first as a punishment to the offender as was the expected custom. Second, as a deterrent to others from building up such unmanageable debts with the sovereign. As was discussed previously in the translation of this verse, some commentators find that the sum was so unreasonable that the original parable may have referred to a smaller amount (Davies & Allison, 1988: 795; De Boer, 1988;

Hultgren, 2002: 24–25). Hagner argues that parables, "by their nature often employ hyperbole for effect, and there is no reason to require that every point correspond to historical reality" (Hagner, 1995: 538).

v.25. Some have suggested that the many may have incurred the debt by tendering for a taxation contract for a certain area. Josephus tells of a certain Joseph who made himself liable for a debt of 16000 talents by bidding for such a taxation contract (Ant. 12.175-176). What is clear is that the venture that the servant had entered into had failed, and that he did not have the funds to repay the debt. The verb in this sentence, ἀποδοθῆναι, means to render what is owed. It is used twice in this verse and again in vv. 26, 28, 29, 30 and 34. This highlights the point of the parable that it is the absence of money, and not the reason for the absence, that matters in this instance. The sovereign, from this point called ὁ κύριος ("the lord"), which emphasizes his legal rights over the servant, but also links to the true King in v.35[82]. As is discussed above, the man is punished as a gesture, not as a matter of settlement for the debt.

v.26. We are told that the slave fell before his master, προσεκύνει ("prostrated himself"). This word is usually used in the context of worship. However, here it should be understood as an attitude of respect, fear and humility as in 8.2, 9.18, 15.25, 20.20. It was a desperate situation, and so we are told that the man pleads with the sovereign for clemency (μακροθύμησον, "be patient", a verb used only here and v.29 in Matthew). The imperfect tense indicates that he kept pleading. He makes the unrealistic promise, καὶ πάντα ἀποδώσω σοι, "and I will pay you everything", with πάντα being in an emphatic position ("everything"). From a structural perspective the servant's plea in v.26 agrees exactly with the fellow servant's plea in v.29, except that the latter does not contain the word πάντα, "everything". In the overall structure of the parable this serves to highlight the injustice that this servant perpetrates against his fellow servant who owes him much less.

v.27. The phrase ὁ κύριος τοῦ δούλου ἐκείνου, "the lord of that servant" occurs once more in 24.50 – in that verse it is related to eschatological judgment. Here ἐκείνου anticipates the ἐκεῖνος of verse 28, in order to distinguish the first servant from the second servant. The next important word to notice is Matthew's use of σπλαγχνισθείς, to be "moved with compassion". Here it refers to the sovereign, but in all other instances in this Gospel it refers to Jesus, 9.36, 14.14, 15.32, 20.34. The sovereign releases (ἀπέλυσεν) the servant from his debt. The use of ἀπέλυσεν relates back to the use of λύσητε and λελυμένα in v.18 drawing these elements together. So, not only is the servant released, but the debt is "cancelled", ἀφῆκεν. This verb is used throughout the Gospel to refer to the cancellation, or more precisely the forgiveness, of sins (cf., 6.12 where the word used for sins, ὀφειλήματα, literally means "debts". Also see, 14-15, 9.2, 5-6, 12.31-32. The metaphor of forgiven debt that is likened to forgiven sin can also be found in Luke 7.4-43, although the phrase τὸ δάνειον only occurs in this verse in the New Testament. What a remarkable act of grace, indeed it is a disruptive act of unmerited mercy that is witnessed here – in response for time to repay the debt, the sovereign cancels the unimaginably massive debt and releases the servant. It is an act of pure grace. Hagner remarks that it is,

82   For a detailed discussion of the employment of the metaphor of the King in New Testament texts in relation to communal ethics and the expectations of obedience, please see *Family of the King: Dynamics of Metaphor in the Gospel According to John*, by Jan van der Watt (Van der Watt, 2000: 376–382).

"not difficult to hear the echo of the gospel of the forgiveness of sins in this verse" (Hagner, 1995: 539).

v.28. In this verse the plot of the narrative takes an unexpected turn. Just as the servant owed money, we discover that he too is owed money by a fellow servant. What is very different in this case, however, is the amount that is owed, merely ἑκατὸν δηνάρια ("one hundred denarii"). This is a very small amount in comparison to what he has just been released from. A denarii was the average daily wages for a workman (BAGD, 179a). There were six thousand denarii to a single talent, as Hagner points out, the forgiven servant had thus been set free from a debt that was 600 000 times greater than what he was owed (Hagner, 1995: 539). We are told that he grabbed the man by the throat, something that may have been common custom among Jews of the time when engaging debtors ἔπνιγεν, "to choke" (Morris, 1992: 475), compare this to 24.49. Regardless of whether it was customary or not, the point of this verse is that while the servant was forgiven a great debt himself, he refuses to show even a comparably small amount of mercy to a fellow servant.

v.29. In this verse the plea of the servant for mercy is deliberately patterned after the plea of the first servant who received mercy from the sovereign, καὶ ἀποδώσω σοι, making this verse a near exact repetition of v.26. The omission of πάντα, "everything", from v.26 could be intended to show the comparatively small amount that is to be repaid, or to highlight the extravagance of the claim made by the first servant. The word παρεκάλει ("pleaded") is more appropriate between fellow servants, persons of equal social stature, than the προσεκύνει ("prostrated") used for the servant in v.26. The point is simply that in this case the plea for patience was a realistic one, it is entirely plausible that the servant would have been able to repay what he owed in a reasonable time.

v.30. The response of the creditor in this verse stands in sharp and drastic relief to the creditor (the sovereign) in v.27. Here we are told that the servant refused to listen, or hear, his fellow servant (οὐκ ἤθελεν, "he would not", the imperfect tense points to a continuing action of the will) which is accentuated by the participle ἀπελθὼν, "having gone away". In other words he walks away and refuses to hear what the fellow servant has to say. He does not accord him a hearing. Thematically this relates back to vv.15-17. The importance of being heard and creating the space for reparation is critical to the community. The second "but" is the strong adversative (as in v.22), instead of forgiving he does the exact opposite. He went away and had the servant thrown into prison, ἕως οὗ ἀποδῷ τὸ ὀφειλόμενον, "until he paid what was owed". This had not only personal consequences, but social consequences as well, since the debt would need to be settled through money that was given by friends and family on his behalf. This represents the very worst of un-forgiveness and injustice on the part of the previously forgiven servant.

v.31. Next the narrative moves to focus on to the other servants of the sovereign, here described as "fellow servants" (σύνδουλοι αὐτοῦ) of the man who was just jailed. We are told that these servants were greatly distressed or distraught, ἐλυπήθησαν σφόδρα, (a phrase that also appears in 17.23 and could mean "very sorry", "very upset" etc.) over what had happened to their fellow servant. They go to the sovereign (τῷ κυρίῳ, still referred to as lord, showing that he has the same relationship to all of the people in this narrative) to inform ("explain", διεσάφησαν cf., 13.36) what has transpired. The reader is assumed to bear knowledge of the cancelled debt of the first servant (v.27). One can see the increasing disease that is developing as this offence touches more and more members of the community.

v.32. As is common in Matthew, he begins the next section of the narrative with τότε, "then", it indicates that what is to come was next in the sequence of events. The sovereign says, λέγει (present for greater vividness), Δοῦλε πονηρέ, "evil servant" (the expression is also used in 25.26, although the two words are reversed in that instance). Wicked, πονηρέ, is a word that Matthew uses frequently, cf., 6.23 where it is translated as "evil". The sovereign reminds him of, πᾶσαν τὴν ὀφειλὴν ἐκείνην, "all the debt" (with the emphasis on πᾶσαν, "all") which was cancelled when he pled for mercy (v.26). The emphasis shows that a huge debt, which could not have been repaid, was cancelled simply when he asked for clemency. Now, however, he was being wicked since a debt which could be repaid was not dealt with in the same way – he had received immense grace, but did not show any grace in return.

v.33. The sovereign asks his servant whether he should not have responded with grace since he had received grace, "οὐκ ἔδει καὶ σὲ ἐλεῆσαι τὸν σύνδουλόν σου, ὡς κἀγὼ σὲ ἠλέησα"? The manner in which the question is phrased anticipates a positive answer. Some translations have "ought you not to have..." The sovereign is however saying something strong than that, he says it is necessary, ἔδει, that the forgiven man shows forgiveness to others (cf., 6.12, 14-15). The sovereign says that he should have shown mercy, ἐλεῆσαι. Of course the sovereign could simply have told the man to cancel the debt, but this shows that there is a meta-process at play in the narrative, Matthew wants to reader to understand not just the act (UR, LR), but the attitude and values associated with mercy (UL, LL). As the disciple judges other people, so he is going to be judged by God, and the measure with which he gives to others he will receive from God in turn (7.2). The point is simply that a servant is to act towards others in the same way as God has acted towards them (cf., Luke 6.36, also see 1 John 4.11 and Jas 2.13 that closely resemble this passage).

v.34. It is not a surprise to read that the sovereign became angry, ὀργισθεὶς ("was filled with anger") and revoked his cancellation of the servant's debt. The wicked servant was handed over to the torturers (τοῖς βασανισταῖς, a word that is only used here in the New Testament, for the cognate verb see 8.29). While torturers were forbidden among the Jews, it was more common among the Romans. When a person faced torture (as opposed to imprisonment) the burden and pressure on friends and family would be heightened to repay the debt. In this instance, given the enormous debt, the imprisonment and torture would have been permanent, this may be a hint at eschatological punishment (particularly in light of v.35). This verse is closely linked to v.30 which describes in similar language how the unfortunate servant was jailed by the unforgiving servant. It is a concrete demonstration that you will be treated how you treat others. Of course this point is made strongly in the next verse.

v.35. Jesus does not always explain the 'truth' of his parables, however in this instance he does. The use of Οὕτως, "so" is intended to show the hearer or reader that the severity of the punishment the unforgiving man received from the sovereign is what all unforgiving sinners could expect from the hand of God. From the application in this verse it becomes clear that king in the parable (v.23) and "master", "lord", or "sovereign" (κύριος – used throughout the pericope) means God and the servants in the parable symbolise the disciples. The large debt forgiven of the first servant points to the forgiveness of sin, in comparison to which the sins others commit against the disciples are to be considered small and petty. As the master revoked the cancellation of the wicked servant's debt, so too Οὕτως ("so", or "thus") God will revoke the forgiveness of the disciples' sins if they do not forgive other disciples their sins. Jesus refers to God as ὁ πατήρ μου ὁ οὐράνιος, "my Father in heaven", stressing a special relationship with God (Father), but also God's sovereignty (in heaven). The verse serves as an inclusion on the question of forgiveness raised by Peter in vv.21-22. God will be our final judge and He will do the forgiving, or unforgiving, as they have done to others. The use of the phrase, "from your hearts", ἀπὸ τῶν καρδιῶν b ὑμῶν, means that the forgiveness must not only have a religious or social validity, but that it must stem from the very heart. It is not just about appearances (UR, LR), but must have deep personal (UL) and religious (LL) convictions behind it for it to be acceptable to the Father (cf., Rom 6.17, 1 Peter 3.4).

Thus, the conduct of the community (UR, LR) is to be patterned on the grace they have received from God (UL), and how they have seen God dealing with them in the community (LL). This is a critical element of a healthy, balanced, community. Just as God freely forgave those who sinned against him, so the members of the community are to freely forgive those who sin against them. The forgiveness is not only to be for appearances (i.e., social UR, LR), it is to be sincere, from the heart and based in faith (UL, LL). The refusal to forgive others will result in God's refusal to forgive the disciple. We can thus see, once again, just how important conduct is as an expression of faith. The manner in which the community behaves is an expression of their true faith.

4.4 Aspects of the social and historical context of the Matthean community

The social setting of the Matthean community[83], as well as that of the author of Matthew, are critical to understanding the communicative intent of Matthew's Gospel in its entirety, and this portion in particular. It is a mistake to think that the manner in which we understand community, forgiveness, intergroup contact and even our Christian faith, is the same as what the original author and the Matthean community understood by these, and many more subtle concepts, contained in Matthew 18.15-35. We would be wise to heed Wolfhart Pannenberg's admonition that, "In a changed situation the traditional phrases, even when recited literally, do not mean what they did at the time of their original formulation" (Pannenberg, 2008: 9). Pannenberg's comment was in response to Gadamer's argument that there

---

83   A number of prominent Biblical scholars and historians have done significant work on explicating and analysing the socio-cultural and socio-historical setting in which Gospel of Matthew was written. The field is exceptional wide and detailed. We will present a sufficiently detailed and careful insight into the world of Matthew and his readers in this section, however, if you wish to read more on this topic please refer to this selection of sources: (Hagner, 1995: 515–541; Mounce, 1995: 173–179; Overman, 1996: 262–276; Carter, 2005: Introduction, 361-375; Viviano, 2007: 193–219; Zimmermann & Dormeyer, 2007: 445–460).

is a need for a carefully understood hermeneutic to "span the distance between the texts and the present" (Pannenberg, 2008: 9)[84].

Matthew's Gospel gives an insight into a social concern that is important for the Matthean community, namely their emerging Christian identity in relation to the Jewish faith out of which early Christianity emerges. The critical element was the emergence of a Christian identity among a people who were not yet conscious of developing in a separate direction to the dominant Hebrew faith[85]. Matthew places a great deal of importance on emphasizing a clear line of connection between the followers of Jesus and the Abrahamic faith tradition (1.1). Hence he starts his Gospel with a genealogy of Jesus that traces back to Abraham (Davies & Allison, 1988; Gundry, 1994). However, Matthew is also careful to show that this new community is also a community for the gentiles (Harding, 2003: 311). The Great Commission, in which the disciples are sent out to all peoples (28.19) is the bookend to the genealogy. These two concepts of identity form a dialectic tension in the Gospel showing that the author is aware of the need to remain close to a deep and rich faith tradition (LL), yet is also conscious of the changing social, cultural and religious setting into which the community is emerging (LR). These two elements offer a measure of texture and complexity to the theology, social values, and community identity that emerge from Matthew's narrative. Many scholars have considered the sermon on the mount discourse (5.1-7.27) to contain the key theological and ethical teaching of Matthew's Gospel. Regardless of whether one gives this discourse such a primary position in the Gospel, it cannot be denied that Matthew engages in complex and subtle theological exercise of reframing the law in the period after the coming of the Messiah and the destruction of Jerusalem. The coming of the Messiah has a socio-religious effect on his theology (LL), whereas the destruction of Jerusalem has a socio-cultural impact on the new community's identity and mission (LR). From a theological perspective, the emphasis of the law shifts from ritual law, notice the absence of emphasis on circumcision and the Sabbath. Yet, Matthew still wants his community to be in the tradition of the Mosaic law, even though it has been theologically reinterpreted by the coming of Jesus the Messiah and the destruction of the temple (5.17-20).

The Gospel gives some insights into the social and psychological pressures that the community is facing after the revolt and the destruction of Jerusalem. Saldarini speculates the following regarding the Matthean community in Jerusalem: "There the community's mission to Israel failed, and eventually, probably in the period preceding the Jewish War of 66-70, they were forced to leave the land of Israel. They found a new home in Syria and began to missionize among the Gentiles." (Saldarini in Luz, 2005: 244). W.D. Davies suggests that Matthew's Gospel was written as a direct consequence to the destruction of the temple in AD 70, and in response to significant social changes in the Jewish community as a result. It is suggested that a number of the dominant themes in Matthew's Gospel directly address the social changes of the time. In summary, after the destruction of the temple and the loss of

---

84 Please see the following source for a discussion on the need for hermeneutics as a bridge between the thought world of the text and the thought world of the contemporary reader (Thiselton, 2006: 465). For a discussion on Pannenberg and Gadamer's understanding of the hermeneutic complexity of gaining contemporary meaning from an ancient text please see, (Thiselton, 2015: 639).

85 For an in depth discussion on the complexity of the emerging identity of the Matthean Christian group please see, (Giversen & Borgen, 1995; Borgen, 1998)

both the priests and ritual sacrifice the Pharisees emerged as the dominant leaders in the Jewish community. They faced a crisis of forming a new identity that would function without access to the temple, and also not foster further confrontation with the gentile Roman rulers. The result was that the expectation of the return of the Messiah was downplayed (since this was one of the expectations that had led to the uprising in Jerusalem). In addition, Jews were encouraged to break all ties with gentiles and retain strict ethnic purity and rigorous observance of the Law (Torah). Several these social and theological characteristics find expression in Matthew's Gospel as he uses his narrative to shape the identity and character of the Matthean community. It is worth noting that since this chapter is traditionally seen as addressing the community its concerns are much more directly focused on shaping the internal structure and identity of the community than the external realities of the context. That being said there is extensive research that shows how the complexities of the social and religious contexts of the Matthean community shaped the communicative intent of the author of this Gospel[86].

This social, political and theological reality has a direct bearing on what we find in Matthew 18, and the particular social and theological emphases that emerge in 18.15-35. L. Michael White comments,

> What may lie behind the social tensions reflected in Matthew's gospel may be the massive population shift that resulted after the first revolt. When most of the Jewish population moved to the Galilean region [in the] north. That's the situation [in] which Matthew's gospel seems to be written. But, as this new population has to be organized, the new political realities of village life begin to produce some new tensions, as well. (*From Jesus to Christ*, 2004).[87]

While the Pharisees were not historically the most prominent grouping in the Jewish community during the lifetime of Jesus (which precedes the first revolt), Matthew places Jesus and Pharisees in constant conflict in his Gospel (Vledder & Van Aarde, 1995: 391)[88]. As this conflict unfolds in Matthew's community he carefully constructs a narrative argument that offers both historical grounds, and theological support, for the emerging identity of the Matthean community (Saldarini, 1994: 5). Jesus is the true Messiah in the line of Abraham. The Matthean community is to live according

---

86 The following article provides a very succinct, and clear, overview of some of this complexity in relation to the communicative intent of the author and the social setting of the receivers of the Matthean text, (Vledder & Van Aarde, 1995)

87 Please find a transcript of the video interview with White, *The Gospel of Matthew: Jesus as the new Moses*. 2004. (From Jesus to Christ: The first Christians). Arlington, VA: PBS (*From Jesus to Christ*, 2004). Also see Sim's commentary on this topic in, *The pacifist Jesus and the violent Jesus in the Gospel of Matthew* (Sim, 2011).

88 Matthew scholarship is popular in South Africa, see (Le Roux, 2011: 1–10) for a discussion of one of the most prominent Matthew scholars, Andries van Aarde from the University of Pretoria. Then also see the work of (Van Aarde & Dreyer, 2010: 1–10) for a reflection on Matthew scholarship at present. I have of course also relied on important earlier works by the South African New Testament scholar Combrink (Combrink, 1983). As you see I have relied extensively on the work of Stellenbosch theologian, Marius Nel, who has worked on forgiveness in Matthew's Gospel (Nel, 2002, 2014a, 2015), then I have also relied on the University of North West (Potchefstroom) theologian Francois Viljoen's work on Matthew (Viljoen, 2006, 2007, 2009, 2011a,b, 2012, 2013, 2016).

to the Torah, but not merely according to the legalistic precepts put forward by the Pharisees, rather they are to follow the teaching of Jesus and live in accordance with the intention of Torah, rather than just obeying the letter of the law.

The relationship between the internal community identity (LL) in relation to the external social situation (LR) comes clearly into focus in Matthew 18. Consider the disciplinary regulations in 18.15-17. If a brother in the community sins against you, tell him about the sin (v.15), if he refuses to listen go back to him with another member of the community (v.16), if the member still does not recant one should take the case to the community / church (v.17), and if the person refuses to listen to the Church he or she should be excommunicated (ἐὰν δὲ παρακούσῃ αὐτῶν, εἰπὲ τῇ ἐκκλησίας ἐὰν δὲ καὶ τῆς ἐκκλησίας παρακούσῃ, ἔστω σοι ὥσπερ ὁ ἐθνικὸς καὶ ὁ τελώνης)[89]. The condemnation is particularly severe, the person is to be treated as a "heathen" or a "tax collector", both of which were considered derogatory social designations among the Jews. It is worth noting that if the outsider is to be considered an ἐθνικὸς (a gentile) then the insiders in the community must hold the view that they are truly Jewish. The expectations here have to do with group orientation. In the social context of the Matthean community group identity, and the importance of belonging to a social group, is of great importance. Not only were such groups important for economic survival and collective social capital, they were also important for religious identity, giving meaning and purpose to the lives of community members. Malina notes,

> Meaning resides in the social system of individuals that is held together by shared culture, shared values, and shared meanings along with social institutions and social roles to realize those values and meanings. (Malina, 1991: 6)

A socio-political reading of Matthew's Gospel shows us that the author employed very specific and powerful thought devices in the writing of the text to shape a sense of identity, a special character that comes from belonging to the 'in group' of the Matthean community. Logically, this social construction of an in-group identity also means that there will be an 'out-group', a group of persons who do not belong, who do not share the character, virtues, identity, privileges and protection of the in-group. Carter explains that if one reads the Gospel text through this socio-political lens one can see the emergence of clear boundaries being drawn between the in-group and the out-group (Carter, 2000: 9–14). Of particular importance is that the Matthean community does not occupy a central space of economic or political power in its context, rather it is a community that is at the edges of society, even marginalised (Carter, 2000: 9–10). Carter says that Matthew's Gospel incorporates "topics of origin, governance and practices to shape and legitimate the marginal identity and lifestyle of a community of disciples" (Carter, 2000: 11). Exclusion of an individual from the protection of the community would be a very severe punishment indeed, as would a disruption of the social cohesion and unity of the community itself.

What is clear is that the social and religious context in which the author and his community find themselves has some important indicators for a faithful reading

---

89 Aland, Barbara ; Aland, Kurt; Black, Matthew; Martini, Carlo M.; Metzger, Bruce M.; Wikgren, Allen: *The Greek New Testament*. 4th ed. Federal Republic of Germany: United Bible Societies, 1993, c1979, S. 50

of the text. If we do not take time to understand the social and religious context in which Matthew collects and writes these parables and sayings of Jesus we could misinterpret their communicative intent for the original audience, and appropriate understandings for our own context that are out of step with the text's original intention and purpose (Kok, 2014b: 9).

Next, let's move from the macro view towards concentrating on several critical concepts that emerge in the passage that is under consideration in this study.

4.5 On forgiveness in the Gospel of Matthew

The theme of forgiveness is of central importance in Matthew's Gospel because of the frequency with which it is dealt with explicitly in the Gospel narrative (1.18-25; 5.21-26; 6.7-15; 9.1-8; 12.22-37; 18.21-35 and 26.26-30)[90]. In addition to this Mbabazi points out that it is important that the author of Matthew's Gospel weaves the theme of forgiveness into the life and teaching of Jesus throughout the Gospel (Mbabazi, 2013: 2–8). Nel goes on to say that the contemporary Biblical scholar will not be able to fully understand either the Gospel, or this theme in the Gospel, without paying careful attention to the theme of forgiveness both in the explicit sayings of Jesus, and also looking for it in the narrative structure of the Gospel itself (Lee & Viljoen, 2010b: 99–100).

> It is therefore important to focus on passages that refer to the teaching of Jesus on forgiveness (e.g. 6.12, 14–15; 18.23–35) and those relating his deeds of forgiveness (e.g. 9.1–8) as well as to where they are placed within the τάξις of Matthew's Gospel. (Nel, 2015: 2).

The thread of forgiveness is first introduced to the reader in the prologue (προοίμιον) of Matthew's Gospel. A number of key themes in the Gospel are introduced in the prologue (1.1-2.23). This already shows the importance of forgiveness as a key theme in the Gospel (Nel, 2015: 2, 4, 6). Most notably for the purposes of this project, Matthew describes the etymology of the name of Jesus in 1.21 (τέξεται δὲ υἱόν, καὶ καλέσεις τὸ ὄνομα αὐτοῦ Ἰησοῦν· αὐτὸς γὰρ σώσει τὸν λαὸν αὐτοῦ ἀπὸ τῶν ἁμαρτιῶν αὐτῶν). Moreover, the prologue and epilogue (ἐπίλογος - 26.1-28.20) are linked by a number of inclusions that form a hermeneutic framework for the interpretation of the sayings and deeds of Jesus in the core of Matthew's Gospel (διήγησις - 3.1-25:46) (Nolland, 2005b: 380; Nel, 2015: 3). One prominent example of such an inclusion is the notion that Jesus would save his people from their sins (1.21) by giving his life as a sacrifice (26.28).

Nel points out that as a result of the interrelatedness of the words and deeds of Jesus in the Gospel narrative, it is necessary to study not only the explicit teaching of Jesus on forgiveness, but also to study his narrated deeds through which he enacts forgiveness (Nel, 2015: 2–4). Richard Burridge developed a convincing and detailed argument to show that Biblical scholars, and ordinary readers of the Biblical text, have often missed important ethical expectations by focussing on the sayings of Jesus only, and neglecting to study his deeds and actions (Burridge, 2007: 25–27,

---

90   It is not being suggested here that forgiveness is the hermeneutic key to understanding the Gospel according to Matthew, for a detailed discussion of the topic of an overarching hermeneutic key please see (Lee & Viljoen, 2010a: 65–67; Nel, 2014a,b).

74–78, 81, 348). Matthew uses events such as the healing of the sick (9.6) and Jesus dining with sinners (9.9-13) as illustrated insights into Jesus' forgiving action. In the next section we will discuss this in some detail, now it need only be mentioned that the concept of a transformed identity (from being an outsider to being an insider) is an important theme related to both forgiveness and community in Matthew's Gospel (Bartchy, S.S., 1992: 796; Hagner, 1993: 238).

We find the introduction to Matthew's διήγησις of Jesus' words and deeds in Matthew 3:1-4:16. Jesus is introduced as the only mediator of forgiveness by John the Baptist in 3.1-12. Nel writes, "According to John, Jesus would not only take the place of contemporary Jewish mediators of forgiveness, but would also surpass his own ministry of repentance" (Nel, 2015: 3), (Ἐγὼ μὲν ὑμᾶς βαπτίζω ἐν ὕδατι εἰς μετάνοιαν, ὁ δὲ ὀπίσω μου ἐρχόμενος ἰσχυρότερός μού ἐστιν, οὗ οὐκ εἰμὶ ἱκανὸς τὰ ὑποδήματα βαστάσαι·αὐτὸς ὑμᾶς βαπτίσει ἐν πνεύματι ἁγίῳ καὶ πυρί - 3:11). He goes on to say that the

> …conflict between John and various Jewish mediators of forgiveness, which is already apparent in the introduction (3:7–12), anticipates the fierce conflict that would develop between them and Jesus in the rest of the Gospel. (Nel, 2015: 3).

In the next part of Matthew's διήγησις (4.17-11.1) Matthew's theology of forgiveness is developed further in the deeds and words of Jesus (Mbabazi, 2013: 32–36). Jesus expounds the notion of forgiveness in the sermon on the mount by reframing it within a proper interpretation of the Law in a variety of social and religious settings (5.3-7.27). Moreover, the link between forgiveness and inclusion in the community is further displayed through acts of miraculous healing (9.1-8) and fellowship with 'outsiders' (sinners) (9.11)[91]. Matthew employs the literary device of inclusion to show that Jesus' words are in accord with his actions, and as such he is an honourable person. The inclusion begins with the announcement of Jesus as the one who will teach and heal (4.23) and concludes with the summary of his ministry (9.35) – thereby Matthew is able to link the narration of Jesus' teaching (5.3-7.27) and the deeds that exemplify his teaching (8.2-9.34). The theme of forgiveness is thus important in Matthew, particularly as it relates to the sayings and ministry of Jesus (most clearly exemplified in the sermon on the mount and Jesus' forgiving of 'sinners' who move from being outsider to insiders) (Kennedy, 1984: 55, 61–62; Burridge, 1997: 524; Mbabazi, 2013: 12–15; Nel, 2015: 3).

The overarching theme of the next portion of Matthew's διήγησις (11.2-13.52) concentrates on the negative response of Israel to the ministry of Jesus, his disciples and the ministry of John. Perhaps the best-known passage in this section, among popular readings of the Gospel, is the section on the unforgivable sin (12.22-37).

---

91 Nel writes, "Whereas the Pharisees used table fellowship in order to signal the exclusion of those they considered being sinners (e.g. tax collectors), Jesus uses it as a means of expressing their inclusion in God's kingdom. This is in line with the function of table fellowship as an important symbol of friendship and reconciliation in the 1st century Mediterranean world" (Nel, 2015: 3). Also see (Hagner, 1993: 238) and the following resources for a detailed discussion of the concept of forgiveness and inclusion of 'outsiders' in the Matthean worldview (Nel, 2002: 197–199), and also this superb article on community composition and dynamics in the Matthean community (Nel, 2014b).

The context of this section is that it forms Jesus' response to the escalating conflict between Jesus and the Jewish leaders who saw themselves as the primary mediators of God's forgiveness. Thus, the themes of forgiveness, community and power are once again of primary concern to Matthew's narrative (Viljoen, 2011a: 331–332). Of course this section also serves to strengthen the notion that an on-going reality of conflict will exist between true followers of Jesus (insiders) and the Jewish leaders (Mbabazi, 2013: 15; Nel, 2015: 4–5).

The next section of Matthew's διήγησις (13.53-16.20) does not expand on the theme of forgiveness directly, rather it focuses on the healing miracles of Jesus and charts the on-going conflict with, and rejection by, the Jewish leaders.

The fourth part of Matthew's διήγησις (16.21-19.2) overlaps with the second phase of Jesus' public ministry. The two phases of Jesus' public ministry each add a different emphasis to Matthew's understanding of forgiveness as related to Jesus. In the first phase of Jesus' ministry (4.17-16.20) Matthew emphasises Jesus' authority to forgive, whereas the second phase (16.21-28.20) emphasises Jesus' weakness, sacrifice and obedience which are also linked to forgiveness[92]. Of course, the focus of this study (18.1-35) falls within this section. As such I will not dwell on it at this point since we have already covered it in detailed in an earlier part of this chapter. All that needs to be said at this point is that it forms the core teaching on how the disciples are to live as a community, thus bringing together the notions of forgiveness and community in a very direct series of narratives (Mbabazi, 2013: 41–42; Nel, 2015: 3).

The fifth part of the διήγησις (19.3-25.46) deals with Jesus ministry in Judea with a particular focus on his journey to Jerusalem. This is another section of critical importance to the unfolding understanding of forgiveness in Matthew's Gospel. It is in this section that Matthew reveals to the reader that Jesus will die for the forgiveness of sins – thus Jesus' teaching is not just an ethical code of forgiveness, it is a performative act that achieves forgiveness, a personal sacrifice at great personal cost. Of course, this has the purpose of strengthening the injunction of 18.35 about the true nature of forgiveness, and that the followers of Jesus will also have to bear a personal cost in order to forgive. This revelation brings the cost of forgiveness into stark focus, but it also opens up the scope of Jesus' forgiveness by showing that Jesus' forgiveness was for a ransom for many, "καὶ δοῦναι τὴν ψυχὴν αὐτοῦ λύτρον ἀντὶ πολλῶν" (20.28b). As has been mentioned earlier, in Matthew the concepts of forgiveness and community are closely linked. The widening of the community and the embracing of outsiders, as well as the regulation of community life inside the community, are all closely related to his presentation of forgiveness in the life and teaching of Jesus.

The Gospel concludes with Matthew's ἐπίλογος (26.1-28.20). The overall inclusio which was opened with the announcement of Jesus' birth and that he would save his people from their sins (1.21), is now concluded and evidenced in the crucifixion (26.28; 27.45-54). After his resurrection Jesus admonishes his disciples to carry on

---

92 Nel writes, "The first phase of his public ministry (4:17-16:20) in which his *authority* to teach, heal and forgive are related to each other is introduced by the same transitional phrase (Ἀπὸ τότε ἤρξατο) that introduces the second phase (cf. 4.17 & 16.21). In the second phase of Jesus' public ministry it is his *weakness*, suffering and sacrifice that are connected to his ability to forgive." (Nel, 2015: 3).

his teaching and example by teaching others to do what he had instructed them to do (28.20a). Nel sums up the theme of forgiveness in Matthew's Gospel as follows:

> The pro- and epilogue are linked by the promise that God would be active in the ministry of Jesus (1:23), and that the resurrected Jesus would always be with his followers (28:20). The final command of the resurrected Jesus to his surviving disciples in the epilogue, viz. to teach all future disciples everything he had taught them (and thus also his ethics of forgiveness), ties the ministry of Jesus to the on-going mission of the church. (Nel, 2015: 8).

It is worth noting at this point that the genre of Matthew's Gospel appears to display the characteristics of an ancient biography (βίος) of Jesus. Van der Watt writes of literary form,

> This type of literature of course, as the word says, focuses on the person of somebody, but not as pure neutral description, but an interested and involved description that also strives for establishing meaning through the description. (Van der Watt, 2012a: 1).

The particular meaning that Matthew intended was for the Matthean community to be formed by the biography of Jesus' life and teaching[93]. Burridge goes as far as saying that the genre of Gospel was in fact a form of βίος (biography or 'lives') (Burridge, 2005: 6, 2007: 24; Smith, 2015: 100), a common form of literature in the ancient near East. Talbert points out that the purpose of these biographies is aimed at instructing and propagandizing – the Gospels as biographies are aimed at dispelling "a false image of the teacher and to provide a true model to follow" (Talbert, 1977: 15–17). This concept is known as 'mimesis' (μίμησις), meaning to imitate (from the Greek root, μῖμος perhaps more commonly known by the Latin imitatio). In a following session we will discuss the notion and intention of mimesis in great detail as it relates to both the literary form and literary intention of Matthew's Gospel. For this current purpose, however, it need only be noted that it was Matthew's intention that the recipients of his narrative would be moulded according to the person, teaching and deeds of Jesus as expressed in this 'biography'. Of central importance in that process was the interrelated aspects of forgiveness and community.

Having considered Matthew's presentation of forgiveness we shall move on to a detailed investigation of Matthew's perspective on community.

---

93 Of course there is a great deal of debate on the literary genre of Matthew's Gospel, see (Lee & Viljoen, 2010a: 65) for a detailed discussion of the various perspectives. I shall simply mention that among the dominant discourses on Matthean genre are, myth (Dibelius & Iber, 1971: 282–285), cultic legend (Bultmann, 1963: 286), a hymn of enthronement (Jeremias, 1958: 38–39; Michel, 1995: 36–37), an Old Testament prophetic pattern of proof (Malina, 1970: 88–91), and a commission (Hubbard, 1974: 62–72; Stuhlmacher, 2000: 25; Lee & Viljoen, 2010a: 64–83). Of course each of these has counter arguments. However, the work of Nel, Mbabazi, Burridge and van der Watt are more than enough to substantiate the credibility of viewing this Gospel as a form of ancient biography (Burridge, 2004: 240–241; Van der Watt, 2012a; Mbabazi, 2013; Nel, 2015).

4.6 On community in the Gospel of Matthew

The theme of community forms another central focus in the Gospel of Matthew. Matthew clearly wrote his Gospel for the community that he calls the Church (ἐκκλησία in 16.18 and 18.17), but he also seeks to address their context with particular reference to the way in which the person, example and teaching of Jesus would find expression in that context (Bartlett, 2001: 75). Nel sums up the way in which Jesus' life and the Matthean community's context are related as follows:

> For Matthew the escalating conflict between Jesus and the Jewish leadership, that had resulted in Jesus making a clear distinction between those who had accepted him and those who did not during his lifetime (12:46-50), reflected his own community's conflict with formative Judaism. (Nel, 2014a: 85).

The Gospel of Matthew contains a narrative tension – within the context of escalating conflict with the Jewish community in the Matthean community (which is related to the conflict that Jesus, John and the disciples had with the Jewish leadership), Matthew needs to provide a clear motivation for the community's mission to all people and all nations (28.19-20).

In order to understand the Matthean community's sensitivity to outsiders it is important to clarify what is understood by the community of Matthew. Did this community for example consist of a single community in a specific context or of a number of different communities facing similar challenges? Can we in other words assume that the outsiders in regards to the Matthean community comprised a specific group in a fixed locale, or were they different groups living across a whole range of localities with which the Matthean communities had varied relationships?

Richard Bauckham (1998:9-48) has challenged the common assumption in this regard, that the Gospels were each written for a specific community that had little or no contact with other Christian communities, or a sense of participation in a broad Christian movement. He instead states that Matthew may have lived in several different and geographically distant Christian communities over the years it took him to compile his Gospel (Bauckham, 1998: 36). If Bauckham is correct,[94] it would mean that Matthew was not only addressing the relationship between his own isolated community and outsiders in their unique context, but rather that of a number of Christian communities within the broader Roman world. In this regard Luz has argued that the evidence of conflict between the Matthean community and formative Judaism in the Gospel of Matthew[95] does not need to be interpreted as indicting a conflict that was limited to a specific geographical area (Luz, Koester & Crouch, 2007: 76–77). A more likely assumption, according to Luz, is that the author of Matthew expected conflict in multiple cities between the followers of Jesus and

---

94 The argument by Bauckham that the Gospels were written for a broad audience has been challenged by a number of scholars. Sim has, for example, objected to his neglect of internal evidence, while Carter has argued that he "seems to confuse [the Gospels'] subsequent effect with their initial focus." (Carter, 2000: 560; Sim, 2001: 268–278).

95 For example the Gospel's polemical characterizations of Israel's leaders and its pointed contrasts between "their synagogues" and "my assembly" (4.23; 6.2, 5; 9.35; 10.17; 12.9; 13.54; 16.18; 23.6, 34) (Luz, Koester & Crouch, 2007: 76–77).

the diaspora Jews as is narrated in Acts.[96] The Matthean community could thus have been comprised of a number of small groups meeting in different locales that were experiencing similar challenges (e.g. conflict with formative Judaism and a growing influx of Gentiles). While it is impossible to ascertain if the thesis of Luz is correct the similar picture that emerges from Acts does give some validity to his suggestion (cf. Burridge, 2007:195).

While the exact homogenous identity of the Matthean community is uncertain, it is clear that they made a distinction between insiders and outsiders, as was common in the Mediterranean ancient near East (Duling, 1999: 15; Nel, 2014b: 730, 733, 2015: 4)[97]. Relationship to Jesus is the point of inclusion or exclusion: wheat or chaff (3.12), good or bad trees (7.16-20), good or bad fish (13.47-48), wise or foolish maidens (25.1-13), sheep or goats (25.31-46). Matthew is very clear, one is for, or against, Jesus (12.30). One either accepts, and adheres, to the ethical and moral principles of Jesus, or one is to be expelled from the community (18.15-17b), at which point you became one of the archetypal outsides, a Gentile (18.17c), "ἔστω σοι ὥσπερ ὁ ἐθνικὸς καὶ ὁ τελώνης". Thus, Matthew's community maintains stringent boundaries between the inside group (who follow (mimesis) Jesus), and the Gentiles who are outside of the community.

4.7 Mimesis and reciprocity in the ancient near east and the Gospel of Matthew

As has been stated earlier, there is some scholarly evidence that the genre of Matthew can fit the pattern of an ancient biography. This is an important point to notice since the genre of biography (βίος) had a particular communicative intent. van der Watt comments that this type of literature,

> ... focuses on the person of somebody, but not as pure neutral description, but an interested and involved description that also strives for establishing meaning through the description. (Van der Watt, 2012a: 1)

Talbert reminds us that biographers would carefully select which materials to include, or exclude, from their biographies in order to teach and instruct their readers, dispelling "a false image of the teacher and to provide a true model to follow" (Talbert, 1977: 15–17). The intention of such biographies was to provide a model that could be copied as an aesthetic, cultural, social, or moral ideal. Morrison notes that the "Greek philosophers had nominated three areas in which *mimesis* occurred, namely, (a) the realm of nature; (b) the realm of art; and (c) the realm of moral reproduction..." (quoted in Harrison, 2013: 215). Simply stated, in ancient

---

96 The promise that Jesus will be present "where two or three are gathered" in his name (18.20) implies according to Ulrich Luz that the Matthean assembly in any given location could be small (Luz et al., 2007: 76–77). The adverb οὗ ("where") allows for a movement meeting in many different locations and thus could envision a movement similar to, and in competition with, the synagogues that were present in every Greco-Roman city.

97 For a detailed scholarly discussion on insiders and outsiders in Matthew's community please see *Mission and ethics - sensitivity to outsiders in Matthew's mission* (Nel, 2014a: 93–112). For more discussion on this topic in the New Testament in general please see the excellent work by Kok, *Insiders versus outsiders: Exploring the dynamic relationship between mission and ethos in the New Testament* (Kok, 2014a)

near eastern culture, the "model represents the standard toward which its copies move" (Castelli, 1991: 22). Both van der Watt and Sörbom point out that mimesis is not a single theory, as such, but rather that it is an identifiable social practice that is particularly strongly presented in the social conduct and the spheres of ethical behaviour in ancient cultures[98] (Sörbom, 2002: 19; Van der Watt, 2014: 1).

Of particular interest for Matthew 18 are the mimetic intentions of the image of the King (cf., 5:7 in relation to 18.23-35, especially v.35), and the concept of reciprocity in forgiveness. Davies and Allison suggest that the notion of conditioned forgiveness that is expressed in 5.7, "Blessed are the merciful (οἱ ἐλεήμονες), for they will receive mercy (ἐλεηθήσονται)" can be linked thematically to 6.12, 14-15 and 18.32b-35 (Davies & Allison, 1988: 802 Vol.2). The principle of reciprocity in forgiveness is established in 7:12, however, in 18.21-35 Matthew goes further by juxtaposing forgiveness and mercy as contingent upon one another (France, 2007: 707–708; Mbabazi, 2013: 184). Mbabazi comments that "God, the king of all, must be imitated in his goodness: the one forgiven should have acted in kind; the one act of mercy should have begotten another" (Mbabazi, 2013: 184).

The text presents a moral expectation to the reader, namely that there is a logical expectation that because of the mercy that the servant with the huge debt had received by being forgiven of his debt by the benevolent king, he should have acted in the same, or at least a similar way to his debtor. Linnemann comments that in this regard, "…mercy is essentially not something which we can accept with a feeling of relief at having got away with it once more, only to let things go on again just as we used to" (Linnemann, 1977: 111). He goes on to state that this narrative appears "to have the character of an ordinance, just as justice is an ordinance" (Linnemann, 1977: 111). The parable communicates a mimetic expectation to the reader, not only in the positive example of the master or king, but also in disappointment (distress, ἐλυπήθησαν) of the fellow slaves at the unforgiveness of their brother (v.31) and the anger (ὀργισθεὶς) of the king when learning of this injustice (vv.32-34). The slave is then handed over to the torturers (βασανισταῖς) to be punished, a contrast to the benevolence (pity, σπλαγχνισθεὶς) and grace that was shown to him the king earlier in the narrative (v.27). Davies and Allison point out that the reversion to torture serves as a *hapax legomenon* to illustrate both the anger of the king at the lack of mercy, and the severity of the resulting punishment (Davies & Allison, 1988: 802 Vol.2). The use of torture in the Roman prison system (a practise that was disallowed by the Jews) was intended to place pressure on the community of the debtor to find a way to settle his debt more urgently (Hagner, 1993: 540; Mbabazi, 2013: 185). The slave would be tortured until his debt was settled entirely, (πᾶν τὸ ὀφειλόμενον v.34) – a similar expression can be found in 5:26, however, it also echoes 18.30 (the very act of injustice which leads this slave to have grace withdrawn and torture enacted upon him). Mbabazi sums it up in saying that this section "clearly teaches that as one treats others, so also will one be treated" (Mbabazi, 2013: 185). This is confirmed in the text itself in v.35 where Jesus concludes his parable by saying, "So

---

98   For a detailed and helpful discussion of mimesis in ancient Greek culture please see the detailed and helpful discussions presented by van der Watt, Sörbom and Castelli (Castelli, 1991; Sörbom, 2002: 19–28; Van der Watt, 2014: 1–4). Also see (Schweiker, 1990; MacDonald, 2001; Scubla, 2005; Van der Watt, 2006, 2012a: 1,b; Van der Watt & Malan, 2006; Watts, 2013)

my heavenly Father will also do to every one of you, if you do not forgive your brother or sister from your heart".

A further element to note is that since the debt owed by the unforgiving slave was so enormous, his imprisonment was likely to be permanent, a hint towards an eschatological punishment for those persons who choose to follow the pattern of the unforgiving servant rather than the gracious king (Davies & Allison, 1988: 803 Vol.2; Hagner, 1993: 540; Mbabazi, 2013: 185). Mbabazi points out, interestingly, that the servant must have recognised his condemned fate since he did not plead once more for mercy as he did in 18.26, and has his fellow slave did in 18.29 (Mbabazi, 2013: 185). The final sentence of the parable takes the form of a summative lesson; it presents the moral of the preceding story.

> Each disciple in the community risks the loss of God's forgiveness in eternal punishment, if he does not forgive a fellow disciple as a heartfelt response to the same generous, merciful, compassionate, and unlimited forgiveness he has received from God. (Carter & Heil, 1998: 121).

The use of the phrase οὕτως καὶ in v.35 is a discourse *deixis* which seems to point to v.34 where the king not only goes back on his mercy to the servant, but also hands him over to the torturers (Mbabazi, 2013: 186). The intention is likely to emphasise the concept of reciprocity since 18.35 can be linked 6.14-15 ("For if you forgive others their trespasses, your heavenly Father will also forgive you; but if you do not forgive others, neither will your Father forgive your trespasses"), which is related to 5.7 ("Blessed are the merciful, for they will receive mercy") and 7.1-2, 12 ("Do not judge, so that you may not be judged. For with the judgment you make you will be judged, and the measure you give will be the measure you get", "In everything do to others as you would have them do to you; for this is the law and the prophets"). Mbabazi notes that the "*logion* in 18.35 also refers to these other interpersonal forgiveness and related texts" (Mbabazi, 2013: 187). Thus, it is plausible to suggest that the translation of the words οὕτως καὶ in v.35 as "so also" emphasises the principles of reciprocity and judgement.

The use of the phrases πατήρ μου ὁ οὐράνιος (my Father in heaven) and ἀπὸ τῶν καρδιῶν (from the heart) in v.35 makes the possibility of misunderstanding the intention of the parable very difficult for its original readers (Gundry, 1994: 375). The use of these phrases "express sincerity and excludes all casuistry and legalism" (Mbabazi, 2013: 187). In other words, if one does not imitate the grace of the king in forgiving others their debts or wrongs, the tone shifts from personal (from the heart) to legal (judgement, jail and torture). According to Luz this requires that there should be a change of heart in the acts of forgiveness and reconciliation – outward reconciliation is not enough, what is needed is a change of heart and full acceptance of the one who has been forgiven (Luz, 2005: 476). This was the failing of the unforgiving servant, he was legally free, yet his actions showed that he had not had a change of heart, and so the king moves from grace to law, from forgiveness to judgement.

Mbabazi sums up the process that Matthew presents as a moral obligation in this parable, in the following manner:

> [1] A wrong is committed [2] The offender does not necessarily seek forgiveness [3] The offended person grants forgiveness as both their *responsibility* towards their fellow human and their *accountability* before their heavenly Father [4] The ultimate goal of the forgiveness demand is to bring harmony within the community. (Mbabazi, 2013: 189 italics in the original).

Thus, from what has been discussed above it is clear that this passage communicates on multiple levels. The first and most obvious level is the text itself. The author chose words, concepts and ideas and placed them in a communicative narrative. Second, the text communicates through its embeddedness in a larger collection of shared cultural, social and historical concepts that make up what one could call the worldview of Matthew and his intended readers. Third, the text communicates on the level of a communicative device – namely the genre of the text as a biographical instrument that was recorded and passed on has certain expectations and understandings associated with it. Most notably, as was mentioned above, the expectation of imitation of the noble aspects of the biography, and avoidance of the ignoble elements of the narrative.

Van der Watt makes the clear point that in the Biblical worldview, and in broader culture at the time of the writing of the Gospels, mimetic texts based their transformational capital not only on religious or theological content, but also very clearly on social expectation (Van der Watt, 2000: 376–382, 2014: 7). He further points out that such texts present themselves with the clear expectation that "'n persoon volgens sy identiteit sal optree. Hierdie aspek van antropologie staan al vanaf Sokrates in die sentrum van diskussie"[99] (Van der Watt, 2014: 7). The expectation of the author is thus that the readers will not only understand the grammar, syntax and narrative, but that they will respond to the narrative mimetically, in a manner which was appropriate to their time and context, not just as a social model, but as a form of concrete structural behaviour. This concept is summed up succinctly by van der Watt who writes[100],

> Navolging of mimesis vorm die skakel tussen die voorbeelde wat God en Jesus stel en die gelowiges wat ook net soos Jesus geleef het, behoort te leef. Etiese gedrag behels inderdaad 'n gehoorsame verhoudingsoriëntasie (mimiek) teenoor Jesus en die Vader en nie die blote nakoming van 'n lys moets en moenies nie. (Van der Watt, 2014: 8).

This is particularly illustrative of an aspect of Matthew's style, most clearly illustrated in the discourse of the sermon on the mount, where Matthew's Jesus points out that faithfulness to God, and true Christian discipleship, is not just a matter of obeying the law, but consists in mimicking the character of the loving God which is fulfilled

---

99   The quotation is translated from Afrikaans to English as follows, "… a person will act according to their identity. This aspect of anthropology has been at the centre of the discussion since Socrates" (Van der Watt, 2014: 7).

100 The quotation is translated from Afrikaans to English as follows, "Emulation or mimesis forms the link between the examples that God and Jesus provide, and the believers who lived in accordance with the example of Jesus. Ethical behaviour involves an obedient relationship orientation towards Jesus and the Father (to mimic) and not the mere fulfillment of a list of do's and don't's" (Van der Watt, 2014: 8).

in the person and life of Jesus (Davies & Allison, 1988: 507, 541 Vol. 1; Morris, 1992: 106–112; Overman, 1996: 77–84; Garland, 1999: 62–77; Talbert, 2010: 72–73).[101] The point is simply that Matthew employs the strategy of mimesis throughout the text, and particularly in Matthew 18 to convey meaning to the reader through the content of the text, the structure of the narrative, the genre of the text, and the its embeddedness in socio-historical network of shared meaning. With regards to the ethical implications of this, van der Watt writes[102],

> Dit beteken dat die etos wat die algemeen aanvaarde gedrag binne die Christengemeenskap verteenwoordig, onder andere veronderstel dat die Vader en Jesus mimeties aan gelowiges, as kinders van God, gebind was… Mimesis word dus verwag, omdat die aangesprokenes hulleself binne die familie bevind. Die veronderstelling is dat binne die betrokke sosiale raamwerk mimeties opgetree moet word. Dit is moontlik omdat mimesis nie 'n sosiale model is nie, maar eerder 'n spesifieke gestruktureerde houding weerspieël. (Van der Watt, 2014: 8).

Up to this point in the discussion we have taken great care to do a detailed reading of the text of Matthew 18, seeking to understand and explicate meaning and intention in the text through a careful study of the textual elements such as grammar and syntax, but also to understand core concepts that arise from an understanding of the genre of the text and its social and historical setting. Of course one could drill ever deeper and deeper into the thought world of Matthew, his readers and his milieu. I trust that this will be a part of my ongoing work in years to come. Now however, having established this foundation it is necessary to shift our focus on a different task. In the section that follows we shall place a lens on the text that we have been studying in order to discuss and understand some contemporary meaning from the text, seeking to understand some of what it may mean to a current reader. The approach that we shall take to the text is an All Quadrants All Levels (AQAL) integrative approach.

---

101 There is a rich corpus of study on this topic, far too much to deal with in this document. I will simply offer two points of illustration, first is the structural narrative of Matthew's Gospel in which Jesus is presented the fulfillment of righteousness (Matthew 3:1-4:17), followed by Jesus' discourse on true righteousness (Matthew 4:18-8:1). These set the scene for the development of a new form of faithfulness and righteousness that progressively unfolds in Matthew's Gospel in accordance with 5:17. This theme is echoed very clearly in our passage in 18.21-22. A second example is the use of "but/and" (δὲ) from 5:22 onwards, where Jesus establishes himself as the fulfillment of the law (Davies & Allison, 1988: 541 Vol. 1). The point is that Jesus is not abolishing the law, but that he is fulfilling it. Thus if the disciple follows both the teaching and the example of a faithful and loving life as seen in Jesus (*mimesis*) she or he cannot go wrong (Davies & Allison, 1988: 507 Vol. 1). For a further helpful discussion on narrative approaches to the Biblical text please see, Tolmie, F. 2012. *Narratology and Biblical narratives: a practical guide*. Wipf and Stock Publishers (Tolmie, 2012).

102 The quotation is translated from Afrikaans to English as follows, "Thus it means that the ethical norms that represented accepted behaviour among Christians, presume that the Father and Jesus are bound memetically to the believers as children of God… Mimesis is thus expected, since those who are being addressed are members of the family. The expectation is that they would behave mimetically within these social boundaries. This is possible, not because mimesis is a social model as such, but rather because it represents a particular attitude (or ethos)" (Van der Watt, 2014: 8).

4.8 An AQAL reading of the text: Establishing the integral possibility of Matthew 18.15-35 for an intercultural Bible reading on forgiveness

As has just been mentioned, this section will build upon the critically important groundwork of Biblical exegesis which was undertaking on Matthew 18.15-35 and consider it through a contemporary theoretical lens – the AQAL integrative framework[103]. It is hoped, and anticipated, that this process will extrapolate perspectives and insights that arise from an interaction of the text and the perspectives on individual and social identity that arise from each of the four quadrants. The concepts that arise from this reading will form traces, conceptual markers, which will be employed in the development of the empirical tools employed with the intercultural reading groups. In addition to this, the concepts that arise from this reading will inform the theological criteria used to map the reader responses to reading the text as individuals and as part of their community, allowing the researcher to explicate meaning and plot a landscape of theological convictions in the readers at varying stages of the intergroup contact process.

As has already been argued, Matthew 18.15-35 is a particularly helpful text on which to do an AQAL reading since it highlights the importance of understanding the theological and practical aspects of the intention of the text in all four quadrants of individual and social identity. Please refer to chapter 2 for a detailed introduction to AQAL integral theory with reference to how it is applied and understood in the context of this project. Moreover, our chosen text illustrates very clearly that the challenges in the Matthean community, and Matthew's addressing of them in the Gospel (especially in chapter 18.15-35) is multifaceted with layers of complexity embedded in the theological and social responses to mimetic faithfulness, sin, justice, honour and shame (cf., 4.8, Forster, 2017).

All Quadrants:

First, this passage highlights the deficiency of a flatland[104] reading of forgiveness. The introductory question posed by Peter (v.21) places forgiveness within the context of the Christian community, "Lord if another member of the Church… (ὁ ἀδελφός

---

103 A portion of this chapter was reworked to publish in a *festschrift* in honour of Prof Jan van der Watt. Please see, Forster, D.A. 2017. A public theological approach to the (im) possibility of forgiveness in Matthew 18.15-35: reading the text through the lens of integral theory. *In die Skriflig/In Luce Verbi*. 51(3):1–10.

104 Flatland is an expression coined by Ken Wilber that explains the process of collapsing one's understanding of all of reality into either the interior realm (psychological, spiritual), or the exterior realm (science, politics, sociology). Wilber suggests that one of the greatest achievements of the Enlightenment was the differentiation of the three realms of being as I (upper left), We (lower left) and It (where 'It' includes both right hand columns of the four quadrants) (1998:24 ff.). As a result of this Wilber sees the task of post-modernity, in relation to modernity, not simply as replacing atomism with holism, but to integrate the "flatland holism with the depth of I and the community of we" (1998:145). This task is urgent since there is a great deal of subtle reductionism in the dualistic world-views of both modern atomism and postmodern holism (c.f. Forster 2006:214-217 for a more detailed discussion of these concepts). Wilber's Holarchic approach, of the four quadrants (presented in section 6 of this paper), attempts to include truth that is derived from each of the four quadrants, the empirical (right hand), constructivist (lower left) and aesthetic (upper left) by "situating them in a truly inclusive embrace" (Snyman 2002:101).

μου)". What we see in this question is an individual (UL) attempting to find meaning amid inner conflict (how many times should I forgive?), which was likely to have been brought on by disharmony in the community (LR) if one considers the place in which this question is found in the narrative of Matthew 18, i.e., just after vv.15-20 which presents a process for dealing with sin or wrongdoing in the community.

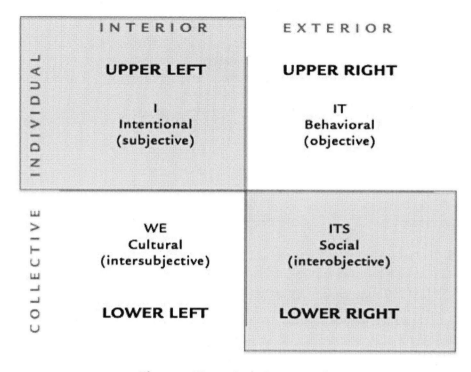

Figure 5: Upper Left, Lower Right

An AQAL approach highlights the textured and nuanced understanding that Matthew applies to the concept of forgiveness, since Jesus's answer to Peter's question adds a further dimension of complexity – namely the reliance of the Matthean community on the Jewish law, (vv.21b-22, "how often should I forgive? As many as seven times?" Jesus said to him, "Not seven times, but, I tell you, seventy- seven times"). Religious law, or regulation, is based upon an understanding of morality that arises from a shared set of theological convictions about what is just and right, and what is unjust and wrong (LL).

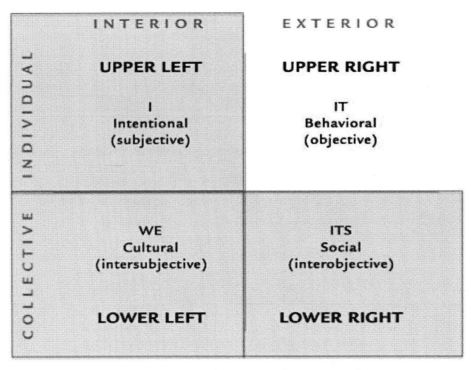

Figure 6: Upper Left, Lower Left, Lower Right

It is generally understood that one of the intentions of Matthew's Gospel was the re-establishment of a new social and religious order based on the understanding that Jesus was the fulfilment of the Jewish law (Davies & Allison, 1988: 507, 541 Vol. 1; Morris, 1992: 106–112; Overman, 1996: 77–84; Garland, 1999: 62–77; Talbert, 2010: 72–73). Jesus is presented as the fulfilment of righteousness which is required by the law (Matthew 3.1-4:17) (UL and UR), followed by Jesus' discourse on true righteousness (Matthew 4.18-8:1). These set the scene for the development of a new form of faithfulness and righteousness that progressively unfolds in Matthew's Gospel in accordance with 5.17 (LL and LR). This theme is echoed very clearly in our passage in 18.21-22. A second example is the use of "but/and" (δὲ) from 5.22 onwards, where Jesus establishes himself as the fulfilment of the law (Davies & Allison, 1988: 541 Vol. 1). The point is that Jesus is not abolishing the law, but that he is fulfilling it. Thus if the disciple follows both the teaching and the example of a faithful and loving life as seen in Jesus (*mimesis*), which is linked to values (UL) and action, (UR), she or he is faithful as a believer (UL), a member in good standing of the new community (LL) and is through their beliefs (UL) and actions (UR) is establishing and upholding the values and virtues of the new community (LR) (Davies & Allison, 1988: 507 Vol. 1). The result is that Matthew presents the shift in identity from individual belief associated with the sin of another, to an integrated understanding of the complex interplay of individual identity (UL), social identity (LL), and individual action (UR) and social harmony (LR).

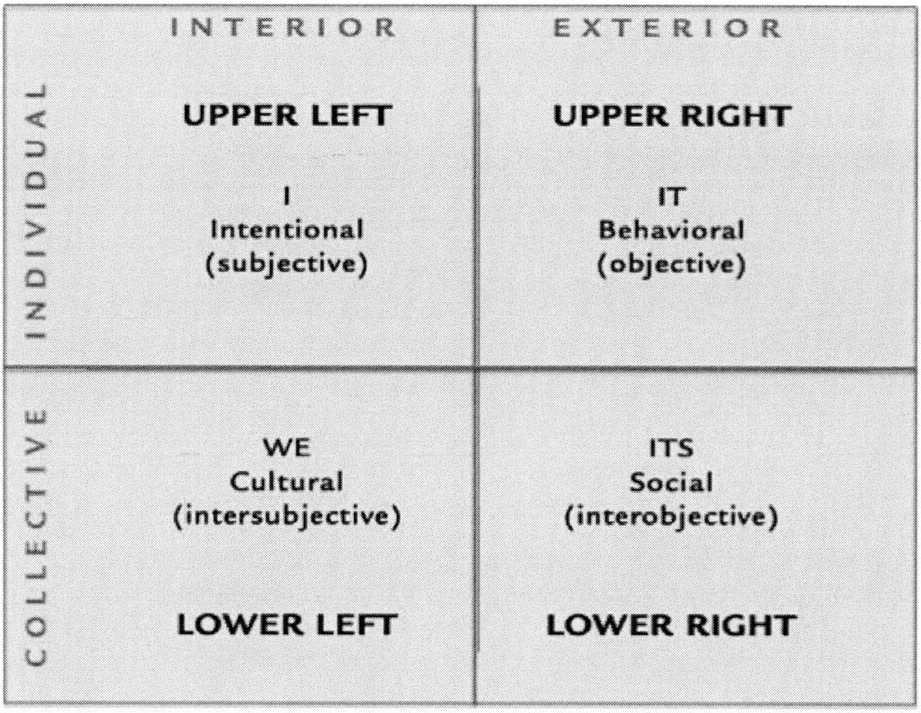

	INTERIOR	EXTERIOR
INDIVIDUAL	**UPPER LEFT** I Intentional (subjective)	**UPPER RIGHT** IT Behavioral (objective)
COLLECTIVE	WE Cultural (intersubjective) **LOWER LEFT**	ITS Social (interobjective) **LOWER RIGHT**

Figure 7: All Quadrants

The importance of this understanding for our study is that it highlights that the intended social cohesion and faith life integration that is advocated in this passage deals with all four of the AQAL life dimensions.

Social harmony and Christian faithfulness requires forgiveness (most easily illustrated in vv.21-22 & v.35), in fact where there is agreement in unity the Lord promises to be among the members of the community ("Again, truly I tell you, if two of you agree on earth about anything you ask, it will be done for you by my Father in heaven. For where two or three are gathered in my name, I am there among them" vv.19-20). Forgiveness cannot be a purely personal matter (UL), although it requires a personal engagement with the particular if there is some sin or wrongdoing that is disturbing both the personal relationship and community harmony. The use of the adjective μόνου (adjective, genitive, singular, masculine) in v.15 emphasises the need for courtesy in the personal engagement, i.e., not to publically humiliate or manipulate the individual. Yet, at the same time it shows that personal engagement is important, "go" (ὕπαγε imperative, present, active, 2nd person, singular) is an UR action of the individual, i.e., "you must go [alone to him]", whereas "between you and him" (μεταξὺ σοῦ καὶ αὐτοῦ) shows both interpersonal presence (LR) and the intention of dealing with the conflict in a shared interpersonal value space (LL) (μεταξὺ is a preposition that can refer either to a physical location as in Acts 12.6, "he was sleeping between to guards", or as an associative interpersonal space as in Acts 15.9, "he made no difference between us and them"). Naturally the flow of the narrative in vv.15-17 shows a progression of identity location from the individuals (the sinner and the sinned against, indicated by the phrase ἀδελφός σου, which indicates relational identity location. Namely, the self and the other who is related to the self, and is also the cause of personal offence, i.e., the sinner who has wronged the sinned against). If the sinner hears the truth (ἀκούσῃ a verb, subjunctive, aorist, active, 3rd person singular, which can mean "to accept", "to believe" and respond) of the sinned against person in the personal engagement (ὕπαγε ἔλεγξον αὐτὸν μεταξὺ σοῦ καὶ αὐτοῦ μόνου), then that person's relational proximity is altered from that of an outsider (v.17, ultimately a "Gentile or a tax collector), to an insider, i.e., one who is "regained". The verb ἐκέρδησας (indicative, aorist, active, 2nd person, singular) indicates a proximal shift in ownership, i.e., to have earned or gained that person for one's self. However, if the person does not hear, the relational interaction moves from subject object engagement (one individual UL, with another individual UR) to an intersubjective (LL) and interobjective engagement (LR). In v.16 the verb παράλαβε (imperative, aorist, active, 2nd person, singular) indicates that one brings along another with one's self (as in Luke 9.28). The taking of another witness (μαρτύρων, noun, genitive, plural, masculine) indicates that the one or ones taken along share a common view of the situation (LL), in other words there is a shared thought world or belief on the matter that is to be addressed with the sinning party. Their presence is intended to act as a social contract (LL), a confirmation of the sinned against person's location on the side of righteousness and truth (σταθῇ verb, subjunctive, aorist, passive, 3rd person, singular). The final progression in the narrative takes the matter to the broader community, the ἐκκλησία (noun, dative, singular, feminine). The ἐκκλησία is viewed as a larger social space (LL) in which deeper and greater truth about the rightness or wrongness of a matter can be established and judged. As in Romans 16.16 the use of this term carries a collective identity and shared thought space, so much so that Paul could say that the "churches of Christ greet you". Furthermore, the term ἐκκλησία not only establishes communal thought boundaries (LL), i.e., the called-out ones, which establishes a boundary between the in-group and the out-group, it also has a socio-historical meaning in common usage that derives form before the Christian era in which it refers to a socio-political entity, like an assembly (Acts 19.39) based in a city or a state (LR). The conclusion of this narrative in vv.17b-19 touches on all four quadrants of individual and social identity. In v.17b Matthew states, "if the offender refuses to listen even to the church, let such a one be to you as a Gentile and a tax collector". As was discussed earlier, the connotation of such a judgement is far reaching. It has consequences for the individual being cast out (UR), for their own belief (i.e., regard them as a Gentile, UL) and belonging in the faith community (LL), and for their future social and economic interaction with the community and broader society (LR, regard them as a tax collector). Some have suggested that the phrase "ἔστω σοι ὥσπερ ὁ ἐθνικὸς καὶ ὁ τελώνης" (v.17b) is an act of formal excommunication from the community, while others have said that it may simply have had religious and interpersonal connotations[105] (Mbabazi, 2013: 153–158). My own reading of this is the narrative is framed thematically by a few important markers that help us to understand what was meant by this phrase. First, the use of the word ἀδελφός throughout the passage places an emphasis on the depth of the relationship and the importance of engaging the sinner to restore interpersonal harmony. Second, the

---

105 Please see Mbabazi's detailed discussion of the 4 general approaches to this topic here, (Mbabazi, 2013: 153–158). Luz has also done an extensive survey of the various approaches to the meaning of this verse in (Luz, 2005: 450–451).

entire discussion is moved along by its location within the Jewish law and Jesus' reinterpretation thereof for the Matthean community (vv.21-22) and the expectation of mimicking the mercy of the father (or king) (v.35). Finally, the social, economic and political setting into which the whole of the Gospel of Matthew enters speaks of an in-group and an out-group identity (Hagner, 1995: 532; Mounce, 1995: 468–469; Carter, 2005: 368). The Matthean community is forming its true identity over against those who do not share their social and religious worldview and heritage. Earlier in this chapter we considered whether the Matthean community, and Matthew, were hostile to the out-group or not, and it was suggested that in light of the evangelists' intentions in the Gospel there is a possibility that the intention and tone of the Gospel speaks of winning over the out-group, rather than outright rejection of them. Carter points out that Jesus frequented with tax collectors and 'heathens' (9.9, 10-13, 11.19), and that he saw such persons as the object of mission, "people to be won over to the community of disciples" (Mounce, 1995: 468–469; Carter, 2005: 368). Regardless of the view of outsiders, it is clear that being an outsider was an undesirable social and religious state to be in. As has already been illustrated, it would have serious and far-reaching consequences for the individual and the community. Significantly, vv.19-20 and v.35 bring in the larger dimension of eternal acceptance or eternal rejection (UL and LL) by God as a result of inclusion or exclusion from the community (UR and LR).

This leads us to the next phase in the narrative of the chosen passage. This next section of the discourse takes on the form of a parable. An approach to understanding parables is to relate certain elements of the parable allegorically to spiritual realities or spiritual/theological constructs (Blomberg, 2009: 46). From a narrative perspective this is significant to note. A parable deals with the notion of forgiveness as a concept differently from a complex social-juristic process to dealing with discipline in the community (UR, LR) (as found in 15-20), or the religious teaching and reframing of a traditional teaching on forgiveness by Jesus (UL, LL) (vv.21-22). Meaning in a parable relies on the author and the reader sharing a common metaphoric thought structure (LL) which creates meaning for the reader (UL) and can find expression in their individual actions (UL) and affirmation and support within the community (LR) (Carter & Heil, 1998: 1–8; Mbabazi, 2013: 160–163)[106]. The application of the parable, which sums up its intention, is to be found in v.35. This verse clarifies the meaning and intention of the preceding narrative.

In Matthew 18.15-35 there is a clear link between a social problem (UR, LR) (the restoration of an individual and communal relationship (vv.15-20) or the cancelling of a debt (vv.23-25)) and a spiritual reality (UL and LL). Jesus answers Peter's question on forgiveness within the community by sharing a parable that can be likened to "the Kingdom of heaven (ἡ βασιλεία τῶν οὐρανῶν)" (v.23). This relationship between the human and the divine, the present and the eschaton, finds expression in the parable of the unforgiving servant in vv.23-35 where heaven, and in particularly the king of heaven, brackets the discussion: the "βασιλεία τῶν οὐρανῶν" (Kingdom of heaven, v.23) and "ὁ πατήρ μου ὁ οὐράνιος" (Jesus' Father in heaven, v.35).

---

106 A great deal of scholarly work has been done on the genre of parables, their intention and usage in the Gospels in general and Matthew's Gospel in particular. Please see, among others, (Linnemann, 1977; De Boer, 1988; Carter & Heil, 1998: 1–8; Liebenberg, 2001; Hultgren, 2002; Jeremias, 2003).

> What this means ... is, for example, that the βασιλεύς and κύριος in the parable is an *analogy* for God, not a *picture* of him; the δοῦλοι, σύνδουλοι and ἀδελφοί are all analogies for the Church. (Mbabazi, 2013: 161)

Matthew's intention in employing this literary style was thus to evoke shared meaning (LL) in the reader by telling a story that could be concretely related to actual experiences (such as insurmountable debt, μυρίων ταλάντων v.24, the witnessing of social injustice, ἰδόντες a οὖν οἱ σύνδουλοι αὐτοῦ τὰ γενόμενα ἐλυπήθησαν σφόδρα v.31). The intended outcome was to draw upon this shared set of community beliefs, to activate a moral and theological change in the individual's beliefs (UL) (οὐκ ἔδει καὶ σὲ ἐλεῆσαι τὸν σύνδουλόν σου v.33a and ἐὰν μὴ ἀφῆτε ἕκαστος τῷ ἀδελφῷ αὐτοῦ ἀπὸ τῶν καρδιῶν b ὑμῶν v.35b). This in turn would change the behaviour of the reader, encouraging her or him not to act like the unforgiving servant, but indeed to act like the merciful king (UL). When vv.21-22 (which introduce the parable) are coupled with the parable narrative, it is clear to see that the intention is not only to alter individual attitudes (UL) and behaviour (UR), but to establish a new moral and religious order (LL) that will bring harmony among the in-group of the Matthean community (LR). Moreover, when one considers all three parts of the text together (vv.15-35) the picture becomes clearer still. Without an integrated shift in belief (καρδιῶν v.35 – the inner self) and action (ἐὰν μὴ ἀφῆτε ἕκαστος τῷ ἀδελφῷ αὐτοῦ v.35) in the individual, the harmony of the community will be eroded (v.17), the unity of the faith will be weakened (vv.18-19), the presence of the Lord in the community will be lost (v.20), and God the heavenly King and Father will be displeased (v.35). The parable elicits in the reader a connection with all four aspects of social and individual identity, individual belief (UL), social values and religious values (LL), individual action (UR), and communal action and social cohesion (LR) – see figure 8 below (from, De Quincey, 2006: 206).

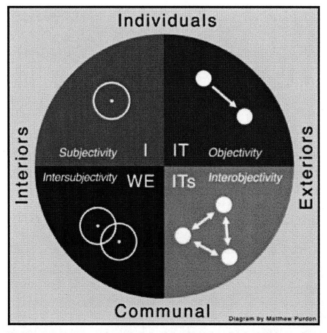

Figure 8: Four aspects of social and individual identity and meaning

Within the context of this study, the AQAL approach makes it possible to identify reader responses to the text that may locate them largely in one or more quadrants of the AQAL integrative theory. For example, if a person had a legalistic reading of the text that sought only to follow the process set out in vv.15-20 (UR, individual confrontation of the sinner, and LR, collective and community confrontation of the sinner), yet they did not understand the intention of the process was the re-establishment of wholisitic harmony in the community (i.e., restoration of the individual relationship, UL; restoration of proximate relationship between the sinner and the sinned against, UR; the deepening of shared values of forgiveness and reconciliation, LL; and the creation and deepening of the benefits of social cohesion, LR), the individual could miss the entire intention of the process, namely to mimic the merciful King and restore true individual and communal harmony by forgiving the brother or sister from one's heart (v.35).

This understanding frames the intention of using Matthew 18.15-35 in the intercultural group readings. It is highly unlikely that any one individual would have a completely integrated understanding of the text (locating meaning in each of the four quadrants and understanding the importance of the interaction between these categories of meaning). However, when a variety of readers engage the text in a safe space, without judgement or competition, it is possible that the various perspectives of the readers could enrich and deepen each other's understanding of both the text, and the communicative intention of the text.

In the final section of this chapter some empirical markers will be identified that arise from an AQAL reading of the text. These markers will be used to 'plot' the reader's responses to concepts and processes of forgiveness that arise from their reading of Matthew 18, as individuals and groups, before, during and after their intergroup contact sessions.

All Levels:

There is one more element to the AQAL theory, and the reading of Matthew 18.15-35 from the perspective of this theory, that requires some discussion. This is the application of the multidimensional understanding of possible levels of meaning and engagement within each quadrant. Please see chapter 2 for a detailed discussion of the theory of embedded heterarchies that are expressed as levels in the AQAL theory.

Let me illustrate the importance of considering heterarchical levels of meaning and understanding to the text by using two examples from the chosen text.

First, in the parable of the merciful King and the unforgiving servant Matthew makes a level comparison to highlight adequate and inadequate levels of forgiveness and mercy. He does this by sharing the example of the adequate response of mercy from the King in cancelling a large debt of one of his slaves (the debt was so large that could not be paid – the equivalent of the wages of 100 000 000 labourers) (δάνειον) (v.27) to the inadequate response of the servant who was unwilling to forgive a small debt (a debt that is the equivalent of 100 days of wages) (ὀφειλόμενον) (v.30) (Snodgrass, 2008: 68; Mbabazi, 2013: 170–172). Forgiveness in this setting is a response to the King. The author employs this literary device of hyperbole to illustrate the incredible mercy of the king and the serious lack of mercy of the unforgiving servant. However, with an AQAL framework it also shows that the level of forgiveness matters. To be forgiven a massive economic debt (UR and LR) (v.27), yet not undergo a change of heart as a result (UL and LL) (vv.28, 30), illustrated in the unwillingness to forgive a much smaller economic debt is a clear violation of the moral principle of the parable, true forgiveness from the heart (v.35). The phrase, "ἐὰν μὴ ἀφῆτε ἕκαστος τῷ ἀδελφῷ αὐτοῦ ἀπὸ τῶν καρδιῶν b ὑμῶν" (v.35) places a spotlight on the fact a certain level, or quality of forgiveness is expected by the Father in heaven, that is, true forgiveness from the heart.

Secondly, the passage shows that forgiveness is not just a matter of following a deontological socio-religious code (v.21 with reference to Genesis 4.24) and then claiming that forgiveness has been realised or enacted. One of the challenges that motivated this study in the South African Christian context is not only that there is not forgiveness among Christian sisters and brothers, but that there are levels or forms of forgiveness that can be equated to unforgiveness. While a process may have been followed (vv.15-20) and some social engagement has taken place (UR, LR), there has not been true and significant forgiveness that can lead to the possibility of reconciliation (UL and LL). It is for this reason that the consideration of levels of forgiveness, as highlighted in Matthew 18.15-35 are an important consideration.

Rather, as the text illustrates, honouring God and one's sister or brother far subtler and textured process that may require multiple instances of forgiveness as one learns to forgive more and remember less (v.22). The heterarchical reading of forgiveness in this text illustrates that true forgiveness and the restoration of spiritual relationships and social harmony involves not only the mind (UL), or some form of action (UR, going to the offending party and engaging them), but perhaps even some form of just restitution (UR, the antithesis of vv.28-30) that will satisfy the community (v.30) (LR), and most importantly a change of heart (τῶν καρδιῶν ὑμῶν) (v.35) (UL and LL). It is a complex process that has social as well as spiritual consequences for both the forgiving and the forgiven parties. The social embeddedness of the narrative suggest that you are bound to the King, therefore you act like the King.

Thus, in conclusion, an AQAL approach to forgiveness in Matthew 18.15-35 allows us to understand the complexity of individual and social identity and expectation in the text. Moreover, it reminds the reader that it is possible to read the text and find meaning in a variety of 'locations' within the four quadrants and a variety of levels in the text. An AQAL reading of the text illustrates the complexity of text reception theory and audience reception theory, and how important it is to have both a theory and a process to gather information, categorise and discuss it for deeper knowledge of both the text and the reader's understanding of the text. Lastly, an AQAL reading of the text emphasises the intention of the metaphor of forgiveness in the text (and embodied process, rather than just a conceptual idea, or a moment of realisation or disconnected action).

4.9 Concluding remarks

This chapter has presented a thorough exegetical engagement with Matthew 18.15-35 using a socio-theological approach, i.e., an approach to the text that focussed specifically on the social aspects (cf., Venter, 1994: 35). In particular, this task was undertaken from the perspective of AQAL integral theory (discussed in chapter 2) and intergroup contact theory and social identity theory (discussed in chapter 3).

This text forms the basis of the intercultural Bible reading process on forgiveness between the two participating communities. This chapter has shown the rich hermeneutic and methodological possibilities that emerge for the contemporary reader in relation to a careful and scholarly reading of the text, taking care not to collapse contemporary concepts and concerns uncritically into the worldview of the author and the intended recipients of the text.

In the chapter that follows the research design of the practice oriented research project in intercultural Bible reading will be presented in detail. The reasoning behind choosing this specific text, and this specific method, will be shown. It will also show how and where the text, and the two preceding theories, were used in the research process.

5   RESEARCH PROBLEM AND DESIGN

5.1 Introduction

In chapter 1 the topic, approach, and intention of this research project was presented. Chapters 2 and 3 presented the two important theoretical foundations on which the research design is predicated, namely AQAL integral theory (chapter 2) and intergroup contact theory (chapter 3). In the previous chapter a thorough technical exegesis of the central Biblical text, Matthew 18.15-35, that shapes this empirical intercultural Bible reading project was conducted. This chapter brings together all of these elements in order to show how the research problem and research objectives were approached in order to gain a deeper understanding of the research problem and engage the questions raised in the research. We shall present an overview of the research design, mapping the logic of the research design process, chosen instruments and processes, data collection plan, and data analysis.

The chapter will deal with the following important elements to explain important aspects of the research design and process:

- The research problem and objectives of the research, which were introduced in chapter 1, will be considered in more detail and depth in relation to the design.

- The selection of the research setting and sampling which is used in this research project. Some further information will be given on the problem owner and the context in which the research is taking place. We will also see how we selected the participants in the project, and why these participants allow for credible empirical research in an intercultural Bible reading project.

- Attention will be given to the theories that informed the research design, the selection of the research method, and the research process – of course some of this was dealt with in chapters 2, 3 and 4. However, in this chapter we shall bring together insights from all three sets of theories (and the Biblical text) that underpin the study, as well as important concepts and ideas from other theorists and theories that shaped the research project. This chapter will also discuss why the particular approach was adopted for this study. In this instance, it was decided to work with a practice oriented approach in the form of empirical intercultural Bible reading groups..

- Finally, the chapter will present some of the smaller and more technical aspects that relate to elements of the data collection plan, such as the instruments and technologies used to capture participant data, measures taken to secure the data, processes used to validate the data with participant samples, the tools and methods used to analyse the data, and the code book that illustrates some of the conceptual elements of the relationship between the research process and the research design.

5.2 Revisiting the research problem

South Africa has a very high percentage of self-identified Christian believers[107], yet it remains a deeply divided nation. Black and White South African Christians hold very different views on the imperative, concepts and processes of forgiveness as the findings in this research project, and the literature show (Chapman & Spong, 2003: 169; Villa-Vicencio & du Toit, 2006: 75–87; Byrne, 2007; Krog, 2010; Elkington, 2011: 5–35, 135–155; Daye, 2012: 8–18; Tutu, 2012: 10–36, 47–60, 92–124). The most significant differences seem to centre around differences in understanding among South Africans as to what the requisites are for true forgiveness to take place. Is forgiveness only a spiritual matter? Is it only about individuals? Does it have political antecedents or consequences (e.g., restitution for wrongs committed, an end to ongoing injustice)? Does it reach beyond the individual to the community?

One significant problem that has been identified is that these un-reconciled persons seldom have contact with each other because of the legacy of the apartheid system which separated persons economically according to class and geographically (Swart, Hewstone, *et al.*, 2010: 312–313). The result is that, as intergroup contact theory shows, each group's social views and religious beliefs become entrenched and the views and beliefs of the 'other' (out-group) are rejected or ignored because they are not understood or engaged across these separating boundaries (Brewer & Kramer, 1985: 219–223; Duncan, 2003: 2, 5; Bornman, 2011: 411–414; c.f., Boesak *et al.*, 2015).

In at least one sense this makes forgiveness almost impossible – not only is it impossible for persons to forgive one another since they have no proximate or authentic social engagement, forgiveness is also a theological impossibility because of deeply held and entrenched convictions about the different nature and processes of forgiveness among different groups in South Africa (Kearney, 2007: 151–152). Paul Ricoeur suggests that what is needed is an act of translation[108] that can bridge the differences in language and the nature of difference experienced between the self and other (Ricoeur & Brennan, 1995: 7)[109]. Kearney comments on the necessity for translation and forgiveness that it,

---

107 Nieman noted that "the 23 main religious groupings… [have] a membership of 37,157,820 in 2001 (84% of the population)" (Nieman, 2010: 37). There have been significant demographic shifts in the South African population in the last 15 years. However, religious affiliation remains very high among South Africans. These statistics are available online <http://www.statssa.gov.za/census01/html/default.asp [Accessed 10 June 2014, 16.01]. For a thorough theological discussion please see (Hendriks & Erasmus, 2005; Forster, 2015b: 9–10). The most recent demographic statistics around religious affiliation and identity in South Africa are to be found in (*General Household Survey 2013*, 2014; Schoeman, 2017: 1–7)

108 "Translation can be understood here in both a specific and a general sense. In the specific sense – the one in common contemporary usage – it signals the work of translating the meanings of one particular language into another. In the more generic sense, it indicates the everyday act of speaking as a way not only of translating oneself (inner to outer, private to public, unconscious to conscious, etc.) but also more explicitly of translating oneself to others." (Ricoeur, 2007: xiv–xv).

109 "The identity of a group, culture, people or nation, is not that of an immutable substance, nor that of a fixed structure, rather, of a recounted story" (Ricoeur & Brennan, 1995: 7).

> ... is only when we translate our own wounds in the language of strangers and retranslate the wounds of strangers into our own language that healing and reconciliation can take place. (Ricoeur, 2007: xx)

Thus, the primary problem that led to the development of this research project is both theological and pragmatic in nature.

First, members of the same faith group (Methodist Christians), who read the same texts, participate in very similar forms of worship and church governance, are divided from one another because they hold different convictions about the nature and processes of forgiveness. This means that they are not able to find common theological ground from which to move forward together. The process of finding that common theological ground is referred to as 'translation' by Ricoeur (Ricoeur, 2007: xx).

The theological convictions that each community holds regarding forgiveness frames their expectation of the 'other', while also giving meaning and identity to themselves and their position. Thus, we find the creation of an 'in-group' / 'out-group' dichotomy as a result of strongly held tacit theological convictions (Tajfel, 1970: 96–103; Pettigrew, 1998: 66–67, 73–74; Zuma, 2014: 40–57).

As chapter 3 presents, intergroup contact theory shows us that such convictions can strengthen prejudices among the in-group concerning the 'other' (an out-group) (Pettigrew, 1998: 69–75; Bornman, 1999: 412; Duncan, 2003: 151). However, when anxiety can be lessened and empathy increased through positive intergroup contact there could be a possibility for a positive shift away from prejudice towards openness and change (Pettigrew, 1998: 67–69; Bornman, 1999: 412; Pettigrew & Tropp, 2005: 951–957).

Thus, the second problem that needed to be addressed was the problem of facilitating, and measuring the value, of a positive intergroup contact between these two communities. Does carefully facilitated, positive intergroup contact (as discussed in chapter 3), help to create a space in which participants of in-groups and out-groups are willing to shift their understandings of forgiveness in the presence of the 'other'? This research proposed that there are a set of social "mediators" and "moderators" (mechanisms) around which representatives from the two communities could encounter one another positively in order to facilitate the possibility for limiting anxiety and increasing empathy for the (Hewstone & Swart, 2011a: 375–376).

It is into this complex contextual reality that this research enters.

5.3 Hypothesis and research questions

The hypothesis of this research project is that the reading Matthew 18.15-35 in an intercultural Bible reading process, employing the carefully facilitated conditions of intergroup contact theory, allows participants to develop a broader and deeper understanding of the concepts and processes of forgiveness (cf., 1.3.1-1.3.3).

The research process is designed in such a manner that it allows for the empirical intercultural Bible reading process to take place under the conditions of positive intergroup contact. As will be shown later in this chapter, data is recorded from the various stages of the research process that allows for a comparison of pre-intercultural engagement and post intervention data. A deductive engagement with these data sets allows for the identification of expected changes, and the identification of unanticipated changes in group understandings of forgiveness from Matthew 18.15-35.

The hypothesis was specified in three research questions (see also 1.5). These research questions will be answered in the empirical research process:

1. To what extent do theological understandings of forgiveness differ among Christians of different race groups?

2. To what extent have theological understandings of forgiveness among Christians of different race groups changed in a more integrative manner after an intercultural bible reading of Matthew 18.15-35?

3. To what extent is the change in theological understandings of forgiveness among Christians of different races (Group A and Group B) stimulated by the mediators and moderators of the intercultural Bible reading practices?

In order to do this empirical research, we had to construct an appropriate theoretical frame. We formulated five theoretical questions to lead this conceptual process:

1. What theoretical framework can be used to understand and explain the complexity of individual and social identity in relation to concepts of forgiveness in an intercultural Bible reading process?

2. How do the social moderators and mediators of intergroup contact theory help to facilitate positive intergroup contact that may lead to an integral understanding of forgiveness among racially diverse Christian groupings reading Matthew 18.15-35 in an intercultural Bible reading process?

3. What is an integral understanding of forgiveness based on a careful Biblical scholarly AQAL reading of Matthew 18.15-35?

4. How do Christians of different races understand forgiveness when reading Matthew 18.15-35?

5. In what ways does intercultural Bible reading under the facilitated conditions of positive intergroup contact contribute towards a more integral understanding of forgiveness in Matthew 18.15-35?

5.5 The scope of the research and the fields of study

At the outset of the project it was hoped that the study would deliver new information on the complexity of understandings of forgiveness among South African Christians reading Matthew 15.15-35. Hence, this is primarily a study in empirical hermeneutics and intercultural Bible reading.

The study envisioned that empirical information on the hermeneutic positions of intercultural Bible readers could aid the problem owner, the Methodist Church of Southern Africa. The problem owner sought to gain some insight into how carefully facilitated intercultural Bible reading processes could facilitate positive intergroup contact. Thus, the aims and objectives of the study necessitated the application of credible processes that could be used to select representative participants of different racial and cultural groupings within the context of the research focus. In addition to this, a research method was required that could yield, capture and present credible and verifiable empirical data on the intercultural Bible reading processes. The design of the processes, and the research instruments, as well as the frameworks for interpreting and presenting the data was predicated on two primary theoretical perspectives that could be related to both the participants in the process as well as the Biblical text. The two theories were discussed in chapters 2 and 3 respectively, whereas the Biblical text was carefully considered in chapter 4 of this study.

5.5.1 Biblical studies, hermeneutics, and interculturality

This research is primarily located within the discipline of Biblical studies. However, the research approach that is used in this study is novel. Some Biblical scholars may ask why an empirical approach was used for a study in intercultural Biblical hermeneutics? First, there is growing academic interest in the arena of intercultural Bible reading and empirical hermeneutics in Biblical studies. A series of scholarly volumes, under the title of *Intercultural Biblical Hermeneutics Series* (c.f., De Wit, 2012; Van der Walt, 2014; Jonker, 2015), is breaking new ground in this field. De Lange sums up the intention of this approach to Biblical studies saying,

> …it has to do with the question of whether reading Bible stories jointly by groups from often radically different cultural and socio-political contexts can contribute to transformation and changed perspectives…. Can cultural differences, when rendered hermeneutically operative, not give such depth to the dialogue on the meaning of stories that faith becomes what it is ultimately meant to be, a searching and reaching for the truth? (De Wit, 2012: 5)

Second, this approach has a longstanding tradition in South Africa and is widely accepted as both valuable and valid by Biblical scholars. Jonker notes:

> I became convinced that intercultural reading of the Bible is a powerful instrument of transformation in South African Reformed churches that are still struggling to unite more than twenty years after apartheid. (Jonker, 2015: ix)

Both of these quotes affirm at least two basic aspects of value to this approach to Biblical studies. First, there is the richness of hermeneutic possibility that emerges from the academic study of intercultural Bible reading processes. How persons interpret texts, and the complex and textured philosophical, social, and emotive reasons that build the bridge between the text and the reader, is of great value to developments in Biblical studies. Second, both of the previous quotations highlight the ethical and pragmatic value that emerges from intercultural Bible reading processes. As we saw in Chapter 4, the Biblical narrators, and their narratives, had some tacit communicative intent – the stories are written for a reason. While the contexts of the ancient authors and their intended readers differ vastly from the contemporary readers and their contexts, the ethical intent of the text can still add value to the lives of contemporary readers and their communities. The interpretative and ethical consequences that emerge from the academic study of "ordinary readers" is extremely valuable in Biblical scholarship (De Wit, 2012: 7). Much of contemporary Biblical scholarship is interested in understanding the complex, and at times contested, relationship between the "privileged position of power" of formal academic readers of the text, and "ordinary readers" (Van der Walt, 2014: 4). As this study shows, the contested understanding, and usage, of the Biblical text is a critical field of research for Biblical scholars who are interested in more than just the protected, or elitist interpretations and uses of the text. Indeed, rigorous and wide reaching scholarship has a responsibility to take seriously a variety of readings and uses of the Biblical text. Punt says,

> The Bible as site of struggle involves, however, more than difference of interpretive opinion. The Bible is involved in the discourse of power and is drawn into a struggle for interpretive control as well as, eventually, ownership thereof. (Punt, 2002: 425)

The "turn to the reader" has proved to be an important and growing focus in recent Biblical scholarship (De Wit, 2012: 8–11). The focus on the empirical reader in Biblical studies has tended to focus on qualitative data such as reading behaviour – how many persons read the Bible, how often do they read it, what do they read? However, that is not the focus of this study. As a theologian engaged in Biblical scholarship, the researcher is far more interested in hermeneutic issues related to the reading of texts. What are the differences in understanding of the social aspects of forgiveness when White middle class South Africans read it? How do Black and Brown South Africans who have suffered the injustices of apartheid understand the same text? Moreover, what changes when these groups read the text together? There are many others who share this same interest (Ukpong, West & Dube, 2000; Dube, 2001; Jonker, 2006; Punt, 2006; De Wit & West, 2008; Jonker, Koopman, Lombard, Naudé & Smit, 2008; Van der Walt, 2010, 2014; Claassens & Juliana, 2011; De Wit, 2012; West, 2014a,c, 2015; Claassens & Birch, 2015). At the heart of many of the projects mentioned previously is a keen understanding of the importance of the relationship between the text and reader's response to the text. Reading the Bible in community can be liberative and life-giving in many communities. However, it can also serve to enforce unjust stereotypes and abusive actions (De Wit, 2012: 11). Texts do something to their readers. Moreover, as has already been noted, in the South African religious context, the Biblical text is a particularly important shaper of both doctrine and ethics, belief and action. Thus, a careful, rigorous, academically sound engagement with the Biblical text and its readers holds great possibility both for scholarship, and for praxis.

5.5.2 Empirical Biblical hermeneutics

In addition to operating within the field of Biblical studies, this project also bears the characteristics of empirical research. While this study produced and presented data that speaks of how the readers interpret the text – what De Wit calls *hermeneuse* – the project is much more expressly focussed on understanding *how* the hermeneutic process functions, and what it may mean (De Wit, 2012: 17). Most Biblical scholars would concur that exegesis, while being critical, is only one aspect of the process of text comprehension. Within the conceptual framework of this project the exegetical aspect (see chapter 4) is critical to understanding what the text may have meant in its historical setting. But there is an intention to this knowledge that informs the rest of the process – namely how do the understandings of contemporary readers of the text relate to that exegetical information. In order to conduct a comparative qualitative analysis of the two sets of understandings some empirical data is needed. The exegetical process yields a rich, textured and valuable set of data. In empirical hermeneutics "we are attempting to map – or at least define - the contours of how flesh-and-blood readers deal with texts" (De Wit, 2012: 17). This second set of empirical data allows for the creation of a rich and textured conversation between the traditionally great interpreters of the text in Biblical scholarship, and the contemporary, ordinary, readers of those texts. This is often referred to as reception criticism. In empirical hermeneutics it "includes an analysis of the appropriation process and is directed at the text in its relationship to local explanation and interpretation, and in its effect on and use by contemporary readers" (De Wit, 2012: 17). Such an analysis highlights the "behaviour potential" of Biblical scholarship.

What is of particular value, and a somewhat recent development in Biblical studies, is the emergence of exegetical-hermeneutical coding. In this process interpretation process is coded (e.g., pietistic, dogmatic, problematizing, liberation focussed etc.) Frequently such approaches allow for an understanding of social and cultural mores, as well as reading and usage strategies. For example, which verses of a pericope are more frequently read, and used, in a certain way by a certain group? What aspects of the narrative are foregrounded under which social reading conditions? What images and concepts do the participants use to fill in the narrative gaps in the text? How do they relate to the actors in the narrative?

Then, one can also gain some fascinating insights when focussing on the elements of appropriate and application of the text in the lives of individuals or communities. For example, if a text is appropriated by a particular community, is the original historical context merely supplanted by the contemporary situation? Or, is there some measure of inter-textuality, or intratextuality, evidenced in the readings (i.e., where the narrative of the contemporary reader, and the narrative of the Biblical text are treated as two equally valid theological informants) (De Wit, 2012: 19). In such approaches one may witness parallelisms between the textual elements, e.g., the unforgiving servant of Matthew 18.28-30 is equated to a contemporary person or group (e.g., White South Africans who are unwilling to part with historical privilege, even after being forgiven for apartheid). Such insights give the researcher a valuable insight into readers' views of the text, but also valuable views of themselves in relation to the text narrative (in-group identity) and to other with whom they are reading the text (out-group identity).

Through empirical research, such as interviews, or focus groups, one can extract this data from the readers. Empirical data that emerges can then be mapped into a descriptive and explanatory schema (in the case of this study, it is the AQAL integral framework). This allows for the researcher to identify, highlight, explain, compare and contrast hermeneutic differences in the intercultural reading process. When one considers this, it becomes evident that the hermeneutic insights can be employed in different ways in an empirical study. In the case of this study it is primarily directed towards two points, stated in the research objectives. They are: First, understanding the interpretations, and interpretive strategies or intentions of the readers in their in-group readings, and in the intergroup readings. Second, using the empirical hermeneutic data to see how the reading of the Biblical text under intercultural Bible reading conditions can serve the processes of theological change among the readers.

In the first instance, the interpretation of the readers, the hermeneutic processes and strategies are normally given descriptive labels: literalist hermeneutics, accommodative hermeneutics, spiritual hermeneutics etc. These labels describe the hermeneutic process, strategy or identifiable theological position of the reader. In the second instance, where hermeneutics is directed at understanding processes of change, a genitive label is given, such as African hermeneutics, women's hermeneutics, liberative hermeneutics etc. The label "refers mainly to the interests of the subject whom the hermeneutical reflection is intended to serve", such as a race group, the poor, women etc. (De Wit, 2012: 20). It is fairly common that the label adopts a surplus value in Biblical scholarship. For example, among feminist theologians, the label "women" is not merely a descriptive label, it also serves as a normative category of reader with the embedded understandings associated with the descriptive category. As an example of this, see Van der Walt's use of "ordinary women" readers *Towards a communal reading of 2 Samuel 13*, (Van der Walt, 2014: 4–5). West employs a similar descriptive strategy in some of his work. See, for example, *Contending for Dignity in the Bible and the Post-Apartheid South African Public Realm* (West, 2015: 78–98).

This is very important in this study, since the use of descriptive *intercultural*, in the intercultural Bible reading aspect of this project has similar normative connotations. De Wit sums it up aptly when he says, "*intercultural* is not solely a way of reading the Bible that crosses geographical boundaries …[it] is an ethically loaded concept" (De Wit, 2012: 20). What such a description conveys about the reading strategy is a matter of the hermeneutic importance of the intercultural encounter for the understanding of the reception of the text in the complex intercultural setting. In other words, this study is less interested in a universal hermeneutic interpretation of forgiveness in Matthew 18.15-35. More directly it is also not entirely directed at a broad a-contextual hermeneutic, e.g., a contemporary South African understanding of forgiveness in the aforementioned text. Neither is the aim to understand only what White, or Black, South Africans understand forgiveness to mean in this passage. The intention is to gain a particular form of hermeneutic knowledge of forgiveness that arises from *intercultural* Bible readings of Matthew 18.15-35 among Black and White contemporary South Africans.

Thiselton rightly points out that in scholarship there is a necessary dialectic tension between the "particular and the universal" in Biblical hermeneutics (Thiselton, 2006: 672). On the first level, there is a crucial difference in the metanarratives of the Biblical text that distinguish it from the metanarratives of contemporary society, such as capitalization of society, globalization etc. However, there are those who hold firmly to the belief that the Christian religion, and the Biblical text in particular, constitutes a "grand narrative" that embraces all metanarratives, since it provides the "norms and criteria for the meaning of lesser narratives" (Thiselton, 2006: 672). The tension is visible, the Biblical narrative and the contemporary narrative are not the same narrative, yet at the same time they are not entirely separate from one another. The Biblical narrative is in a form of dialectic tension with the contemporary narratives – this is the first level. The second level relates to the relationship that the Biblical narrative has with particular contemporary metanarratives, for example the narratives of women, as opposed to the narratives of men. Or, the narratives of Africans, as opposed to the narratives of Europeans. It is a mistake to assume that there is not a different form of dialectic tension between the "grand narrative" of the Bible and the many particular metanarratives of contemporary readers that relate to it. In an attempt to avoid that mistake, De Wit notes that some have argued for a form of "relativism" that counters the oppressive and monolithic "universalism" of uncritical approaches (De Wit, 2012: 20–21). Whereas the grand narrative dominates in universalism (as if there is no difference among readers and their contexts), the contextual has prominence in hermeneutic relativism. This describes some of the tension that exist in Biblical scholarship. Eurocentric (Western) hermeneutics has tended to present itself as a dominant, even "universal", hermeneutic position. Whereas Africa, Asian and Latin-American hermeneutics have been viewed as less valuable since they are considered as being too contextual in nature, and so too relativistic to have wide spread value. In such a space certain readings, and readers, are excluded since their perspectives are evaluated as invalid, or less valid, by universal hermeneutic standards.

It is in this context the empirical intercultural Bible reading, such as that offered in this project, can offer some value. It does so, according to De Wit, by holding onto two important concepts: interactive diversity and eccentricity (2012: 21).

Interactive diversity suggests that we recognise the value of diversity in different readings of the Biblical text. When this principle is operative it allows for critical engagement with entrenched and powerfully supported views of 'truth'. Surely, when done in a credible and careful scholarly manner this is the very work of Biblical scholarship, to engage established views and perspectives in a robust manner to seek for deeper truth and meaning? Different perspectives on the text, and the scholarly understanding of the motivations, reasoning, and concepts that allow for, or support, such understandings is, invaluable in innovating Biblical scholarship and taking the discussion of the Biblical text and its use forward.

The second important concept is the notion of eccentricity. The philosophy of eccentricity stipulates that "people are never completely reducible to themselves" (De Wit, 2012: 22). Eccentric anthropology shows, as was suggested in Wilber's AQAL theory, that the 'self' is never in isolation of the other (Wilber, 2001a: 20–21; c.f., Birx, 2010: 515). As a result, it is important to consider individuals in relation to interactions with others. Thus, eccentricity suggests that persons are not only products of their interpretations of the Bible, they can also engage with, consider, and understand the interpretations of others. As a result, even if a particular person's interpretation is narrow, or largely closed to others, the person can never be fully reduced to that interpretation. As long as there is a commitment to engagement, a seeking after a greater truth, there is the opportunity to develop nuance, critique, and even new interpretations through interaction with others.

In this project the process element of the intergroup engagement, structured through intercultural Bible reading, was designed to facilitate hermeneutic engagement, and the explication of meanings through the engagements, in the form of empirical data. The data serves to understand both cross-sectional insights into particular hermeneutic positions among certain individuals or groups at particular moments (e.g., the pre-intercultural engagement reading of the text). However, the empirical hermeneutic data also allows for comparative theological engagement between different points of engagement to what differences there are, and seek to understand not only what is different, but how different it is and why it is different.

5.6 Research method

The research is built upon a Practice Oriented Research method that seeks to bridge the gap between theory and praxis (Hermans & Schoeman, 2015a: 26–29, 42–43) – this is will take the form of a qualitative empirical engagement with data that is sourced from the participants in the research process. The use of qualitative research methods, such as focus group meetings, data validation, data analysis and cross pollination between the practice stream and the theory stream, are employed in order to understand the dynamics and mechanisms at work within the individual participants and the two groups in this study. Practice oriented research is particularly helpful when the problem owner recognises a discrepancy between the factual situation (F) and the desired situation (D) and there is no clear understanding of the journey from the factual to the desired (Verschuren, 2009a: 155; Hermans & Schoeman, 2015a: 26–28). Ypma notes that in order to understand a problem in practice one can follow five steps (c.f., Schilderman, 2004: 201–206; Verschuren, 2009a: 159–162; Ypma, 2014: 29):

i. Describe and analyse the problem within the current situation (F). In this step the problem is framed in practice and established in a theoretically rigorous manner within the context.

ii. The second step is diagnostic, seeking to identify the background causes and contributors towards the problem.

iii. In the design phase the researcher (together with the problem owner) designs an intervention that could resolve the problem.

iv. The plan is implemented in the intervention phase.

v. In conclusion, the intervention is critically evaluated and data is produced to ascertain what changes have taken place towards reaching the desired goal (D). This allows the researcher and the problem owner to ascertain to what extent the problem has been solved, and what is still necessary to further understand and engage the problem in future research and intervention cycles.

The problem of culturally and racially diverse South African Methodist Christians not engaging one another, and one another's understandings of the conditions and processes of forgiveness, is what predicated this particular study.

Hence, the primary reason for this research was to seek to gain necessary insight to understand the complexity of different understandings of forgiveness between two communities in a divided Church context. This is the identified problem in practice (see point (i) of the practice oriented research process above). The desired outcome of the research process is to be able to feed the knowledge gained through the research intervention (points (iii) and (iv) in the practice oriented research process) and the analysis of the interventions (v) back into the communities in order to facilitate a shift from the identified current reality (ii) – (F) to the desired reality (D).

The problem owner in this case is the Methodist Church of Southern Africa, and in particular the Helderberg Circuit, of which both of these congregations are part. The knowledge generated in this research process intends to help the problem owner to develop the witness and work of the Church in this community (Somerset West). It is important to note that unity in the Church is not only a pragmatic concern, i.e., the practical development of social witness and work. Rather forgiveness has a much deeper and more significant foundation for Christians, namely the witness of Christian scripture and ecclesiology within Christian theology.

While this practice oriented research projected may not be able to solve this complex problem entirely, it will shed some light on the kinds of understandings of forgiveness (supported by negative intergroup social prejudice) that hinder progress. It will also shed light on some mechanisms that can be used contextually to facilitate positive intergroup contact among these two communities to moderate the conditions of positive change in their understandings of shared forgiveness.

As will be shown in the analysis of the pre-intercultural engagement focus group meeting data (cf., 6.3.2, 6.2), each of the two cultural groupings had a largely in-group understanding of the conditions and processes of forgiveness from Matthew 18.15-35. Moreover, each group held preconceived prejudices of the expectations of the out-group in relation to forgiveness in relation to Matthew 18.15-35. This aspect of the research cycle correlates to points (i) and (ii) above, namely identifying the problem (i) and understanding the problem in practice (ii). Next, the researcher, together with the problem owner (the Methodist Church of Southern Africa, Helderberg Circuit) designed a research intervention to gain further insight into the problem and evaluate the hypotheses that arose from the identification of the problem and its analysis – points (i), (ii) and now (iii).

As part of the research design phase (iii) It was decided that a focus groups meetings would be best suited to both facilitating the intercultural Bible reading process, but also extracting empirical data for the qualitative aspect of the research intervention. The reason that focus groups were chosen as an observational tool is because of their capacity to bring together groups in facilitated ways that can yield results that are identifiable and thus can be evaluated and analysed. Given writes of the approach, that focus groups can be,

> ...used for exploratory research, where the participants are relatively free to discuss the topic as they see fit, or they can be used in a more structured fashion, where the interviewer or moderator takes a more active role in controlling the issues to be discussed. (Given, 2008: 352).

The next part of the practice oriented research process was to implement the intervention (iv). In this case, as will be discussed in greater detail below, the intervention required the following elements:

- A process that could bring together the two representative cultural groupings in a setting where they could read, reflect upon, and discuss concepts and processes of forgiveness in relation to Matthew 18.15-35.

- A process that would allow for the introduction of the mechanisms of positive intergroup contact theory where the intergroup contact mediators could be incorporated to positively allow the intergroup contact moderators to develop. (see the discussion of the intergroup contact moderators and mediators in sections 3.3.3, 3.3.6 of this book).

- The process necessitated three critical aspects:
  - The gathering the required empirical data for qualitative analysis (achieved through recording, transcribing, validating, coding and analysing the focus group sessions).
  - The facilitation of intercultural Bible readings of Matthew 18.15-35 to explicate empirical intercultural hermeneutic information (this was achieved through the use of the "Dwelling in the word" Bible reading process described below).
  - The structuring of the intercultural Bible reading processes according to the principles of positive intergroup contact theory (again, this was possible through the designed and facilitated intercultural Bible reading focus groups conducted with the introduction of the positive intergroup contact mediators).

The final stage of the practice oriented research cycle is the evaluation of the research intervention (v) (Hermans & Schoeman, 2015a: 40–42). This book is the outcome of that process. In particular, the findings and analysis of the data in chapter 6 present a rigorous and meticulously articulated understanding of what took place, and why it is believed to have happened.

Once all of the above has been completed, the findings of this project will be communicated to the problem owner (the Methodist Church of Southern Africa) and the participants. This is discussed in the conclusion of this book as an avenue that may lead to further research (cf., 7.4.1-7.4.3).

The value of this method is that it seeks to address a problem in practice in an academically rigorous and scientifically sound manner. At the same time, it develops critical knowledge and new information for the problem owner and the participants in the intercultural Bible reading process. Moreover, it develops new knowledge and theory for academic professionals in Biblical studies that is both of a methodological and a content development nature.

Thus, it was decided that this approach was best suited to engaging, and contributing towards the solving, of the identified problem.

5.7 The Intervention: topic, social context, designing intervention practices

5.7.1 The topic of forgiveness

Why the topic of forgiveness was chosen? There are two answers to this question. There is a narrative and a meta-narrative. The meta-narrative concerns the purpose of academic research. The Christian faith maintains that the positive transformation of society for the common good is both necessary and important. Over the last number of years I have had the privilege of focussing my research on topics that have attempted to address some of the most besetting and destructive ills of our time – economic injustice, global poverty and corruption. What this experience has shown is that these causes are best served by academically rigorous, theoretically sound, practice oriented interventions. There is a critical place in society, and in the academy, for the development of knowledge for knowledge's sake. However, my conviction has been to apply what abilities and opportunities I have to produce knowledge for the sake of change that is of value in a variety of "publics"; the public of the academy, the public of the church, and the public of broader society (cf., Forster, 2017: 1–10). As such I share Verschuren's conviction that the type of research that is done primarily for the sake of change ought to produce results that can be measured according the criterion of utility (Verschuren, 2009b: 1). This conviction led me to focus on the topic of forgiveness in general terms.

5.7.2 The context of a contested social reality: Somerset West

The social context of South Africa is extremely complex. A detailed analysis of the macro, mezzo and micro contexts of South Africa's social past and current context is a topic that could be a study all on its own. For my most recent research on the current reality of social transformation and living conditions among South Africa's diverse population please see *What hope is there for South Africa?* (Forster, 2015a).

At this point it will suffice to say that South African society remains divided along racial, social and economic lines (Durrheim & Foster, 1995: 387–402; Wale & Foster, 2007: 45–69; Steyn & Foster, 2008: 25–51; Anon, 2011) in spite of the fact that 83% of South Africans indicated that they are Christian in the last census that charted religious affiliation (Forster, 2015a: 9–10; Schoeman, 2017: 1–7)[110].

Of course there are a myriad of reasons for this lack of social harmony in South African society; many of them are valid. What is of most interest in this research, however, is the way in which South African Christians understand the imperative for forgiveness and reconciliation which is a cornerstone of the Christian faith in general, and a necessary element of Christian ecclesiology in particular (Migliore, 2004; Gowan, 2010; McGrath, 2011; Tutu, 2012). This issue offers very significant insights into the theology of South African Christians – what is forgiveness? What are the criteria for forgiving someone? What is the consequence of forgiveness? Furthermore it offers rich insights into other important ancillary theological issues, such as the nature of sin, the nature of Christian community, Christian justice, restorative justice etc.[111]

It is within this social context that we focus on a particular example, and expression, of the need of forgiveness, namely the Somerset West Methodist Church at Church Street, and the Somerset West Methodist Church at Coronation Ave[112]. We begin by locating these two churches within the broader context of Southern African Methodism and its history, and then move on to discussing the specific history of these two congregations and the pain of their division.

---

110 Also see (Forster, 2008a: 70–99; Nieman, 2010: 37; Erasmus, 2012: 48–50, 55). A theological critique of this data is available in Hendriks, J & Erasmus, J. Religion in South Africa: 2001 population census data. *Journal of Theology for Southern Africa,* Vol 121. (Hendriks & Erasmus, 2005: 88–111) and for a theological consideration of the 2013 General Household Surevey data see, (Schoeman, 2017: 1–7).

111 For a more detailed discussion on the complexity of the witness of the Church in relation to justice in South Africa please see, *Justice and the Missional Framework Document of the Dutch Reformed Church,* (Botha & Forster, 2017: 1–9).

112 Community narratives are important aspects of the formation of social identity, theological beliefs and ethical practices please see – please see, *Religious stories we live by: Narrative approaches in theology and religious studies,* for a detailed discussion of this (de Haardt, 2013: 209–220; Ganzevoort, de Haardt & Scherer-Rath, 2013).

The Methodist Church of Southern Africa serves the 6 nations of Southern Africa. The denomination is known for its progressive stance against apartheid in South Africa (De Gruchy, 2005: 14; See Forster, 2008c: 411–434). Moreover, the denomination sought to overcome racial, ethnic and social divisions and remain "one and undivided" (Balia, 1991: 86; Forster, 2008c: Section 4.1.; Forster & Bentley, 2008: 14, 148; Bailie, 2009: 42–43; Mtshiselwa, 2015: 4–5). Sadly the reality is that in spite of such efforts congregations of the denomination remain largely separated according to race, culture, language and socio-economic standing. Forster writes, "while the top structures of the church officially addressed the evils of apartheid and opposed the state, there were not many congregations that were truly racially integrated" (Forster, 2008c: 421). The disconnect between the official policy of the denominational church and the reality of the local congregation is a common phenomenon[113].

In South Africa this disconnect on congregational level is compounded by a number for factors. First, the enforcement of the group areas act after 1950 in South Africa forced persons of different ethnic groups to live in separate geographical locations (De Gruchy, 2005: 37; Forster & Bentley, 2008: 87). This geographical separation entrenched cultural identity and linguistic preference in congregational worship and activity. Moreover, there was a time when it was not legally permissible for persons of different race groups to gather together for worship. Such restrictions, when combined with the convenience of attending a church service within geographic proximity of one's home caused many churches to remain ethnically and linguistically exclusive. Second, the formation of the Methodist Church in Southern Africa was as a result of missionary activity. In the 19th century it was common practice for missionaries to establish separate services for English speaking settlers and vernacular speaking indigenous groupings (See Grassow in Forster & Bentley, 2008: 13–24). It was a common belief among missionaries of the time that the Gospel needed to be inculturated[114] for the indigenous population so that faith could be assimilated into the life of the community without having to overcome the barriers of a foreign culture and social framework. The London Missionary Society missionary Dr John Philip was an advocate of this approach (De Gruchy, 2005: 75–79). Sadly, this reasoning was appropriated by the Apartheid state to maintain separation between the races in later years. Nevertheless, this practice, at the very formation of the churches in Southern Africa, led to the development of different theological and liturgical preferences and traditions between predominantly White and predominantly Black churches within the same denomination or church tradition. In the Methodist Church of Southern Africa, for example, predominantly White congregations tend not to have a responsive liturgy, with extemporary prayers led by a minister in English. Whereas predominantly Black Methodist congregations have a sung liturgy (normally the *Siykudumisa Thixo*, a version of the 1654 service for Morning Prayer in the Anglican tradition) which is sung in Xhosa with congregational responses. In most instances the liturgy is led by a liturgist and

---

113 For a full discussion of this disconnect between congregations and denominations see (Smit, 1996) and (Forster, 2008c: 420–421, 2010c: 9–12).

114 Niebuhr's book *Christ and culture* (Niebuhr, 1956) was a seminal work in understanding the relationship between faith and culture. It opened up a whole new discourse in theology on this topic. A great deal of work has been done on this topic since then.

the church choir and not the minister. This means that in both instances there is both the difference of language as well as the style of worship to overcome.

What is even more painful in some instances is that there are circuits in which churches that were racially and culturally integrated from foundation decided to separate along racial lines. This is the case in the Helderberg Circuit where the current research took place.

The Methodist work began in Somerset West in 1837 (according the Whiteside) with the establishment of a mission station to minister to freed slaves who were emancipated in the South African colony in 1834 (Moister, 1871: 232; Whiteside, 1906: 89; Welsh, 2000: 35–36). The work began as part of the Cape Town Circuit in an old "wine-store" that was purchased and transformed into a place of worship (Whiteside, 1906: 89). By 1847 the building had to be enlarged to accommodate 500 persons. The historic Church Street Methodist Church building was completed in 1861 under the pastorate of Rev Ridgill. There were regular weekly services for the whole community. At this stage there was only one congregation that served the entire population of the area, both Black and White, although even by this early stage a separate 'European' service had begun at Church street Methodist Church on Sunday evenings (Whiteside, 1906: 89). Later this would lead to a split in the congregation as the White members moved to a new Church building that they built at the top of Main Road, Somerset West in 1934. This White congregation later built Coronation Avenue Methodist Church (opened on 16 November 1969) when the Main Road Church building became too small.

With the promulgation of the Group Areas Act legislation in 1958 the racial divide was sanctioned by law and the pain of separation was intensified as members of the White Methodist grouping reaped the rewards of job reservation, economic protection, access to land and education and preference before the law.

This development in the history of the two Methodist congregations in Somerset West left lasting and painful scars – this is evidenced in the empirical datasets for Group A (D1:63, 64, D2:19, 41, 50, and D6:3, 30, 33). During the painful years of apartheid the pain was worsened as members of the Church Street congregation suffered under the weight of state sanctioned oppression (cf., D6:25, D5:19).

The result is a complex set of social, economic, cultural and religious divisions between the predominantly White Coronation Ave congregation and the predominantly Black (Brown / Coloured) Church street congregation (please see the discussion of the pre-intercultural engagement and post-intercultural engagement findings in 6.2-6.3).

A visit to either of the congregations on a Sunday will show that even some 23 years after the end of political apartheid in South Africa each of these congregations remains homogenous in terms of race and culture. This is surprising since there are not any major differences in either language or liturgical style between the two communities. Both are English speaking, and both follow traditional and contemporary forms of accepted Methodist worship in their Sunday services. The systems of Church governance and polity are also similar in that both congregations are members of the same Circuit (the Helderberg Circuit) and submit to the Laws and Discipline of the Methodist Church of Southern Africa.

Of course there have been some laudable attempts at bridging the divide between the two congregations. These have included social events, such as Church fetes, special celebration services as well as shared worship service on Feast days (such as Easter). However, these have not had any lasting transformational effects on the two communities (cf., D6:25, 27, 29). They remain largely independent from one another in their congregational life and ministry within the community.

Naturally this situation has caused a great deal of pain among both the members and leadership of each of the communities. There are great possibilities for mutual enrichment, growth and the strengthening of their collective work and witness, if the two churches were able to find a path towards forgiveness and reconciliation.

Since both congregations belong to the same denomination and share the same basic theological outlook, one must assume that there are some subtle and textured elements held by each of the communities that prohibit the journey of forgiveness and reconciliation.

This is where this research fits in – can a carefully facilitated engagement between these two groups in an intercultural Bible reading process of Matthew 18.15-35 create the conditions for a positive shift in conviction towards a discovery of the 'other' and the possibility of forgiveness?

5.7.3 Theoretical design plan for the intervention practices

The design of the intervention is informed by three theoretical perspectives.

5.7.3.1 *AQAL integrative theory*

The second question is why the AQAL integral approach was chosen as an underpinning theory in this research process? This theory, and the choice to use it, is discussed in detail in chapter 2 of this book. At this point we shall simply relate to pertinent elements of AQAL theory that are important for understanding the research design.

First, the AQAL theory allows for a textured and nuanced understanding of individual identity and the expression of convictions and ideas that can be mapped into a four quadrants model (the interior, the exterior, the individual and the social). This allowed for the deduction of codes that were used in the analysis of the data gathered from the intercultural Bible reading practices. It was shown in chapter 2 that this theory deals with all of the primary aspects of identity and being (individual interior – such as thoughts and beliefs; individual exterior – race, gender, physical ability; collective interior – faith community, social identity; and collective exterior – social geography, economic standing etc.) (Wilber, 2003: 22–49; Ferreira, 2010: 1–8; Forster, 2010a: 2–3). Since the problem of forgiveness and reconciliation in South Africa is embedded in a spiritual, social, political and economic context it is critical to engage as many aspects of identity as possible to extrapolate a rich, nuanced and dense set of theological and sociological data. Second the AQAL approach allows for hierarchical gradation in the development and complexity of thought and behaviour without having to denigrate, or elevate, different levels in relation to one another (Wilber, 1998: 49; Snyman, 2002: 73–75; Forster, 2006: 167–174; Ferreira, 2010: 1–8). This approach is a very helpful schema to engage such a complex set of issues responsibly and effectively and it was deemed to be particularly sensitive of the expectation of managing prejudice that is predicated in the intergroup contact theory (which was discussed in chapter 3)

The integrative philosophy of the AQAL approach allows for an intellectually robust theoretical model that can be used to plot the complex understandings of the processes and concepts of forgiveness in the Biblical text, as well as in the two groups and the individual participants. This allows the researcher to design research instruments and processes that can extrapolate data at various stages in the research process. The data can then be analysed and compared to other sets of data (the AQAL reading of the Biblical text, and the pre-intercultural engagement and post-intercultural engagement AQAL mappings of concepts of forgiveness). Such an analysis allows for a credible empirical hermeneutic engagement as necessitated by (v) in the practice oriented research design[115].

5.7.3.2 *Intergroup contact theory*

Chapter 3 of this book deals with the content of intergroup contact theory, and the reasons for its choice in detail. In this section we shall only highlight those aspects that are of direct correlation to the research design process. Please refer to chapter 3 for a detailed and critical presentation of the theory and its constituent elements.

As part of the research design of this practice oriented research project it was decided to employ intergroup contact theory to shape the intercultural Bible reading engagements between the two communities (Bornman, 2011; Pettigrew & Tropp, 2011; Adams *et al.*, 2012; Amodio & Hamilton, 2012; Brown, 2012; cf., Cakal, 2012). There are two primary reasons for this.

First, intergroup contact theory is a widely accepted and highly regarded social identity theory that is applied in the academy for understanding how groups form their primary individual and social identities (Bornman, 2011; cf., Pettigrew & Tropp, 2011; Amodio & Hamilton, 2012; Brown, 2012) and also how this identity formation affects the possibility of engagement between in-group identity and out-group identity (Bornman, 2011; Amodio & Hamilton, 2012; cf., Brown, 2012; Kuchenbrandt *et al.*, 2013).

Second, there is a wealth of accepted empirical research that shows that carefully structured and facilitated intergroup engagements are not only helpful in gathering data about the self-understanding of groups and their perceptions of others, but also that such engagements can facilitate the possibility for positive change in intergroup relationships (Islam & Hewstone, 1993; Pettigrew, 1998; Miller, 2002; Pettigrew & Tropp, 2005; cf., Kuchenbrandt *et al.*, 2013; Ypma, 2014: 21).

As a result, it was decided to make use of intergroup contact theory since it is hypothesised that this approach will allow for the development and implementation of necessary mechanisms (intergroup contact mediators) that lessen anxiety and increase empathy (intergroup moderators) among in-groups and out-groups. This facilitates the desired shift from the current factual situation identified in the problem (F) to the desired state expressed by the problem owner (D).

---

115 Please refer to 6.2, 6.3, 6.3.4 for detailed information on how this theoretical perspective informed the intervention practices in the intercultural Bible reading process. Please also refer to section 5.7.3 below.

The application of intergroup contact theory within the intercultural Bible reading interventions has the intention of facilitating a positive space of encounter with 'the other' that could allow for the possibility of theological shifts in the understanding of forgiveness to take place among the participants – namely gaining understanding of what is required to shift from (F) to (D). Intergroup contact theory suggests that change is possible between in-groups and out-groups when a number of requisite conditions are facilitated (Allport, 1954; Pettigrew, 1998; Pettigrew & Tropp, 2011). These include at least the following, "…equal group status within the situation, common goals, intergroup cooperation and authority support" (Pettigrew, 1998: 65). This was discussed, and considered, in detail in section 3.3.6.

The focus group interventions, referred to as intercultural Bible readings, that were developed in this research process allowed for the creation of a shared task, equality of status (namely the interpretation of a Biblical text by non-technical, "ordinary" Bible readers (De Wit, 2012: 9–11)), a common goal (seeking to understand what forgiveness from Matthew 18.15-35 could mean in an intercultural Bible reading group), participation with the permission of authorities (the nomination of the participants by their pastors) (Brewer & Kramer, 1985; Pettigrew, 1998; Pettigrew & Tropp, 2011; Amodio & Hamilton, 2012). In particular, the interpretation of a text by "ordinary" readers is a perfect tool to facilitate these conditions and this process (Van der Walt, 2014: 52–54). The use of "dwelling in the word" as a facilitated process for this intervention is discussed in the next section of this book (c.f., Ellison & Keifert, 2011; Nel, 2013b).

5.7.3.3 Readings of Matthew 18.15-35

In order to ascertain what the text suggest about forgiveness in its varied and complex forms it was necessary to do a close reading of Matthew 18.15-35. The exegetical exercise (see chapter 4) provided numerous insights into possible understandings and readings of forgiveness that emerged from the text (see 4.8, and Forster, 2017 in particular). These could be correlated with other scholarly engagements with this passage in its social and historical context. Naturally it was necessary to consider the identity and context of the author of the text, as well as the identity and social context of the intended readers of the text. To fully grasp the complexity of the issues raised in Matthew 18.15-35, without simply collapsing the worldview and concerns of the ancient near east into current social paradigms, it was important present both a social and historical review of the issues that the author sought to address. Some significant questions were raised that hold importance for the current research project. What were the intergroup challenges that were faced by the Matthean community (Hagner, 1995; Overman, 1996; Nel, 2002, cf., 2014a, 2015; Carter, 2005; Zimmermann & Dormeyer, 2007)? What are the spiritual and theological conditions and consequences of forgiveness (Gowan, 2010; Hägerland, 2011; Mbabazi, 2013; Nel, 2015). In addition to the social world view it was also important to gain an understanding into social identity theory in the New Testament, particularly as it relates to Matthew's gospel and the chosen text (Malina & Rohrbaugh, 1993; Duling, 1999; Kok, 2014a; Kok, Jacobus (Kobus), 2014; Nel, 2014a; Tucker & Baker, 2014).

At the conclusion of this close reading of the text some preliminary remarks and conclusions were discussed in relation to the AQAL theory of Ken Wilber (Taylor, 2001; Paulson, 2008; Ferreira, 2010; Forster, 2010a). This was made possible through mapping the Biblical text and doing a qualitative textural analysis in ATLAS.ti using the same set of codes that were identified for the focus group engagements. Some of the questions that were presented to the text were: How do individual and collective elements of forgiveness relate to one another? How do spiritual and social aspects of reconciliation and restitution interact? What are the processes related to forgiveness? What are the ethical and spiritual expectations of mimicking the authorial intent of the text? These important concepts allowed the text to act not only as a 'safe space' within which the conditions for intergroup contact could be developed, but also allowed the text to act a theological 'reflective surface' that could be used to offer insight, texture and meaning to the AQAL engagement with the reader's theological responses in the intercultural Bible reading interventions (Van der Walt, 2014: 52–54).

This study is focussed on facilitating an intervention (a series of intergroup engagements in the form of intercultural Bible readings of Matthew 18.15-35) that could mediate the effects of positive intergroup contact among the two groups[116]. It is hypothesised, based on the empirical research of intergroup contact theory (see chapter 3) that such a process could lead to increased social cohesion between in-group and out-group participants of the two communities.

The evaluation of this intervention relies on the AQAL mapping of understandings of forgiveness that emerge from the reading of Matthew 18.15-35 with individual readers and carefully designed and facilitated process of intercultural Bible reading which are structured in accordance with the requirements of intergroup contact theory.

The structure of the intercultural Bible reading processes allowed for the positive intergroup engagement to take place within a religious framework that adds the value of a shared task or objective, as well as the opportunity of gaining authoritative permission for participation (through the nomination of participants by their respective pastors). Such an approach within a religious setting has proven, in research, to be effective (Burch-Brown & Baker, 2016: 1–24).

Moreover, it is argued in sections 4.1-4.2 that the Biblical text plays a significant normative role as an informant of both identity and moral action for South African Christians.

Thus, it is necessary to consider the participants' theological understanding of the concept of forgiveness within the framework of the reading of Matthew 18.15-35 that was used as the reflective surface and space within which the intergroup engagements took place (Van der Walt, 2014: 6, 52–54, 65).

In chapter 3 it was shown that positive intergroup contacts can take place in a situation where a number of mediating criteria are met (c.f., Levine & Hogg, 2009: 468–469). Reading the text together, (known as "dwelling in the word"), is the space within which these characteristics of positive intergroup contact were facilitated (c.f., Ellison & Keifert, 2011; Nel, 2013b). That was however a matter of structural process

---

116 The intervention, which is structured as part of the practice oriented research project – as presented above in 5.6, was designed to engage specific theory in practice and to build upon that theory in its context to contribute towards the opening up of a problem in practice, cf., (Hermans, 2003, 2004: 21–52, 2014: 123–125; Hermans & Moore, 2004; Hermans, Graham & Rowlands, 2005: 219; Anthony, Hermans & Sterkens, 2007: 100–128; Verschuren, 2009a, b: 1–9, Hermans & Schoeman, 2015b: 45–63, c: 8–25, a: 26–44; Schoeman & van den Berg, 2016: 213)

facilitation in the intervention design. What is at stake in this section of the research relates to content – how do the respective communities understand and articulate concepts of forgiveness when reading Matthew 18.15-35 with one another?

5.7.4 Design plan for the data collection and intervention practices

5.7.4.1 *Sampling: Identifying participants*

The identification of participants for this research had to fulfil a number of important criterion. First, the participants needed to be independent volunteers who freely participated in the research. However, they also needed to be representatives from one of the two Churches who are the problem owners of this research (namely, either members from Church Street Methodist church or members from Coronation Ave Methodist church). Moreover, the participants needed to represent, in some manner at least, the social identities of the two communities participating in the intercultural Bible reading process.

These requirements allowed for the selection of participants to participate as one of two different Church groups, an important condition that was necessary to test the intergroup contact intervention. The research required the social conditions of difference that leads to the formation of a social identity as an in-group engaging an out-group (see the discussion of these terms in sections 3.3-3.4). In this case, each group would have viewed itself as an in-group among its Church peers since it shared some common social and psychological perspectives and identifiers. The other group, would have been regarded as the out-group. The nature of this study required that the two communities have differences to allow for diversity in interaction. The one community comes from a demographic that is described as having suffered directly under the racially oppressive policies of apartheid South Africa (Church street Methodist Church). This community was almost entirely comprised of Brown (at times identified as Black) South Africans (Duncan, 2003; Cakal *et al.*, 2011: 606–608). The second community came from a privileged South African constituency – these are predominantly White South African Christians who still experience the privileges and benefits of whiteness in South Africa. Privilege in this instance is characterised by socio-economic status, level of education, and race – since in South Africa White South Africans received preferential treatment in all of these aspects of social life under the Apartheid system (Terreblanche, 2002: 55, 143, 387). These two communities were treated as "knowing subjects" since "the perspectives of the various partners and their differences of opinion are important for the process of discovery; objectivity and neutrality must be replaced by reflective subjectivity" (Bergold & Thomas, 2012). In this process it is assumed that there is value in the perspectives, insights and personal history of the participants.

In the selection process the researcher also wanted to meet the requirement of the participants having official, authoritative, sanction for their participation in the research project (Pettigrew, 1998: 65–85). As such the researcher met with the pastors (ministers) of the two churches and we discussed the research project, its design and objectives. They each agreed to nominate a number of participants that they would approach and invite to join the intercultural Bible reading process as formal representatives of their respective congregations, with the sanction of the Church's leadership. No specific criteria were given for the selection of members from each Church. I also did not have any part in the decision of who was invited to participate. However, since the ministers were aware of the research project, and its area of investigation, it was evident that they had attempted to select a spectrum of representatives from their communities (namely, male, female, younger and older members).

A letter of invitation was sent by the respective pastors to approximately 12 persons in each of their respective congregations. Out of those 24 persons 12 participated in the process (two groups of 6 persons from each congregation representing Church Street Methodist church and Coronation Ave Methodist church). Please see a copy of the letter of invitation in Appendix A. Please refer to section 5.7.4 for an overview and discussion of the demographic information of the participants in the project.

A total of 12 persons participated in the intercultural Bible Reading process. As discussed in chapter 5 these participants were selected and nominated for participation by the ministers of their respective congregations – communities A and B. There were two reasons for this. First, it served to ensure that the researcher did not contaminate the process of participant selection and so influence the research process or findings. Second, it fulfilled one of the criteria of positive intergroup contact theory, namely that the participants felt that they were selected to participate in the process with the formal sanction of their leadership and community (c.f., 3.3.6). All of the participants agreed to participate in the process out of their own free will and were given the option of withdrawing from the process at any stage without any recourse. Each participant signed the ethical disclaimer form (see Appendix B for an example of this form).

The names of the participants were anonymized in the transcription of the data for the group meetings by assigning each participant a randomized identifier (P1-P12). The table below offers specific demographic information on the participants in the study. The participants self-identified in these demographic categories.

Table 4: Demographic information of participants

Participant	Community	Race	Gender
P1	Church Street	White	Female
P2	Coronation Ave	White	Female
P3	Church Street	Black	Male
P4	Coronation Ave	White	Male
P5	Church Street	Black	Female
P6	Coronation Ave	White	Female
P7	Church Street	Black	Male
P8	Coronation Ave	White	Male
P9	Church Street	Black	Male
P10	Coronation Ave	White	Female
P11	Coronation Ave	White	Female
P12	Church Street	Black	Male

Each community thus had an equal number of participants – six participants from Church Street Methodist Church (Group A) and six participants from Coronation Ave Methodist Church (Group B). There were an equal number of female participants and male participants in the collective group. However, Church Street Methodist Church had four male participants and two female participants, whereas Coronation Ave Methodist Church had two male participants and four female participants. The racial composition of the respective communities was largely representative of their membership demographics, with Church Street Methodist having five Coloured participants (identified as Black participants in this study[117]) and one White participant. While Coronation Ave Methodist Church had six White participants. All of the participants (from both communities) are English speaking.

To protect the anonymity of the participants their ages are not listed next to their demographic details. However, one of the participants was aged under 30 years of age, one was aged between 30 and 40 years, four persons were aged between 40 and 50 years, three persons between the ages of 50 and 60 years, and the remaining four persons were over the age of 60.

The demographic makeup of the respective groups approximates the demography of the adult membership of each of the two churches. This meant that, with the exception of one participant, all of the persons who participated in this study had experienced life under South Africa's apartheid system.

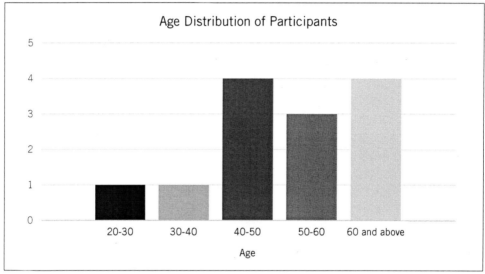

Figure 9: Age distribution of participants

5.7.4.2 *Data collection*

In order to answer the three research questions it was necessary to design a means of collecting data from the participants in the research project at three different stages, or points, of the research process[118]. The theories that informed the research project also required that certain types of data would need to be sourced for analysis. In this section we shall get a brief overview of the design of data collection in light of the above.

---

117 For a more detailed description of how the complex and contested notion of race was approached in this study please refer to section 1.10 in the introduction.
118 For reasons of scientific integrity, the possibility of verification, and potential reuse, the dataset underlying this study can be retrieved from http://dx.doi.org/10.17026/dans-x9b-379m. You may require permission to access some aspects of the data – you will receive information on this process via the previously listed DOI link.

Since this study focusses on intercultural Biblical hermeneutics it was necessary collect hermeneutic data from the participants in the study. In this case, the hermeneutic data that was collected was necessary in order to gain insights into how the participants understood concepts and processes of forgiveness when reading Matthew 18.15-35.

Moreover, since social identity complexity theory plays such an important role in intercultural hermeneutics, it was necessary to gather the data in a social, or group, reading context. Each of the two participating groups were largely homogenous in terms of race and culture (please see previous section for how the sampling of participants was designed and implemented). Demographic information was an important component in ascertaining to what extent social identity categories (such as race and culture) influence the hermeneutic perspectives of the participants. The participants self-reported their race, age and gender in an individual information session that took place before the first group meeting.

In order to gain data from the participants related to their intercultural Biblical hermeneutic views of forgiveness, the researcher designed a series of group readings of the Biblical text in which the participants had the opportunity to read the text and then share their understandings of forgiveness with the researcher and the rest of the group (Ellison & Keifert, 2011; Nel, 2013b). These group readings where structured in the form of focus group encounters (Pettigrew, 1998; Pettigrew & Tropp, 2011), in which the conversations were recorded by means of an audio recording device and then transcribed for later analysis (please refer to the next section for a detailed description of the design of the intervention practices at the various stages of the project).

The transcribed data was made anonymous (so as to protect the identity of the participants while maintaining coded identifiers that could be linked to the social identity and demographic information of the participants). Once the data had been transcribed, participants from each of the groups where asked to review the transcripts in order to verify that they reflected an accurate record of group meeting and conversations that took place. Upon agreement from the reviewing participants the transcriptions were finalised and secured for later analysis. Standard procedures for the storing and protection of the data were followed (in keeping with the standards of ethical clearance for Radboud University and the University of Stellenbosch – please refer to Appendix B for an outline of the processes and procedures that were followed).

Please refer to the next section (5.7.4.3) to see the relationship between the design of data collection and the design of the intervention practices. Then, please refer to the design of analysis section (5.8) to see how the collected data was utilised in the analysis of the research process.

5.7.4.3 Intervention practices

The use of focus group encounters was important in this project since it allowed for a structured understanding of contextual meaning and the dynamism of social interaction within the two groups, as they met separately, but also between the two groups as they encountered one another in an intercultural Bible reading process (Pettigrew, 1998; Pettigrew & Tropp, 2011). A number of elements of focus group research were kept in mind as this project unfolded. These are discussed under the headings below.

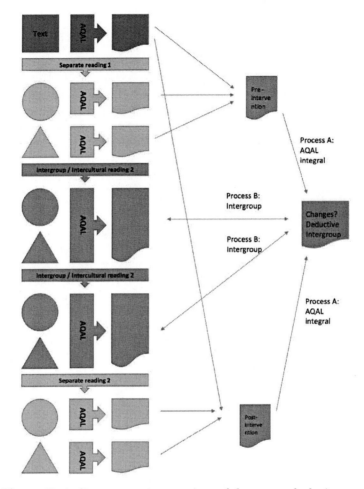

Figure 10: A diagrammatic overview of the research design and intervention process

5.7.4.3.1 The pre-intercultural engagement test: Information, ethical clearance and opening conversation

The researcher arranged to meet each of the 12 participants separately in their home or in their own Church to:

- Give them basic information about the intercultural Bible reading process.
- Gain their ethical clearance and consent to participate in the research project.
- Engage in an opening conversation that covered:
  - Demographic information.
  - Their view of the Biblical text as a source of theological and ethical authority.
  - Specific information on the participant's pre-intercultural engagement understanding of forgiveness (which was analysed by applying an AQAL

lens using a Computer Assisted Qualitative Data Analysis Software (CAQDAS) program). Each participant had been given a copy of Matthew 18.15-35 in advance of the meeting and asked to read it and come prepared to discuss their understanding of forgiveness in relation to this text. (Please see Appendix B for the Ethical Clearance consent form, and Appendix C for the Radboud University letter confirming ethical clearance).

5.7.4.3.2 First separate focus group meetings: 'in group' reading of Matthew 18.15-35

The researcher met with each of the two communities separately for the first focus group meetings. The purpose of this first group meeting was to introduce the participants to the process of communal Bible reading of Matthew 18.15-35 that would be employed in the group interventions going forward namely, "Dwelling in the word" (Ellison & Keifert, 2011; Nel, 2013b). The separate meetings took place in each group's home church setting.

These pre-intercultural engagement focus group meetings had two stages:

1. The participants were asked to introduce themselves to one another and to share some personal biographical and historical information about themselves. Although most of the participants already knew the members of their in-group, this was an important part of the process since it would be required in the intergroup setting at a later stage. This exercise served both to gather data about the participants and their understandings of themselves, but also to facilitate a safe and engaging space for the focus group to begin to communicate freely through a sense of shared identity, an egalitarian power structure, the value of their perspective in the common task etc.

2. The participants were then invited to read Matthew 18.15-35 using the "Dwelling in the word" approach (Ellison & Keifert, 2011: 7–8; Nel, 2013b: 1–8).

    i.   The approach requires that the Biblical text is read through aloud twice by two different readers (Ellison & Keifert, 2011: 7).

    ii. Next the participants are given a chance to read the text through on their own in silence and note any important words, verses, concepts or thoughts that arise around forgiveness (Ellison & Keifert, 2011: 7).

    iii. Next, they paired themselves with another participant ("a reasonably friendly looking stranger" (Ellison & Keifert, 2011: 7–8; Nel, 2013b) in the words of the designers of this approach). The intention of this aspect of the process is to create a space for their partner to share what they had heard, read or experienced in reading the text.

    iv. Then each participant offers feedback on behalf of their partner. This achieves two important goals; first it removes the pressure to have to offer a 'clever' or impressive reading of the text since one is not representing one's own perspective in the feedback. This accords with the mediating principles of intergroup contact theory (removing competition, participating towards a common goal, removing hierarchies of expertise, and lessening anxiety while increasing cognitive empathy). More importantly, however, it forces the participant to listen very carefully to the other to hear their perspective and report it clearly and accurately to the larger group in the last part of this process (Ellison & Keifert, 2011: 8). As mentioned this was a crucial part of the process since it decreased anxiety and increased cognitive empathy, two of the intergroup contact moderators facilitated in this intervention.

v.   Once all of the groups had reported on what they heard and read, the interviewer asked some questions of the participants that were designed to chart the participants' understanding of the concept of forgiveness within the AQAL framework and notions of in-group and out-group identity.

The data gained form the first focus group gatherings was plotted using the AQAL theory codes, and interpreted in relation to intergroup theory codes. A qualitative interpretation and evaluation is presented and discussed in chapter 6 of this book.

5.7.4.3.3 *Second and third group meetings: Intercultural Bible reading*

The researcher next met with the two communities together in intergroup focus group sessions on two further occasions. Whereas the previous separate group meetings each took place in the respective Church of the participating group, this meeting took place in a neutral venue. These intergroup contact sessions were structured as intercultural Bible reading engagements between the two communities.

This intergroup contact meeting followed the following process:

1.   The communities were invited to meet in a neutral venue seated around a large round table. Participants were allowed to seat themselves where they felt comfortable around the table. Equal numbers of participants from each church grouping were present.

2.   The participants from the two communities were invited to introduce themselves to the rest of the group and share some personal biographical and historical information with one another. This served both to gather data in the intergroup setting, but also to facilitate a safe and engaging space for the focus group to begin to communicate freely. It also gave some insight of the differences that exist between the participants (age, gender, race, and which church they belong to).

3.   The participants were then invited to read Matthew 18.15-35 using the "Dwelling in the word" approach (described in detail above).

4.   On this occasion, it was particularly insightful since each of the participants was invited to pair up with a "friendly stranger" from the other Church group and listen to them share their perspectives on forgiveness in the text. They then reported what they had heard from their partner. The recordings of the focus group conversations show that numerous points of growth and learning took place in these conversations and in the process of listening and reporting what they had heard from one another. The data is presented and discussed in chapter 6.

5.   Finally, after all the members had reported back the researcher posed a set of questions that were designed to chart the participants' understanding of the concept of forgiveness when reading the text in a safe space in the presence of the 'other'. These questions solicited both theological information about the text and psychosocial information about the intergroup engagement.

The data gained from the first focus group gatherings was interpreted in relation to intergroup theory and AQAL theory and a qualitative interpretation and evaluation is presented and discussed later in this book (cf., 6.2).

The researcher did some comparison between the first sets of pre-intercultural engagement data that was recorded in the interviews and separate group readings and the second set of data recorded in this intercultural Bible reading to highlight and interpret any similarities or differences that may have arisen in the process.

The process above was repeated on a second occasion one week later than the previous intercultural Bible reading. It was already evident that each time that the group met together their friendship was developing, anxiety was decreasing and empathy increased which allowed for fascinating data to be recorded for description and analysis. The effectiveness of the intergroup contact mediators and moderators was evidenced in the data.

5.7.4.3.4 Fourth group meeting: Post-intercultural engagement separate group meetings

In this final meeting the researcher once again met with the communities separately for the final focus group discussions and the completion of a post-intercultural engagement group meeting. At this meeting three activities took place. Each of the communities was invited to read Matthew 18.15-35 in the same manner as the previous sessions were facilitated ("Dwelling in the word"). Next, they were invited to give personal responses to a set of questions which were designed to chart their growing in understanding of the concept of forgiveness when reading the text, and the influence and effectiveness of the facilitated intergroup contact sessions. Then, the group discussed their experiences of both their growth in understanding of the concept of forgiveness as well as the process of intercultural Bible reading and intergroup contact that allowed shifts to take place.

The respective group meetings with each of the church groups ended with some general discussion about future opportunities for contact and other opportunities for growth and the creation of reconciling spaces that may follow separately from this research project. The research participants were thanked and notified of the process going forward after which they will be briefed on the findings and included in a final celebration and act of thanksgiving for their participation.

The data gained form this third separate set focus group meetings was interpreted and a qualitative interpretation and evaluation based on intergroup theory and AQAL theory was analysed and discussed (cf., 6.2-6.4). The researcher also compared this set of data to the data gained in the pre-intercultural engagement interviews and first separate focus group interviews, as well as the two intercultural Bible readings (meetings two and three). The intention of this process was to highlight and interpret any similarities or differences that may have arisen out of the process, paying particular attention to transformative mechanisms that can be described and understood as part of the intervention cycle.

5.8 Design of Analysis

The analysis was designed in accordance with the research questions that shaped this study. The process of reasoning that informed the analysis design is described below, while the technical detail of the design and its contents are discussed in the section on the theoretical codes that follows (5.9), and in the analysis of the data itself (chapter 6).

1. To what extent do theological understandings of forgiveness differ among Christians of different race groups?

It was necessary to design an analytical process that could explicate information from the pre-intercultural Bible reading data (i.e., where Group A and Group B read the text separately from one another) in order to answer this research question. The primary objective of the analysis design in this sense was to ascertain whether the participants from different race groups held different theological understandings of forgiveness.

The AQAL theory (discussed in chapter 2) allowed for the articulation and description of concepts and categorizations of understanding and identity in relation to the participants' race identity, and their hermeneutic understandings of forgiveness. These concepts were developed into analytical codes that could be used to engage the data to identify and explain understandings of identity and theological understanding among the participants. For example, it was possible to apply this theory to an analysis of the data in order to identify whether Group A primarily held a social identity, while Group B held a form of primary individual identity. Moreover, the AQAL theory informed the design of theological concepts and theological language that allowed the researcher to analyse understandings of forgiveness from participants' reading of Matthew 18.15-35. By relating what was observed in the pre-intercultural engagement datasets (D1 and D2) to an AQAL reading of the text (cf., 4.8), it became possible to identify, analyse, and describe differing understandings of forgiveness between the two groups.

2. To what extent have theological understandings of forgiveness among Christians of different race groups changed in a more integrative manner after an intercultural bible reading of Matthew 18.15-35?

To answer the second research question, it was necessary to design a form of analysis that would allow for the identification of changes in understandings of forgiveness within the participants between their pre-intercultural engagement and post-intercultural engagement readings of the text. For example, did understanding of forgiveness identified, analysed and described in relation to research question 1 differ among the same group of participants after they had read the text together in a positive intergroup contact intercultural Bible reading setting? Here the AQAL was once again employed to map understandings of forgiveness in the post-intervention group readings (datasets D5 and D6). The theory provided theological language and concepts, in conjunction with the AQAL reading of the text in 4.8, that could allow for the identification of difference between datasets D1 and D6 (Group A before and after the intercultural Bible reading engagement) and D2 and D5 (Group B before and after the intercultural Bible reading engagement).

3. To what extent is the change in theological understandings of forgiveness among Christians of different races (Group A and Group B) stimulated by the mediators and moderators of the intercultural Bible reading practices?

The final research question necessitated the development of a form of analysis that required insight from positive intergroup contact theory in relation to the findings of the analysis in relation to research questions 1 and 2 above. In order to answer request question 3 it was necessary to ascertain whether the introduction of positive intergroup contact mediators and moderators in the intercultural Bible reading engagement could be observed, and whether the observation of these practices in datasets D3 and D4 has any correlation to the findings of the analysis of research question 1 and 2. Thus, the theory informed the development of a series of analytical codes related to the mediators and moderators of positive intergroup contact. The codes were used to identify instances of the operation of the mediators and moderators of intergroup contact in the intercultural Bible reading practice, and then ascertain whether there was any correlation between the identification of these instances and changes in understandings of forgiveness among the participants.

De Vos notes that qualitative research analysis is particularly suited to help the researcher "understand reality by discovering the meanings that people, in a specific setting attach to it", and "understand phenomena within a particular context" (De Vos, 1998: 241–242). Qualitative analysis is thus well suited to identifying and explicating relationships of meaning within a complex system of interactions (Tuckey, 2015: 41). A critical function of the research is to deal with the data in a responsible and sensitive manner so as not to place information into, or onto, the data sets. As such, the clear identification and development of qualitative codes was necessary. These codes where then used in the qualitative research environment (ATLAS.ti) to carefully and systematically go through the data to identify, highlight and relate specific themes and events in the research intervention process. This process was undertaken numerous times, both to test the validity of the initial findings, but also to deepen and texture the networks of interactions and relationships between ideas, events, and mechanisms.

The researcher was aware of his own bias, and the desired outcome of the problem owner, in conducting the research. As such the concept of bracketing was employed. Bracketing is a way to manage the "tension between subjectivity and objectivity and the problems that arise when undertaking emotionally and ethically challenging research" (Rolls & Relf, 2006: 286). Through an awareness of the researcher's own bias, and a careful application of bracketing in the data analysis, the researcher attempted to remain open and objective to the research participants, the research process, and the data and findings that emerged as a result.

In order to establish a measure of objective reliability in the research process and findings, the code book (discussed below), coded datasets, and findings in the data were reviewed by three ATLAS.ti qualitative empirical research experts to establish interrater reliability for the coding of the datasets (cf., Pope, Ziebland & Mays, 2000: 114; Hwang, 2008: 519–527; Lu & Shulman, 2008: 105–117; Castro, Kellison, Boyd & Kopak, 2010: 342–360; DeCuir-Gunby, Marshall & McCulloch, 2011: 136–155). These persons independently evaluated the coding strategy, the code descriptions, and the application of the codes to the datasets in order to ascertain the credibility of the research analysis process. Naturally, the researcher will have a more nuanced understanding of both the codes (and the theories that inform them), as well as the research participants, the research process, and the findings. Yet, it was important to establish the integrity of the data analysis processes according to acceptable academic standards by means of an interrater approach (cf., Tinsley & Weiss, 1975: 358–362; James, Demaree & Wolf, 1984: 85; McHugh, 2012: 276–282). The following formula for kappa was used (please see Appendix D for details):

$$\text{Kappa} = \frac{(\text{Observed Agreement} - \text{Expected Agreement})}{1 - \text{Expected Agreement}}$$

The interrater reliability score, calculated according to Cohen's kappa, delivered the following results:

Table 5: Calculation of interrater reliability (Cohen's Kappa)

Interraters	Calculation of Kappa
R3 and R1	0,73
R3 and R2	0,68
R1 and R2	0,68

5.9 Definitions of codes

Since this research applied a practice oriented approach to qualitative data analysis, it was necessary to develop and define a number of key codes that could be used to cluster, analyse and interpret the data that emerged from the intergroup contact sessions and the AQAL approach to the perspectives of the participants and the Biblical text (Saldaña, 2011: 93–94). The codes that are listed below emanate from two general processes. First, several of the codes below are theory based (as described in the previous section). These codes are related to the two primary theories that shape the research project, its design, and implementation – namely Ken Wilber's integral AQAL theory (chapter 2) and intergroup contact theory (chapter 3), as well as understandings of forgiveness from an AQAL reading of the Biblical text (cf., 4.8). Second, a number of the codes listed below emerged during the process of reading the transcribed data from the focus group meetings – these are empirical codes. As the transcripts were read a number of patterns emerged from the data that served as analytic tools (Saldaña, 2011: 91). In addition to this the patterns were also able to be clustered into analytical categories (Saldaña, 2011: 91–92). The codes are necessary to be able to identify and group sections of the data, and also to show interactions, interplay and interrelationships between the categories and themes within the data (Given, 2008: 150; Saldaña, 2011: 92–93).

Theoretical Codes

5.9.1 AQAL codes – mapping theological understandings of forgiveness in the reading of the text

The first set of empirical codes that will be presented are the codes that address the AQAL integrative theory. As has already been discussed in some length, this theory allows for the articulation and explication of identity and meaning by defining and placing responses of the participants, and concepts found in the Biblical text, with one or more of the four AQAL quadrants.

The intention of the codes was to allow the researcher to carefully work through the data sources, in the light of AQAL theory, and develop clusters of relationships between ideas, expressions, actions, and interactions.

The first necessary category descriptor was to be able to identify the manner in which participants in the research project, as well as the Biblical text that was used in the process, understood and expressed their understandings of forgiveness.

An integral understanding of forgiveness, and integral expressions of meaning and identity: Primary level codes for AQAL theory: *_AQAL_

- Description: This category description aims to bring together specific understandings or definitions of forgiveness, and expressions of meaning and identity, that can be related to an aspect, or various aspects, of the AQAL integrative theory discussed in chapter 2. AQAL theory posits that the description and categorisation of meaning and identity can be expressed in relation to four descriptive categories or sets of characteristics. The categories are: Individual Interior (UL), Collective Interior (LL), Individual Exterior (UR), Collective Exterior (LR). The asterisk (*) serves in place of the specific research data set, for example the data set for the first group meeting (D1) is 1_AQAL_. Each data set is assigned a number and specific codes are used for that data set (e.g., data set D2 is coded as 2_AQAL_ and so forth).

- Characteristics: Since this code category aims to group together, or offer understandings of expressions, definitions or actions of forgiveness, meaning or identity, that arise from the text, or readings of the text, it can be characterised as relating to personal (UL and UR) forgiveness or subjective (interior) identity and meaning, or social and political understandings or expressions of forgiveness, or expressions of identity and meaning, (LL) and (LR). Further sets of sub codes are developed to better understand finer variations of this general code category.

The table below offers a succinct reference for how the AQAL codes are related to the four quadrants of meaning and identity in AQAL integral theory:

Table 6: AQAL codes

UL – Individual Interior	UR – Individual Exterior
*_AQAL_UL	*_AQAL_UR
• Belief • Personal forgiveness • Private • Me • Prayer • Confession • Faith conviction	• You are • Confront • I act
LL – Collective Interior	**LR – Collective Exterior**
*_AQAL_LL	*_AQAL_LR
• Our faith • God expects • Us • Religious law • Community ideal • In Group	• Political • Restitution • Communal (we are) • Public • Them • Out Group

The individual interior state (UL) - *_AQAL_UL

- Description: This code identifies expressions of personal identity, or theological conviction, based on internalised individual subjective criteria (c.f., Wilber, 1997: 77). It also identifies understandings of forgiveness as individual subject states of belief or knowledge (e.g., spirituality, belief, religion, personal identity).
- Characteristics: Personal, emerges from the individual interior (UL) (belief, conviction, emotion), individual, subjective – spiritual conviction, personal repentance, personal piety. Lacks social engagement and transformative agency.
- Examples:
  - Sin as spiritual bondage, forgiveness as spiritual liberation. D1:21 "Even when you are in bondage, God forgives, when you ask forgiveness and he set us free and when we are free".
  - A separation of forgiveness from concrete social and personal action. D1:26 "sometimes we tend to look at what he did...**I:** mmmhmm **P7:** at what the person did, but we don't look at the person, because that what he did, is not important."

The collective interior state (LL) - *_AQAL_LL

- Description: This code identifies expressions of social identity, shared belief, group theological conviction, customs, practices or laws that are common to a group. It is based on collective internalised subjective criteria (c.f., Wilber, 1997: 77). Furthermore, this code identifies forgiveness as a shared set of communal beliefs or values (e.g., shared spirituality, culture, custom, shared identity, shared belief, religion, law). For example, there cannot be communal harmony while there is strife between community members – this is a shared conviction, a cultural belief.
- Characteristics: The collective subjective expresses a shared belief, identity, set of values, principles (LL) (culture, theological tradition, collective identity).
- Examples: "We believe...", "It is our custom..."
  - A shared set of values that are considered as normative 'truths'. D1:20 "Never go alone. [silent] talk to people, so that, as a group... so that people will see the truth that will be reflected".
  - Shared beliefs and community harmony. D1:70 "So I think part of what this is saying is, it could have been what Matthew was trying to say to the community is to make sure as a community, that you have the same heart, and identity as that of God."

Individual exterior (UR) - *_AQAL_UR

- Description: This code identifies expressions of individual action or object identified meaning. These might include individual characteristics (such as maleness, whiteness), or individual actions, (such as confronting another, pointing out the fault of another), or observations of another (an act, a series of actions, object characteristics). The code further identifies the responsibility of the individual in facilitating or enacting forgiveness in action.

- Characteristics: Objective, individual, observational, based on interpretation of sensory data, quantifiable, identifiable in an objective sense, personal agency, personal responsibility, activity based, direct towards another.
- Examples: "I see…", "You look like…", "I must confront…", "You must…"
  - Engage the individual to point out her or his sin. D1:6 "go and tell somebody he has done wrong…"

Collective exterior (LR) - *_AQAL_LR

- Description: This code identifies collective action, or the classification of external observations related to structures. These might include collective actions or observations (political action, social action, geography etc.) In addition, the code identifies the social (policy, political) aspects of forgiveness. Forgiveness is more than just personal action; it requires institutional sanction and support to facilitate and sustain it (e.g., collective action, political action, consequences of a legal system, reparation).
- Characteristics: Objective, observational, based on interpretation of sensory data, quantifiable, identifiable in a collective objective sense.
- Examples: "You look like…", "We must…"
  - Social implications of mercy as justice. D2:11 "he didn't do anything illegal [silent] but he, although he forgave, he didn't really get the drift of it in other words, there was no mercy really, he didn't fully understand, he hadn't learnt the lesson".

5.9.2 Intergroup Contact codes – identifying, clustering and discussing mechanisms of intergroup engagement among the participants

As was stated earlier, this research hypothesised that positive and constructive developments of intergroup contact could be facilitated through a carefully constructed and facilitated intergroup contact intervention (in this instance, through the intercultural Bible reading engagements under the conditions of positive intergroup contact). The hypothesis specifically suggested that if anxiety could be lessened through meeting in a neutral location, the performing of a shared task, that participants engage in the process having the permission of authority figures, and that participants have a relatively equal status in the situation, then empathy between the participants could be increased. The process of decreasing anxiety and increasing empathy would be a critical mechanism for facilitating positive intergroup contact that allows for the broadening and deepening of understandings of forgiveness between 'in groups' and 'out groups'.

Under the headings below, several codes are presented based on the theory of intergroup contact (this theory is discussed in detail in chapter 3). These theoretical codes serve as descriptors and identifiers of key aspects of intergroup contact theory that will be employed in engaging the qualitative research data that was gathered from focus group interventions. There are three broad categories of codes: positive intergroup contact mediators, positive intergroup contact moderators, and observations of shifts in the mediators (e.g., from an exclusive 'in group' understanding of forgiveness, to the adoption of the ideas or concepts of forgiveness that are characteristic of the 'out group' that can be related to the process of intergroup contact).

Concept: Primary code level for Intergroup contact theory: *_IG_

- Description: This descriptor indicates that the code which is being employed is based on, or describes, an aspect of intergroup contact, or the theory that described and informed the understandings of intergroup contact. This theory is discussed in detail in chapter 3. The asterisk (*) serves in place of the specific research data set, for example the data set for the first group meeting (D1) is 1_IG_. Each data set is assigned a number and specific codes are used for that data set (e.g., data set D2 is coded as 2_IG_ and so forth).

Dimension: Secondary code level for Intergroup Contact Theory Mediators: *_IG_MED_

- Description: As explained in chapter 3.3.1, positive intergroup contact is mediated by a decrease in anxiety and an increase in affective empathy and, or, cognitive empathy (3.3.3). This secondary code level is used to identify aspects of the intergroup contact mediators in the research data.

Aspects: The positive intergroup contact mediator codes are:

Decrease in anxiety: *_IG_MED_ANXIETY_DOWN

- Description: This code is used to identify instances in which one can identify a decrease in anxiety among the participants. For a discussion of intergroup contact anxiety please see 3.4.7.
- Characteristics: Within the intergroup contact environment one may identify a decrease in anxiety among the participants through their willingness to participate freely in discussions, to share personal information or narratives, to make themselves vulnerable, through instances of shared humour, or personal connection.
- Example:
  - Expressing an openness to the other and the perspectives of the other. D3:31 "...and learn, you know, different things from it, uuhhhh, you know the point of it, is to keep an open perspective of the other, cos as we've seen already there's richness it that you know, but also to be able to say... listen here's something that I feel strongly about and I need you folks to hear it, you know?"

Increase in affective empathy: *_IG_MED_EMPATHY_AFFECTIVE_UP

- Description: Affective empathy is the capacity to connect with, and to some measure, experience the emotions of the other. Empathetic mediators identify an increase in this capacity among the individuals, or within the groups. Increased empathy is a critical element of effective intergroup contact that leads to helpful and effective engagement with the other (Pettigrew, 1998: 71–71; Ricoeur, 2007: xvii–xix; Kearney, 2013). For a detailed discussion of intergroup contact empathy, in its various forms, please see 3.4.8.

- Characteristics: A deeper connection with the emotional experience of the other. Feeling aspects of what the other is feeling more deeply and understanding the emotional experience more fully. Imagining how the other may be feeling.
- Example:
  - An expression of attempting to feel what another person may feel. D5:19 "If I was Coloured or Black now and I experienced the apartheid regime, would I have been as humble or as forgiving as what these people are?"

Increase in cognitive empathy: *_IG_MED_EMPATHY_COGNITIVE_UP

- Description: Cognitive empathy is identified as a second step in the empathic process. Once a person is able to empathise with the emotional experience of another, it sometimes leads to that person imagining how the other person makes meaning of their situation (i.e., a shift from affective experience, to cognitive meaning making) (Swart, Turner, et al., 2011: 189). This often adds texture and nuance to the in-group perspective in relation to the concepts and ideas of the out-group. It is associated with the deconstruction of prejudice and cognitive bias.
- Characteristics: Examples may include the retelling of concepts, notions or ideas of the other or the out-group in the words of the in-group. Ideas, concepts and language of the out-group are validated and at times adopted or affirmed.
- Example:
  - Thinking differently because of an encounter with the ideas of another person. D5:12 "we got different views on what forgiveness should be and what it should be all about, um, but the two points I put down here, that, um, that I, that I got on the first time, I think we met with the Church street crowd was that, um, there were two points, that sound like quite basic when you read it, but it hadn't, like, dawned on me as clear".

Dimension: Secondary code level for Intergroup contact theory moderators: *_IG_MOD_

The moderation of positive intergroup contact depends on the introduction of intergroup mechanisms, known as contact moderators (3.3.6). They are:

Equal status within the situation: *_IG_MOD_EQUALSTATUS

- Description: This code is used to identify instances in the intergroup contact engagements where hierarchies are flattened and inequality of power is balanced. It identifies instances in which equal status among the participants is either facilitated or equality is expressed.
- Characteristics: Examples may include instances in which participants directly express equal status in the reading community, or where the facilitator explains that all of the readers have equal status in the reading community because of the nature of the task and setting.
- Example:
  - Expressing how group equality made the process of engagement safe and more effective. D5:47 "I was going to say, for me in the whole area of forgiveness, is that safe ground as well, I think that the important... it is that

we were on neutral ground and we felt safe, we weren't vulnerable in any way, we'd had sort of… we knew they were church people, we knew was… who they were and they sort of knew who we were".

Common goals: *_IG_MOD_COMMONGOALS

- Description: Positive intergroup contact requires that the participants feel that they are working together towards common goals. This set of codes identifies instances in the data where participants either express that they are working towards common goals, or the processes is facilitated in such a manner that they cooperate with one another to reach common goals.
- Characteristics: Participants express an understanding that they are working towards the same objective or goal.
- Example:
  - Since there is a common goal, the participants felt safe to participate with persons who were different. D5:44 "I have a sense that… uhh… even though there must be diversity, it must be safe diversity. [group agreement] **I:** you don't want to go into a space where… if you walk in and it's let's say, it's two different races, you under attack… **P10:** yes **P8:** mmm **I:** So there was something about the safeness of our diversity".

Intergroup cooperation: *_IG_MOD_IGCOOPERATION

- Description: This code is used to identify instances in which members of the groups work together, assist one another, or seek solutions and agreement, within the intercultural Bible reading process.
- Characteristics: Participants engage in activities that support one another, they display a willingness to listen to each other, or help each other.
- Examples:
  - As with the previous code, in this instance, cooperation was expressed as a necessary aspect for reaching the common goal. D5:44 "I have a sense that… uhh… even though there must be diversity, it must be safe diversity. [group agreement] **I:** you don't want to go into a space where… if you walk in and it's let's say, it's two different races, you under attack… **P10:** yes **P8:** mmm **I:** So there was something about the safeness of our diversity".
  - The common goal, and the cooperation, is expressed as a condition for freedom to participate in the process. D5:45 "we knew that we had a common task, we knew that, that group wasn't more powerful than this group, we had a neutral venue, some of those things were quite important… in **P8:** mmm **I:** allowing us to give a little bit of ourselves… give a little bit… I can give a little bit of ground… because that actually does make sense to me and in this context, I, I can take it on without, without uhhh being embarrassed, or uh, threatened, or uh, vulnerable… **P4:** and be yourself, I mean…".

Support of authorities, law or custom: *_IG_MOD_SUPPORT

- Description: As discussed in section 3.3.6, positive intergroup contact research shows that it is more effective when the participants feel that they have the support or sanction of authorities to participate freely and with commitment in the intergroup contact process. This code identifies expressions of such support, either from among the participants, or in the structuring and moderation of the intergroup contact sessions.

- Characteristics: Expressions of support from figures of authority (the ministers of the respective congregations), or sanction from an official body (i.e., the minister or Church council has nominated the participants or encouraged them to participate in the process).

- Example:
  □ An expression that the task is being undertaken with the sanction and support of church authorities. D5:44 "So there was something about the safeness of our diversity, the fact that, that we were… am I correct in that… **P2:** very much so **I:** we were doing this with the sanction of our churches…"

5.9.3 Coding and analysis

After the six group meetings had taken place, the recordings of the meetings were transcribed, made anonymous, and read through three times completely by the researcher. The purpose of this initial reading was twofold: First, it served to try to eliminate any typographical errors in the transcribed text, ensuring that the text matched the recordings accurately. Second, it served to reintroduce the researcher to the events of the group meetings, and allowed him to identify some interesting patterns and aspects of the encounter that may hold possible value for the more technical research process that would follow[119]. The transcripts were then verified with a sampling of six participants (three from each community for the pre-intercultural engagement and post-intercultural engagement meetings, and six participants, equally representing the two participating communities, for the two intercultural Bible reading meetings in which the intervention was introduced). This process was undertaken to establish the reliability of the transcripts as a record of the group meetings.

Next the transcripts were converted and imported into ATLAS.ti for analysis. The ATLAS.ti software assigned a designation to each dataset (D1-D6).

The pre-intercultural engagement and post-intercultural engagement datasets (D1, D2, D5 and D6) were then coded using the theoretical codes for the AQAL integral theory (see chapter 2 for a detailed presentation of the AQAL theory, and chapter 5.9.1 for a discussion of the AQAL codes). This process was extremely insightful as it allowed for the identification and selection of data from the group sessions that highlighted how the participants understood concepts of forgiveness as found in the reading and discussion of Matthew 18.15-35 and their interaction around their theological ideas and convictions. The coding process was repeated multiple times (up to 7 times on some documents) to sharpen the identification and capturing of aspects of the participants' understandings of forgiveness in relation to the text and the group interaction in more precise and textured ways. The findings of this process will be discussed in detail in the sections that follow.

---

119 This approach was informed by Friese's NCT approach (Noticing things, Collecting things, Thinking about things) that is also used in this research to engage the empirical data in a qualitative analytical process in a more formal manner later in the research process (Friese, 2014: 12–14).

This method was necessary to establish a baseline of findings and data at the start of the process (*before* the intercultural Bible reading process was facilitated under the conditions of positive intergroup contact theory). Then, it was necessary to establish a clear set of findings and data for how the participants understood forgiveness in relation to the reading of text and their interaction *after* the intercultural Bible reading process, facilitated under the conditions of positive intergroup contact theory, had taken place. The pre-intercultural engagement data and the post-intercultural engagement data was analysed separately (as will be shown below). Once the findings of the pre-intercultural engagement and post-intercultural engagement readings had been established, the two data sets and the findings from them were compared with one another in a variance approach (cf., sections 5.7.3-5.7.4 of the research design).

The final step in the process, related to research questions two and three, was to identify where shifts in understandings of forgiveness had taken place and account, to some measure at least, for the possible reasons why such shifts may have occurred. It was also important to identify instances in which anticipated shifts either did not take place at all, or did not take place in the manner, or to the extent, that was anticipated. This comparative analysis, and the evaluation of why shifts may, or may not, have taken place as anticipated was done by means of the use of the application of positive intergroup contact theory (presented in detail in chapter 3). A series of theoretical codes, based on this theory (cf., 5.9.2), was related to the data sets to identify and analyse what had taken place, linking the anticipated, or unanticipated, changes to events in the intercultural Bible reading process. This process was undertaken on datasets D3 and D4 primarily, since these were the group meetings where the two groups encountered one another and the reading of the text took place under the conditions of positive intergroup contact. However, in the final post intervention meetings (recorded in datasets D5 and D6) the participants also reflected on the effects and importance of aspects of the positive intergroup contact experience in the intercultural Bible reading meetings. Once again, this coding was undertaken several times to refine and sharpen the gathered data for analysis and presentation in the finds below. The code book, coded datasets, and findings in the data were reviewed by two independent ATLAS.ti qualitative empirical research experts to establish interrater reliability for the coding of the datasets (cf., Pope *et al.*, 2000: 114; Hwang, 2008: 519–527; Lu & Shulman, 2008: 105–117; Castro *et al.*, 2010: 342–360; DeCuir-Gunby *et al.*, 2011: 136–155). These persons had the task of evaluating the design, implementation, and reliability of the coding strategy in relation to the datasets, the code book, and the analytical findings. As was mentioned in section 5.7.4, the researcher will naturally have a more detailed and textured understanding of the research problem, the theoretical informants of the research design and processes, and the research participants. However, it was of great importance to establish credibility for the process and findings through interrater evaluation – see the finding of Cohen's kappa, and the calculation table in Appendix D.

5.10   Concluding remarks

This chapter has shown how the research project was conceptualised, designed and implemented. It placed the research problem within a particular social and historical context. The chapter showed why the practice oriented research method was favoured to engage this project. It also showed why qualitative empirical research design was best suited to a research project engaged in empirical hermeneutic intercultural Bible reading.

The research mechanisms, and the research process, were explained and placed within their respective theoretical frameworks. An effort was made to show the scientific rigour and objectivity of the research process and the researcher. This was done by explaining the ethical implications of participant selection, the design of the intercultural Bible reading sessions according to intergroup contact theory, how data was gathered, treated and analysed.

Clear links were drawn between the research problem, the research objectives, the research design and the theoretical frameworks that shape this study.

In the next chapter we shall do an in depth and critical analysis of the data that was gathered during the research process. Based on that analysis and evaluation some findings, and their relevance and importance, will be presented and discussed.

6 THE FINDINGS

6.1 Introduction

This study is as a practice oriented research project that employs a socio-theological[120] approach to present and analyse the findings of the research from the data (Venter, 1994: 35). Hence, this chapter we shall present, analyse and consider the findings of the engagement with the two Church communities (identified as Group A and Group B) in relation to the three research questions. The first research question sought to understand to what extent theological understandings of forgiveness differ among Christians of different race groups? The hypothesis of the study in relation to each group's pre-intercultural engagement understanding of forgiveness will be revisited, after which there will be a detailed presentation of the data that emerged from each meeting. Finally, there will be a presentation of the findings and an analysis of each group's pre-intercultural engagement data.

The second research question sought to ascertain to what extent theological understandings of forgiveness among Christians of different race groups changed in a more integrative manner after an intercultural bible reading of Matthew 18.15-35? In order to answer this question we shall follow a process where we introduce and analyse the post intervention data of Group A and Group B. A narrative overview of the post-intercultural engagement intercultural Bible reading meeting will be presented. Then, the theoretical hypothesis of the expected understandings of forgiveness for each group in the post-intercultural engagement meetings will be presented, after which the data from the respective meetings will be presented in detail and analysed. These findings will be presented as post-intercultural engagement findings for Group A, and post-intercultural engagement findings for Group B.

Next, there will be a comparative analysis of the differences in the data between the pre-intercultural engagement and post-intercultural engagement understandings of forgiveness in Group A and Group B. A variance approach[121] will be used in this regard – hence, it will be necessary to see what changes or shifts took place between the pre-intercultural engagement and the post-intercultural engagement intercultural Bible group readings. Where anticipated variances (based on the theories discussed in chapters 2 and 3, and the AQAL reading in chapter 4) are identified they will be analysed in relation to the theoretical underpinnings and the data from the intercultural Bible reading gatherings that took place under the

---

120 Please see the discussion in 4.3 on the specific methodological approach that was employed in relation to the text (i.e., that a choice was made to focus particularly on the social aspects of the text). Venter describes the usage of such approaches in relation to theological considerations of the social aspects of the text as a "socio-theological" approach (Venter, 1994: 35).

121 For a discussion of a variance approach in a qualitative empirical research studies please see the discussion on p.70 in (Blatter, 2008: 68–71). For a discussion of how the variance approach to data analysis was used in this research project please refer to sections 5.7.3-5.7.5.

conditions of positive intergroup contact theory. Where anticipated variances are not present, some discussion will take place in which possible explanations are offered for why such anticipated changes were not realised, or not realised to the extent that was anticipated, as per the research hypotheses.

Having arrived at some findings from the data a detailed analysis will allow for some conclusions in relation to intergroup contact theory moderators and mediators in the intercultural Bible reading engagement. This will allow us to gain some answers to research question three which seeks to ascertain to what extent changes in theological understandings of forgiveness among Christians of different races (Group A and Group B) were stimulated by the mediators and moderators of the intercultural Bible reading practices.

The next chapter (chapter 7) will present a consideration of the theological significance of this socio-theological analysis of the intercultural Bible reading process on forgiveness, conducted under the conditions of positive intergroup contact.

6.2 First research question

To what extent do theological understandings of forgiveness differ among Christians of different race groups?

In order to answer this question, it was necessary to analyse the data of the first two group meetings. Before the structured intercultural Bible reading meetings took place (recorded in datasets D4 and D5), the two homogenous communities met at separate times, in their home Churches (a safe and familiar environment), to engage in the process of reading Matthew 18.15-35. The dataset for the Church Street Methodist Church meeting is recorded in dataset D1. While the Coronation Avenue Methodist Church meeting is recorded in dataset D2. ATLAS.ti software was used, along with a set of theoretical codes (AQAL codes, cf., section 5.9.1) to manage and analyse the data. This process allowed for the identification of themes in the data, and also allowed the identified themes to be categorised for deeper analysis and discussion in relation to AQAL integral theory (discussed in chapter 2) and the thorough exegetical reading of Matthew 18.15-35 (discussed in chapter 4). The section that follows presents some of the more important findings from this aspect of the research process.

6.2.1 Group A: Church Street Methodist Church

6.2.1.1 *Demographic and narrative description of the meeting*

The first meeting took place with the identified participants from Church Street Methodist Church (P1, P3, P5, P7, P9, P12). There were six participants present, two female and four male. Since this meeting was intended to gather data from the participants on how they understood forgiveness within their homogenous and familiar surroundings and relationships, the meeting was held at their Church building. The setting was familiar to the participants, and all the participants knew each other well as members of the same church community. The participants and the researcher met seated around a large table to avoid hierarchal categorisation of importance. The structure of this meeting was the same as all the meetings that would follow. Here is an overview of the structuring of the meeting:

- The members were welcomed.
- They introduced themselves to one another.
- The researcher explained the process of this group meeting. Attention was given to explaining:
  - That they were nominated to participate in the process (ensuring an understanding that they were participating with the *sanction* of their Church authority).
  - That their perspectives and understandings of forgiveness and the text were important and contextually helpful and that we were interested in understanding the text together (this accentuated *equality* within the group and that they were participating towards a *common goal* and that they would need to *cooperate* with one another to achieve the goal).
  - That all participants were equal i.e., there were no 'expert readers' (this was important to ensure an understanding of equal status as Biblical readers and interpreters).
  - This meeting was explained in relation to the overall process (i.e., that the other group would have a similar meeting, then there would be two combined meetings in a neutral venue, and then each group would have a final separate meeting in their own church building at the end of the process). While the process was explained, the intentions behind the research processes were not explained to the participants in detail until after the research was completed.
- The Biblical text was handed out. At each meeting the researcher made printed copies of Matthew 18.15-35 available in the New Revised Standard Version (NRSV). This ensured that all participants were reading the same version of the Biblical text.
- The researcher explained the 'Dwelling in the Word' Bible reading process (see 5.7.3). The text was read aloud by the researcher. Participants were then given time read the text for themselves and note any aspects they wished to discuss.
- Once the text had been read and the participants had reflected on it personally they paired into groups of two. In these pairings, the participants shared what they had understood about forgiveness in reading the Biblical text. After sufficient time had passed the participants shared what they had read, understood, and discussed with the group. Where appropriate the researcher asked clarifying questions and moderated the discussion so that all of the members had a chance to participate in the open discussion.
- Once this discussion was complete the administrative and logistical arrangements for the next meeting were discussed and agreed upon, and the meeting was closed.

6.2.2.2 *Hypothesis*

Previous research on some of the characteristics of social identity and hermeneutic approaches to meaning making in the Biblical text of predominantly Black Christian groupings (c.f., 1.3.1-1.3.4, 5.3), suggests that the participants from this community would largely view their identity in a social manner (LL) (c.f., Forster, 2010b: 243–253, 2017: 1–10). In relation to this such persons, by virtue of a primarily social worldview, would understand forgiveness in a social and political manner. As such the hypothesis was that this group would understand forgiveness to have social requirements (LL and LR), such as the restoration of community harmony (LL), restitution for wrong caused, and the establishment (or re-establishment) of a just social, political and economic order (LR) (see sections 2.4.5 and 4.7, 4.8 for a discussion aspects of these views).

While the data largely concurs with this hypothesis, it also shows some variance. The extent to which participants had a shared social identity differed among participants, as did the extent to which they understood forgiveness to have social requirements or consequences. This was expected. The findings and an analysis of the findings follows.

6.2.3 Results: Group A

The data from the Church Street Methodist Church group meeting (D1) showed the following:

6.2.3.1 *The link between community harmony (intersubjective social identity) and forgiveness*

A total of 19 quotations where identified that indicated an aspect of intersubjective identity expression (1_AQAL_LL) that finds expression as a form of communal harmony. The study participants expressed that their identity was understood in social and communal forms such as a shared faith perspective (D1:12, 21, 24, 34 65, 85), or shared memory or history (D1:27, 65, 88). Snyman described this intersubjective meaning making as "shared background, contexts and worldviews" (Snyman, 2002: 96; c.f., Wilber, 2011b: 16–17). The data shows that to some extent this shared experience, and the expectation of forgiveness being dependent on community harmony, has been formed as a result of a shared experience of South Africa's apartheid history (D1:55, 87, 88). In particular, the participants expressed the notion that true forgiveness requires harmony (LL) between the members of the community or in-group and out-group communities. This was most often tied to hermeneutic interpretations of aspects of the narrative of Matthew 18.15-35.

Quotation	Analysis
D1:34 in verse 16 it says take another one or two with you errmm and she said you know this is what constitutes the church, the Bible says "wherever two or three are gathering in my name there I am in the midst of them". So when we do this, we take the other persons with us, **P1** was saying, Jesus is there to listen. <u>Suddenly it becomes church, when he's there...</u> that struck me you know. eeerrr <u>up until that point it's just two people in conflict.</u>	Shared identity in Christ creates a new reality and new possibilities for forgiveness and the resolution of conflict. When faith identity is shared, "Suddenly it becomes Church when he's there" (LL) the conflict between two individuals is transformed and new possibilities emerge, "until that point it's just two people in conflict".
D1:165 P1: And yet you know .... Errr <u>forgiveness is so important</u> because [silent] when you take the sacraments you take the blood, the body and blood of Christ, and he says <u>before you can do that, go on and forgive your brother, before you can drink my blood and eat my body. Go and forgive your brother...</u> so if we are going to take sacraments <u>and there is unforgiveness here...[silent] its bouncing back, it's not reaching Him.</u> Mmmm It is just bouncing back all the time, because you're going to the altar and receiving the blood and the the blood of Christ the the body and these... <u>my brother is sitting there still unforgiven but we change them, the sacraments</u> [coughing]	The shared faith perspective (LL) creates a necessity for forgiveness, "forgiveness is so important...". However, if one does not forgive, within the context of this shared faith experience (the sacrament of communion, and the "blood" and "body" of Christ), then the expression of faith is deemed to be less valid, or even changes the efficacy of the sacrament (LR). If there is unforgiveness one's prayer and faith is "bouncing back" and it means "we change them, the sacraments".

Quotation	Analysis
D1:170 So I think part of what this is saying is, it could have been what <u>Matthew was trying to say to the community is to make sure</u> as a community, that <u>you have the same heart, and identity as that of God.</u>	This understanding of forgiveness in the text is expressed clearly as a form of social harmony (LR, LL), "Matthew was trying to say to the community..." you have to have "the same heart, and identity as that of God".
D1:185 <u>I have forgiven totally, but is there is</u>... daar is nog [there still is] .... P3:...well it doesn't just disappear P3: <u>is there a worteltjie [a root] somewhere in the grounds</u> .... P3: ... that just proves and just shows you still that <u>you still recognize it as the evil it was,</u> because once you look at something like that, and you got no emotions that means...	In this quotation two community members were discussing the complexity of forgiving the sins of racism and the economic and social consequences of apartheid in light of the Biblical text (LR). The quote shows the complexity of aspiring for complete forgiveness, yet there is still a "worteltjie [a root]" of pain and brokenness (LL, LR). Harmony has not yet been restored, and the memory of wrongdoing still evokes an emotive response, "you still recognize it as the evil it was" (LR).

6.2.3.2 *The link between forgiveness and concrete social, economic or political action (LR)*

The data showed that this aspect was one of the strongest expressions of understandings of forgiveness in the pre-intercultural engagement Bible reading among participants in Group A. The necessity of social action (restitution, recompense, economic engagement, political change etc.) was identified as being expressed 49 times by the participants (1_AQAL_LR). This is presented as an inter-objective engagement in AQAL theory (Snyman, 2002: 96; c.f., Wilber, 2011b: 16–17).

The strongest expressions of this were in relation to the interpretation of the first section of the text (Matthew 18.15-20). The participants expressed the need to engage wrongdoers in a collective manner "Never go alone. [silent] talk to people, so that, as a group so that people will see the truth that will be reflected" (D1:20, cf., also D1:7, 9, 10, 19, 23).

Quotation	Analysis
D1:29 so that we <u>don't expose them,</u> don't <u>humiliate them or embarrassed them</u>	Once again, the intention of this engagement was to restore harmony with the offending party (LR), as one participant mentioned, that one should go with just one or two persons, in private so that you "don't expose them... humiliate or embarrassed [sic] them" (LL).

However, there was also a clear understanding that forgiveness is not only the restoration of psychological harmony (LL) but also setting right social, economic and structural wrongdoing (LR).

Quotation	Analysis
D1:53 How can I in the concept I am living in now, you know iiii in a month or two's time I will be sixty. How do I read this and be a good Christian <u>coming from a background, from apartheid and fff for the last twenty one years that I have been free.</u> I have come to the conclusion where I would say, you know because I hate it, in as much you know within me	In this quotation the participant was discussing their understanding of the mistake that the 'unforgiving servant' made (cf., Matthew 18.21-35). The discussion revolved around the issue that while political changes had meant the end of political apartheid in South Africa, this participant was turning 60 years old, yet still did not have true social and economic freedom (LR).

D1:162 But also I must admit and this is the question for you and the rest, many times when I look at certain things when I watch a movie when the reality of South Africa... There still comes something within me, did I forgive perfectly or am I fooling myself?

The complexity of the expectation for full forgiveness (UL, LL), and the reality that there has not yet been social, economic and political transformation that expresses social harmony (LR, LL), evoked this dissonant response from one participant, "did I forgive perfectly or am I fooling myself?" This discussion was in the context of Matthew 18.35 where there is a clear expectation of full forgiveness. For this participant, it is clearly a complex spiritual, social and political / economic matter (UL, LL, LR).

D1:163 But then they come again and they bring cold ice water and they throw it all over me, then I get revived, I feel new again to fight the battle again. When I get tortured again and get you know, so something comes and sits within me. Again I think, you know? Is this really over, do I really, did I really forgive because there comes a little bit of a pain within me as well?

This quotation is one of the clearest expressions of the complexity, and difficulty, of forgiving the 'other' who is seen as the source and cause of ongoing pain (in this context, it was discussed in relation to unlimited forgiveness (Matthew 18.21-22), and the unmerciful servant (v.31)). The participant expressed a re-emergence of pain and memory when he experiences ongoing social and economic inequality among Christians (LL). It is an experience of being "tortured again" that causes him to ask, "is this really over"? Behind his question is whether true forgiveness is possible while he continues to experience injustice (akin to v.31) (LR), or must he continue to forgive in spite of a lack of social, political and economic change (akin to vv.21-22) (UL, LL).

6.2.4 Variance from the hypothesis

As can be expected, there were some participants in this group who identified as not fully agreeing with, or making meaning in ways that differ from, the views discussed above. First, there was one participant in the group who held a view that differed from the general view of the group, namely, that forgiveness in Matthew 18.15-35 was an expression of communal harmony (LL) and could be achieved through social, political and economic engagement with the causes of social disharmony (LR). This participant viewed the problem primarily as related to individual sinfulness and "Spiritual bondage" (cf., D1:9) (i.e., being in bondage to evil spirits) which is an UL (individual, spiritual) understanding of forgiveness.

Quotation

D1:9 I: ...so will that be a sort of spiritual slavery...
P5: Spiritual slavery...
P9: ...Spiritual slavery really...
I: ...Spiritual bondage?...
P9:...Spiritual bondage and various activities and various things that enslaves in that...

Analysis

Participant P9 felt that the challenges that were faced in South Africa at present were as a result of "Spiritual slavery", and "Spiritual bondage". This places forgiveness within the realm of the individual and the spiritual (UL). The individual is enslaved spiritually, and the solution to this enslavement is to find spiritual freedom. The context within this discussion took place was the pericope on unlimited forgiveness (Matthew 18.21-22), and the unforgiving servant (translated as "slave" in some translations), (vv. 23-34).

Another participant held a view that differed from the general interpretation of the necessity for social, political, or economic transformation as a requisite for forgiveness (LR). This participant suggested that such activities are "not important". Rather since persons matter more than social conditions, and forgiveness is necessary (v.35), it must be given in spite of such social brokenness.

Quotation	Analysis
D1:26 Like the parable of the unforgiven servant... [silent]... sometimes we tend to look at what he did... I: mmmhmm P7: at what the person did, but we don't look at the person, because that what he did, is not important. The person is important, we must look through the eyes of mercy.	This participant was discussing an understanding of Matthew 18.32-33, 35. The participant emphasised that "mercy" is more important than justice or social expectation in relation to forgiveness. This is a display of individual spiritual (UL) or social spiritual (LL) primary theological categorization of forgiveness.
D1:173 So when you go into a house, this is the house, when you go you must bind up the strong man, so you bind the unforgiveness, the spirit of unforgiveness, in that person. So when you bind that spirit that strong man of unforgiveness, then you lose him from the consequences of unforgiveness.	Participant P9 expressed the notion that a spiritual action (UL) (biding "up the strong man") frees persons from the "consequences of unforgiveness".

The analysis of the data thus shows a great deal of theological complexity in relation to social identity complexity. The participants in the respective groups do tend to display understandings of forgiveness that are theological expressions of their social identity informants. Yet, at the same time, there are some subtle differences, and even questions, related to their views. We shall see in the sections that follow that this complexity increases with intercultural engagement.

6.2.5 Conclusions

The results of dataset D1 (Group A, pre-intercultural engagement reading of Matthew 18.15-35) shows evidence of two expected social and hermeneutic phenomena that were discussed in the hypotheses (cf., 1.3, 5.3). First, that there is a strong expression of the need for a shared experience of social harmony and shared identity as an expression of forgiveness (LL). This is an expectation that forgiveness, as expressed and understood in this text, requires that Christians should have "the same heart, and identity as that of God" among each other (D1:170). This characteristic, i.e., shared intersubjective identity, was most common among participants in this group.

The other identifiable characteristic was the expectation among the participants that forgiveness would have a social expression or requirements. Restored harmony between persons would be because of concrete engagement with the causes of hurt and harm (e.g., addressing racism, economic inequality, political abuse) (cf., D1:20, cf., also D1:7, 9, 10, 19, 23, 52, 162, 163).

Of the 6 participants, one participant differed from the general intersubjective hermeneutics of the group (LL) with strong social hermeneutics (LR). This participant viewed forgiveness primarily as an individual spiritual phenomena (UL) that freed the person from "Spiritual slavery" and "Spiritual bondage" (D1:9). Furthermore, this participant, and one other, differed with the group in the understanding that forgiveness required concrete social restoration (LR) and saw forgiveness as primarily a spiritual phenomenon (UL) (D1:140-143, 148, 173). These views, however, were a variance from the general views of the other participants in the group.

Thus, the predominantly Black Christian grouping understood forgiveness in Matthew 18.15-35 in a collective manner. Forgiveness is understood as an expression of the restoration of social harmony in the community (LL) with clear expectations of social, economic and political transformation (LR).

6.2.6 Group B: Coronation Ave Methodist Church

The data from the Coronation Ave Methodist Church group meeting (D2) showed the following:

6.2.6.1 *Demographic and narrative description of the meeting*

The second group meeting of the research process took place later on the same day as the meeting discussed in 6.2 above. This meeting was with the participants from the Coronation Ave Methodist Church (P2, P4, P6, P8, P10, P11) – Group B. There were six participants present in this meeting, four female and two male participants. Once again, the intention of this meeting was to gather data from the participants on how they understood forgiveness within their homogenous group identity (in-group), familiar surroundings and relationships. The meeting was held at their Church building. The setting was familiar to the participants, and all the participants knew each other well as members of the same church community. The participants and the researcher met seated around a large table to avoid hierarchal categorisation of importance. The structure of this meeting was largely the same as that discussed in 6.2, and set the pattern for all the meetings that would follow. I shall not repeat the entire description for each group meeting unless there is some variance, or a reason to explain a particular aspect of the meeting structure. However, since this was the first meeting of this group I will explain the structure and content of the meeting in similar detail to how it was presented in 6.2.

- The members were welcomed.
- They introduced themselves to one another.
- The researcher explained the process of this group meeting. Attention was given to explaining:
  - That they were nominated to participate in the process (ensuring an understanding that they were participating with the *sanction* of their Church authority).
  - That their perspectives and understandings of forgiveness and the text were important and contextually valid and that we were interested in understanding the text together (this accentuated *equality* within the group and that they were participating towards a *common goal* and that they would need to *cooperate* with one another to achieve the goal).
  - That all participants were equal i.e., there were no 'expert readers' (this was important to ensure an understanding of equal status as Biblical readers and interpreters). In this group, however, there were three participants who had participated in more in depth lay Bible study programs (the 'Disciple' course). However, the intention of the course was thematic insight into

the Biblical text, rather than the development of technical skills for critical academic Biblical scholarship[122].

    □   This meeting was explained in relation to the overall process (i.e., that the other group had already met in a similar meeting. It was explained that there would be two combined meetings in a neutral venue in the next two weeks, and then each group would have a final separate meeting in their own church building at the end of the process).

- The Biblical text was handed out. At each meeting the researcher made copies of Matthew 18.15-35 available in the New Revised Standard Version. This ensured that all participants were reading the same version of the Biblical text.

- The researcher explained the 'Dwelling in the Word' Bible reading process (see 5.7.3). The text was read out loud by the researcher. Participants were then given time read the text for themselves and note any aspects they wished to discuss.

- Once the text had been read, and the participants had reflected on it personally, they paired into groups of two. In these pairings, the participants shared what they had understood about forgiveness in reading the Biblical text. After sufficient time had passed the participants shared what they had read, understood, and discussed with the group. Where appropriate the researcher asked clarifying questions and moderated the discussion so that all of the members had a chance to participate in the open discussion.

Once this discussion was complete the administrative and logistical arrangements for the next meeting were discussed and agreed upon, and the meeting was closed.

6.2.6.2 *Hypothesis*

As discussed in section 1.3 and 5.3 it was hypothesised that identity in this group would be predominantly individual (UL), while the hermeneutic approach to forgiveness would be largely spiritual in nature (UL, LL) (c.f., Forster, 2010b: 243–253, 2017: 1–10). If there was any expectation of action in relation to forgiveness it would largely be individual action (UR), rather than social, economic or political transformation (LR) (Gibson & Gouws, 2000: 278–292; Walker, 2005: 41–54; Swartz, 2006: 551–570; Forster, 2010b: 243–253; Bowers du Toit & Nkomo, 2014: 1–8; le Roux, 2014: 1–16; Williams & Stroud, 2014: 277–293).

In summary, it was expected that this group would largely view forgiveness as a spiritual phenomenon (UL) with very little understanding, or expectation, for social, economic or political engagement to enact or facilitate the process of forgiveness (LR). In this instance the dataset D2 concurs with some aspects of the hypothesis, while it displays different findings in relation to others. These findings will be discussed and analysed in the section below. The intention, at the end of this section, is to be able to account, to some measure at least, for the manner in which the participants in this group understood forgiveness in relation to their reading of Matthew 18.15-35 from within their social and theological context.

---

122 For more information on the *Disciple* Bible reading course please see (Wilke & Wilke, 2003) – the course is described as "Thirty-four lessons on biblical themes from the Old and New Testaments."

6.2.7 Results: Group B

The data that was collected from the pre-intercultural engagement group meeting with the participants from Coronation Ave Methodist Church (D2) will be presented below.

6.2.7.1 *Forgiveness as an individual spiritual concern (UL)*

The data showed that most of the participants in this group understood forgiveness as primarily a matter of being restored in relationship to God (D2:14, 15, 20, 33, 36, 43). The purpose of forgiveness was to restore one's relationship with God, which may have been damaged by sinning against another person. This suggests that they saw forgiveness as primarily a spiritual matter (restoration of spiritual harmony between the individual and God, UL) rather than a social matter in which social harmony is restored in the community or society (LR).

Quotation	Analysis
D2:14 Ja for me [silent] the reason why I said that, that was the most important for me because, for me the toughest part of this whole Bible reading was probably the last four, five lines where it says ermm ermm especially where it says "so our err heavenly father will also do to every one of you if you not forgive your brother or sister from your heart", so [silent] for me God will not turn you away, if you truly repentant and ask for forgiveness for you sins, so and the example that I use, let's say now I'm an alcoholic and I klap [hit] my wife every night and err bad to the kids, kick the dog and every night I say to God "hey God I'm sorry" but the next day I carry on. God will turn his face away from you and that's the part that I understand. He'll cut you off, and that's the decision that you make. But the day that I sit and I say "you know what God I'm really serious about this now", and he knows your heart, and he knows you're being truly repentant, truly want to turn a 180 [degrees] on what you've doing wrong, that's when this debt, for me, where they say they were tortured until there entire debt is paid.[silent] For me that's when your debt is paid. When you truly repented an and and God can see you know what, this guy truly wants to turn around and that's for me, when the forgiveness kicks in. So for me, the thing that almost negates, or softens this thing for me, is the forgiveness part and that's all I been focusing on for a last week. Is, it doesn't matter what I do or anybody else does.	First, this quotation illustrated the principle that the participants largely understood forgiveness as a spiritual process that is intended to restore spiritual harmony between the sinner and God (UL). This discussion was in the context of first pericope of the text (Matthew 18.15-20). The 'sinned against' (i.e., the object or subject of the wrongdoing) did not feature at all in the process of forgiveness. The focus was placed on the relationship between the individual sinner and God. Note the illustrative example about spousal abuse. The "debt" is allocated in reference to God, not the injured spouse. The pre-requisite for forgiveness is being "truly repentant", which is described as God knowing your "heart" (interior resolve (UL) as opposed to exterior action (UR, LR)). The conclusion of the quote summarises this view of forgiveness "it doesn't matter what I do or anybody else does".
D2:15 … be careful that we don't judge others… because it is not for us to judge. God is the judge, so we shouldn't be judging others because they will probably judge us back	The statement in this quote is framed in relation to Matthew 18.31. The participant is expressing a conviction that "… it is not for us to judge. God is the judge" of sin, and that "we shouldn't be judging others". This interpretation shows a theological conviction that sin, and judgement of sin, are purely spiritual matters (UL, LL). The judging of what is right or wrong is between the individual and God (UL) and is not a matter of social agreement (LL) or individual or social action (UR, LR).

Quotation	Analysis
D2:47 P2: ... I think for me, thinking about the country, a lot of what happened in the country, I lived in Somerset West all my life I: Yes P2:... Which <u>nothing happened in Somerset West way back then</u> you can imagine, <u>it didn't affect my life</u>... I: Yes P2:... so <u>how could I, forgive something that I personally didn't do?</u>	One of the clearest expressions of a separation between faith life (UL) and social life (LR) is expressed in this quote. The participant explains that he/she was not 'involved' in apartheid and so could not forgive "something that I personally didn't do", "it [apartheid] didn't affect my life". What it shows is that the understanding of culpability for sin, and the expectation of forgiveness, is directed towards God and is viewed in individual terms ("my life") (UL). Even though the consequences of apartheid are evident in society, because the participant does not feel he/she has wronged God there is nothing for which forgiveness needs to be given or sought. This discussion took place within the context of Matthew 18.21-22, and 35.

The quotes extracted and referenced in this section show that in large measure the participants in this group interpreted the Biblical text in a manner that views forgiveness as an individual phenomenon that operates between the person seeking forgiveness and God (UL). Forgiveness is thus a spiritual 'transaction' in which the debt incurred as a result of wrongdoing is cancelled by God (UL). Forgiveness does not involve other persons, or the consequences of sin (LR). It is thus largely understood as an individual spiritual phenomenon.

6.2.7.2 *Forgiveness as a social (LR) spiritual concern (LL)*

Some participants in this group displayed a tendency to separate their faith life and faith convictions (LL) from the rest of their lives (UR, LR) (c.f., D2:16, 22, 23). The consequence of this is that forgiveness is seen as a purely spiritual phenomenon that does not have any bearing on economic, politics or social concerns – such views can be likened to what the Kairos South Africa document termed 'Church theology'[123]. This hermeneutic approach was common among White South Africans during the apartheid era, and seems to have remained a characteristic within the contemporary Bible reading community.

Quotation	Analysis
D2:16 also what I had that **P2** also brought up is you know <u>is this passage meant only for people in the church?</u> So... so what **P2** was saying was <u>what what kind of advice would God then give, saying that what kind of advice God then give or what kind of counsel will you gives to somebody that's done something wrong outside the church?</u>	This quotation shows that the participants interpreted Matthew 18.15-20 as only having authority for "people in the church" (UL and LL). The expressed assumption is persons whose actions are not faith related (or related to the life or community of the church), i.e., "outside the church" would require different "counsel" and "advice".

123 The Kairos document, penned in 1985 at the height of South Africa's apartheid abuses, identified three types of dominant theologies that operated at that time: A state theology that sought to uphold and support the ideology of the state through the church and belief systems of South African Christians. Next Kairos described a church theology that either sought a middle, "third way" of compromise without justice (i.e., placing peace above justice), or was completely disengaged from what was taking place in society and the political realm (Kairos Theologians, 1985: 15–17; De Gruchy in, Forrester, Storrar & Morton, 2004: 51; Huber & Fourie, 2012: 110–114; Boesak, 2015: 15).

However, there were several participants in the group whose perspective varied from the general hermeneutic characteristics of the group. These persons had a clear understanding that faith conviction and everyday life need to be aligned for forgiveness to be real and possible (cf., D2:24, 31, 41). This is discussed under the heading that follows.

Quotation	Analysis
D2:31 well that first received the mercy and yet he didn't extend it. And he he didn't follow through on it. He was he was given a huge amount of mercy and yet he couldn't follow throw on it. <u>So we sort of think that he actually internalized what had actually been, what had been the grace that has been given to him, and he hadn't really understood it</u>. He just sort of felt, <u>OK move on now and get back to my normal way of behaving</u> and that was not very merciful [silent] and that's the point.	Here a participant clearly shows unless there is consistency between belief (LL) and a transformed social situation expressed in action or a changed life (LR), then he hadn't "understood" forgiveness. Rather, he had "internalized" it and gone back to a "normal way of behaving". These statements were made in relation to the unforgiving servant who had received much, yet was not willing to show mercy (Matthew 18.23-34).

6.2.8 Unexpected results

As with the previous group, there were also persons, and instances, of variance from the general hypothesis. The hypothesis was that the members of this group (Group B) would largely see forgiveness in individual spiritual terms (UL and LL). The previous sections show that this is largely true. However, there was one participant who viewed forgiveness differently from the other general views of the group participants. This participant had worked in a predominantly Black educational setting (D2:48, 49). This could account for the self-awareness of race, and the recognition of the pain of others.

Quotation	Analysis
D2:46 P4: …Well, can I just say, I mean Peter Storey [a prominent Methodist Bishop and social activist] talks about the <u>corrosive effect of White power and I, so I really do relate to that</u>.	This participant engaged one of the other participants about the hermeneutic perspective from which the participant was interpreting the text in an individual, spiritual manner (UL) – the section in question was Matthew 18.21-22, 23-35. The participant highlighted the hermeneutic influence of whiteness as "White power" in misinterpreting the text.
D2:50 P4: … and therefore we need to, we need to take cognisance of that and we need to sort of almost … write that into the way that we behave, <u>we can't just say that if they don't come to us, you know, therefore, it is not our problem</u>… P10: …its not what I said … P4: I know, I know, I agree with you, I'm say we need to maybe it take it to a different level to say, '<u>we recognise their pain and that hurt and then… our response needs to be different</u>. I I agree you didn't say that fortunately …	Here the participant makes the clear point that a social response is necessary to deal with the consequences of apartheid. Forgiveness is not possible as long as White Christians say "it is not our problem". Rather they should "recognise their pain" (LL) and then their "response needs to be different" (LR).

6.2.9 Conclusions

An analysis of the data from the Coronation Ave, pre-intercultural engagement reading of Matthew 18.15-35 (D2) shows some support for the expected social and hermeneutic phenomena that were discussed in the hypotheses (see 1.3 and 5.3). In particular, the data shows that this group largely interpreted forgiveness in the text in relation to their own world view and experience (D2:47 and D2:50 as two clear, yet very different examples of this phenomenon).

The majority of the group tended to understand forgiveness as an individual spiritual phenomenon that was enacted between the sinning party and God (cf., D2:14, 15, 20, 33, 36, 43). Thus, they found it difficult to identify with the pain and struggle of others (the persons sinned against) as a condition for forgiveness (LL, LR cf., D2:47). A second aspect of the hypothesis that was confirmed in the data is that members of this group largely separated their faith life from South Africa's social, economic and political reality (c.f., D2:16, 22, 23). This tended to further 'spiritualise' forgiveness. It made it difficult for the participants to empathise with the pain and concern of South African's who had suffered, and continue to suffer, the consequences of apartheid.

However, there was some variance from the hypothesis (cf., D2:46, 48, 49, 50). This participant was cognisant of both White identity and the hermeneutic influence of such identity on interpreting the text. He encouraged the other participants to develop a measure of cognitive and affective empathy in relation to persons who may have suffered under apartheid (D2:50).

In conclusion, the data from this group meeting confirms that this Christian group largely understood forgiveness in spiritual and individual terms without much understanding of the social, economic and political expectations around forgiveness.

6.3 Second research question

The second aim of this study was to gain an understanding of the extent to which theological understandings of forgiveness among Christians of different race groups changed in a more integrative manner after an intercultural bible reading of Matthew 18.15-35.

To facilitate this research process, it was necessary to conduct pre-intercultural engagement group meetings with each group on their own (represented in datasets D1 and D2). Then at the end of the process, after the intervention had taken place, it was necessary to once again have separate group meetings with each of the groups (represented in datasets D5 and D6). Please refer to 5.8 for a detailed discussion of the design of analysis.

Next, we shall engage the data from datasets D5 and D6, which accounts for the post-intercultural engagement understandings of forgiveness in the separate homogenous groups (Group A and Group B). In addition, the pre-intercultural engagement and post-intercultural engagement datasets (D1 and D6; D2 and D5) will be compared to one another to ascertain what may have changed in the participants' understandings of forgiveness, and what may possibly account for such change.

6.3.1 Group A: Church Street Methodist Church

We now move on to a presentation of aspects of the post-intercultural engagement data from Church Street Methodist Church (Group A, dataset D6).

The participants in this group meeting were the same as those recorded in dataset D1. Thus, it is not necessary to repeat the demographic and social description of the group again – please refer to 5.7.3 and 6.2.1 for this information.

6.3.1.1 *Narrative of the meeting*

The intention of this meeting was to gather the participants from Group A in a context that could be described as an 'in-group' setting. This meant that the meeting took place in their Church building, only the participant members from their Church grouping and the interviewer / researcher were present. The participants sat around a large table so that all of the members could see one another and there was no hierarchical difference among the participants. The structure of the meeting was largely the same as the previous meetings (see 6.2.1) with two exceptions. First, the interviewer used a small portion of time at the end of the meeting to express his thanks to the participants for their involvement in the process. As part of this wrap up he also explained the process that would follow the conclusion of the meeting which would involve the validating of the transcriptions, the analysis of the data, and writing it up in this manuscript. Second, the interviewer introduced two questions about the intercultural Bible reading process at the start of the meeting: A) could the participants identify any differences in their understandings of forgiveness in relation to Matthew 18.15-35 as a result of the process (cf., D6:73)? B) Could they identify any specific moment, event, or action that helped to facilitate this change (cf., D6:72, 74)? The first question relates to integral hermeneutics, and possible shifts in theological understandings of forgiveness. The second question sought to probe the value of the intercultural Bible reading process conducted under the conditions of positive intergroup contact.

6.3.1.2 *Hypothesis*

In sections 1.3 and 5.3 of this study it was proposed that positive intergroup contact between the two groups of participants would bring about changes in the way in which the in-group understood forgiveness when reading Matthew 18.15-35 together. This is premised on Allport's contact hypothesis. Allport et.al. propose that positive intergroup contact reduces prejudice of the 'other' by decreasing contact anxiety and increasing affective and cognitive empathy (cf., Allport, 1954; Swart, Turner, *et al.*, 2011; Swart & Hewstone, 2012). The theoretical underpinnings of this hypothesis were discussed at length in 3.1 and 3.2. In the context of positive intergroup contact it is suggested that the participants of the in-group will be more willing, and more capable, of considering alternative or even conflicting understandings of forgiveness that are held by the out-group (cf., the discussion in 3.3.3). The dataset was studied to see if the dominant hermeneutic and social identity characteristics were changed in a more integrated manner after the intercultural Bible reading intervention from the perspective of intergroup contact theory. In particular, are there any identifiable shifts between the characteristics identified in dataset D1 where the participants' understandings of forgiveness were largely characterised as social (LL) and political (LR) and D6 (where the hypothesis would suggest some awakening to the individual and spiritual aspects of forgiveness, (UL) should be evidenced)?

6.3.2 Results: Group A

The dataset D6 (Group A, Church Street Methodist Church, Post-intercultural engagement group reading) rendered the following results. The participants indicated directly (e.g., D6:1) and indirectly (e.g., D6:5) that their understandings of forgiveness had been challenged and changed as a result of the intercultural

Bible reading process. The result is thus that there is evidence of a broadening understanding of forgiveness (i.e., a more integral understanding) within this group.

6.3.2.1 *A broadening of understandings of forgiveness – shared views (LL).*

First, there are clear indications in the data that participant perspectives had been broadened to include views they had not previously held, or had in common with the 'out-group' (6_AQAL_UL – 35 quotations, which are discussed in the section that follows this one). These notions were largely reflected in collective interior (intersubjective) understandings and approaches to making meaning (6_AQAL_LL – 18 quotations). Simply stated, the data shows that in large measure this group had adopted views common to the 'out-group' (UL), and thus had a new shared identity, or integral, understanding of forgiveness between the in-group and out-group readings (LL).

Quotation	Analysis
D6:1 Uhm, <u>did your understanding of forgiveness change in any way err as a part of this process</u> and and if it did, err can you maybe give us an idea of how it changed, from this to to that. Anybody... **P7:** I always, I always found it very hard to forgive... **I:** Ja **P7:** But, <u>while I was reading with others here and the other group errr my... a lot of my concepts about forgiveness changed</u>.	Participant P7 expressed clearly that the process of reading the text in the intercultural Bible reading process had changed her / his views of understandings of forgiveness in relation to Matthew 18.15-35, "while I was reading with others... a lot of my concepts of forgiveness changed".
D6:4 I: What, give me a little... <u>can you express what might've changed, what was it that made that change, what helped the change happen?</u> **P7:** Because <u>you found others also thinking in the same way</u> that you thought, that you were thinking and others also seeing that that we we mustn't be apart, we must be one. <u>We call ourselves the Methodist people</u>.	The participant accounted for the change in understanding of forgiveness in two ways. First, the participant indicated that a measure of cognitive empathy had taken place, "you found others also thinking the same way" (UL). However, there is also an expression that the change took place as a result of a shared faith identity (LL), "we must be one", and "We call ourselves the Methodist people" (LL). This participant was discussing these shifts in relation to the expectation for community harmony in Matthew 18.15-19, 35.
D6:46 P1: Ja, for me the group reading process was very informative, um, and and <u>it was good, because I saw, I saw, uh how people see things differently to me</u> **I:** mmm **P1:** and you know, <u>it's differently, but it is one if you know what I mean</u> mmm **P9:** mmm **P1:** and and and, it was, it... it was a learning process for me, <u>because I learnt what the next person had to had to say, and I hope they learnt what I had to say as well</u>	This participant expressed the notion of intersubjective change very clearly as a result of the intercultural Bible reading process (LL). The participant expresses that the process "was good" because he/she discovered that other persons "see things differently", but also that there are some points of shared experience and interpretation, "but it is one if you know what I mean". The exchange of ideas within the shared experience was valuable and meaningful. Of particular importance in this quote is that this person felt that they had contributed to the 'other', "I hope they learnt what I had to say as well".

The group largely concurred on this particular point. Their views were enriched, and even changed, because of the opportunity of reading the text in group with a variety of experiences from different identities and contexts. Participant P9 said the following, "so therefore, you know, when you get different people, reading it from a perspective it gives a different meaning around the table" (D6:57). This is quite remarkable in light of the earlier reflection on this participant and their views. It is clear from the selected data above that the participants in this group developed more integral understandings of forgiveness as will be shown below.

6.3.2.2 *A broadening towards individual-spiritual understandings of forgiveness (UL)*

One of the more important aspects of the hypothesis is that the participants from this group, who largely understood forgiveness in collective (LL) and social terms (LR) (cf., the discussion of dataset D1 in 6.2), would develop a fuller understanding of forgiveness in the individual-spiritual category (UL). There was clear evidence in the direct admissions of the participants, and in their theological expressions, that such a development had taken place.

Quotation	Analysis
D6:11 P9: Ja, mine is plain and simple. What I've learned… the more and more I was reading reading through this and on the conversation, it doesn't matter how great your sins or hatred are, if you seek sincere and honest forgiveness, it will be granted	Previously participant P9 had expressed a clear understanding that forgiveness had clear social requirements – communal harmony need to be restored in practical and pragmatic ways (such as the confrontation of sinful or destructive behaviour) before forgiveness could be realised (LR) (cf., D1:6). However, at this stage the participant spiritualises forgiveness by making some allowance for the fact it can be separated from "how great your sins or hatred are". The participant indicates that "if you seek sincere and honest forgiveness, it will be granted" (UL). This comment was in relation to a discussion of Matthew 18.15-19, 20-22, 35.
D6:12 P9: In, in our discussion too you know, and this is basically you know, forgiveness, forgiveness comes from God	This quotation comes from a discussion about the conditions that would be necessary for forgiveness, Matthew 18.20-22, 23-35 (LR) (cf., D6:13). However, the participant prefaces the discussion by saying the only person (or place) from which forgiveness can ultimately come is "from God" (UL). At the end of the narrative the participant said "If I keep on rejecting your forgiveness, I'm not free" (D6:21).
D6:22 I: There's one thing here that strikes me, um **P9** in what I heard from you, is to say that there is a, I'm hearing you saying that there is a connection between, um, this [pause] spiritual [pause] imperative, you, you know we have to forgive, this is, this is, we, we won't be free the other person won't be free **P9:** we won't be free	The researcher sought to clarify that the participant was now expressing his understanding of forgiveness as including a clear individual spiritual element (UL), "spiritual… imperative". The participant responded in the affirmative, "we won't be free". This was a new interpretation of Matthew 18.19-20 from this participant.

D6:36 P1: <u>I can't do this on my own, but I can do it with Christian help, you've got to ask the Lord to strengthen you, to be able to perhaps forgive that person,</u> you can't in your own strength you can't	This participant expressed the understanding that true forgiveness is a matter of a shared belief and value system (LL), "I can't do this on my own, but I can do it with Christian help" (cf., vv.16-17, 19-20). However, the participant went further to say that it also requires personal belief and the help of God (UL), "you've got to ask the Lord to strengthen you".
D6:41 P1: <u>First have the love of God and then I forgive you</u> [**group collective:** mmmm (<u>agreement</u>)]	In a later quotation, the participant expressed it simply as, "First have the love of God and then I forgive you". To which the whole group agrees. This is a significant shift in understanding forgiveness in individual spiritual terms for this participant.

In total there were 35 quotations under the code 6_AQAL_UL which expressed a clear and significant shift in understanding the importance of an individual-spiritual understanding of forgiveness. In the discussion of the third research question we shall draw some links between these shifts of understanding in forgiveness and introduction of practices and mechanisms related to positive intergroup contact theory.

6.3.3 Unexpected results

The analysis shows that there were at least two anticipated shifts in relation to the hypothesis discussed in 1.3 and 5.3. First, there had been a shift from a narrow in-group (LL) understanding of forgiveness, to include the out-group within the shared, and broader, understanding of forgiveness (cf., D6:1, 4, 46, 57). Second, there had been a growth in the understanding of the necessity of an individual-spiritual understanding of forgiveness – which was not a characteristic of this group's general hermeneutic approach in the pre-intercultural engagement group reading (cf., section 6.2.5). The individual-spiritual understanding of forgiveness (UL), (which was predominantly a Group B perspective in dataset D2, cf., 6.2.9), was much more widely expressed as an acceptable and important understanding of forgiveness in relation to Matthew 18.15-35 (cf., D6:11, 12, 26, 56).

However, there is also at least one instance of variance from the hypothesis. In this instance, it was that a participant did not hold the predominant view of forgiveness that was more characteristic with their in-group, Group A (i.e., LR and LL understandings of forgiveness as social harmony that is facilitated through pragmatic engagement with personal or structural sin). This participant did not need to undergo a shift in order to be open to the individual-spiritual view of forgiveness (UL) that was largely characteristic of Group B. The variance was that this participant expressed a strong affinity for an individual-spiritual view of forgiveness in the pre-intercultural engagement group meeting (cf., D1:2, 3, 4, 8) and this view was maintained as a dominant perspective throughout the intercultural Bible reading process. It is possible that since this person has their primary identity within the social, political and economic context of Group A, there was no significant challenging of the hermeneutic perspective in the encounter with the 'other' in Group B, since they largely shared the individual-spiritual perspective of forgiveness to begin with.

6.3.4 Coronation Ave Methodist Church

This section will present some pertinent of aspects of the post-intercultural engagement data from Coronation Ave Methodist Church (Group B, dataset D5).

At this group meeting the same participants were present as in dataset D2. Thus, it is not necessary to repeat the demographic and social description of the group again – please refer to 6.2 for this information.

6.3.4.1 *Narrative of the meeting*

As with Group A, reported in the previous section, the intention of this meeting was to gather the participants from this group (Group B) in a context that could be considered an 'in-group' setting. In other words, the persons who participated in this group were all of the members of Coronation Ave Methodist Church who were nominated and identified for participation in this process by their Church and minister. We met at the Coronation Ave Methodist Church in surroundings that were familiar to the group participants. The meeting took place around a large table so that all of the participants could see one another. This also meant that all of the participants had equal status around the table. The meeting was structured in largely the same manner as all of the previous meetings, so I shall not repeat all of those details here (cf., 6.2.1). However, there were two additions in this meeting. First, the interviewer / researcher used a small portion of the meeting time at the end of the process to express thanks to the participants for their involvement in the research project. The steps that would follow this last meeting were also outlined and questions were answered. The participants were informed that after this meeting the recordings of all of the meetings would be transcribed, made anonymous, validated by a sampling of the participants, the data would be analysed and the findings would be written up in this manuscript. Second, the interviewer introduced two questions that were not present in the earlier meetings: A) were the participants able to identify any differences in their understandings of forgiveness in relation to Matthew 18.15-35 as a result of the process (cf., D5:51)? B) Could they identify any specific moment, event, or action that helped to facilitate this change (cf., D5:52)? As previously stated, the first question sought to probe changes in theological understandings of forgiveness in Matthew 18.15-35 after the completion of the intercultural Bible reading process. The second question sought to establish whether the intervention had any value for the participants' growth in understandings of forgiveness in reading this text with one another.

6.3.4.2 *Hypothesis*

As indicated above, the intention in this section of the study was to ascertain to what extent, or not, the hypothesis about Group B's participants in this process would be found plausible (cf., 1.3 and 5.3). In summary, it was suggested that in light of positive intergroup contact theory (cf., chapter 3) that the intercultural Bible reading process, facilitated under the conditions of positive intergroup contact, would lessen contact anxiety between the participants of Group B and Group A (cf., Allport, 1954; Swart, Turner, *et al.*, 2011; Swart & Hewstone, 2012). Together with this, it was suggested that positive intergroup contact would facilitate the reduction of prejudice of the 'out group' by increasing affective and cognitive empathy (discussed in detail in 3.1 and 3.2). As a result there should be some evidence in the data of a shift in theological understanding from the dominant perspectives of the participants identified in dataset D2 (cf., 6.2.9). In the pre-intercultural engagement group meeting (recorded in dataset D2) the participants in this group largely understood forgiveness in the reading of Matthew 18.15-35 in individual-spiritual terms (UL) (cf., D2:14, 15, 20, 33, 36, 43), without much affinity for the social, economic and political expectations around forgiveness (LR and LL) (c.f., D2:16, 22, 23). The latter expectations were largely characteristic of the pre-intercultural engagement perspectives of Group A. Hence this dataset was worked with to establish what the dominant hermeneutic and social identity characteristics were among participants in Group B after the intercultural Bible reading intervention from the perspective of AQAL integral theory. Moreover, the intention was to ascertain if there were any identifiable shift between the characteristics identified in dataset D2 (where predominantly individual and spiritual understandings of forgiveness (UL) were evidenced) and D5 (where it is hoped that evidence of more social (LL) and political (LR) understandings will be evidenced)?

6.3.5 Results: Group B

We shall now look at the findings in dataset D5 (Group B, Coronation Ave Methodist Church, Post-intercultural engagement group reading). Once again, as with the discussion of dataset D6, this group once again report directly (cf., D5:11), and indirectly (cf., D5:4), that they had experienced changes in their understandings of forgiveness.

6.3.5.1 *A broadening towards shared understandings of forgiveness (LL)*

One of the aspects in the data that confirms that there has been a change in the participants of Group B's understanding of forgiveness after the intervention has taken place, is that certain participants made clear concessions that they had developed new shared expressions of intersubjective meaning (LL) with Group A. In the section that follows this one we shall examine the nature of these new shared perspectives of forgiveness (which will be shown to be social and political (LR) perspectives, which are more common to Group A).

Quotation	Analysis
D5:19 If I was Coloured or Black now and I experienced the apartheid regime, would I have been as humble or as forgiving as what these people are so, cos often we sit here in this church, and we think those guys are thinking so bad of us low of us, or whatever, but it was a revelation to me that it's not actually like that. That they actually very humble and, and you know, how would I be?	This participant's self-identity was challenged through the process of intercultural Bible reading. The participant begins with a statement of affective empathy "If I was Coloured or Black now...". Within this frame of reference the participant asks, "would I have been as humble or forgiving"? This realisation shows that there has been a shift in personal identity (UL) that has been altered to incorporate a larger form of shared identity (LL) that allows for the questioning of current beliefs and values, "it was a revelation to me that it's not actually like that". Moreover, this question shows that the individual has come to understand the theological necessity of some form of social transformation as a condition for forgiveness (this is particularly in the context of the discussion of the unforgiving servant (vv.23-34)).

D5:4 P6: and… <u>trying to really recognise the other person's hurt</u>… and trauma maybe, in the, in the situation. Cos so often, <u>it's so easy to see it from your own point of view and not from the others point of view. That just brought that home to me again.</u>	This participant expressed both a change in cognitive empathy "it's so easy to see it from your own point of view and not from the others point of view", and affective empathy "trying to really recognise the other person's hurt", that shifted his/her understanding of forgiveness as a result of the intercultural Bible reading encounter (LL and LR).
D5:7 P4: and it is, its… in a contemporary context, I've… <u>the question I've asked, are we the unforgiving servants… White South Africans perhaps…</u>	The process of reading the Biblical text also elicited new hermeneutic possibilities within the participants. This comment was made in relation to the reading of Matthew 18.32. The participant asks whether the in-group (Group B) are not inadvertently "unforgiving servants", who have received much, but done little in return (LR).
D5:27 P11: So, I think, <u>the strongest thing for me was change and transformation,</u> forgiveness isn't just, isn't just a process of forgiving, <u>it's forgiving and changing to, to stop it happening again</u>	In this quotation one of the other participants expressed a similar notion. The participant recognises that there is a need to be transformed and changed ("change and transformation" of the self) (LL) for forgiveness to be achieved, or at least embarked upon. This portion of the discussion was particularly in light of the reading of vv.30-31.

There was a consensus of data from this group meeting, that the intercultural Bible reading process had helped the participants to widen their understanding of forgiveness by taking on the experiences and ideas of participants from Group A (cf., D5:1, 2, 4, 6, 7, 12, 19, 21,27). This broadening of shared belief and identity challenged some entrenched or strongly held ideas of certain participants in Group B (cf., D5:7, 27). In some instances the new experience and insight (affective and cognitive empathy) led to the development of new understandings of forgiveness and the requirements for forgiveness (cf., D5:4, 19). In relation to the findings of dataset D2, it was suggested that this group had initially struggled to connect faith and life in relation to forgiveness and South Africa's social, political and economic context (cf., D2:16, 22, 23). The findings above show that there has been an awakening to the non-dual nature of faith and life (cf., D5:7, 27). It can thus be concluded that this aspect of the hypothesis was plausible in these instances – participants from Group B had broadened their social identity and hermeneutic perspectives (LL) to include perspectives on forgiveness that were more characteristic of Group A in dataset D1.

6.3.5.2 *Developing an understanding of the social, economic and political understandings of forgiveness (LR)*

As was pointed out in the conclusion of the discussion of dataset D2, Group B largely viewed forgiveness in individual-spiritual terms as taking place between the party who had sinned and God (cf., D2:14, 15, 20, 33, 36, 43) (UL). It was shown that these participants generally did not have a strong or developed understanding of the social, political, or economic expectations of forgiveness (cf., D2:47). Their tendency to individualise and spiritualise forgiveness made it difficult for them to recognise, and address, the suffering and pain of those who were (and remain) disadvantaged because of apartheid. This was a significant stumbling block to forgiveness.

However, an analysis of dataset D5 shows that participants in Group B had broadened their understandings of forgiveness (which were predominantly UL in D2) to include aspects of the social, economic and political (LR) as a result of the intercultural Bible reading process. Two powerful examples of this where presented in the previous section where quotations D5:4 and D5:7 were discussed. In those instances, the participants engaged complex social issues such as whiteness and it's political and economic effects in South Africa. They also addressed the needs to lead to both personal change in racial and social attitudes (cf., D5:16) and structural change (cf., D5:27). In the quotations and analysis below we shall consider some specific examples of what changes took place in the participants' understandings of forgiveness as a social, economic and political phenomenon, in relation to their post-intercultural engagement reading of Matthew 18.15-35.

Quotation	Analysis
D5:11 and the first one was, um, <u>If a person does not acknowledge his or her fault, then he or she cannot receive forgiveness</u>	This quotation is an extension of the discussion captured in D5:7 in which the participant questioned whether "White South Africans" are not possibly the "unforgiving servants" mentioned in Matthew 18.32. The participant makes the point in this quotation: "If a person does not acknowledge his or her fault, then he or she cannot receive forgiveness". This is a significant shift towards a recognition of social culpability in relation to forgiveness (LR). Since the context within which the acknowledgement is placed is race relationships (cf., D5:7) rather than merely a relationship with God (as was expressed in D2:14, 15, 20, 33, 36, 43). Hence, one is able to witness a shift from an individual spiritual understanding of forgiveness (UL) to a social and political understanding of the process and consequences of forgiveness (LR).
D5:15 And then, the, the next point, is <u>when we receive forgiveness there should be a transformation</u> I: mmm P8: And for me that was also a revelation, because often, you know like, people use the word love cheaply, <u>you know forgiveness is also used just as cheaply</u>, now, if you forgive somebody, um, then then, <u>there should be transformation in your life and their life</u>, it shouldn't be that forgiveness is a curb, but <u>there's not change now</u>…	The participant goes on to explain the content of the acknowledgement, and here it becomes clear that the requirement for forgiveness is not only repentance to God (UL), but "transformation" that is not "cheap", but that transforms "your life and their life" (LR) (cf., Matthew 18.24-25). The emphasis on the cost of transformation is significant. It shows that the participant had grappled with the pragmatic requirements, and consequences, of forgiveness in the presence of a wounded or "angered" other (cf., D5:17, 19). True forgiveness has a social, economic and political component (LR). The participant further says that it cannot be that forgiveness (repentance) comes without true change ("but there's not change now") (in reference to vv.30-31). This is also a reference to the current situation of economic, geographic and social exclusion among White and Black South Africans (cf., D5:19 and D5:6).

D5:11 P11: Um, but then, on the other side, <u>If I am</u> <u>constantly sinning, sinning against someone and somebody</u> <u>is constantly forgiving me, then I need to catch a wake up</u> <u>and I need to make the change to stop, stop doing the same</u> <u>thing to them</u>
I: mmm
P11: So, I think, the strongest thing for me was change and transformation, <u>forgiveness isn't just, isn't just a process</u> <u>of forgiving, it's forgiving and changing to, to stop it</u> <u>happening again</u>

In the first part of this quotation the participant expresses a realisation that true forgiveness has a strong social component (LL) that is linked to concrete actions (LR) "I need to make the change to stop, stop doing the same thing to them" (this was in relation to the actions of the unforgiving servant in v.30). In addition to this the participant shows insight that forgiveness has a political element that is oriented towards a better future, "forgiveness isn't just, isn't just a process of forgiving, it's forgiving and changing to, to stop it happening again" (cf., vv. 30-31, 35).

6.3.6 Variance of the hypothesis

These examples illustrate a clear shift in the participants' understanding of forgiveness in relation to Matthew 18.15-35 as having a social, political and economic component (LL and LR). In total there were 38 quotations that were captured under the code 5_AQAL_LR, which expressed this understanding either directly, or indirectly. The participants linked their capacity to shift their understanding of forgiveness, and take on aspects of how members of Group A viewed it (this shows a new shared understanding of forgiveness, 5_AQAL_LL had a total of 13 quotations in the data). (cf., D5:4, 19).

There was one participant who clearly expressed that she/he had not changed in understanding either the shared identity or hermeneutic space with Group A, or the political, economic and social aspects of forgiveness. "For me, in reading with the group and realising that there were different hurts, and getting back to sort of some of the apartheid hurts, and I could hear their hurts, but it never affected me. I've always lived in Somerset West, I was always outside of everything. I didn't implement any of those issues" (D5:33). This is a clear variance from the rest of the participants in the group who had expressed some cognitive and affective empathetic shift between datasets D2 and D5.

In conclusion, however, it is reasonable to say that the group largely developed a more integrated understanding of forgiveness within the process of intercultural Bible reading.

6.4 Third research question

As anticipated there was a variance in the understandings of forgiveness among the participants between datasets D1 and D5 (Church Street Methodist church participants), and D2 and D6 (Coronation Ave Methodist church participants). However, as has already been discussed in the previous sections the variance between the pre-intercultural engagement and post-intercultural engagement datasets do not show exactly what was hypothesised 1.3. In the section that follows we shall discuss what was observed in the data. This will lay a foundation for the consideration of whether there was any correlation between the changes that did, or did not, take place and the intercultural Bible reading intervention under the conditions of positive intergroup contact theory.

6.4.1 Observed shifts in hermeneutic understandings of forgiveness

The third aim of this study was to understand to what extent the changes in theological understandings of forgiveness among Christians of different races (Group A and Group B) could be correlated to the mediators and moderators of the intercultural Bible reading practices?

The hypothesis of the study was that changes in theological understandings of forgiveness would only become possible if the intercultural group contact is facilitated as a form of positive intergroup contact (cf., section 3.3). In other words, mere contact between the participants from two different homogenous race groups would not be sufficient to facilitate a positive integral shift in hermeneutic and theological understandings of forgiveness in Matthew 18.15-35. As discussed in 3.3 mere contact between in-groups and out-groups can serve to heighten intergroup contact anxiety, which in turn make affective and cognitive reframing (empathy) very difficult. Moreover, negative intergroup contact could lead to an increase in anxiety between the in-group and out-group participants (from both group perspectives). Rather than allowing for a positive, more integrated and culturally diverse Biblical hermeneutic to develop, it could lead to a closed, more entrenched, or more strongly held in-group perspective on the interpretation of forgiveness in the text, and the in-group views of out-group participants.

Thus, the hypothesis is that if the intercultural Biblical reading process takes place under conditions in which the mechanisms for positive intergroup contact are introduced with care, the participants will experience a decrease in intergroup contact anxiety and an increase in affective empathy and cognitive empathy, that could facilitate the conditions under which participants are willing re-evaluate their own hermeneutic perspectives of forgiveness in the light of the perspectives of members from the other group that is in conflict with other out-group perspectives.

In sections 6.3.3 and 6.3.6 of this chapter we presented and discussed that there were shifts in understandings of forgiveness among participants from both Group A and Group B respectively (this is seen in the findings of the post intervention datasets D5 and D6). As such, we know that hermeneutic shifts did take place among the participants after the intercultural Bible reading engagement. Here is a summary of those findings:

GROUP A: Church Street Methodist church participants

In datasets D1 and D6 (Church Street Methodist church participants) the data showed that two anticipated shifts had taken place.

In the first instance the participants had broadened their shared understandings of forgiveness (LL) including concepts and understandings of forgiveness that were more characteristic of the out-group. This is evidenced in the manner in which they viewed the theological and social expectations and consequences of forgiveness (LL and LR) (cf., D6:1, 4, 46, 57). This would seem to make sense in light of the contention of certain positive intergroup contact theorists, that carefully facilitated contact between in-group and out-group participants can facilitate the conditions of both affective and cognitive empathy to operate, which are the conditions under which cognitive reframing can take place[124] (the changing of beliefs or ideas) (Levine & Hogg, 2009: 471–472).

Hence, a hermeneutic shift was identifiable in the post intervention data among participants in this group. In the pre-intercultural engagement dataset (D1) the characteristic understanding of forgiveness displayed a largely collective (LL) and social / political (LR) hermeneutic approach to understandings of forgiveness in Matthew 18.15-35 (cf., the discussion in 6.2.5 and quotation D1:20, and also D1:7, 9, 10, 19, 23, 52, 162, 163). Whereas the post intervention dataset displayed a growing awareness of individual-spiritual understandings of forgiveness (UL). Thus, in a theological sense, members of this group had understood that forgiveness is not only a matter of social harmony and the restoration of social, economic and political wellbeing in the community (LR / LR), it also has a transcendent spiritual element that requires God's involvement in the process of making the impossible possible (UL) (cf., D6:11, 12, 26, 56).

GROUP B: Coronation Ave Methodist church participants

A careful study and analysis of datasets D2 and D5 (Coronation Ave Methodist church participants) also showed instances of the anticipated shifts taking place between the pre-intercultural engagement and post-intercultural engagement Bible readings.

Once again, participants of this group indicated that their encounter with the out-group had made an impression on them that facilitated an increase in both affective empathy (cf., D5:19) and cognitive empathy (cf., D5:4). In particular, this was expressed in the participants' articulation of changes in their racial and social attitudes towards members of the out-group (LL) (cf., D5:16) and the awakening to the need for structural change and social transformation (LR) in South Africa as a necessary aspect of making forgiveness possible between Black and White Christians (cf., D5:27). Thus, we see an expanded perspective of shared in-group identity (LL) that evidences new integral understandings of forgiveness as a social and political concept (LR), "If I was Coloured or Black now and I experienced the apartheid regime, would I have been as humble or as forgiving as what these people are" (D5:19). The majority of participants in this group have started to develop a more dominant shared understanding of justice (LR) as an aspect of forgiveness. As this shared desire for justice was recognised among the participants (LL) (cf., D5:1, 2, 4, 6, 7, 12, 19, 21,27), and strengthened from different perspectives the members, and understandings of forgiveness, of the out-group began to be identified as insiders, and their views as acceptable (cf., Roccas & Brewer, 2002: 90; Kok, 2014b: 3).

This shift allowed members of this group to adopt aspects of the out-group's understanding of forgiveness to aggregate, or replace, their own views. As discussed in 3.3.8 this process is called "perspective taking" (Swart, Turner, et al., 2011: 188). It breaks down the stereotype, or prejudgment, of the other and their ideas and opens

---

124   Kok (2014) suggests that under certain conditions it may even be possible to create a "merger" of in-group and out-group social identities to facilitate a new shared social identity (cf., Roccas & Brewer, 2002: 90; Kok, 2014b: 3). This is not the purpose of this study, although there is some possibility of observing such a 'shared in-group' emergence in the data (cf., D6:57, 66)

the possibility for an increase in cognitive empathy. Thus, members of this group characteristically broadened their hermeneutic understanding of the expectations, conditions, and consequences of forgiveness to include economic, political and social realities (a shift from UL to LR) (cf., D5:16, 27). This is an example of a broader integral interpretation of forgiveness in Matthew 18.15-35. In quotation D5:7 the participant interprets the in-group as possibly being unforgiving servant of Matthew 18.32. This is a significant and radical hermeneutic shift from a largely individual spiritual interpretation in dataset D2 (cf., D2:14, 15, 20, 33, 36, 43).

The examples that are discussed above are encouraging observations since they show that for these communities some new possibilities Biblical hermeneutical perspectives on forgiveness have emerged. The possibilities include a new way of theological reflection on forgiveness in the Biblical text[125]. These new hermeneutic possibilities emerged as the participants adopted a more integral view of forgiveness that textured their previously held interpretations of the text and incorporated perspectives on understanding forgiveness from the perspective of the 'other' in the intercultural Bible reading process. This seems both plausible, and responsible, when one considers the range of possible understandings of forgiveness that are present in Matthew 18.15-35 (cf., Lee & Viljoen, 2010a: 65–67; Mbabazi, 2013: 32–36; Nel, 2014a,b). These possibilities were discussed in detail in 4.5 and 4.8.

6.4.2 Unexpected results among participants

In each of the post-intercultural engagement datasets (D5 and D6) there were examples of anticipated shifts that did not take place.

First, not all of the participants in Group A (Church street Methodist Church) expressed theological views that could be comparable with the views of Group B. A careful study of the pre-intercultural engagement data shows that the one participant did not fit the general shift in hermeneutic pattern that was common for this group (c.f., 6.3.3). The analysis shows that this participant did not need to make the change since the participant already identified with the theological and hermeneutic perspectives of forgiveness held by Group B in the pre-intercultural engagement test (i.e., largely individual spiritual), (cf., D1:2, 3, 4, 8 and the discussion in 6.2.4 and 6.3.3). Thus, while the other participants in this group made hermeneutic shifts to adopt aspects of the individual-spiritual understanding of forgiveness (UL) between dataset D1 and D6, this participant held their pre-intercultural engagement viewpoint. The researcher had not anticipated this set of conditions in the group sample and so this is a variance from the general hypothesis.

Second, there was a participant in Group B who also did not show any evidence of a hermeneutic shift between the pre-intercultural engagement dataset (D2) and the post-intercultural engagement dataset (D5). This participant held a strong view of separation between faith and life (UL), and so did not concede any culpability in relation to pain suffered by members of Group A under apartheid (LR / LL) (cf.,

---

125 It is possible that such new, even shared, understandings of forgiveness emerge among participants in this study as a result of an emerging intergroup social identity (Hermans, 2000: 135–136; Harré, 2002: 611–612; Kok, 2014b: 2, 8). However, this is not the focus of this study, and so it is only a speculation, and not necessary to ascertain in relation to the findings discussed above (which are primarily theological in nature and do not require any conclusions on social identity complexity among the participants).

D5:33). In fact the participant expressed an awareness of the expression of hurt by members of Group A (LL), but said that this did not evoke any affective or cognitive empathy, "I could hear their hurts, but it never affected me" (D5:33). The researcher was unable to find any reasonable explanation in the data for this lack of change in this participant. Thus, in this instance, this was a variance from the general hypothesis of change that was postulated 1.3.

6.4.3 Unexpected results in hermeneutic shifts

The researcher worked through the data a number of times in relation to the two theories (AQAL theory, chapter 2, and intergroup contact theory, chapter 3), and the exegetical reading of the text (chapter 4) to try to identify any obvious shifts that took place that were not anticipated in the research hypothesis or design. These were discussed in some detail in the previous sections. As was mentioned above in sections 6.4.1-6.4.2 the two instances of participant variance, one in Group A and one in Group B, were un-anticipated.

In addition to this, however, the research was encouraged by the *extent* to which the participants in Group A and Group B were willing to engage the experiences and ideas of the other group in the positive intergroup contact intercultural Bible reading process (see datasets D3 and D4). A merger on complex social identity is when, "convergent group memberships are simultaneously recognized and embraced in their most inclusive form" (Roccas & Brewer, 2002: 91). This was very clearly expressed in D6:4, "we mustn't be apart, we must be one. We call ourselves the Methodist people". The convergent denominational (religious) identity (LL) was a strong motivator to the participants to understand and work towards possibility of forgiveness.

The affective element of the necessity of forgiveness was expressed using powerful spiritually laden language (UL and LL) by a member of Group A, which had initially held an almost exclusive social, political and economic understanding of forgiveness (LR), "you've got to ask the Lord to strengthen you, to be able to perhaps forgive that person" (D6:36). The statement was made in the context of a discussion of Matthew 18.35. This statement contained a surprising expression that forgiveness may be made possible through growing deeper in love with God (not just engaging the economic, political or social reality in the life of the 'other'). This shows a shift from a LR view to the inclusion of UL understandings of the process of forgiveness for this participant from Group A. From Group B there was equally surprising an unanticipated insight into the necessity for pragmatic transformation and change, "when we received forgiveness there should be a transformation" (D5:15). This statement was in light of the discussion of the actions of the unforgiving servant (vv.30-31). The quotation that most explicitly exemplified the radical shift in social and hermeneutic understanding (UL to LR) was "the question I've asked, are we the unforgiving servants… White South Africans perhaps…" (D5:7). This is a remarkable insight from a member of Group B that had largely held a spiritual hermeneutic and individual social identity (UL) before the intercultural Bible reading intervention.

The use of the word "perhaps" in both of the illustrative quotations (D6:36, D5:7) is very telling. It shows that the participants are wrestling with the possibility of forgiveness, one can almost hear them asking "what could I do, what could my people do, to make forgiveness possible?" The depth and strength of these hermeneutic shifts was very surprising for the researcher and elicited a measure of hope for what may lie ahead between these two communities.

6.4.4 The relationship between positive intergroup contact mechanisms and the intercultural Bible reading process

This project hypothesised that carefully facilitated intergroup contact can be effective in addressing in-group and out-group anxiety, and thus facilitating the conditions under which both affective empathy and cognitive empathy can emerge (Hewstone & Swart, 2011a: 375–376). It was suggested that these are the conditions under which participants might be willing to reappraise their views of the 'other' and amend their own social and theological perspectives. The social "mediators" and "moderators" of positive intergroup contact (discussed in 3.3.6) are identified as "mechanisms" for positive group engagement in the literature (Paolini *et al.*, 2004: 770–786, 2006).

The literature shows that intergroup contact mediators (or social conditions / mechanisms) need to be facilitated in an intergroup contact setting in order to positively change the social moderators (i.e., to decrease anxiety (*_IG_MED_ANXIETY_DOWN) and increase affective empathy (*_IG_MED_EMPATHY_AFFECTIVE) and cognitive empathy (*_IG_MED_EMPATHY_COGNITIVE) among participants).

Pettigrew's research on these mechanisms shows that in order to make such positive shifts possible the following should take place: learning about the out-group, changing perceptions of behaviour of the out-group, generating affective ties (friendship, concern etc.), and engaging in a reappraisal of the values and identity of the in-group (Pettigrew, 1998: 70–73). This was the aim of the intercultural Bible reading intervention (recorded in datasets D3 and D4).

In this section of the findings we shall keep Allport's four "situational specifications" (that were identified as positive intergroup contact mechanism within the research design of this project) in mind as we analyse the findings of the intercultural Bible reading process. In summary, we shall seek to identify the presence and operation of the following intergroup contact mechanisms in the data (c.f., Levine & Hogg, 2009: 468–469):

- Equal status in the situation (equality among participants and groupings) (*_IG_MOD_EQUALSTATUS)

- Common goals (shared goals) (*_IG_MOD_COMMONGOALS)

- Intergroup cooperation (*_IG_MOD_IGCOOPERATION)

- Sanction from formal authorities (*_IG_MOD_SUPPORT)

Positive intergroup contact theory suggests that mechanisms need to be present and operable in the intergroup contact situation in order to mediate a change in the affective mediators of intergroup contact (psychological processes) (Levine & Hogg, 2009: 468–469). Thus, these mechanisms were carefully built into the intergroup contact interventions of this research through the structure of the meetings, the social nature of the Bible reading project using the "Dwelling in the Word" approach, and the frequent reframing of the primary authority of the Biblical text as a shared identity space and reflective surface. As was pointed out in chapter 5, the practice oriented research approach is particularly well suited to identifying and analysing "specific mechanisms and pathways between causes and effects" (Blatter, 2008: 69).

6.4.5 Results: Positive intergroup contact mediators

We shall now move on to discussing what was observed in relation to the introduction of positive intergroup contact mediators in intercultural Bible reading processes. We shall pay particular attention to instances in which participants express, or reflect upon, their personal emotional experience in the intercultural Bible reading encounter (specifically in relation to a decrease in in-group and out-group anxiety) and whether this can be correlated to the findings of the post-intercultural Bible reading session findings of changed understandings of forgiveness. Thus, we shall highlight and consider instances in the intercultural encounter (recorded in datasets D3 and D4), and in the final group meetings (D5 and D6 respectively), in which participants expressed an increase in affective empathy or cognitive empathy that can be correlated to a change in their understanding of forgiveness.

6.4.5.1 *Anxiety*

The theory suggest that where anxiety can be lessened, and open, vulnerable and safe contact can be facilitated between in-group and out-group participants, the participants will be better predisposed towards an increase in empathy (Batson *et al.*, 2002: 1656–1666; Turner, Hewstone & Voci, 2007: 369; Swart, Turner, *et al.*, 2011: 187–189). This may either entail "affective empathy", i.e., the ability to feel, or imagine, the emotional experience of the other or it may take the form of "cognitive empathy" (what the literature refers to as "perspective taking") (Swart, Turner, *et al.*, 2011: 187). In some instances, both forms of empathy are evidenced to varying degrees. Batson *et al.*, have identified three steps in the empathetic process (Batson *et al.*, 1997: 105–118) (cf., the discussion in 3.3.3). However, in all instances a decrease in anxiety is important.

Within the data instances in which the participants expressed a decrease in intergroup anxiety were coded using *_IG_MED_ANXIETY_DOWN. There were 6 instances recorded in dataset D3 and 7 instances in dataset D4. Some examples will be cited and analysed below.

Quotation	Analysis
D3:52 I: That's one of the gifts of this process, hey, because when you listen, and you had to listen to P6, you have to listen for her context you know. ... **P9:** If... probably YOU read it, you find for example you find it completely different what I would say that I was reading it, because then perhaps if we were to have a one on one conversation, we will, we will differentiate miles apart, **I:** mmm **P9:** but for me it made sense, because I find myself in that point, or find myself in that position, and I find conclusion and I find rest and I find peace in that portion.	This quotation from participant P9 shows evidence of a decrease in anxiety, "I find rest and I find peace" (UL). In this instance it is directly linked to having a "one on one conversation" with a participant from the out group (UL). This reframes the participant's understanding of forgiveness from a conflicting view to s a shared view (LL). There is a clear correlation between the encounter with the 'other' ("you have to listen for her context"), the change in understanding of forgiveness ("for me it made sense") and the experience of peace in the participant ("I find peace").

Quotation	Analysis
D4:29 I: Um, I mean we've <u>received such a gift to meet one another</u>. That's the <u>gift I think, is, is meeting people</u> [collective agreement] **I:** Not churches, not concepts of a community here, one there, we not looking at ideas in our heads, we've got faces here, hey? It's beautiful.	In this quotation, we see the group expressing collective agreement to the fact that meeting people (in-group and out-group contact) has been "a gift" to one another (LL). The data further shows that the gift is not only new ways of understanding forgiveness (UL) in the text, but also the gift of seeing the world from a different perspective (LL and LR) (affective and cognitive empathy).
D4:17 P3: Okay, <u>P4 was like a bubbling fountain today</u>, so I couldn't… [laugh]	By the time the two groups had met for their second intercultural Bible reading session they had become quite familiar with one another. Participant P3 points out that P4 was talking freely "like a bubbling fountain", which is met with laughter from the group – it shows the emergence of a new 'shared' integral thought space (LL). This is another instance where it shows that positive intergroup contact and lessening of anxiety can be correlated with one another.

The examples cited above are not intended to be normative. They simply illustrate that in certain instances, under certain conditions, there had been a lessening of anxiety among the participants, which in turn allowed for the participants to reframe their theological and hermeneutic understandings of forgiveness in a more integral manner (UL / LL / LR).

6.4.5.2 *Empathy*

In the section that follows we shall consider where there was evidence of either cognitive empathy, or affective empathy (or both) in the data, and how this may be correlated to the reframing of understandings of forgiveness among the participants.

6.4.5.2.1 Cognitive empathy

In datasets D3 and D4 the code * _IG_MED_EMPATHY_COGNITIVE_UP was used to identify in stances in which participants expressed forms of cognitive empathy (what the literature calls "perspective taking") (Swart, Turner, *et al.*, 2011: 187).

Again, the intention here is not to prove any causal relationship, but simply to highlight instances in which members expressed this tendency during the intercultural Bible reading process.

Quotation	Analysis
D3:7 P8: Well, from **P3**, as well <u>I heard something</u> very… <u>it seemed so obvious after he had said it</u>, but I hadn't really… <u>like it hadn't shown up as clear as what he said and, he was saying…</u>	Here a participant from Group B is expressing that he/she was able to take on an expression of the understanding of forgiveness as if it were his/her own experience (a shift from UL to LR), "it seemed obvious after he said it". This new perspective is described as a deepening clarity as a result of the engagement with participant P3 from Group A.

Quotation	Analysis
D3:53 P4: If I can just respond to that, I think that's so important, but we must realise that sometimes, <u>we are seeing it because of where we are at that point</u> **P5:** mmm **P4:** and it's so <u>important then that we don't judge others,</u> **P9:** Yes **P4:** <u>too often I hear in the church, about now this is the way that it is, and it is the way that it is</u> **[general agreement]**	This quotation displays cognitive empathy from a different vantage point. Participant P4 (Group B) is imploring the participants to awaken to their own cognitive and contextual biases ("we are seeing it because of where we are at that point"). She/he goes on to encourage the participants not to "judge others", but rather to understand that there may be alternative perspectives, "now this is the way that it is" followed by general group agreement. This is already a shift from a purely spiritual understanding of forgiveness (UL) which is common to Group B participants, towards an understanding that requires social openness to the 'other' (LL).

The participants had a general sense of agreement that when they "read the Bible together… it is far more rich" (D3:66) – this is a shift towards a shared hermeneutic (LL). This richness stems from the new insights gained through approaching the understanding of the text from the perspective of the 'other', it brings a deepened "clarity" (D3:7), and greater tolerance for the perspectives and views of others (D3:53).

6.4.5.2.2 Affective empathy

The code * _IG_MED_EMPATHY_AFFECTIVE_UP was employed throughout the datasets to identify instances in which participants expressed affective empathy for one another. As will be shown in the selected quotes below, this presented itself as expressions of friendship, deepening concern, and engaging in a reappraisal of the values and identity of the in-group in relation to the out-group (Pettigrew, 1998: 70–73). There is some finding of correlation between these instances and the reframing of theological notions of forgiveness among the participants. In total there were 9 identifiable instances of this in dataset D3 and 4 instances in dataset D4.

Quotation	Analysis
D5:17 I found the Church Street crowd very humble in actual fact, <u>I felt, um, embarrassed,</u> cos, I thought that <u>they shouldn't be feeling so humble</u>, if anything, <u>they should be feeling a bit more</u>…	In this instance the participant was able to imagine what it may be like to be a member of the 'out-group' (LL). This was expressed as a form of embarrassment over how the participant viewed the members of the out-group as being "humble". What is significant is that this statement is made by a member of Group B, who held an almost exclusively individual spiritual view of forgiveness (UL). Now, however, in the encounter the participant begins to express an understanding that forgiveness has an emotive and social element that is shared with the other (LL).

D3:61 P8: And for me I was actually sad when I saw that, uh, obviously, I was glad that the church was been fixed and everything, <u>but in my mind I was almost saddened by the fact that we didn't make use of that opportunity to become that one church</u>

This quotation shows a participant expressing remorse over the lack of unity between the two communities "I was almost saddened by the fact that we didn't make use of that opportunity to become that one church". The outcome is that this participant from Group B moves from an individual spiritual understanding of forgiveness (UL) to a collective and social view of forgiveness (LL/LR), "didn't make use of that opportunity to become that one church".

D5:23 P2: That <u>we just going to have to keep forgiving and keep forgiving and keep forgiving</u>
I: mmm
P2: <u>Even if it is the same hurt, it's different aspects of that hurt,</u>
I: mmmm
P4: Sjoe <u>That's a, that's a new insight for me now, you've, I know you've mentioned it before, but that's just taken a little bit</u>...
P2: Ja
P8: It's like you keep chipping away at that thing until it's gone

Here participant P4 expresses a different perspective on his or her own hurt as a result of a new insight gained from participant P2, "I know you've mentioned it before, but that just taken a little bit..." In this instance the empathetic act of "sharing" "different aspects of that hurt" with one another (affective empathy) (LL) allowed for a perspective shift to take place, "that's a new insight for me now" (cognitive empathy). In this instance, the participant from Group A, whose view of forgiveness was predominantly social and political (LL and LR) moves towards a more individual psychological and spiritual view of forgiveness, "we just going to have to keep forgiving and keep forgiving and keep forgiving".

The data thus shows some instances in which the participants entered into one another's emotional experience to some extent (LL), imagining what it would be like to "be the other". "For me, in reading with the group and realising that there were different hurts, and getting back to sort of some of the apartheid hurts, and I could hear their hurts" (D5:33). "If I was Coloured or Black now and I experienced the apartheid regime, would I have been as humble or as forgiving as what these people are... how would I be?" (D5:19). There is some clear correlation in the data between these instances of affective empathy and changes in hermeneutic understandings of forgiveness. In the quotations above the findings relate to members of Group A and Group B who showed more integral views of forgiveness as a result of affective empathetic engagements (UL to LL/LR, and LL/LR to UL). These examples from the data illustrated that affective empathy operated within the group and that it could be correlated to "perspective reframing" (cognitive empathy), as in D5:23, D5:19.

6.4.6 Results: Positive intergroup contact moderators

In the sections that follow we shall discuss what can be identified as the positive intergroup contact moderators that are evidenced in the datasets D3 and D4, and which participants pointed out as beneficial to positive intergroup contact, in relation to the reframing of their theological perspectives on forgiveness, in datasets D5 and D6. The conditions that Allport identified, "...involved equal status among the participants, cooperation on common goals between groups, and institutional support" (Hewstone & Swart, 2011a: 375). If you are not yet familiar with the positive intergroup contact moderators, please refer to section 3.3.6 for a discussion of each of the moderators in detail. Please also refer to 5.7.3.2 for a discussion of how these moderators informed the research design.

6.4.6.1 *Equal status*

The research shows that where intergroup contact participants experience equality of status, their prejudice is significantly reduced. This allows for the operation of both affective and cognitive empathy among the participants, thereby lessening prejudice of the 'other'(Allport, 1954: 281). Two strategies were used in the intercultural Bible reading process to facilitate an experience of equality of status among the participants. First, every group meeting began with an explanation that none of the participants had greater or lesser exegetical and hermeneutic expertise than the others. "There are no right or wrong answers. We are not looking for technical exegesis or Greek or Hebrew or anything like that, our task is simply to listen to one another and listen for the voice uhh of God in our midst, so there are no right or wrong answers, we're just doing this together, we're a team together" (D4:3). Second, the "Dwelling in the Word" approach to intercultural Bible reading was used (cf., D4:4). As explained in 5.7.3 this approach ensures that the pressure is taken off participants to have to impress the group with their knowledge or skill. Rather, the emphasis is placed upon listening to the other as they speak of their engagement with the text (Ellison & Keifert, 2011: 7–8; Nel, 2013b). The participants expressed that they experienced the encounter with one another, in this equal space, as a great gift that allowed learning and growth to take place - "there has been a sense all along that all of these things, this understanding happens better when we do it together" (D5:3). The shared understanding that resulted (LL) allowed for members of Group A to engage perspectives on forgiveness that were common to Group B, i.e., LL/ LR to UL (c.f., 6.3.3). It also allowed members of Group B to engage perspectives of forgiveness that were more characteristic of Group A, i.e., UL to LL/LR (c.f., 6.3.6).

6.4.6.2 *Common Goals*

A second important mechanism for positive intergroup contact is that the participants needed to understand that they were working together towards a common goal. Without this understanding the engagement may have become distrustful or competitive. In order to facilitate an understanding of the shared goal, or purpose, of the intercultural Bible reading process, the participants were informed of the purpose of the meetings, and the reasons for their selection, in the letter of invitation (cf., Appendix A). In addition to this the process was explained to the participants, by means of an explanation of the "Dwelling in the word" approach to intercultural Bible reading. There is evidence of the fruit of this mechanism being present as the following quotation shows:

Quotation

D5:47 P2: I was going to say, for me in the whole area of forgiveness, is that safe ground as well, I think that the important… it is that we were on neutral ground and we felt safe, we weren't vulnerable in any way, we'd had sort of… we knew they were church people, we knew was… who they were and they sort of knew who we were
I: yes, ja
P2: and I think that's the importance
I: ja
P2: It's the safe…. The compassionate ground, the… for forgiveness to happen
P8: ja, ja

Analysis

Participant P2 expresses how much she / he appreciated the understanding among the group that their common goal was the working together "on neutral ground" in a "safe" environment to develop understandings of forgiveness. In fact, the participant expresses directly that, "It's the safe…. The compassionate ground, the… for forgiveness to happen". This common goal allowed "forgiveness to happen". This is a significant shift for this participant she/he is from Group A which had a strong social and political understanding of forgiveness in the pre-intercultural Bible reading engagements (LL/LR). Now, however, the participant displays a view of forgiveness that is individual, spiritual, and psychological (UL), the "compassionate ground… for forgiveness to happen".

Here one can see a correlation between participation towards a common goal and a shift in an understanding of forgiveness. Whereas previously the participant (from Group A) may not have been willing to forgive unless the social, economic, and political conditions of forgiveness were met (LL/LR), now there is a willingness for "forgiveness to happen" because of safe space that was created by the shared goal of forgiveness among the participants (UL).

6.4.6.3 *Cooperation*

A further mechanism that the research suggests is necessary for positive intergroup contact is a sense of cooperation among the participants (Allport, 1954: 281). The letter of invitation that the ministers sent to the participants in their respective Churches signalled the intention of participating and cooperating together towards a greater purpose or goal. It said, "the participants are helping to test an approach to reading the Bible that Rev Forster has developed in order to see whether this method works, or does not, and if it does work, where it works and why it works, and where it does not work, why this is so. You will be helping to test this approach to reading the Bible." (see Appendix A). One particular quotation illustrates how the participants experienced the importance of this mechanism in engaging in the process of intercultural Bible reading on forgiveness:

Quotation

D5:44 even though there must be diversity, it must be safe diversity.
[group agreement]
I: you don't want to go into a space where… if you walk in and it's let's say, it's two different races, and you are under attack…
P10: yes
P8: mmm
I: So there was something about the safeness of our diversity, the fact that, that we were… am I correct in that…
P2: very much so

Analysis

In this quotation, the interviewer is probing the importance of intergroup cooperation as a mechanism for reducing anxiety and increasing empathy. The interviewer expresses the importance of "the safeness of our diversity", that there must be a space where the participants agree to encounter one another without feeling "under attack" (LL). Three different participants representing both groups agree to this statement as an expression of the importance of group cooperation towards a common task.

In this illustrative example it is important to note that participants from both Group A and Group B agree with the importance of cooperating with one another (LR) in order to achieve a common understanding (UL) and experience or reality of forgiveness (LL).

6.4.6.4 *Support of authorities*

Allport's research in positive intergroup contact shows that the effects of prejudice reduction are "greatly enhanced if this contact is sanctioned by institutional support (i.e., by law, custom or local atmosphere)" (Allport, 1954: 281). The mechanism of support from authorities was also introduced in the intercultural Bible reading research design process, and the intercultural Bible reading intervention itself. In terms of the design, the participants for the project were identified by their respective ministers, sanctioned as official participants and representatives of their communities in this process, and encouraged the participate fully and freely towards the common goal of forgiveness. The participants were notified of this in the letter of invitation to participate written by their minister (see Appendix A), and also in the ethical clearance form supplied by the researcher (see Appendix B). The participants were reminded that they had been carefully selected, and sanctioned, for participation at the start of each Bible reading session (cf., D3:2, D4:2, D5:44). The participants accepted the responsibility of engaging one another for the purposes of developing understanding of forgiveness as representatives of their respective communities.

One of the clearest illustrations of this is to be found in this quotation: "the people around this table all represent the Methodist church. …I mean if someone had to ask me that's new to Somerset West, why there's two Somerset West Churches, I'd say, I'd say, I don't know, they'd say but that's not cool, and I'd have to agree and leave it at that" (D3:63). This is a significant statement by the participant from Group B, since it shows how the commitment to participation in the project began to illicit understandings that forgiveness would only be possible in a shared setting (hence a move from UL to LL/LR).

Another participant expressed the desire for change and reconciliation in the following manner: "…I'm hoping that this can maybe be the, be the start of another, of a new initiative, it has to happen, it must happen, it's a scar in the, on the face of the church" (D3:60). The participant from Group A felt a sense of responsibility to engage with 'the other', and to face the challenging issues of their racially divided past, in order to work together for forgiveness. This is an instance of correlation between the intergroup contact moderator of the sanction and support of authorities towards a new shared process and understanding of forgiveness (from LL/LR to include UL).

6.5 Concluding remarks

This chapter presented the findings of the research process and analysed them in relation to the research questions. It was only possible to do so because a theoretical foundation had been laid for this task in the preceding chapters.

Ken Wilber's Integral AQAL theory (discussed in chapter 2) gave the language and philosophical framework that made it possible to plot the theological perspectives of forgiveness in the text (cf., 4.8), and the theological perspectives of the participants at various stages. This theory enabled the researcher to identify views of forgiveness in relation to the four quadrants of meaning construction and identity (UL, UR, LL, LR). Having this language and structure made it possible to present the pre-intercultural engagement findings of the participants in datasets D1 and D2, and the post-intercultural engagement datasets D5 and D6, and to identify shifts in the data between the pre-intercultural engagement and post-intercultural engagement datasets.

The intercultural Bible reading intervention itself was designed the light of the insights gained from positive intergroup contact theory (discussed in detail in chapter 3). The positive intergroup contact mechanisms (mediators and moderators of positive intergroup contact) were identified in the intercultural Bible reading intervention (datasets D3 and D4).

Importantly, since this is a study of how ordinary readers interpret a particular text (Matthew 18.15-35), it was necessary to present a thorough exegetical reading of the text (see chapter 4). This section of the study showed the possible understandings of the text, placing it within its historical and social setting.

The presentation and analysis of the findings of this research process thus built on these theoretical informants to establish how the participants from the communities understood forgiveness in the text before the intervention (this is in relation to the first research question). We also presented and analysed their understandings of the text after the intercultural Bible reading intervention (this was related to the second research question). Then, we considered how the introduction of positive intergroup contact moderators and mediators informed the process of intercultural Biblical engagement (this was in relation to the third research question). In the final section of the chapter the findings were evaluated in relation to the project design and implementation.

In the last chapter of this manuscript we shall revisit the research objectives, provide some tentative answers to the research questions, and summarise the findings and importance of the findings and this project for the problem owner and the academic discourse.

Discussion and conclusions

7.1 Introduction

This research project sought to engage the complexity of understandings of forgiveness in Matthew 18.15-35 within the context of an intercultural Bible reading process. The study began by problematizing the concept of forgiveness (cf., 1.1-1.2). It was suggested that South Africans, and South Africa, could benefit from more nuanced understandings of forgiveness. Such knowledge may help them to move towards the possibility of persons from diverse histories, cultural identities, racial identities, and economic classes, grasping what forgiveness may entail (cf., Thesnaar, 2008: 53–73, 2014: 1–8; van der Borght, 2009: 9, 26; Tutu, 2012: 47–48, 74, 218).

Considering the above, an aim of this study was to produce rigorous, textured, and credible theological insight into the complexity of differing understandings of forgiveness in Matthew 18.15-35 from among members of different cultures in an intercultural Bible reading intervention (cf., 1.4). The primary objectives were:

A. To gain theological insight into the hermeneutic understandings of forgiveness when participants in the project read the chosen text in an in-group setting, then in an intercultural Bible reading setting, and once again in an in-group setting after the intercultural Bible reading intervention had taken place.

B. Moreover, the researcher sought to gain some insight into the ways in which social moderators and mediators of positive intergroup contact constructively facilitate the conditions for integral understandings of forgiveness to develop among the intercultural Bible reading participants (this was termed the 'posibilising' of forgiveness).

The hypothesis of the study was that the pre-intercultural engagement Bible reading sessions, undertaken in relatively homogenous in-group Bible reading settings, would deliver hermeneutic results that are in keeping with the social identity of the readers. Thus, Group A, (a predominantly Black (Coloured) group) would understanding forgiveness in the chosen text as being social and political. Whereas Group B, (a White population group) tended to individualise and spiritualise understandings of forgiveness in the text (cf., sections 1.3.1 and 5.6 for a discussion of the constituent conceptual formulations of this aspect of the hypothesis). This hypothesis was engaged through the first research question.

Moreover, it was further hypothesised that a carefully facilitated intercultural Bible reading intervention in which the mechanisms of positive intergroup contact are introduced (cf., 1.3.3 and 3.3) would allow for the conditions in which members of the two groups developed more integral understandings of forgiveness. The notion of integral meaning construction, and more integral concepts of forgiveness, were discussed in 2.4-2.5 and 4.8. The hermeneutic shifts in understandings of forgiveness in the above hypothesis were engaged through research question two. The correlation between such shifts and the conditions of the introduction of positive intergroup contact moderators and mediators in an intercultural Bible reading process, was addressed through research question three.

To undertake a credible scholarly engagement with the content and processes of forgiveness that may emerge from persons of different cultures and contexts reading Matthew 18.15-35 in in-group and intercultural settings, a practice oriented research intervention was conceived. The research design (discussed in chapter 5) was thus envisaged in such a way that it moved between the theoretical and the practice streams (van Weert & Andriessen, 2004) to design and implement the intercultural Bible reading intervention, to solicit credible and verifiable data from the process, and to analyse and present the findings from gathered data.

Three theories informed the research design. First, Ken Wilber's AQAL integral theory was used as a philosophical framework that provided language and structure to 'plot' the theological understandings of forgiveness in the text, and in the reading of the text (see chapter 2 for a discussion of the theory, and chapter 6.3-6.4 for a presentation of the findings from the datasets employing insights from this theory). Second, intergroup contact theory was used to identify the mechanisms and processes for positive intergroup contact that informed the intercultural Bible reading sessions (see chapter 3 for a discussion of the theory, and 6.2-6.4 for a discussion and analysis of the findings from the data that relate to the application of this theory in the research process). Third, the Biblical text was engaged in a scholarly exegetical process (see chapter 4) so as to avoid collapsing the thought world of the text into the contemporary context. This is a critical aspect of a credible engagement with the Biblical text. This process allowed for the construction of a hermeneutic bridge to link aspects of the text to aspects of the interpretive insights of the contemporary readers engaged in this research project.

The major observations of the study will be discussed in section 7.2.1 and evaluated in 7.2.3. We shall unpack these findings, and what the analysis of the findings showed, in the conclusion below.

7.2 A discussion of the findings in relation to the research questions

In 6.2-6.4 we presented aspects of the findings in the data from the pre-intercultural engagement and post-intercultural engagement Bible reading sessions. We also discussed and analysed the introduction of the conditions of positive intergroup contact during the intercultural Bible reading process. Each of these sections sought to engage one of the research questions. In the section that follows we shall offer a summary of the major observations in relation to the research questions.

7.2.1 Summary of major observations

The research design was predicated on three primary research questions. We shall briefly refer to the findings of the research process in relation to each of the research questions in the section that follows.

1. To what extent do theological understandings of forgiveness differ among Christians of different race groups?

In answer to research question 1, it is concluded that an analysis of the data shows that to a significant extent the social and cultural identities of the participants in the respective communities influenced their hermeneutic and theological understanding of forgiveness in Matthew 18.15-35.

In Group A, which is a predominantly Black / Coloured community, forgiveness is largely understood in a collective and social manner (cf., 6.2.1-6.2.5). In other words, forgiveness is not only an individual concern, it has social consequences and social expectations within the community (LR and LL). Moreover, this group understood that forgiveness is not only a matter of spiritual restoration between the individual (or community) and God. Rather, it should be evidenced in the restoration of relationships and structures in the community (LR and LL). For this group, forgiveness can only be authentic if the conditions for forgiveness are evidenced in the community. This is in keeping with notions of intersubjective identity that are more common in Black and Coloured South African communities (Adhikari, 2005; cf., Shutte, 2009; Forster, 2010a,b; Cakal *et al.*, 2011).

An analysis of the results showed that Group B, which is an entirely White community, largely understood forgiveness in an individual and spiritual manner (UL) (cf. 6.2.6-6.2.9). For the majority of participants in this group, the pre-intercultural engagement data showed that they viewed forgiveness as being primarily a matter of restoring their spiritual relationship with God (UL). They did not initially consider that forgiveness may need to engage the party against whom the sin (or grievance) was committed. Forgiveness would have been enacted when God had set them free from the guilt and spiritual culpability of their actions (UL), it would not necessarily entail the restoration of relational harmony among members of the community (LL) or the restitution of social, political or economic structures in the community (LR).

2. To what extent have theological understandings of forgiveness among Christians of different race groups changed in a more integrative manner after an intercultural bible reading of Matthew 18.15-35?

The findings of the post intervention research data and analysis shows that to a large extent (except for minor variations which are discussed in 7.2.2) the participants of the intercultural Bible reading intervention developed more integral understandings of forgiveness. This means that participants were far more open to accepting understandings of forgiveness that were not held within their in-group, but were more common among members of the out-group. For example, members of Group A were willing to aggregate their social and political understandings of forgiveness (LL, LR) with individual and spiritual understandings (UL). In Group B, members who had held almost exclusively individual and spiritual understandings of forgiveness (UL) were open to understandings of forgiveness that had social and political implications and consequences (LL, LR). This does not necessarily mean that the participants gave up the views they initially held (although there is evidence some instances of this), rather, that their adapted their views in relation to the views of others.

Thus, in answer to research question two:

The data showed that the majority of participants underwent a shift in theological understandings of forgiveness between datasets D1 and D6 (cf., 6.2.5 and 6.3.3), and

D2 and D5 (cf., 6.2.9 and 6.3.6) respectively. The "extent" of the shift was significant both in the theological content of how understandings of forgiveness changed and in the number of participants that expressed such hermeneutic shifts (cf., 6.4). Moreover, the "theological understanding" of forgiveness was more integral for the majority of participants i.e., the participants expressed more theologically integrated expressions of forgiveness that included the individual and the collective (UL, LL), as well as the spiritual (UL) and the political (LR). This is in keeping with an AQAL reading of the possibilities of understanding forgiveness in Matthew 18.15-35 (cf., 4.8 for a presentation of this reading of the text).

3. To what extent is the change in theological understandings of forgiveness among Christians of different races (Group A and Group B) stimulated by the mediators and moderators of the intercultural Bible reading practices?

The stated objective of the intercultural Bible reading intervention (designed in accordance with the mechanisms of intergroup contact theory) was to facilitate positive intergroup contact among the participants (cf., 5.5, 5.7.3.2, 5.7.3, 5.9.2). Allport's intergroup contact theory suggested that certain types of contact could contribute towards what is called an "optimal contact strategy" in which the prejudice between groups is reduced, and the possibility of social harmony is increased (Allport, 1954: 264; Dixon *et al.*, 2005: 699). Since this is a practice oriented research project with a limited number of participants and a limited number of intergroup contact sessions, the findings are not conclusive or normative in nature, but they are insightful and valid for this study (cf., 1.8).

The data does show that the mechanisms of positive intergroup contact (discussed in 3.3.6) were introduced in the intercultural Bible reading sessions with effect (cf., datasets D3 and D4, as well as the discussions in 6.4 and 6.4.4). In addition, the data shows that there were shifts in understandings of forgiveness in the readings of the text, towards a more integral hermeneutics of forgiveness, among the majority of participants after the intercultural Bible reading intervention that was facilitated under the conditions of positive intergroup contact (cf., 6.4-6.5). This is not a causal conclusion. However, it is a correlational observation. In other words, under these conditions, the participants in this research project, did develop their theological understandings of forgiveness in the reading of Matthew 18.15-35 after reading the text under the conditions of positive intergroup contact in an intercultural Bible reading setting. It is credible to conclude that in this case there is a correlation between the "goals and content of the reading practices" in this intercultural Bible reading process, and the "change in theological understanding of forgiveness among Christians of different races", to quote from the second research question.

In summary, the primary conclusion of this study is that more integral theological understandings of forgiveness were evidenced among the majority participants in this intercultural Bible reading process which was conducted under the conditions of positive intergroup contact.

Thus, there are a number of very interesting and useful findings in both the pre-intercultural engagement and post-intercultural engagement datasets. Moreover, the comparative findings (between the pre-intercultural engagement data and the post-intercultural engagement data) show some important and significant hermeneutic shifts in the understandings of forgiveness among the participants who were members of the intercultural Bible reading engagements.

7.2.2 Unexpected findings

In evaluating the findings of the research there were a number of points that were not anticipated or expected from the research process and findings.

- The researcher did not anticipate that such limited intercultural contact under the conditions of positive intergroup contact would deliver such significant hermeneutic shifts in understandings of forgiveness between the pre-intercultural engagement and post-intercultural engagement data. In 3.3.5 it was suggested that a higher frequency and deeper quality of intergroup contact can lead to an "optimal contact strategy", which can "elucidate the conditions under which contact works most effectively to reduce prejudice and, by implication, to increase the possibility of social harmony" (Dixon *et al.*, 2005: 699). The two participating communities only had two intercultural Bible reading engagements together. While the findings resulting from these meetings make a valuable contribution to the scholarly discourse and offer some helpful insights, it would be valuable to conduct further research on the impact of the frequency and quality of such positive intergroup contact engagements on hermeneutic shifts between participants. This would naturally necessitate a different research project.

- As explained in 6.4.3 the researcher never anticipated that there would be significant hermeneutic differences among some participants in their pre-intercultural engagement in-group settings. For example, the participant in Group A who held an individual and spiritual view of forgiveness in the pre-intercultural engagement dataset (D1), and did not significantly shift that view on the post-intercultural engagement dataset (D6). Another example is the participant in Group B who maintained, and even strengthened, an understanding of forgiveness that did not account for the social, political and economic dimensions of forgiveness in the post-intercultural engagement dataset D5. In future research such variances in in-group identity will be anticipated in relation to social identity complexity theories.

7.2.3 Discussion of the findings

Some valuable insights have been gained because of this research project.

First, it is shown that changes in hermeneutic perspectives are possible among members from in-group / out-group communities who have engaged in an intercultural Bible reading intervention. Having established this shift, it could be studied in much greater detail and depth in future projects to ascertain where exactly the shifts took place, why they took place, and whether there are identifiable mechanisms of practices that can account for change under a certain set of conditions.

Second, the researcher values the insights that were gained into the dominant hermeneutic perspectives of participants from the two communities in the pre-intercultural engagement readings of Matthew 18.15-35. This warrants much greater reflection and study. It cannot be contended that communities with a similar history and demographic makeup will present with the same, or even similar, understandings of forgiveness to those found in datasets D1 and D2. However, it would be extremely valuable and interesting to engage a much larger sampling of readers in this process in an inductive study. This has the possibility of delivering much more nuanced and detailed understandings of how members of such communities construct meanings of forgiveness in relation to this text. The outcome of such a study would provide valuable theological information for Churches and academic theologians in fields such as Biblical Studies, Systematic Theology, Ethics and Public Theologies.

Third, while not reported in this study directly, (since it is not related to the research objective), the data shows that the participants valued the process of intercultural Bible reading a great deal. The research has communicated this to the ministers of the two communities. The participants hope that they may find further opportunities to read texts together and in so doing come to a deeper and fuller understanding of both the texts under consideration, and one another.

In a critical sense, an evaluation of the research process and findings uncovered some limitations that could be addressed in future research.

Firstly, since this is a limited scope practice oriented research project, the findings of the research are limited to the participants and variables in question. With greater resources, more time, and a larger sampling, much more valuable insights could be gained for Biblical scholarship, and the problem owner (the Methodist Church of Southern Africa, Helderberg Circuit).

Secondly, since this was the first time that the researcher had engaged in a research process of this nature the research process was not as smooth and economical as it could have been. With the value of hindsight some different choices may be made in future in relation to the sampling of participants (either for them to be more representative of their constituent communities, or for them to be more equally matched demographically). It may also be wise to combine focus groups with other forms of data gathering, such as requesting the participants to keep a structured journal of their experiences, or conducting structured interviews at various points in the intervention cycle.

Thirdly, this research project formed part of a formal research process which was to be examined for the awarding of an academic degree. In conducting the research, and writing up the research findings, the researcher recognised that there are some constraints (and naturally also positive opportunities) that arise from conducting research that is to be examined. No doubt every research project has its own theoretical constraints (publication, institutional requirements, resources etc.) Wherever possible these need to be considered in both the planning and the evaluation of the research process in order to avoid diminishing the possible contribution of the project.

In conclusion, however, this has been a most valuable and insightful project that has delivered superb findings and resulted in significant insights for the problem owner, the communities that were involved, and the researcher. It is hoped that the readers will also find some value in this manuscript.

7.2.4 A reflection on the theological possibilities

At the start of this process it was suggested that forgiveness is an extremely complex theological notion. This study has opened up some aspects of this complexity among the participating communities. Vosloo noted that the complexity of understandings and approaches to forgiveness in public discourse in South Africa complicates the task of working towards a more reconciled nation (Vosloo, 2015: 363). It was suggested that one aspect that complicates this task is that Black and White Christians seldom have opportunities to encounter one another in safe spaces, and under positive intergroup contact conditions, that allow for honest and constructive engagement. Among many other things, this is one of the social realities that makes forgiveness almost impossible in South Africa. Since people cannot encounter one another in a way that allows for the "translation" of the beliefs and experiences of the other, they hold to their untested and entrenched theological and social points of view (Kearney, 2007: 151–152).

This project has shown that it is possible to bring together persons who hold different, and even conflicting, theological perspectives in a manner that allows for honest and safe engagement around those views. The data shows that the participants found great value in the reading, interpreting and discussing of the Biblical text. For some participants it led to new discoveries in the experiences of others (cf., D5:19). For other participants it opened up new ways of understanding and reading the Biblical text, and in particular new understandings of forgiveness as a concept and as a process that has spiritual, political, individual and social contents and expectations (cf., D5:42, D6:47). It is plausible to conclude that one outcome of this research is that it highlights an aspect of the theological importance of reading the text in community with "the other". As Koopman says,

> This joint listening to the Word wills us to develop a common story which belongs to all of us. This common heritage corrects our racial ideologies, but also liberates, encourages and energizes us to work for a new society which reflects something of the biblical ideals. (Koopman, 1998: 165).

The participants did discover that the Biblical concept of forgiveness is a shared concept, and that each of us approaches it form a different vantage point (whether socially, historically, or theologically). They discovered that their own theologies can be enriched, deepened, and even changed, when reading the text with others. An outcome of this process is not only a deeper understanding of forgiveness in Matthew 18.15-35, but also a strengthening of the possibility of forgiveness between the two participating communities (D6:3, 13, 64).

7.3 Contributions of this research to theory

Taking the above findings into account, it can be concluded that this research project has made some contributions towards theory and our conception of how theological understandings of a theological notion (in this case the notion of forgiveness) can change among readers of a Biblical text (Matthew 18.15-35) in an intercultural Bible reading process. We shall highlight some of the contributions that this study has made in under the headings below.

7.3.1 New Testament studies

It is contended that this study has contributed to the field of New Testament studies in the following manner:

7.3.1.1 *Empirical Intercultural Biblical Hermeneutics*

First, the study has shown that a practice oriented research design approach can yield valuable and empirically credible theological insights into the hermeneutic understandings of readers of the Biblical text. This study illustrates a novel a methodological contribution in the field of New Testament studies. It adds new theoretical knowledge to the corpus of scholarly research on empirical intercultural Biblical hermeneutics (cf., Van der Walt, 2010, 2012, 2014; De Wit, 2012; Jonker, 2015). This holds great promise for Biblical scholars and theologians who seek credible and rigorous scholarly methods for identifying, explicating, and discussing complex hermeneutic and theological concepts emerging from readers of the Biblical text.

7.3.1.2 *Social identity theories and Biblical studies*

Second, this study produced data that contributes towards understandings of how the participants from two racially distinct Christian communities interpret the same text (Matthew 18.15-35) and arrive at different understandings of forgiveness in relation to the text. The findings showed that to a large extent the hermeneutic approaches of the respective communities were informed by their primary social identity (cf., 6.2.3 for Group A and 6.2.7 for Group B). The design of the project further shows that there is a clear logic that informs and upholds the theological and hermeneutic positions of the Biblical reader. This hermeneutic logic can be identified and engaged in a qualitative empirical manner. Hence, this is a novel theoretical contribution to the field of intercultural Biblical hermeneutics and social identity approaches to contextual Biblical scholarship (cf., West, 1991, 2014c, 2015, Van der Walt, 2010, 2012, Kok, 2014a,b, 2015, 2016; Kok & Dunne, 2014).

7.3.1.3 *AQAL integral theory and Biblical studies*

Third, the theoretical lens of Ken Wilber's integral AQAL theory was applied to explicate innovative understandings of forgiveness in Matthew 18.15-35 (cf., 2.5, 4.8). This hermeneutic lens allowed the researcher to engage aspects of the theology of the text without losing sight of its primary social and historical context. The AQAL reading of Matthew 18.15-35 built on traditional scholarly readings of the text, while building a bridge between the "then" and the "now" (Burridge, 2007: 356; Kok, 2016: 20). Indeed, some of what was presented in these sections of the research bears a strong semblance to traditional theological perspectives and exegetical strategies. However, there were some aspects that were both new and transformative in relation to the scholarly field and the context of this study (cf., Forster, 2017: 1–10).

7.3.2 Positive Intergroup contact in South African communities

The second major area in which it is suggested that this study has contributed to theory is in the production of knowledge related to positive intergroup contact as facilitated among the religious communities that participated in the study. The findings of the research showed that mere contact is not sufficient to deal with prejudice, fear and distrust. Something more is needed to facilitate the conditions that make it possible for members to aggregate, or amend, their judgements of the out-group, or shift in their theological understandings of forgiveness. What is required is a form of contextually aggregated positive intergroup contact. In an article published out of the process and findings of this research (cf., Forster, 2017: 1–10), it was suggested that Biblical scholarship of this nature holds promise for the emerging approach of Public Theology in Biblical scholarship[126]. Koopman rightly points out, in the line of David Tracy (Tracy, 1975: 287; Ruiter, 2007) and Jürgen Habermas (Smit, 2007b, 2017: 67–94; Dreyer & Pieterse, 2010), that the language, intention, and tone of theology changes (and needs to vary) depending on the public from which it emerges, and the public for which it is intentioned. This study was predicated upon the notion that it wished to produce some findings that would be of value to the "problem owner" (cf., 5.6).

The theoretical conceptualization, findings, and analysis of the findings, in this research have helped to contribute new understandings of how intergroup contact theory may be applied to intercultural Bible reading interventions as a form of Public Theological engagement. The particular approach that was adopted in this study is novel and so holds promise for both methodological development, as well as an interrogation, testing, and refinement of the specific intergroup contact theory findings in the data (cf., 6.4.4-6.5).

Nonetheless, it must be noted that because this is a limited scope practice oriented research project, there are limitations that must be kept in mind when evaluating or engaging the findings of this study.

7.3.2.1 *Limitation of the findings*
This study was intentionally conceptualised as a practice oriented research project that was aimed at engaging specific communities with a particular problem – hence the findings are modestly limited to these parameters. The limitations of the study are discussed in 1.8 and 5.7. The design limitations of the project are set as a result of the limited sample of participants, the limited duration of the intervention, and the nature of the research objectives.

The intention of the study was not to work towards the production of evidence, or conclusive statements that span a wide and complex range of contexts across South Africa or the world. Rather, this case aimed to gain a deeper, more nuanced understanding of a particular set of theological insights related to understandings of forgiveness among racially diverse participants reading the same Biblical text. The selection of the participants and the set of conditions of the research process were chosen in order to gain in-depth and theological information about this particular phenomenon. In summary, the observations contained in this study are not proofs of any specific process or concept. Rather, they form helpful insights into this case and the theological ideas of the participants in this case over the period of this intercultural Bible reading intervention. Naturally this has some value beyond the limited scope of this study since it shows the possibility of such an approach for a much larger, and much more intricate study, of this nature that may have a larger

---

126 Biblical scholarship is of particular importance in relation to notions of Christian orthodoxy and matters of public theological concern. For a more thorough and detailed discussion of the notion of Christian Orthodoxy in relation to Public Theology please refer to, *Moderne orthodoxie: Verdediging van een denkvorm voor de publieke theologie* (Hübenthal, 2015).

sampling, a broader range of Biblical methods and empirical research designs. Thus, it is suggested that this study lays the groundwork for further studies along the same trajectory.

7.3.2.2 Social identity complexity theory and intercultural Biblical hermeneutics

This research project was designed with the intention of addressing the research questions noted above (cf., 7.2). During the process of conducting the research the researcher realised that there are many other possible ways in which this theological problem (cf., 1.3) could have been approached. In this instance the research was designed to gain insight into the theological understandings of forgiveness among participants from two communities before and after a process of intercultural Bible reading was undertaken. The research thus relied on an approach to social identity theory that was presented in detail in chapter 2 – namely, Ken Wilber's AQAL theory.

It was noted that Wilber's work needed to be considered critically. The critiques of scholars such as Schneider in particular, but also Rich, Paulson, Meyerhoff, Brys and Bokor, have highlighted and considered some of the deficiencies and weakness in Wilber's integral theory as a form of integral social identity construction (c.f., Schneider, 1987: 196–216, 1989: 470–481, 2012: 120–123; Rich, 2001; Paulson, 2008; Meyerhoff, 2010; Brys & Bokor, 2013). However, such critique notwithstanding, the researcher made a case for the use of Wilber's AQAL theory for the task at hand. It was argued that while Wilber's approach will have its detractors and critics, it is regarded as a credible approach that is used and appreciated within the scholarly discourse (cf., Rich, 2001; Snyman, 2002; Paulson, 2008; Saiter, 2009; Ferreira, 2010; Forster, 2010a; Meyerhoff, 2010; Brys & Bokor, 2013). In addition, the author sought to nuance and texture Wilber's approach by relying on the work of African and South African social identity scholarship, as is evidenced in chapter 2.

Similarly, it was noted in section 3.3 that intergroup contact theory also has its critics and detractors (Parkin & Forbes, 1999; Wright, 2003: 409–430; Dixon et al., 2005: 697–711; Prestwich, Kenworthy, Wilson & Kwan-Tat, 2008: 575–588; Wright & Lubensky, 2009: 291–310; Hewstone & Swart, 2011a: 379–380). One critique that will need to be considered in furthering the research findings of this project is the tendency to minimize the value of difference and conflict in intergroup contact interventions.

Some scholars have raised the concern that some approaches to intergroup contact may avoid, suppress, or minimize necessary conflict between groups. In addition to this, the interventionist nature of intergroup contact could be seen as a form of social engineering – e.g., bringing about engagement between persons or communities in processes without actually addressing the ideological underpinnings of prejudice. On the issue of power relations, some have argued that facilitated intergroup contact may inadvertently strengthen strong groups and further weaken the position of weaker minorities. These challenges were noted in both the research design, and its implementation, so as to avoid inadvertently invalidating real and necessary concerns among groups or individuals, or to subtly protect the majority at the expense of minority views (Dixon et al., 2005: 697–711).

This project has thus sought to make a contribution by being informed by two social identity theories that provided language and philosophical structures around which to conceptualize and engage the complexity of Biblical hermeneutics and text reception in relation to individual and social identity in a particular South African setting. Naturally many other theories, and theorists, could be employed to approach this task from a variety of different perspectives and for various purposes. This may be a task for future research.

Having noted the above, one area that does deserve further investigation is the notion of social identity complexity theory in relation to both the assumed author and recipients of the Biblical text, as well as the contemporary readers of Biblical texts and their hermeneutics. Kobus Kok's work on social identity complexity theory is an important beacon in this regard (both for the treatment of social identity complexity in the text, and in the contemporary readers of texts) (cf., Kok, 2014a,b, 2016; Kok & Dunne, 2014). It was not possible to delve into the many rich avenues of theological possibility that this field contains within the scope of this project. However, the research process did attempt to acknowledge, and note, the importance of social identity complexity theory in both the Biblical text and the reading communities engaged in this project.

7.4 Possibilities for future research

As is common, this research process has arrived at some findings, and uncovered many other avenues and points of interest that are worth engaging, considering, and researching in future projects. The previous section pointed out that the research was designed in such a way that the findings would be limited so as to ensure credibility, to allow for theological depth, and in order to engage and answer the specific research objectives. Under the headings that follow several points will be mentioned that could warrant further, or future, research in relation to this project and its findings.

7.4.1 Different sample of participants

This project was deliberately contained to a manageable sampling of participants to ensure the successful completion of the practice oriented research cycle. This choice is in keeping with practice oriented research design criteria (Blatter, 2008: 68; Bryman, 2012: 69). However, the findings of this study could be textured, enriched, and even tested, if a larger sampling of participants were engaged in such processes of intercultural Biblical hermeneutics under the conditions of positive intergroup contact. Such an enlarged sampling of participants, while more complicated to work with, will lend far greater depth, variety, and theological texture to enrich our understanding of intercultural Biblical hermeneutics.

7.4.2 Test the intervention and findings in different contexts

A second area in which this research could be developed and taken further, is to test the research design intervention, and the findings of this intervention, with different groups in different contexts. This project was undertaken to develop understanding around a particular set of theological and social conditions. That is, the project focussed on understandings of forgiveness in the reading of Matthew 18.15-35 among two racially and culturally distinct Methodist communities in Somerset West. The unique variables of this project (theological background of the participants, denominational identity, South African history, the topic of forgiveness, the Biblical text (Matthew 18.15-35) etc.) allowed for particular engagements that led to a contextual set of findings. These findings are not normative for all intercultural Bible reading engagements. Rather, what would be valuable is for the project to be presented, refined, and even tested in different contextual settings with different variables (e.g., different communities, different topics, different Biblical texts). This could lead to a much more nuanced and valuable understanding of intercultural Biblical hermeneutics, and of the role of positive intergroup contact in facilitating theological shifts in the understandings of Bible readers from different races and cultures. The outcome of such projects could lead to a series of mechanisms, or even frameworks for engagement, that could aid diverse communities to learn together and deepen their theological understandings of Biblical texts in community.

7.4.3 Engaging the datasets with different objectives or questions in mind

As was seen in presentation and analysis of the findings from the datasets, only a limited number of illustrative examples from the data were presented for analysis. Naturally it is necessary to make choices about what is chosen to illustrate support or disapproval of the hypothesis of the study. This meant that even though the data was worked through extensively, it was done with a particular research aim in mind. The full datasets could be worked through in later research to extract different information or reach other conclusions. They present a rich and textured source of information that is sure to hold value for text reception theories, Biblical hermeneutics, and intergroup contact approaches to intercultural Bible reading in South Africa.

7.5 Reflection on the research process and findings

This project has produced several important and insightful findings. Yet, the scope and nature of the findings are limited to the case under consideration. The problem owner for this project, the Methodist Church of Southern Africa, Helderberg Circuit, will have access to a rich resource of data as a result. This data is can be classified under two broad categories:

- *Intercultural Biblical Hermeneutics*: The first contribution that this research project realised is a series of insights into how the participants in this project understood forgiveness in Matthew 18.15-35 at various stages in the research process. The findings allow the Church, and other academics, to see how the participants formed their understandings of forgiveness in relation to their social identity, and also how these understandings shifted after an intercultural Bible reading process had taken place. The research does not account for the causes of the changed theological perspectives on forgiveness. That will need to be dealt with in a future research project. However, it does show that changes did take place, and that the participants did largely tend towards the adoption of more integral understandings of forgiveness in the post-intercultural engagement readings of Matthew 18.15-35.

- *Positive intergroup contact*: The second significant set of findings that this research presents relate to the design and implementation of the conditions for positive intergroup contact as a part of an intercultural Bible reading process. The research shows that the majority of participants in this study experienced a decrease in intergroup contact anxiety, and an increase in affective empathy and cognitive empathy when positive intergroup contact was facilitated in a manner that included the following conditions, "…equal group status within the situation, common goals, intergroup cooperation and authority support" (Pettigrew, 1998: 65). This is not a causal finding. However, there is some correlation between the conditions for positive intergroup contact and the intercultural Bible reading hermeneutic findings before and after the intervention.

The nature and scope of this project have proven valuable to the researcher. A great deal of insight has been gained into Biblical hermeneutics and the interpretive possibilities of reading the text in an intercultural Bible reading setting. The findings and processes that result from the findings should also hold some value for the two participating communities, and the Helderberg Circuit of the Methodist Church of Southern Africa.

Indeed, the participants in the study also expressed their appreciation for the intercultural Bible reading process, and how it was facilitated. As one participant noted, "there has been a sense all along that all of these things, this understanding, happens better when we do it together" (D5:3, cf., D5:44, 47).

Having read through the datasets (D1-D6), as well as coding the datasets multiple times, the researcher has gained a deep appreciation for the sincerity and commitment that the readers have for the task of working to make forgiveness possible between them. This makes the study truly worthwhile!

7.6 Conclusion

This study began with an acknowledgement that forgiveness is a complex and contested issue in South Africa. In particular, the point was made that while it is a necessary and important process for South Africans, our different hermeneutic understandings of what the Bible says about forgiveness, contribute towards our inability to forgive and be forgiven.

Does this mean that forgiveness is impossible?

This study showed that one could give content to, and explicate, the theological perspectives, and the hermeneutic informants, of readers of the Biblical text. This helps the 'problem owner', i.e., the Methodist Church of Southern Africa, Helderberg Circuit, to understand what some of the barriers to shared understandings of forgiveness may be. Moreover, it allowed for the design of the intercultural Bible reading intervention under the conditions of positive intergroup contact. The data showed that in this case, the participants of this study mostly became more open to the theological understandings of forgiveness of the 'other'.

Nussbaum suggests that such processes of hermeneutic translation remain important when she writes:

> [T]he ability to imagine the experience of another – a capacity almost all human beings possess in some form – needs to be greatly enhanced and refined if we are to have any hope of sustaining decent institutions across the many divisions that any modern society contains. (Nussbaum, 2010: 10).

It is hoped that this project facilitated such an act of translation, even if only in a modest form, between the two participating communities, and that it contributes some new knowledge to scholarly research in this field.

So, to answer the previously stated question, 'Is forgiveness impossible?' In a modest and limited manner, this study has shown that as far as theological understandings of forgiveness among culturally diverse readers of Matthew 18.15-35 is concerned, the journey toward shared understandings of forgiveness may indeed be a possibility.

REFERENCES

Adams, B.G., Van de Vijver, F.J.R. & De Bruin, G.P. 2012. Identity in South Africa: Examining self-descriptions across ethnic groups. *International Journal of Intercultural Relations*. 36(3):377–388.

Adhikari, M. 2005. *Not White Enough, Not Black Enough: Racial Identity in the South African Coloured Community*. Athens, OH: Ohio University Press.

Aland, B., Aland, K., Universität Münster, Institut für Neutestamentliche Textforschung & Deutsche Bibelgesellschaft. 2005. *Greek-English New Testament: Greek text Novum Testamentum Graece, in the tradition of Eberhard Nestle and Erwin Nestle*. Stuttgart: Deutsche Bibelgesellschaft.

Allen, O.W.J. 2013. *Matthew*. Philadelphia: Fortress Press.

Allison, D.C. 2005. Structure, Biographical Impulse, and the Imitatio Christi. In Grand Rapids, MI: Baker Academic *Studies in Matthew: Past and Present*. 135–157.

Allport, G.W. 1954. *The Nature of Prejudice*. Boston, MA: Addison-Wesley.

Amodio, D.M. & Hamilton, H.K. 2012. Intergroup anxiety effects on implicit racial evaluation and stereotyping. *Emotion*. 12(6):1273–1280.

Anon. 2011. The clashing rainbow colours; South Africa and race. *The Economist* (London). 4 June.

Anthony, F.-V., Hermans, C.A.M. & Sterkens, C. 2007. Religious practice and religious socialization: Comparative research among Christian, Muslim and Hindu students in Tamilnadu, India. *Journal of Empirical Theology*. 20(1):100–128.

Aronson, E. 1978. *The jigsaw classroom*. Thousand Oaks, CA: Sage.

Austin, J.L. 1975. *How to do things with words*. Vol. 367. New York, NY: Oxford University Press.

Bacon, B.W. 1930. *Studies in Matthew*. New York: Holt.

Bailie, J. 2009. The impact of liberation theology on Methodism in South Africa with regard to the doctrine of Christian perfection. Unpublished PhD Thesis. University of South Africa. [Online], Available: http://uir.unisa.ac.za/handle/10500/2600 [2015, July 20].

Balcomb, A. 1993. *Third Way Theology: Reconciliation, Revolution, and Reform in the South African Church during the 1980s*. Pietermaritzburg: Cluster Publications.

Balcomb, A.O. 1996. Modernity and the African experience. *Bulletin for Contextual Theology in Southern Africa & Africa*. 3(2):12–20.

Balia, D.M. 1991. *Black Methodists and White Supremacy in South Africa*. Durban: Midiba Publications.

Baloyi, B. & Isaacs, G. 2015. *#FeesMustFall: What are the student protests about? - CNN.com*. [Online], Available: http://www.cnn.com/2015/10/27/africa/fees-must-fall-student-protest-south-africa-explainer/index.html [2015, November 20].

Barlow, F.K., Louis, W.R. & Hewstone, M. 2009. Rejected! Cognitions of rejection and intergroup anxiety as mediators of the impact of cross-group friendships on prejudice. *British Journal of Social Psychology*. 48(3):389–405.

Barrow, J.D. & Tipler, F.J. 1988. *The Anthropic Cosmological Principle*. Oxford, UK: Oxford University Press.

Bartchy, S.S. 1992. Table Fellowship. In J.B. Green, S. McKnight, & I.H. Marshall (eds.). Leciester: InterVarsity Press *Dictionary of Jesus and the Gospels*. 796–800.

Barthes, R. 1990. Texte. In Vol. 22. Paris *Encyclopaedia Universalis*. 370–374.

Bartlett, D. 2001. *Ministry in the New Testament*. Eugene, OR: Wipf & Stock Publishers.

Batson, C.D., Polycarpou, M.P., Harmon-Jones, E., Imhoff, H.J., Mitchener, E.C., Bednar, L.L., Klein, T.R. & Highberger, L. 1997. Empathy and attitudes: can feeling for a member of a stigmatized group improve feelings toward the group? *Journal of Personality and Social Psychology*. 72(1):105–118.

Batson, C.D., Chang, J., Orr, R. & Rowland, J. 2002. Empathy, Attitudes, and Action: Can Feeling for a Member of a Stigmatized Group Motivate One to Help the Group? *Personality and Social Psychology Bulletin*. 28(12):1656–1666.

Bauckham, R. 1998. *Gospels for All Christians*. London: Bloomsbury Academic.

Bauer, D. 1989. *Structure of Matthew's Gospel: A Study in Literary Design*. New York, NY: Continuum.

Benner, D.G. & Crabb, L. 2004. *Sacred Companions: The Gift of Spiritual Friendship & Direction*. Downers Grove, IL: IVP Books.

Bergold, J. & Thomas, S. 2012. Participatory Research Methods: A Methodological Approach in Motion. *Forum Qualitative Sozialforschung / Forum: Qualitative Social Research*. 13(1). [Online], Available: http://www.qualitative-research.net/index.php/fqs/article/view/1801 [2013, December 03].

Biko, S. 2002. *I Write What I Like: Selected Writings*. Chicago, Il: University of Chicago Press.

Birx, H.J. 2010. *21st Century Anthropology: A Reference Handbook*. Thousand Oaks, CA: SAGE Publications.

Blatter, J.K. 2008. Case Study. In Vols 1 & 2. L.M. Given (ed.). London: SAGE Publications *The SAGE encyclopedia of Qualitative Research Methods*. 68–71.

Blomberg, C.L. 2009. *Interpreting the Parables*. Downers Grove, IL: InterVarsity Press.

Boesak, A. 2008. And Zaccheus remained in the tree: reconciliation and justice and the Truth and Reconciliation Commission. *Verbum et Ecclesia*. 29(3):636–654.

Boesak, A.A. 2015. *Kairos, Crisis, and Global Apartheid: The Challenge to Prophetic Resistance*. London: Palgrave Macmillan.

Boesak, A., Fitchue, E.J., Fitchue, L.G., Fluker, W.E., Harris, F.E., Koopman, N., Mingo, A., Nel, R., et al. 2015. *Contesting Post-Racialism: Conflicted Churches in the United States and South Africa*. R.D. Smith, W. Ackah, A.G. Reddie, & R.S. Tshaka (eds.). Jackson: University Press of Mississippi.

Bohm, D. 1993. Science, spirituality and the present world crisis. *Revision*. 15(4).

Bohm, D. 2002. *Wholeness and the Implicate Order*. Reissue edition ed. Abingdon: Routledge.

Boleyn-Fitzgerald, P. 2002. What should "forgiveness" mean? *The Journal of Value Inquiry*. 36(4):483–498.

Borgen. 1998. *Early Christianity and Hellenistic Judaism*. New York, NY: Continuum.

van der Borght, E. 2008. *Christian identity*. Vol. 16. Leiden: Brill.

van der Borght, E. 2009. [Online], Available: https://research.vu.nl/files/2632701/Oratie%20 Borght.pdf [2017, May 07].

van der Borght, E. 2010. *The unity of the church: A theological state of the art and beyond*. Vol. 18. Leiden: Brill.

Bornman, E. 1999. Self-image and Ethnic Identification in South Africa. *The Journal of Social Psychology*. 139(4):411–425.

Bornman, E. 2011. Patterns of intergroup attitudes in South Africa after 1994. *International Journal of Intercultural Relations*. 35(6):729.

Botha, J. & Forster, D.A. 2017. Justice and the Missional Framework Document of the Dutch Reformed Church. *Verbum et Ecclesia*. 38(1):1–9.

Bowers du Toit, N.F. & Nkomo, G. 2014. The ongoing challenge of restorative justice in South Africa: How and why wealthy suburban congregations are responding to poverty and inequality. *HTS Theological Studies*. 70(2):1–8.

Brewer, M.B. & Kramer, R.M. 1985. The Psychology of Intergroup Attitudes and Behavior. *Annual Review of Psychology*. 36(1):219–243.

Bridge, S.L. 2004. *Getting the Gospels: Understanding the New Testament Accounts of Jesus' Life*. Grand Rapids, MI: Baker Books.

Brown, J.K. 2002. *The disciples in narrative perspective: The portrayal and function of the Matthean disciples*. Vol. 9. Leiden: Brill.

Brown, R. 2012. Liking more or hating less? A modest defence of intergroup contact theory. *The Behavioral and brain sciences*. 35(6):428.

Brown, R.E. 1986. *Birth of the Messiah*. London: Bloomsbury Publishing.

Bryman, A. 2012. *Social research methods*. Oxford; New York: Oxford University Press.

Brys, Z. & Bokor, P. 2013. Evaluation of Ken Wilber's Integral Psychology From a Scientific Perspective. *Journal of Spirituality in Mental Health*. 15(1):19–33.

Buitelaar, M. 2006. "I Am the Ultimate Challenge" Accounts of Intersectionality in the Life-Story of a Well-Known Daughter of Moroccan Migrant Workers in the Netherlands. *European Journal of Women's Studies*. 13(3):259–276.

Bultmann, R.K. 1963. *The history of the synoptic tradition*. New York, NY: Harper & Row.

Burch-Brown, J. & Baker, W. 2016. Religion and reducing prejudice. *Group Processes & Intergroup Relations*. (March, 9):1–24.

Burridge, R.A. 1997. The Gospels and Acts. In S.E. Porter (ed.). Leiden: Brill *Handbook of Classical Rhetoric in the Hellenistic Period - 330 B.C. - A.D. 400*. 507–532.

Burridge, R.A. 2004. *What Are the Gospels?: A Comparison with Graeco-Roman Biography*. Grand Rapids, MI: Wm. B. Eerdmans Publishing.

Burridge, R.A. 2005. *Four Gospels, One Jesus? A Symbolic Reading*. 2nd ed. Grand Rapids, MI: William B. Eerdmans Pub.

Burridge, R.A. 2007. *Imitating Jesus: an inclusive approach to New Testament ethics*. Grand Rapids, MI: William B. Eerdmans Pub.

Byrne, M. 2007. *Trauma and Forgiveness: Lessons from South Africa and East Timor*. Alexandria, NSW: Australian Catholic Social Justice Council.

Cairns, E. & Hewstone, M. 2002. The impact of peacemaking in Northern Ireland on intergroup behaviour. *The nature and study of peace education*. 217–228.

Cairns, E., Hewstone, M. & Tam, T. 2006. Forgiveness in northern Ireland. *A Sampling of Research Results*. 20.

Cakal, H. 2012. Unpacking intergroup anxiety. *INTERNATIONAL JOURNAL OF PSYCHOLOGY*. 47:687.

Cakal, H., Hewstone, M., Schwär, G. & Heath, A. 2011. An investigation of the social identity model of collective action and the "sedative" effect of intergroup contact among Black and White students in South Africa. *British Journal of Social Psychology*. 50(4):606–627.

Capra, F. 1996. *The Web of Life: A New Scientific Understanding of Living Systems*. New York, NY: Anchor Books.

Carter, W. 1992. Kernels and Narrative Blocks: The Structure of Matthew's Gospel. *The Catholic Biblical Quarterly*. 54(3):463–481.

Carter, W. 2005. *Matthew and the Margins*. London: Bloomsbury Academic.

Carter, W.C. 2000. *Matthew and the margins*. Vol. 204. (Journal for the study of the New Testament. Supplement series). Sheffield: Sheffield Academic Press.

Carter, W. & Heil, J.P. 1998. *Matthew's Parables: Audience-Oriented Perspectives*. Washington, DC: Catholic Biblical Association of America.

Castelli, E.A. 1991. *Imitating Paul: A discourse of power*. London; Louisville, KY: Westminster John Knox Press.

Castro, F.G., Kellison, J.G., Boyd, S.J. & Kopak, A. 2010. A methodology for conducting integrative mixed methods research and data analyses. *Journal of mixed methods research*. 4(4):342–360.

Catchpole, D. 1983. Reproof and Reconciliation in the Q Community: A Study of the Tradition-history of Mt 18,15-17.21-22/Lk 17, 3-4. *STUDIEN ZUM NEUEN TESTAMENT UND SEINER UMWELT*. 8:83–84.

Cezula, N.S. 2013. Identity formation and community solidarity : second temple historiographies in discourse with (South) African theologies of reconstruction. Thesis. Stellenbosch : Stellenbosch University. [Online], Available: https://scholar.sun.ac.za/handle/10019.1/80038 [2015, October 29].

Cezula, N.S. 2015. Reading the Bible in the African context: Assessing Africa's love affair with prosperity Gospel. *Stellenbosch Theological Journal*. 1(2):131–153.

Chapman, A. & Spong, B. 2003. *Religion & Reconciliation in South Africa*. West Conshohocken, PA: Templeton Foundation Press.

Christ, O., Schmid, K., Lolliot, S., Swart, H., Stolle, D., Tausch, N., Al Ramiah, A., Wagner, U., et al. 2014. Contextual effect of positive intergroup contact on outgroup prejudice. *Proceedings of the National Academy of Sciences*. 111(11):3996–4000.

Christopher, M. 2010. *A Source critical Edition of the Gospels of Matthew and Luke in Greek and English: Vol. 1 Matthew - Vol. 2 Luke*. Rome: Gregorian Biblical BookShop.

Claassens, J. & Birch, B. 2015. *Restorative readings: Old Testament, Ethics, Human Dignity*. Eugene, OR: Wipf and Stock Publishers.

Claassens, L. & Juliana, M. 2011. Human dignity in the prophetic traditions: Upholding human worth in a context of dehumanisation. *Nederduitse Gereformeerde Teologiese Tydskrif*. 52(1). [Online], Available: http://ngtt.journals.ac.za/pub/article/view/4 [2014, October 24].

Cloke, K. 1994. *Mediation: Revenge and the magic of forgiveness*. 2nd. ed edition ed. London: Center for Dispute Resolution.

Coakley, S. & Stang, C.M. 2011. *Re-thinking Dionysius the Areopagite*. Hoboken, NJ: John Wiley & Sons.

Cochrane, J., De Gruchy, J. & Martin, S. 1999. Faith, struggle and reconciliation. In J. Cochrane, J. De Gruchy, & S. Martin (eds.). Cape Town: David Philip Publishers *Facing the truth. South African faith communities and the Truth and Reconciliation Commission*. 1–11.

Collier, K.L., Bos, H.M.W. & Sandfort, T.G.M. 2012. Intergroup contact, attitudes toward homosexuality, and the role of acceptance of gender non-conformity in young adolescents. *Journal of Adolescence*. 35(4):899–907.

Combrink, H.B. 1983. The structure of the Gospel of Matthew as narrative. *Tyndale Bulletin*. 34:61–90.

Combrink, H.J.B. 1982. The macrostructure of the Gospel of Matthew. *Neotestamentica*. 1–20.

Critchley, S., Kearney, R., Dooley, M. & Hughes, M. 2001. *On Cosmopolitanism and Forgiveness*. Routledge London.

Damasio, A. 2008. *Descartes' error: Emotion, reason and the human brain*. New York, NY: Random House.

D'Aquili, E.G. & Newberg, A.B. 1999. *The Mystical Mind: Probing the Biology of Religious Experience*. Philadelphia: Fortress Press.

Davies, W.D. & Allison, D.C. 1988. *A critical and exegetical commentary on the Gospel according to Saint Matthew*. Edinburgh: T&T Clark.

Davies, W.D. & Jr, D.C.A. 2004. *Matthew 8-18*. London: A&C Black.

Davis, M.H. 1994. *Empathy: A Social Psychological Approach*. Boulder, CO: Westview Press.

Daye, R. 2012. *Political Forgiveness: Lessons from South Africa*. Eugene, OR: Wipf & Stock Publishers.

De Boer, M.C. 1988. Ten Thousand Talents? Matthew's Interpretation and Redaction of the Parable of the Unforgiving Servant (Matt 18:23-35). *Catholic Biblical Quarterly*. 50(1):214–232.

De Chardin, P.T. 2008. *The Phenomenon of Man*. New York, NY: HarperCollins.

De Gruchy, J.W. 2002. *Reconciliation: Restoring Justice*. London: Fortress Press.

De Gruchy, J.W. 2005. *The Church Struggle in South Africa*. Twenty-fifth anniversary ed., 1st Fortress Press ed ed. Minneapolis: Fortress Press.

De Gruchy, J.W. 2013. *Led into mystery: faith seeking answers in life and death*. London: SCM Press.

De Quincey, C. 2006. *Radical Knowing: Understanding Consciousness through Relationship*. San Francisco, CA: Inner Traditions / Bear & Co.

De Vos, A.S. 1998. *Research at grass roots: a primer for the caring professions*. 1st ed ed. Pretoria: J.L. van Schaik : Academic.

De Wit, J.H. 2012. *Empirical Hermeneutics, Interculturality, and Holy Scripture*. Elkhart, IN: Institute of Mennonite Studies.

De Wit, J.H. de & West, G. 2008. *African and European Readers of the Bible in Dialogue: In Quest Of a Shared Meaning*. Leiden: Brill.

Dea, W. 2010. *Igniting Brilliance: Integral Education for the 21st Century*. Boston, MA: Integral Publishers.

DeCuir-Gunby, J.T., Marshall, P.L. & McCulloch, A.W. 2011. Developing and using a codebook for the analysis of interview data: An example from a professional development research project. *Field methods*. 23(2):136–155.

Derrida, J. 2007. A certain impossible possibility of saying the event. *Critical Inquiry*. 33(2):441–461.

Descartes, R. & Cress, D.A. 1993. *Meditations on First Philosophy (Third Edition)*. Indianapolis, IN: Hackett Publishing.

DeYoung, C. & Boesak, A.A. 2012. *Radical Reconciliation: Beyond Political Pietism and Christian Quietism*. Maryknoll, NY: Orbis Books.

Dibelius, M. & Iber, G. 1971. *Die Formgeschichte des Evangeliums*. Tübingen: Mohr.

Dixon, J., Durrheim, K. & Tredoux, C. 2005. Beyond the Optimal Contact Strategy: A Reality Check for the Contact Hypothesis. *American Psychologist*. 60(7):697–711.

Dovidio, J.F., Glick, P. & Rudman, L. 2008. *On the Nature of Prejudice*. Hoboken, NJ: John Wiley & Sons.

Dovidio, J.F., Eller, A. & Hewstone, M. 2011. Improving intergroup relations through direct, extended and other forms of indirect contact. *Group Processes & Intergroup Relations*. 14(2):147–160.

Dreyer, J.S. & Pieterse, H.J.C. 2010. Religion in the public sphere: What can public theology learn from Habermas's latest work? *HTS Teologiese Studies / Theological Studies*. 66(1).

Du Toit, C.W. Ed. 2004. *The Integrity of the Human Person in an African Context: Perspectives from Science and Religion*. Pretoria: Research Institute for Theology and Religion.

Du Toit, F. & Doxtader, E. 2010. *In the balance: South Africans debate reconciliation*. Auckland Park, South Africa: Jacana Media.

Dube, M.W. 2001. *Other ways of reading: African women and the Bible*. Society of Biblical Literature Atlanta. [Online], Available: http://ngkok.co.za/vbo/e-mouton/RoseAbbey2001_IamtheWoman.pdf [2015, March 11].

Dube, Z. 2013. Teaching the Bible at public universities in South Africa: A proposal for multidisciplinary approach. *HTS Teologiese Studies / Theological Studies*. 69(1).

Duffy, M. 2009. *Paul Ricoeur's pedagogy of pardon*. London: Continuum.

Duling, D.C. 1999. Matthew 18:15-17: Conflict, Confrontation, and Conflict Resolution in a "Fictive Kin" Association. *Biblical Theology Bulletin: A Journal of Bible and Theology*. 29(1):4–22.

Duling, D.C. 2002. Matthew as marginal scribe in an advanced agrarian society. *HTS Teologiese Studies / Theological Studies*. 58(2).

Duncan, N. 2003. "Race" talk: discourses on "race" and racial difference. *International Journal of Intercultural Relations*. 27(2):135–156.

Durrheim, K. & Foster, D. 1995. The Structure of Sociopolitical Attitudes in South Africa. *The Journal of Social Psychology*. 135(3):387–402.

Eagly, A.H., Baron, R.M., Hamilton, V.L. & Kelman, H.C. 2004. *The social psychology of group identity and social conflict*. (APA decade of behavior volumes). Washington, DC: American Psychological Association.

Elkington, R. 2011. *Transformation: Race, Prejudice and Forgiveness in the New South Africa*. New York, NY: Lulu.com.

Elliott, J.H. 1993. *Social Scientific Criticism of the New Testament*. Augsburg: Fortress Press.

Ellison, P.T. & Keifert, P. 2011. *Dwelling in the word: a pocket handbook*. Minnesota: Church innovations.

Erasmus, J. 2012. Religious demographics in post-apartheid South Africa. In Stellenbosch, South Africa: AFRICAN SUN MeDIA *Welfare, Religion and Gender in Post-apartheid South Africa: Constructing a South-North Dialogue*. 43–64.

Eubank, N.P. 2012. Wages of righteousness: The economy of heaven in the Gospel of Matthew. Unpublished Thesis. Duke University.

Farmer, W.R. 1976. *The Synoptic Problem: A Critical Analysis*. Macon, GA: Mercer University Press.

Ferreira, I. (Naas) W. 2010. Die ontwikkeling van die menslike bewussyn: Ken Wilber se AQAL-teorie. *HTS Teologiese Studies / Theological Studies*. 66(1):1–8.

Finlay, K.A. & Stephan, W.G. 2000. Improving Intergroup Relations: The Effects of Empathy on Racial Attitudes1. *Journal of Applied Social Psychology*. 30(8):1720–1737.

Ford, D.F. 2005. *The Modern Theologians: An Introduction to Christian Theology Since 1918*. Hoboken, NJ: Wiley.

Forrester, D.B., Storrar, W. & Morton, A. 2004. *Public Theology for the 21st Century: Essays in Honour of Duncan B. Forrester*. London: A&C Black.

Forster, D. 2005. Post-human Consciousness and the Evolutionary Cosmology of Pierre Teilhard de Chardin. *Grace and Truth: A Journal of Catholic Reflection for Southern Africa*. 22(2):29–44.

Forster, D.A. 2006. Validation of individual consciousness in strong artificial intelligence: an African theological contribution. PhD. University of South Africa. [Online], Available: http://uir.unisa.ac.za/handle/10500/2361 [2015, July 13].

Forster, D.A. 2007. Identity in relationship: The ethics of Ubuntu as an answer to the impasse of individual consciousness. In C.W. Du Toit (ed.). Pretoria: Research Institute for Theology and Religion *The impact of knowledge systems on Human Development in Africa*. 245–289.

Forster, D.A. 2008a. God's mission in our context: Critical questions, healing and transforming responses. In W. Bentley & D.A. Forster (eds.). Kempton Park: AcadSA Publishers *Methodism in Southern Africa: A celebration of Wesleyan mission*. 70–99.

Forster, D.A. 2008b. Why you can't simply trust everything you read. In W. Bentley & D.A. Forster (eds.). Cape Town: Methodist Publishing House *What are we Thinking? Reflections on Church and Society from Southern African Methodists*. 25–46.

Forster, D.A. 2008c. Prophetic witness and social action as holiness in the Methodist Church of Southern Africa's mission. *Studia Historiae Ecclesiasticae*. XXXIV,(1):411–434.

Forster, D.A. 2010a. A generous ontology: Identity as a process of intersubjective discovery – An African theological contribution. *HTS Teologiese Studies / Theological Studies*. 66(1):1–12.

Forster, D.A. 2010b. African relational ontology, individual identity, and Christian theology An African theological contribution towards an integrated relational ontological identity. *Theology*. 113(874):243–253.

Forster, D.A. 2010c. The Church has AIDS: Towards a Positive Theology for an HIV+ Church. *EPWORTH REVIEW*. One(Two):6–24.

Forster, D.A. 2015a. What hope is there for South Africa? A public theological reflection on the role of the church as a bearer of hope for the future. *HTS Teologiese Studies / Theological Studies*. 71(1):1–10.

Forster, D.A. 2015b. What hope is there for South Africa? A public theological reflection on the role of the church as a bearer of hope for the future: original research. *HTS: Theological Studies*. 71(3):1–13.

Forster, D.A. 2017. A public theological approach to the (im) possibility of forgiveness in Matthew 18.15-35: Reading the text through the lens of integral theory. *In die Skriflig/In Luce Verbi*. 51(3):1–10.

Forster, D.A. & Bentley, W. 2008. *Methodism in Southern Africa: A celebration of Wesleyan Mission*. 1st ed. Kempton Park: AcadSA Publishers.

Forster, D.A. & Oostenbrink, J.W. 2015. Where is the church on Monday? Awakening the church to the theology and practice of ministry and mission in the marketplace: original research. *In die Skriflig: The George Lotter Dedication*. 49(3):1–8.

France, R.T. 2007. *The Gospel of Matthew*. Grand Rapids, MI: Wm. B. Eerdmans Publishing.

Friese, S. 2014. *Qualitative data analysis with ATLAS.ti*. London: SAGE.

The Gospel of Matthew: Jesus as the new Moses. 2004. (From Jesus to Christ: The first Christians). Arlington, VA: PBS. [Online], Available: http://www.pbs.org/wgbh/pages/frontline/shows/religion/story/matthew.html [2013, October 13].

Ganzevoort, R.R., de Haardt, M. & Scherer-Rath, M. 2013. *Religious stories we live by: Narrative approaches in theology and religious studies*. Brill.

Garland, D.E. 1999. *Reading Matthew: A Literary and Theological Commentary on the First Gospel*. Macon, GA: Smyth & Helwys Publishing, Inc.

Gebser, J. 1985. *The Ever-Present Origin*. Athens, OH: Ohio University Press.

General Household Survey 2013. 2014. (Statistical Information 1). Pretoria, South Africa: Statistics South Africa. [Online], Available: http://www.statssa.gov.za/publications/P0318/P03182013.pdf [2015, June 11].

Gesthuizen, M.J.W., Scheepers, P.L.H. & Savelkoul, M.J. 2011. Explaining relationships between ethnic diversity and informal social capital across European countries and regions: Tests of constrict, conflict and contact theory. 40(4):1091–1107.

Gibson, J.L. & Gouws, A. 2000. Social Identities and Political Intolerance: Linkages within the South African Mass Public. *American Journal of Political Science*. 44(2):278–292.

Given, L.M. 2008. *The SAGE Encyclopedia of Qualitative Research Methods*. Los Angeles, CA: SAGE Publications.

Giversen, S. & Borgen, P. Eds. 1995. *The New Testament and Hellenistic Judaism*. Aarhus, Denmark; Oakville, Conn.: Aarhus University Press.

Gobodo-Madikizela, P. 1997. Healing the racial divide? Personal reflections on the Truth and Reconciliation Commission. *South African Journal of Psychology*. 27(4):271–272.

Gobodo-Madikizela, P. 2002. Remorse, forgiveness, and rehumanization: Stories from South Africa. *Journal of humanistic psychology*. 42(1):7–32.

Gobodo-Madikizela, P. 2003a. *A human being died that night: A South African story of forgiveness*. Boston, MA: Houghton Mifflin.

Gobodo-Madikizela, P. 2003b. Alternatives to revenge: Building a vocabulary of reconciliation through political pardon. *The provocations of amnesty: Memory, justice and impunity*. 51–60.

Gobodo-Madikizela, P. 2008a. Trauma, forgiveness and the witnessing dance: Making public spaces intimate. *Journal of Analytical Psychology*. 53(2):169–188.

Gobodo-Madikizela, P. 2008b. Transforming trauma in the aftermath of gross human rights abuses: Making public spaces intimate through the South African Truth and Reconciliation Commission. *Social psychology of intergroup reconciliation*. 57–75.

Gobodo-Madikizela, P. 2008c. Empathetic Repair after Mass Trauma When Vengeance is Arrested. *European Journal of Social Theory*. 11(3):331–350.

Gobodo-Madikizela, P. 2011. Intersubjectivity and Embodiment: Exploring the Role of the Maternal in the Language of Forgiveness and Reconciliation. *Signs*. 36(3):541–551.

Gobodo-Madikizela, P. 2012. Remembering the past: Nostalgia, traumatic memory, and the legacy of apartheid. *Peace and Conflict: Journal of Peace Psychology*. 18(3):252.

Gobodo-Madikizela, P. & Merwe, C.V.D. 2009. *Memory, Narrative and Forgiveness: Perspectives on the Unfinished Journeys of the Past*. Cambridge: Cambridge Scholars Publishing.

Goldin, I. 2014. The reconstitution of Coloured identity in the Western Cape. In S. Marks & S. Trapido (eds.). New York, NY: Routledge *The politics of race, class and nationalism in twentieth century South Africa*. 156–181.

Goodacre, M. 2004. *The Synoptic Problem: A Way Through the Maze*. London: A&C Black.

Goosen, A. 2011. Comparing cross-group and same-group friendships amongst white South African students at Stellenbosch University. Thesis. Stellenbosch : University of Stellenbosch. [Online], Available: https://scholar.sun.ac.za/handle/10019.1/6735 [2015, October 29].

Gowan, D.E. 2010. *The Bible on forgiveness*. Eugene, OR: Pickwick Publications.

Green, J.B. 2006. Conversion in Luke-Acts: The Potential of a Cognitive Approach. *Consultation on the Use of Cognitive Linguistics in Biblical Interpretation, Conversion in Luke-Acts (SBL). wpd*. 1–28.

Greenstein, G. & Zajonc, A. 2006. *The Quantum Challenge: Modern Research on the Foundations of Quantum Mechanics*. Boston, MA: Jones & Bartlett Learning.

Griffiths, B. 1990. *A New Vision of Reality: Western Science, Eastern Mysticism and Christian Faith*. Springfield, Il: Templegate Publishers.

Grigsby, J. & Stevens, D. 2000. *Neurodynamics of Personality*. New York, NY: Guilford Press.

Grof, S. & Valier, M.L. 1984. *Ancient Wisdom and Modern Science*. Albany, NY: SUNY Press.

Gundry, R.H. 1994. *Matthew: A Commentary on His Handbook for a Mixed Church Under Persecution*. Grand Rapids, MI: Wm. B. Eerdmans Publishing.

de Haardt, M. 2013. Visual Narratives: Entrance to everyday religious practices. In R.R. Ganzevoort, M. de Haardt, & M. Scherer-Rath (eds.). Leiden: Brill *Religious stories we live by: narrative approaches in theology and religious studies*. 209–220.

Hägerland, T. 2011. *Jesus and the Forgiveness of Sins: An Aspect of his Prophetic Mission*. Cambridge: Cambridge University Press.

Hagner, D.A. 1993. *Matthew*. Dallas, TX: Word Books.

Hagner, D.A. 1995. *Word Biblical Commentary, Vol. 33b: Matthew 14-28*. Dallas, TX: Thomas Nelson.

Hammett, D. 2010. Ongoing contestations: the use of racial signifiers in post-apartheid South Africa. *Social Identities*. 16(2):247–260.

Hannoum, A. 2005. Paul Ricoeur On Memory. *Theory, Culture & Society*. 22(6):123–137.

Harding, M. 2003. *Early Christian life and thought in social context: a reader*. London; New York: Sheffield Academic Press.

Harré, R. 2002. Public sources of the personal mind social constructionism in context. *Theory & Psychology*. 12(5):611–623.

Harrison, J.R. 2013. The imitation of the "great man" in antiquity: Paul's inversion of a cultural icon. In S.E. Porter & A.W. Pitts (eds.). Leiden: Brill *Christian origins and Greco-Roman culture*. 213–254.

Heilbron, H.L. 2012. Christians and religious diversity? : a theological evaluation of the meaning of an ethic of embrace in a context of religious diversity. Thesis. Stellenbosch : Stellenbosch University. [Online], Available: https://scholar.sun.ac.za/handle/10019.1/19920 [2015, October 29].

Hendriks, J. & Erasmus, J. 2005. Religion in South Africa: 2001 population census data. *Journal of Theology for Southern Africa*. 121:88–111.

Hermans, C.A.M. & Moore, M.E. Eds. 2004. *Hermeneutics and empirical research in practical theology: the contribution of empirical theology by Johannes A. van der Ven*. (Empirical studies in theology no. v. 11). Leiden ; Boston: Brill.

Hermans, C.A.M. 2000. Analysing the dialogic construction of identity of religiously affiliated schools in a multicultural society. *International Journal of Education and Religion*. 1(1):135–165.

Hermans, C.A.M. 2003. *Participatory learning*. Vol. 9. Leiden: Brill.

Hermans, C.A.M. 2004. When theology goes "practical". From applied to empirical theology. In C.A.M. Hermans & M.E. Moore (eds.). Leiden: Brill *Hermeneutics and empirical research in practical theology: the contribution of empirical theology by Johannes A. van der Ven*. 21–52.

Hermans, C.A.M. 2014. From Practical Theology to Practice-oriented Theology. *International Journal of Practical Theology*. 18(1):113–126.

Hermans, C. & Schoeman, W.J. 2015a. Practice-oriented research in service of designing interventions. *Acta Theologica*. 35:26–44.

Hermans, C. & Schoeman, W.J. 2015b. Survey research in practical theology and congregational studies. *Acta Theologica*. 35:45–63.

Hermans, C. & Schoeman, W.J. 2015c. The utility of practical theology: Mapping the domain, goals, strategies and criteria of practical theological research. *Acta Theologica*. 35:8–25.

Hermans, C.A.M., Graham, E. & Rowlands, A. 2005. A pragmatic practical theology as public theology. *Pathways to the public square: Practical theology in an age of pluralism*. 219–228.

Herzog, W. 1992. Sociological Approaches to the Gospel. In S. McKnight & J.B. Green (eds.). Downers Grove, IL: InterVarsity Press *Dictionary of Jesus and the Gospels*.

Hewstone, M. 1996. Contact and Categorization: Social Psychological. *Stereotypes and stereotyping*. 323.

Hewstone, M. 2009. Living Apart, Living Together? The Role of Intergroup Contact in Social Integration. In R. Johnston (ed.). British Academy *Proceedings of the British Academy, Volume 162, 2008 Lectures*. 242–300. [Online], Available: http://www.britishacademypublications.com/view/10.5871/bacad/9780197264584.001.0001/upso-9780197264584-chapter-9 [2016, July 20].

Hewstone, M. & Swart, H. 2011a. Fifty-odd years of inter-group contact: From hypothesis to integrated theory. *British Journal of Social Psychology*. 50(3):374–386.

Hewstone, M. & Swart, H. 2011b. Fifty-odd years of inter-group contact: From hypothesis to integrated theory: Fifty-odd years of inter-group contact. *British Journal of Social Psychology*. 50(3):374–386.

Hewstone, M., Cairns, E., Voci, A., McLernon, F., Niens, U. & Noor, M. 2004. Intergroup forgiveness and guilt in Northern Ireland. *Collective guilt: International perspectives*. 193–215.

Hewstone, M., Kenworthy, J.B., Cairns, E., Tausch, N., Hughes, J., Tam, T., Voci, A., Von Hecker, U., et al. 2008. Stepping stones to reconciliation in Northern Ireland: Intergroup contact, forgiveness and trust. *The social psychology of intergroup reconciliation*. 199–226.

Hofmeyr, J.H. & Govender, R. 2015. *SA Reconciliation Barometer 2015: National Reconciliation, Race Relations, and Social Inclusion*. Cape Town: Institute for Justice and Reconciliation. [Online], Available: http://www.ijr.org.za/uploads/IJR_SARB_2015_WEB_002.pdf.

Howard, L. 2005. *Introducing Ken Wilber: Concepts for an Evolving World*. Bloomington, In: AuthorHouse.

Hubbard, B.J. 1974. *The Matthean redaction of a primitive apostolic commissioning: An exegesis of Matthew 28: 16-20*. Society of Biblical Literature.

Hübenthal, C. 2015. *Moderne orthodoxie: Verdediging van een denkvorm voor de publieke theologie*. Nijmegen: Radboud Universiteit.

Huber, W. & Fourie, W. 2012. *Christian Responsibility and Communicative Freedom: A Challenge for the Future of Pluralistic Societies : Collected Essays*. Münster: LIT Verlag.

Huizenga, L.A. 2009. *The new Isaac: tradition and intertextuality in the Gospel of Matthew*. Vol. 131. Leiden: Brill.

Hultgren, A.J. 2002. *The Parables of Jesus: A Commentary*. Grand Rapids, MI: Wm. B. Eerdmans Publishing.

Huxley, A. 1945. *The Perennial Philosophy*. New York, NY: Harper Collins.

Hwang, S. 2008. Utilizing qualitative data analysis software: A review of Atlas.ti. *Social Science Computer Review*. 26(4):519–527.

Islam, M.R. & Hewstone, M. 1993. Dimensions of contact as predictors of intergroup anxiety, perceived out-group variability, and out-group attitude: An integrative model. *Personality and Social Psychology Bulletin*. 19(6):700–710.

James, L.R., Demaree, R.G. & Wolf, G. 1984. Estimating within-group interrater reliability with and without response bias. *Journal of applied psychology*. 69(1):85.

Jantsch, E. 1980. *The self-organizing universe: scientific and human implications of the emerging paradigm of evolution*. Oxford: Pergamon Press.

Jenkins, P. 2006. Reading the Bible in the global south. *International Bulletin of Missionary Research*. 30(2):67–73.

Jeremias, J. 1958. Jesus' Promise to the Nations: The Franz Delitzsch Lecturesfor 1953. *Studies in Biblical Theology*. 24.

Jeremias, J. 2003. *The Parables of Jesus*. London: S.C.M. Press.

Jones, L.G. 2008. *Transformed Judgement: Toward a Trinitarian Account of the Moral Life*. Eugene, OR: Wipf & Stock Publishers.

Jonker, L. 2006. From multiculturality to interculturality : can intercultural biblical hermeneutics be of any assistance? : colloquium on. [Online], Available: http://reference. sabinet.co.za/sa_epublication_article/script_v91_a3 [2015, July 02].

Jonker, L. 2015. *From adequate Biblical interpretation to transformative intercultural hermeneutics: Chronicling a personal journey*. (Intercultural Biblical Hermeneutics Series no. 3). Elkhart, IN: Institute of Mennonite Studies.

Jonker, W.D., Koopman, N., Lombard, C., Naudé, P. & Smit, D. 2008. *Die relevansie van die kerk: teologiese reaksies op die vraag na die betekenis van die kerk in die wêreld*. Cape Town: Bybel-Media.

Kairos Theologians. 1985. *Challenge to the Church: A Theological Comment on the Political Crisis in South Africa*. Johannesburg: Kairos Theologians. [Online], Available: http://www. sahistory.org.za/archive/challenge-church-theological-comment-political-crisis-south-africa-kairos-document-1985.

Kaplan, D.M. 2008. *Reading Ricoeur*. New York, NY: State University of New York Press.

Kearney, R. & Zimmermann, J. Eds. 2015. *Reimagining the Sacred: Richard Kearney debates God with James Wood, Catherine Keller, Charles Taylor, Julia Kristeva, Gianni Vattimo, Simon Critchley, ... Studies in Religion, Politics, and Culture)*. New York, NY: Columbia University Press.

Kearney, R. 2007. Paul Ricoeur and the Hermencutics of Translation. *Research in phenomenology*. 37(2):147.

Kearney, R. 2013. Forgiveness as the limit: Impossible or possible. In F. O'Rourke (ed.). Notre Dame, IN: University of Notre Dame Press *What happened in and to moral philosophy in the twentieth century: Philosophical essays in honour of Alasdair Macintyre*. 305–320.

Keepin, W. 1993. Lifework of David Bohm-River of Truth. *Revision*. (Summer):1–22.

Kennedy, G.A. 1984. *New Testament interpretation through rhetorical criticism.* Chapel Hill: University of North Carolina Press.

Kessler, R. 2004. From Bipolar to Multipolar Understanding. *Through the Eyes of Another: Intercultural Reading of the Bible.* 452–459.

van Kesteren, M.T.R., Rijpkema, M., Ruiter, D.J., Morris, R.G.M. & Fernández, G. 2014. Building on Prior Knowledge: Schema-dependent Encoding Processes Relate to Academic Performance. *Journal of Cognitive Neuroscience.* (April, 4):1–12.

Kim, D.-H. 2014. The homiletical appropriation of biblical passages in the light of speech act theory: preaching as a performance of the biblical text. Unpublished PhD Thesis. Stellenbosch University. [Online], Available: https://scholar.sun.ac.za/handle/10019.1/96016 [2015, July 12].

Kim, S. & Kim, K. 2008. *Christianity as a World Religion.* London: Bloomsbury Academic.

Kim, S.C., Kollontai, P. & Hoyland, G. 2008. *Peace and reconciliation: in search of shared identity.* Surrey, UK: Ashgate Publishing, Ltd.

Kingsbury, J.D. 1989. *Matthew: Structure, Christology, Kingdom.* Philadelphia: Fortress Press.

Kloppenborg, J.S. 2014. *Synoptic Problems: Collected Essays.* Tübingen: Mohr Siebeck.

Kok, J. (Kobus). 2012. A Theology of Reconciliation in Contexts of Conflict and Change. *Churchman.* 126(3):227–246.

Kok, J. (Kobus). 2014a. *Sensitivity to Outsiders: Exploring the Dynamic Relationship between Mission and Ethics in the New Testament and Early Christianity.* Tübingen, Germany: Mohr Siebeck.

Kok, J. (Kobus). 2014b. Social identity complexity theory as heuristic tool in New Testament studies. *HTS Theological Studies.* 70(1):1–9.

Kok, J. (Kobus). 2015. The radicality of early Christian oikodome: A theology that edifies insiders and outsiders. *Verbum et Ecclesia.* 36(3):1–12.

Kok, J. (Kobus). 2016. Drawing and transcending boundaries in the Dutch Reformed Church: A social identity and critical correlatory perspective on missional challenges in Post Apartheid South Africa. PhD. University of Pretoria.

Kok, J. (Kobus) & Dunne, J.A. 2014. *Insiders Versus Outsiders: Exploring the Dynamic Relationship Between Mission and Ethos in the New Testament.* New Jersey, NJ: Gorgias Press.

Kok, J (Kobus). 2014. Insiders versus outsiders: Exploring the dynamic relationship between mission and ethos in the New Testament an introduction. In J. (Kobus) Kok & J.A. Dunne (eds.). (Perspectives on Philosophy and Religious Thought no. 14). New Jersey, NJ: Gorgias Press *Insiders versus outsiders: Exploring the dynamic relationship between mission and ethos in the New Testament.* 1–14.

Konstan, D. 2010. *Before Forgiveness: The Origins of a Moral Idea.* Cambridge: Cambridge University Press.

Koopman, N. 1998. Racism in the Post-Apartheid South Africa. In L. Kretzschmar & L.D. Hulley (eds.). Pretoria: J.L. van Schaik Publishers *Questions About Life and Morality: Christian Ethics in South Africa Today.* 153–168. [Online], Available: http://philpapers.org/rec/KOORIT [2015, January 21].

Köster, H. 1990. *Ancient Christian gospels.* Edinburgh: Trinity Press International.

Krog, A. 2010. *Country Of My Skull*. New York, NY: Random House.

Kuchenbrandt, D., Seidel, S.K. & Eyssel, F. 2013. Cooperation makes it happen: Imagined intergroup cooperation enhances the positive effects of imagined contact. *Group Processes & Intergroup Relations*. 16(5):635–647.

Kuhn, T.S. 2012. *The structure of scientific revolutions*. Chicago, Il: University of Chicago press.

Laszlo, E. 1987. *Evolution: The Grand Synthesis*. Boulder, CO: Shambhala Publications, Incorporated.

Lategan, B.C. 2015. *Hermeneutics and Social Transformation – A selection from the essays of Bernard C. Lategan*. D.J. Smit (ed.). (Beyers Naudé Centre Series on Public Theology). Stellenbosch: SUN Press.

Le Roux, J. 2011. Andries van Aarde's Matthew Interpretation. *HTS Teologiese Studies / Theological Studies*. 67(1):1–10.

Lee, K. & Viljoen, F.P. 2010a. The ultimate commission: the key for the gospel according to Matthew. *Acta Theologica*. 30(1):64–83.

Lee, K. & Viljoen, F.P. 2010b. Gentiles in Matthew's infancy narrative. *Dutch Reformed Theological Journal= Nederduitse Gereformeerde Teologiese Tydskrif*. 51(1 & 2):99–108.

Leithart, P.J. 2012. Jesus as Israel: The Typological Structure of Matthew's Gospel. [Online], Available: http://www.leithart.com/pdf/jesus-as-israel-the-typological-structure-of-matthew-s-gospel.pdf.

Levine, J.M. & Hogg, M.A. 2009. *Encyclopedia of Group Processes and Intergroup Relations*. Thousand Oaks, CA: SAGE Publications.

Lewis, C.L. 2014. A between-subjects comparison of same-group and cross-group friendships amongst Coloured South African students at Stellenbosch University. Thesis. Stellenbosch : Stellenbosch University. [Online], Available: https://scholar.sun.ac.za/handle/10019.1/86223 [2015, October 29].

Liebenberg, J. 2001. *The Language of the Kingdom and Jesus: Parable, Aphorism, and Metaphor in the Sayings Material Common to the Synoptic Tradition and the Gospel of Thomas*. Berlin: Walter de Gruyter.

Linnemann, E. 1977. *Parables of Jesus: Introduction and Exposition*. London: SPCK.

Lohr, C.H. 1961. Oral techniques in the Gospel of Matthew. *Catholic Biblical Quarterly*. 23(403):35.

Lovejoy, A.O. 2011. *The Great Chain of Being: A Study of the History of an Idea*. Piscataway, NJ: Transaction Publishers.

Lu, C.-J. & Shulman, S.W. 2008. Rigor and flexibility in computer-based qualitative research: Introducing the Coding Analysis Toolkit. *International Journal of Multiple Research Approaches*. 2(1):105–117.

Luz, U. 2004. Intertexts in the Gospel of Matthew. *Harvard Theological Review*. 97(2):119–137.

Luz, U. 2005. *Studies in Matthew*. Grand Rapids, MI: Wm. B. Eerdmans Publishing.

Luz, U., Koester, H. & Crouch, J.E. 2007. *Matthew 1-7: a commentary*. Philadelphia, PA: Fortress Press.

Lybaek, L. 2002. *New and Old in Matthew 11-13: Normativity in the Development of Three Theological Themes*. Göttingen, Germany: Vandenhoeck & Ruprecht.

MacDonald, D. 2001. *Mimesis and Intertextuality in Antiquity and Christianity*. London: Bloomsbury Academic.

Makhulu, A.M. 2016. Reckoning With Apartheid: The Conundrum of Working Through the Past, An Introduction. *Comparative Studies of South Asia, Africa and the Middle East.* [Online], Available: http://dukespace.lib.duke.edu/dspace/handle/10161/12663 [2016, December 05].

Malina, B. 1991. Reading Theory Perspective: Reading Luke-Acts. In J.H. Neyrey (ed.). Peabody, MA: Hendrickson Publishers *The social world of Luke-Acts: Models for interpretation.* 3–23.

Malina, B.J. 1970. The Literary Structure and Form of Matt. xxviii. 16–20. *New Testament Studies.* 17(1):87–103.

Malina, B. & Rohrbaugh, R.L. 1993. *Social Science Commentary on the Synoptic Gospels.* Philadelphia: Fortress Press.

Masenya, M., Phiri, I.A. & Nadar, S. 2005. The Sword that Heals! The Bible and African Women in African-South African Pentecostal Churches. *On being Church: African women's voices and visions.* 47–59.

Matera, F.J. 1987. The plot of Matthew's Gospel. *The Catholic Biblical quarterly.* 49(2):233–253.

Mbabazi, I.K. 2013. *The Significance of Interpersonal Forgiveness in the Gospel of Matthew.* Eugene, OR: Wipf and Stock Publishers.

Mbembe, A. 2015. Achille Mbembe on The State of South African Political Life. [Online], Available: http://africasacountry.com/2015/09/achille-mbembe-on-the-state-of-south-african-politics/ [2016, January 02].

McGrath, A.E. 2011. *Christian Theology: An Introduction.* Hoboken, NJ: John Wiley & Sons.

McHugh, M.L. 2012. Interrater reliability: the kappa statistic. *Biochemia medica.* 22(3):276–282.

Meiring, P. 1999. Reconciliation: dream or reality? *Missionalia: Southern African Journal of Mission Studies.* 27(2):241–244.

Meiring, P. 2002. Leadership for reconciliation: A Truth and Reconciliation Commission perspective. *Verbum et Ecclesia.* 23(3):719–735.

Meiring, P. 2014. *Chronicle of the Truth and Reconciliation Commission: A Journey through the Past and Present into the Future of South Africa.* Eugene, OR: Wipf and Stock Publishers.

Meyerhoff, J. 2010. *Bald Ambition: A Critique of Ken Wilber's Theory of Everything.* Boston, MA: Inside the Curtain Press.

Michel, O. 1995. The conclusion of Matthew's gospel: A contribution of the history of the Easter message. In 2nd ed. G. Stanton (ed.). Edinburgh: T & T Clark *The interpretation of Matthew.* 39–51.

Migliore, D.L. 2004. *Faith Seeking Understanding: An Introduction to Christian Theology.* Grand Rapids, MI: Wm. B. Eerdmans Publishing.

Miller, N. 2002. Personalization and the Promise of Contact Theory. *Journal of Social Issues.* 58(2):387–410.

Moister, W. 1871. *A history of Wesleyan missions, in all parts of the world, from their commencement to the present time.* 3d. and rev. ed. ed. London: Hardpress. [Online], Available: http://hdl.handle.net/2027/uc2.ark:/13960/t91837g90.

Morris, L. 1992. *The Gospel According to Matthew*. Grand Rapids, MI: Wm. B. Eerdmans Publishing.

Mounce, R.H. 1995. *Matthew*. Vol. 1. Peabody, MA: Hendrickson.

Mtshiselwa, N. 2011. Towards an indigenous (Xhosa) South African biblical scholarship. *Old Testament Essays*. 24(3):668–689.

Mtshiselwa, N. 2014. A Re-Reading of 1 Kings 21: 1-29 and Jehu's revolution in Dialogue with Farisani and Nzimande: Negotiating socio-economic redress in South Africa. *Old Testament Essays*. 27(1):205–230.

Mtshiselwa, N. 2015. The emergence of the Black Methodist Consultation and its possible prophetic voice in post-apartheid South Africa: original research. *HTS: Theological Studies*. 71(3):1–9.

Muller, R. 2008. Rain rituals and hybridity in Southern Africa. *Verbum et Ecclesia*. 29(3):819–831.

Murphy, M. 1992. *The Future of the Body: Explorations Into the Further Evolution of Human Nature*. New York, NY: J.P. Tarcher.

Nadar, S. 2006. "Hermeneutics of transformation?"A critical exploration of the model of social engagement between biblical scholars and faith communities: general. *Scriptura: International Journal of Bible, Religion and Theology in Southern Africa*. 93:339–351.

Negru, T. 2007. Gadamer-Habermas debate and universality of hermeneutics. *Cultura International Journal of Philosophy of Culture and Axiology*. 4(1):113–119.

Nel, M.J. 2002. *Vergifnis en versoening in die evangelie volgens Matteus*. Stellenbosch: Unpublished DTh, University of Stellenbosch.

Nel, M.J. 2013a. The Forgiveness of Debt in Matthew 6: 12, 14–15. *Neotestamentica*. 47(1):87–106.

Nel, M.J. 2013b. The influence of dwelling in the word within the Southern African partnership of missional churches. 34(1):1–8.

Nel, M.J. 2014a. Mission and ethics - sensitivity to outsiders in Matthew's mission. In J. (Kobus) Kok & J.A. Dunne (eds.). (Perspectives on Philosophy and Religious Thought no. 14). New Jersey, NJ: Gorgias Press *Insiders versus outsiders: Exploring the dynamic relationship between mission and ethos in the New Testament*. 85–105.

Nel, M.J. 2014b. The presence of religious virtuosi and non-virtuosi in the Matthean community. *Dutch Reformed Theological Journal= Nederduitse Gereformeerde Teologiese Tydskrif*. 55(3 & 4):729–746.

Nel, M.J. 2015. The motive of forgiveness in the Gospel according to Matthew. *In die Skriflig/In Luce Verbi*. 49(1):9.

Neville, D.J. 1994. *Arguments from Order in Synoptic Source Criticism: A History and Critique*. Macon, GA: Mercer University Press.

Nhemachena, A. 2016. Rhodes Must Fall: Nibbling at Resilient Colonialism in South Africa. *Journal of Pan African Studies*. 9(4):411–416.

Niebuhr, H.R. 1956. *Christ and Culture*. New York, NY: HarperCollins.

Nieman, A. 2010. Churches and social development in South Africa. In I. (Naas) W. Swart, H. Rocher, J. Erasmus, & S. Green (eds.). Stellenbosch, South Africa: SUN Press *Religion and social development in post-apartheid South Africa*. 37–44.

Nkurunziza, D. 2014. *Making Friends Across the Boundaries of Religious Differences: Religions Building Peace for a New World Order*. Bloomington, IN: Xlibris Corporation.

Nolland, J. 2005a. *The gospel of Matthew*. Vol. 1. Grand Rapids, MI: Wm. B. Eerdmans Publishing.

Nolland, J. 2005b. *The Gospel of Matthew: a commentary on the Greek text*. Grand Rapids, MI: W.B. Eerdmans Pub. Co. ; Paternoster Press.

Nussbaum, M.C.C. 2010. *Not For Profit: Why Democracy Needs the Humanities*. Princeton, NJ: Princeton University Press.

Overman, J.A. 1996. *Church and Community in Crisis: The Gospel According to Matthew*. London: Bloomsbury Academic.

Pannenberg, W. 2008. *Basic Questions in Theology*. Philadelphia: Augsburg Fortress, Publishers.

Paolini, S., Hewstone, M., Cairns, E. & Voci, A. 2004. Effects of direct and indirect cross-group friendships on judgments of Catholics and Protestants in Northern Ireland: The mediating role of an anxiety-reduction mechanism. *Personality and Social Psychology Bulletin*. 30(6):770–786.

Paolini, S., Hewstone, M., Voci, A., Harwood, J. & Cairns, E. 2006. Intergroup contact and the promotion of intergroup harmony: The influence of intergroup emotions. [Online], Available: http://psycnet.apa.org/psycinfo/2006-21411-011 [2016, July 19].

Paolini, S., Hewstone, M. & Cairns, E. 2007. Direct and indirect intergroup friendship effects: Testing the moderating role of the affective-cognitive bases of prejudice. *Personality and Social Psychology Bulletin*. [Online], Available: http://psp.sagepub.com/content/early/2007/08/06/0146167207304788.short [2016, July 19].

Parker, J.E. 1968. The interaction of negroes and whites in an integrated church setting. *Social forces*. 46(3):359–366.

Parkin, A. & Forbes, H.D. 1999. Ethnic Conflict: Commerce, Culture and the Contact Hypothesis. *International Migration Review*. 33(4):1109.

Paulson, D.S. 2008. Wilber's Integral Philosophy: A Summary and Critique. *Journal of Humanistic Psychology*. 48(3):364–388.

Pelikan, J. & Fadiman, C. 1990. *The World Treasury of Modern Religious Thought*. Boston, MA: Little, Brown.

Pettigrew, T.F. 1997. Generalized intergroup contact effects on prejudice. *Personality and social psychology bulletin*. 23(2):173–185.

Pettigrew, T.F. 1998. Intergroup contact theory. *Annual review of psychology*. 49(1):65–85.

Pettigrew, T.F. & Tropp, L.R. 2005. Relationships Between Intergroup Contact and Prejudice Among Minority and Majority Status Groups. *Psychological Science*. 16(12):951–957.

Pettigrew, T.F. & Tropp, L.R. 2006. A meta-analytic test of intergroup contact theory. *Journal of personality and social psychology*. 90(5):751–755.

Pettigrew, T.F. & Tropp, L.R. 2011. *When Groups Meet: The Dynamics of Intergroup Contact*. 1 edition ed. New York, NY: Psychology Press.

Philander, N.C. 2011. Die rol van die kerk as een van die instellings in die samelewing wat mense moreel vorm. *Dutch Reformed Theological Journal / Nederduitse Gereformeerde Teologiese Tydskrif*. 52(1 & 2):174–185.

Phiri, I.A. & Nadar, S. 2012. *African women, religion, and health: Essays in honor of Mercy Amba Ewudziwa Oduyoye*. Wipf and Stock Publishers.

Piaget, J. 1976. *The Grasp of Consciousness: Action and Concept in the Young Child*. Abingdon: Routledge and Kegan Paul.

Pope, C., Ziebland, S. & Mays, N. 2000. Analysing qualitative data. *British medical journal*. 320(7227):114.

Popper, K.R. 2002. *Conjectures and Refutations: The Growth of Scientific Knowledge*. Hove, UK: Psychology Press.

Powell, M. 1992. Toward a Narrative-Critical Understanding of Matthew. In D.R.A. Hare (ed.). (Interpretation). Louisville, KY: John Knox Press *Matthew*. 341–346.

Powers, B.W. 2010. *The Progressive Publication of Matthew: An Explanation of the Writing of the Synoptic Gospels*. Nashville, TN: B&H Publishing Group.

Prestwich, A., Kenworthy, J.B., Wilson, M. & Kwan-Tat, N. 2008. Differential relations between two types of contact and implicit and explicit racial attitudes. *British Journal of Social Psychology*. 47(4):575–588.

Punt, J. 2002. From re-writing to rereading the Bible in post-colonial Africa: Considering the options and implications. *Missionalia*. 30(3):410–442.

Punt, J. 2006. Using the Bible in post-apartheid South Africa: Its influence and impact amidst the gay debate. *HTS Teologiese Studies / Theological Studies*. 62(3).

Rausch Albright, C. 2000. The "God module" and the complexifying brain. *Zygon®*. 35(4):735–744.

Relations, U. of O.I. of G. & Sherif, M. 1961. *Intergroup conflict and cooperation: The Robbers Cave experiment*. Vol. 10. University Book Exchange Norman, OK. [Online], Available: http://psychclassics.yorku.ca/Sherif/chap7.htm?wptouch_preview_theme=enabled [2016, July 22].

Rich, G.J. 2001. Anthropology, Consciousness, and Spirituality: A Conversation with Ken Wilber. *Anthropology of Consciousness*. 12(2):43–60.

Riches, J.K., Telford, W. & Tuckett, C.M. 2001. *Synoptic Gospels*. London: A&C Black.

Ricoeur, P. 2007. Introduction: Ricoeur's philosophy of translation. In Translated by Eileen Brennan. New York: Routledge *On Translation*. vii–xx.

Ricoeur, P. 2009. *Memory, History, Forgetting*. Chicago, Il: University of Chicago Press.

Ricoeur, P. & Brennan, E. 1995. Reflections on a new ethos for Europe. *Philosophy & social criticism*. 21(5–6):3–13.

Rieger, J. 2001. *God and the Excluded: Visions and Blind Spots in Contemporary Theology*. Philadelphia: Fortress Press.

Roccas, S. & Brewer, M.B. 2002. Social identity complexity. *Personality and Social Psychology Review*. 6(2):88–106.

Rolls, L. & Relf, M. 2006. Bracketing interviews: addressing methodological challenges in qualitative interviewing in bereavement and palliative care. *Mortality*. 11(3):286–305.

le Roux, A. 2014. "We were not part of apartheid": rationalisations used by four white pre-service teachers to make sense of race and their own racial identities. *South African Journal of Education*. 34(2):1–16.

Ruiter, D.J. 2007. Notions of the Public and Doing Theology. *International Journal of Public Theology*. 1(3):431–454.

Saiter, S.M. 2009. Universal Integralism: Ken Wilber's Integral Method in Context. *Humanistic Psychologist*. 37(4):307–325.

Saldaña, J. 2011. *Fundamentals of qualitative research*. (Understanding qualitative research). New York, NY: Oxford University Press.

Saldaña, J. 2013. *The coding manual for qualitative researchers*. Los Angeles: SAGE.

Saldarini, A.J. 1994. *Matthew's Christian-Jewish Community*. Chicago, Il: University of Chicago Press.

Sanders, E.P. 2006. *The Tendencies of the Synoptic Tradition*. Cambridge: Cambridge University Press.

Sanderson, C.A. 2010. *Social psychology*.

Schilderman, J. 2004. *Normative claims in pastoral ministry research*. Leiden: Brill.

Schmitt, C.B. 1966. Perrenial Philosophy: From Agostino Steuco to Leibniz. *Journal of the History of Ideas*. 505–532.

Schneider, K.J. 1987. The Deified Self A" Centaur" Response to Wilber and the Transpersonal Movement. *Journal of Humanistic Psychology*. 27(2):196–216.

Schneider, K.J. 1989. Infallibility Is So Damn Appealing A Reply to Ken Wilber. *Journal of Humanistic Psychology*. 29(4):470–481.

Schneider, K.J. 2012. Existentialism and the transpersonal: A rejoinder. *Existential Analysis*. 23(1):120–123.

Schoeman, W.J. 2017. South African religious demography: The 2013 General Household Survey. *HTS Teologiese Studies / Theological Studies*. 73(2):1–7.

Schoeman, W.J. & van den Berg, J.A. 2016. Practical Theology exploring interdisciplinary practices: The quest for engaging with lived religion in the South African context. *Theology and the (post) apartheid condition: Genealogies and future directions*. 1:213.

Schrödinger, E. 2012. *What is Life?: With Mind and Matter and Autobiographical Sketches*. Cambridge: Cambridge University Press.

Schweiker, W. 1990. *Mimetic reflections*. New York, NY: Fordham University Press.

Scubla, L. 2005. The Bible, "Creation," and Mimetic Theory. *Contagion: Journal of Violence, Mimesis, and Culture*. 12–13(1):13–19.

Searle, J.R. 1969. *Speech acts: An essay in the philosophy of language*. Vol. 626. Cambridge: Cambridge University Press.

Searle, J.R. 1975. Indirect speech acts. *Syntax and semantics*. 3:59–82.

Searle, J.R. 1976. *A taxonomy of illocutionary acts*. Trier: Linguistic Agency University of Trier.

Searle, J.R. 1985. *Expression and meaning: Studies in the theory of speech acts*. Cambridge: Cambridge University Press.

Senior, D. 1987. Matthew 18:21-35. *Interpretation*. 41(4):403–407.

Setiloane, G. 1998. Towards a biocentric theology and ethic – via Africa. In C. Du Toit (ed.). Pretoria: Research Institute for Theology and Religion *Faith science and African culture: African cosmology and Africa's contribution to science*.

Shutte, A. 1993. *Philosophy for Africa*. Cape Town: UCT Press.

Shutte, A. 2001. *Ubuntu: An Ethic for a New South Africa*. Cluster Publications.

Shutte, A. 2009. Ubuntu as the African Ethical Vision. In M.F. Murove (ed.). University of Kwazulu-Natal Press *African Ethics: An Anthology of Comparative and Applied Ethics*. 85–99.

Sim, D.C. 2001. The social setting of the Matthean community: New paths for an old journey. *HTS : Theological Studies*. 57(1 & 2):268–280.

Sim, D.C. 2009. Matthew and the Pauline Corpus: A Preliminary Intertextual Study*. *Journal for the Study of the New Testament*. 31(4):401–422.

Sim, D.C. 2011. The pacifist Jesus and the violent Jesus in the Gospel of Matthew. *HTS Teologiese Studies / Theological Studies*. 67(1).

Smit, D.J. 1996. Oor die kerk as 'n unieke samelewingsverband. *Tydskrif vir Geesteswetenskappe*. 2(36):119–129.

Smit, D.J. 2007a. *Essays in Public Theology: Collected Essays 1*. Stellenbosch, South Africa: AFRICAN SUN MeDIA.

Smit, D.J. 2007b. What does "Public" mean? Questions with a view to Public Theology. In 1st ed. SUN Press *Christian in public aims, methodologies, and issues in public theology*. 11–47.

Smit, D.J. 2017. Does it matter? On whether there is method in the maddess. In 1st ed. S.C.H. Kim & K. Cannon (eds.). Leiden: Brill *A companion to Public Theology*. 67–94.

Smith, J.I. 2007. *Muslims, Christians, and the Challenge of Interfaith Dialogue*. Oxford University Press, USA.

Smith, J.M. 2015. *Why βίος? On the Relationship Between Gospel Genre and Implied Audience*. London: Bloomsbury Publishing.

Snodgrass, K. 2008. *Stories with Intent: A Comprehensive Guide to the Parables of Jesus*. Grand Rapids, MI: Wm. B. Eerdmans Publishing.

Snyman, K. 2002. Myth, mind, Messiah: exploring the development of the Christian responsibility towards interfaith dialogue from within Ken Wilber's integral hermeneutics. University of South Africa. [Online], Available: http://uir.unisa.ac.za/handle/10500/1050 [2015, July 20].

Sörbom, G. 2002. The classical concept of mimesis. *A Companion to Art Theory*. 19–28.

South African Science and Religion Forum. 2007. *The Impact of Knowledge Systems on Human Development in Africa*. Pretoria: Research Institute for Theology and Religion, University of South Africa.

Stephan, W.G. & Stephan, C.W. 1985. Intergroup anxiety. *Journal of Social Issues*. 41(3):157–175.

Steyn, M. 2001. Whiteness in the Rainbow: Experiencing the loss of privilige in the New South Africa. In C.V. Hamilton, L. Huntley, N. Alexander, A.S.. Guimarães, & W.. Boulder (eds.). London: Lynne Rienner Publishers *Beyond Racism: Race and Inequality in Brazil, South Africa, and the United States*. 85–103.

Steyn, M. & Foster, D. 2008. Repertoires for talking white: Resistant whiteness in post-apartheid South Africa. *Ethnic and Racial Studies*. 31(1):25–51.

Stuhlmacher, P. 2000. Matt 28:16-20 and the course of mission in the apostolic and postapostolic age. In J. Ådna & H. Kvalbein (eds.). Tübingen: Mohr Siebeck *The mission of the early church to Jews and gentiles*. 18–43.

Surmon, K., Juan, A. & Reddy, V. 2016. Class over race: new barriers to social inclusion. *HSRC Review*. (9258). [Online], Available: http://www.hsrc.ac.za/en/review/hsrc-review-april-to-june-2016/class-over-race [2016, December 05].

Swart, H. & Hewstone, M. 2012. Forgiveness, intergroup. In Hoboken, NJ: Wiley *The encyclopedia of peace psychology*. [Online], Available: http://onlinelibrary.wiley.com/doi/10.1002/9780470672532.wbepp112/full [2016, July 19].

Swart, I. & De Beer, S. 2014. Doing urban public theology in South Africa: introducing a new agenda: original research. *HTS: Theological Studies*. 70(3):1–14.

Swart, H., Hewstone, M., Christ, O. & Voci, A. 2010. The impact of crossgroup friendships in South Africa: Affective mediators and multigroup comparisons. *Journal of Social Issues*. 66(2):309–333.

Swart, H., Hewstone, M., Christ, O. & Voci, A. 2011. Affective mediators of intergroup contact: A three-wave longitudinal study in South Africa. *Journal of Personality and Social Psychology*. 101(6):1221–1238.

Swart, H., Turner, R., Hewstone, M. & Voci, A. 2011. Achieving forgiveness and trust in postconflict societies: The importance of self-disclosure and empathy. In L.R. Tropp & R.K. Mallet (eds.). Washington, DC: American Psychological Association *Moving beyond prejudice reduction: Pathways to positive intergroup relations*. 181–200. [Online], Available: http://psycnet.apa.org/books/12319/009 [2016, July 19].

Swart, I. (Naas) W., Rocher, H. & Erasmus, J. 2010. *Religion and Social Development in Post Apartheid South Africa: Perspectives for Critical Engagement*. Stellenbosch, South Africa: SUN Press.

Swart, I. (Naas) W., Gouws, A., Pettersson, P., Erasmus, J. & Bosman, F. 2012. *Welfare, Religion and Gender in Post-apartheid South Africa: Constructing a South-North Dialogue*. AFRICAN SUN MeDIA.

Swartz, S. 2006. A long walk to citizenship: morality, justice and faith in the aftermath of apartheid. *Journal of Moral Education*. 35(4):551–570.

Tajfel, H. 1970. Experiments in intergroup discrimination. *Scientif. Amer*. 223(5):96–103.

Tajfel, H., Billig, M.G., Bundy, R.P. & Flament, C. 1971. Social categorization and intergroup behaviour. *European Journal of Social Psychology*. 1(2):149–178.

Talbert, C.H. 1977. *What is a Gospel?: The Genre of the Canonical Gospels*. Macon, GA: Mercer University Press.

Talbert, C.H. 2010. *Matthew*. Grand Rapids, MI: Baker Academic.

Taylor, A.M. 2001. Ken wilber's a theory of everything: Some societal and political implications. *World Futures*. 57(3):213–237.

Taylor, C. 1992. *Sources of the Self: The Making of the Modern Identity*. Cambridge: Cambridge University Press.

Terreblanche, S.J. 2002. *A History of Inequality in South Africa, 1652-2002*. Pietermaritzburg: University of Natal Press.

The Holy Bible: containing the Old and New Testaments. 1989. New York: Oxford Univ. Pr.

Thesnaar, C. 2008. Restorative Justice as a Key for Healing Communities. *Religion and Theology*. 15(1):53–73.

Thesnaar, C.H. 2013. Embodying collective memory : towards responsible engagement with the "other". *Embodying collective memory : towards responsible engagement with the "other"*. 112:1–15.

Thesnaar, C.H. 2014. Seeking feasible reconciliation: A transdisciplinary contextual approach to reconciliation. *HTS Theological Studies*. 70(2):1–8.

Thiselton, A.C. 2006. *Thiselton on Hermeneutics: The Collected Works and New Essays of Anthony Thiselton*. Surrey, UK: Ashgate Publishing, Ltd.

Thiselton, A.C. 2015. *The Thiselton Companion to Christian Theology*. Grand Rapids, MI: Wm. B. Eerdmans Publishing.

Thomas, R.L. 2002. *Three Views on the Origins of the Synoptic Gospels*. Kregel Academic.

Tinsley, H.E. & Weiss, D.J. 1975. Interrater reliability and agreement of subjective judgments. *Journal of Counseling Psychology*. 22(4):358.

Tolmie, F. 2012. *Narratology and Biblical narratives: a practical guide*. Eugene, OR: Wipf and Stock Publishers.

Tracy, D. 1975. Theology as public discourse. *The Christian Century*. 92(10):287–291.

Tracy, D. 2014. Three Kinds of Publicness in Public Theology. *International Journal of Public Theology*. 8(3):330–334.

Tucker, J.B. & Baker, C.A. 2014. *T&T Clark Handbook to Social Identity in the New Testament*. London: A&C Black.

Tuckey, E.C. 2015. An ethical investigation of the teaching and practice of moral formation at St Augustine College, the College of the Transfiguration and the South African Theological Seminary. Thesis. [Online], Available: http://uir.unisa.ac.za/handle/10500/20103 [2016, June 12].

Turner, R.N., Hewstone, M. & Voci, A. 2007. Reducing explicit and implicit outgroup prejudice via direct and extended contact: The mediating role of self-disclosure and intergroup anxiety. *Journal of personality and social psychology*. 93(3):369.

Turner, R.N., Hewstone, M., Voci, A., Paolini, S. & Christ, O. 2007. Reducing prejudice via direct and extended cross-group friendship. *European review of social psychology*. 18(1):212–255.

Tutu, D. 2012. *No Future Without Forgiveness*. New York, NY: Random House.

Tymieniecka, A.-T. 1991. *Husserlian Phenomenology in a New Key: Intersubjectivity, Ethos, the Societal Sphere, Human Encounter, Pathos Book 2 Phenomenology in the World Fifty Years after the Death of Edmund Husserl*. Dordrecht: Springer Netherlands.

Ukpong, J.S., West, G.O. & Dube, M. 2000. Developments in biblical interpretation in Africa: Historical and hermeneutical directions. *The Bible in Africa: Transactions, trajectories and trends*. 11–28.

Van Aarde, A.G. & Dreyer, Y. 2010. Matthew studies today – a willingness to suspect and a willingness to listen. *HTS Teologiese Studies / Theological Studies*. 66(1):1–10.

Van Der Meer, T.W., Te Grotenhuis, M. & Scheepers, P.L. 2009. Three types of voluntary associations in comparative perspective: The importance of studying associational involvement through a typology of associations in 21 European countries. *Journal of Civil Society*. 5(3):227–241.

Van der Riet, L. 2014. Reconciliation, Justice, Spirituality: In Conversation with John W. de Gruchy. Stellenbosch University.

Van der Walt, C. 2010. Ideologie en mag in Bybelinterpretasie: Op weg na'n kommunale lees van 2 Samuel 13. Stellenbosch: University of Stellenbosch. [Online], Available: http://scholar.sun.ac.za/handle/10019.1/4019 [2015, July 03].

Van der Walt, C. 2012. Close encounters: creating a safe space for intercultural Bible reading-Part I. *Scriptura: International Journal of Bible, Religion and Theology in Southern Africa*. 109:110–118.

Van der Walt, C. 2014. *Toward a Communal Reading of 2 Samuel 13*. Elkhart, IN: Institute of Mennonite Studies.

Van der Watt, J.G. 2000. *Family of the King: Dynamics of metaphor in the Gospel according to John*. Vol. 47. Leiden: Brill.

Van der Watt, J.G. 2006. Ethics and Ethos in the Gospel according to John. *Zeitschrift für die Neutestamentliche Wissenchaft und die Kunde der Älteren Kirche*. 97(2):147.

Van der Watt, J.G. 2012a. Mimesis or imitation in ethical dynamics. In J.G. Van der Watt & R. Zimmermann (eds.). Tübingen: Mohr Siebeck *Rethinking the Ethics of John*. 395.

Van der Watt, J.G. 2012b. Power through language in 1 John/Mag deur taal in 1 Johannes. (Original Research). *HTS Teologiese Studies*. 68(1).

Van der Watt, J.G. 2014. Navolging van Jesus, mimesis en 1 Johannes. *In die Skriflig/In Luce Verbi*. 48(1).

Van der Watt, J.G. & Malan, F.S. 2006. *Identity, ethics, and ethos in the New Testament*. Vol. Bd. 141. (Beihefte zur Zeitschrift für die neutestamentliche Wissenschaft und die Kunde der älteren Kirche). Berlin: Walter de Gruyter.

Vanhoozer, K.J. 1990. *Biblical narrative in the philosophy of Paul Ricoeur: a study in hermeneutics and theology*. Cambridge: Cambridge University Press.

Vanhoozer, K.J. 1998. *Is there a meaning in this text? The Bible, the reader, and the morality of literary knowledge*. Leicester, England: Apollos.

Vanhoozer, K.J. 2005. Lost in interpretation? Truth, scripture, and hermeneutics. *Journal of the Evangelical Theological Society*. 48(1):89–114.

Venter, D. 1994. The formation and functioning of racially-mixed congregations. Thesis. Stellenbosch : University of Stellenbosch. [Online], Available: http://scholar.sun.ac.za/handle/10019.1/15576 [2016, October 09].

Verkuyten, M. 2010. *Identiteit en diversiteit : De tegenstellingen voorbij*. Amsterdam: Amsterdam University Press.

Verschuren, P.J.M. 2009a. *Praktijkgericht onderzoek: ontwerp van organisatie-en beleidsonderzoek*. Amsterdam: Boom. [Online], Available: http://repository.ubn.ru.nl/handle/2066/78476 [2015, July 15].

Verschuren, P.J.M. 2009b. Why a methodology for practice-oriented research is a necessary heresy. In Vols 1–9. Radboud University, Nijmegen: Unpublished Lecture *Farewell lecture delivered at Radboud University, Nijmegen*.

Vezzali, L., Hewstone, M., Capozza, D., Giovannini, D. & Wölfer, R. 2014. Improving intergroup relations with extended and vicarious forms of indirect contact. *European Review of Social Psychology*. 25(1):314–389.

Viljoen, F. 2016. The Torah in Matthew. PhD (published). Radboud University.

Viljoen, F.P. 2006. Jesus' teaching on the Torah in the Sermon on the Mount. *Neotestamentica*. 40(1):135.

Viljoen, F.P. 2007. Fulfilment in Matthew. *Verbum et Ecclesia*. 28(1):301–324.

Viljoen, F.P. 2009. A contextualised reading of Matthew 6: 22-23:'Your eye is the lamp of your body'. *HTS Theological Studies*. 65(1):0–0.

Viljoen, F.P. 2011a. Power and authority in Matthew's Gospel. *Acta Theologica*. 31(2):329–345.

Viljoen, F.P. 2011b. The foundational statement in Matthew 5: 17-20 on the continuing validity of the law. *In die Skriflig: Festschrift: Tjaart van der Walt*. 45(2 & 3):385–407.

Viljoen, F.P. 2012. Interpreting the visio Dei in Matthew 5: 8. *HTS Theological Studies*. 68(1):1–7.

Viljoen, F.P. 2013. Jesus' halakhic argumentation on the true intention of the law in Matthew 5: 21-48. *Verbum et ecclesia*. 34(1):70–81.

Villa-Vicencio, C. & du Toit, F. 2006. *Truth & Reconciliation in South Africa: 10 Years on*. Cape Town: New Africa Books.

Visser, F. 2012. *Ken Wilber: Thought as Passion*. Albany, NY: SUNY Press.

Viviano, B. 2007. *Matthew and His World: The Gospel of the Open Jewish Christians : Studies in Biblical Theology*. Göttingen: Vandenhoeck & Ruprecht.

Vledder, E.-J. & Van Aarde, A.G. (Andries G.). 1995. The social location of the Matthean community. [Online], Available: http://repository.up.ac.za/handle/2263/17868 [2013, December 05].

Vosloo, R. 2015. Difficult Forgiveness? Engaging Paul Ricoeur on Public Forgiveness within the Context of Social Change in South Africa. *International Journal of Public Theology*. 9(3):360–378.

Vosloo, R.R. 2012. Traumatic memory, representation and forgiveness: Some remarks in conversation with Antjie Krog's Country of My Skull. *In die Skriflig*. 46(1).

Wade, J. 1996. *Changes of Mind: A Holonomic Theory of the Evolution of Consciousness*. Albany, NY: SUNY Press.

Wale, K. & Foster, D. 2007. Investing in discourses of poverty and development: How white wealthy South Africans mobilise meaning to maintain privilege. *South African Review of Sociology*. 38(1):45–69.

Walker, M. 2005. Race is nowhere and race is everywhere: narratives from black and white South African university students in post-apartheid South Africa. *British Journal of Sociology of Education*. 26(1):41–54.

Watts, J.L. 2013. *Mimetic Criticism and the Gospel of Mark: An Introduction and Commentary*. Wipf and Stock Publishers.

van Weert, T. & Andriessen, D. 2004. Onderzoeken door te verbeteren Overbruggen van de kloof tussen theorie en praktijk in HBO-onderzoek. *www.lectoren.nl.* [Online], Available: http://www.narcis.nl/publication/RecordID/oai:hbokennisbank. nl:inholland%3Aoai%3Arepository.samenmaken.nl%3Asmpid%3A10547 [2017, February 14].

Welsh, F. 2000. *A history of South Africa.* New York, NY: HarperCollins.

Weren, W. 2006. The Macrostructure of Matthew's Gospel: A New Proposal. *Biblica: Commentarii Periodici Pontificii Instituti Biblici.* 87:171–200.

West, G. 2014a. Liberation hermeneutics after liberation in South Africa. *Studies in World Christianity and Interreligious Relations.* (48):341.

West, G.O. 1991. *Biblical Hermeneutics of Liberation Modes of Reading the Bible in the South African Context.* Maryknoll, NY: Orbis Books. [Online], Available: http://philpapers.org/rec/WESBHO [2016, February 18].

West, G.O. 2014b. Locating "Contextual Bible Study" within biblical liberation hermeneutics and intercultural biblical hermeneutics. *HTS Theological Studies.* 70(1):1–10.

West, G.O. 2014c. Locating "Contextual Bible Study" within biblical liberation hermeneutics and intercultural biblical hermeneutics: original research. *HTS : Theological Studies.* 70(1):1–10.

West, G.O. 2015. Contending for Dignity in the Bible and the Post-Apartheid South African Public Realm. In J. Claassens & B. Birch (eds.). Eugene, OR: Wipf & Stock Publishers *Restorative readings: Old Testament, Ethics, Human Dignity.* 78–98.

West, G.O. & Dube, M.W. 1996. An Introduction. How We Have Come To "Read With". *Semeia.* 73:7–17.

West, G.O. & Dube, M.W. 2001. *The Bible in Africa.* Amsterdam: Brill Academic Publishers.

Whiteside, J. 1906. *History of the Wesleyan Methodist Church of South Africa.* London: Hardpress.

Wilber, K. 1975. Psychologia perennis: The spectrum of consciousness. *Journal of Transpersonal Psychology.* 7(2). [Online], Available: http://www.atpweb.org/jtparchive/trps-07-75-02-105.pdf [2015, July 25].

Wilber, K. 1993. *The spectrum of consciousness.* Wheaton, IL: Quest Books.

Wilber, K. 1996a. *Up from Eden: a transpersonal view of human evolution.* Wheaton, IL.: The Theosophical Pub. House.

Wilber, K. 1996b. *A brief history of everything.* Boston, MA: Shambhala.

Wilber, K. 1997. An integral theory of consciousness. *Journal of consciousness studies.* 4(1):71–92.

Wilber, K. 1998. *The Essential Ken Wilber: An Introductory Reader.* 1st ed ed. Boston, MA: Shambhala.

Wilber, K. 2000a. *Waves, Streams, states and self: A summary of my psychological model.* Vol. 3. Boston, MA: Shambhala.

Wilber, K. 2000b. *One Taste.* Boston, MA: Shambhala Publications.

Wilber, K. 2001a. *Sex, Ecology, Spirituality: The Spirit of Evolution, Second Edition*. 2 Revised ed. Boston, MA: Shambhala.

Wilber, K. 2001b. *Eye to Eye*. San Francisco, CA: Shambhala Publications.

Wilber, K. 2003. Waves, streams, states, and self: An outline of an integral psychology 1. *The Humanistic Psychologist*. 31(2–3):22–49.

Wilber, K. 2004. *The Simple Feeling of Being : Embracing Your True Nature*. Boston, MA: Shambhala.

Wilber, K. 2007. *A Brief History of Everything*. 2nd ed. Boston, MA: Shambhala.

Wilber, K. 2011a. *Integral Spirituality: A Startling New Role for Religion in the Modern and Postmodern World*. Boston, MA: Shambhala Publications.

Wilber, K. 2011b. *The Eye of Spirit: An Integral Vision for a World Gone Slightly Mad*. 3 Sub edition ed. Boston, MA: Shambhala Publications.

Wilber, K. 2012. *The Spectrum of Consciousness*. 2nd edition ed. Wheaton, IL: Quest Books.

Wilber, K. 2014. *The Atman Project: A Transpersonal View of Human Development*. Wheaton, IL: Quest Books.

Wilber, K. & Wilber, K. 2000. *Integral psychology: consciousness, spirit, psychology, therapy*. Boston, MA: Shambhala.

Wilcox, C. 2011. *Bias: The Unconscious Deceiver*. Bloomington, IN: Xlibris Corporation.

Wildman, W.J. 2010. *Religious philosophy as multidisciplinary comparative inquiry: Envisioning a future for the philosophy of religion*. Albany, NY: Suny Press.

Wilke, R.B. & Wilke, J.K. 2003. *Disciple: Becoming Disciples Through Bible Study*. Abingdon: Abingdon Press.

Williams, Q.E. & Stroud, C. 2014. Battling the Race: Stylizing Language and Coproducing Whiteness and Colouredness in a Freestyle Rap Performance. *Journal of Linguistic Anthropology*. 24(3):277–293.

Williams Jr, R.M. 1947. The reduction of intergroup tensions: a survey of research on problems of ethnic, racial, and religious group relations. *Social Science Research Council Bulletin*. 57(xi):153.

Wright, S.C. 2003. Strategic Collective Action: Social Psychology and Social Change. In R. Brown & S.L. Gaertner (eds.). Oxford, UK: Blackwell Publishers Ltd *Blackwell Handbook of Social Psychology: Intergroup Processes*. 409–430. [Online], Available: http://doi.wiley.com/10.1002/9780470693421.ch20 [2016, July 20].

Wright, S.C. & Lubensky, M.E. 2009. The struggle for social equality: Collective action versus prejudice reduction. In S. Demoulin, J. -P, & J.F. Dovidio (eds.). New York, NY, US: Psychology Press *Intergroup misunderstandings: Impact of divergent social realities*. 291–310.

van Wyngaard, C. 2014. The Language of "Diversity" in Reconstructing Whiteness in the Dutch Reformed Church. In R.. Smith, W. Ackah, & A.G. Reddie (eds.). New York, N.Y.: Palgrave Macmillan *Churches, Blackness, and Contested Multiculturalism: Europe, Africa and North America*. 157–170.

Young, I.M. 2011. *Justice and the Politics of Difference*. Princeton University Press.

Ypma, M. 2014. Diversiteit in de hulpverlening: Een praktijkonderzoek naar de rol van vooroordelen en onbewuste attituden in de relatie tussen cliënten en hulpverleners van een Utrechts buurtteam. Radboud University.

Zimmermann, R. & Dormeyer, D. 2007. *Kompendium der Gleichnisse Jesu*. München: Gütersloher Verlagshaus.

Zohar, D. 1991. *The Quantum Self*. New York, NY: HarperCollins.

Zuma, B. 2014. Contact theory and the concept of prejudice: Metaphysical and moral explorations and an epistemological question. *Theory & Psychology*. 24(1):40–57.

APPENDIX A

Dear [participant name],

I trust that this email finds you well?

I am writing to ask whether you would consider participating in short term research project being conducted by one of our ministers, Revd. Dr. Dion Forster – it is hoped that the outcome of the research will be of value to the churches in our Circuit and to the broader Methodist family across Southern Africa.

What is the research project?

This project aims to understand how a sampling of South African Christians read and understand the Bible. The aim is to have 12 people participating in the project (some from Church Street Methodist Church and some from Coronation Ave Methodist Church), of which I would be grateful if you would consider being one of the participants.

You will be invited to participate in a few group discussions of the Biblical text at which some questions will be asked of the participants to understand how you, and the rest of the group, understand the meaning of the passage we are reading. We are not looking for trained Biblical scholars. The aim of the research is to understand how regular members of our churches would read and make meaning of a text in their normal faith life.

Please note that the research is not intended to 'test' the participants. Rather, the participants are helping to test an approach to reading the Bible that Rev Forster has developed in order to see whether this methods works, or does not, and if it does work, where it works and why it works, and where it does not work, why this is so. You will be helping to test this approach to reading the Bible.

What commitment will be required?

It is envisioned that you will have to be able to commit a total of 5 – 6 hours over a period of about 4 weeks.

Meeting 1: Explain the research project, answer any questions, get the consent of the participants, fill in a questionnaire.

Meeting 2: Meet with the larger group to read the Biblical text and discuss it.

Meeting 3: Meet with the larger group again to read and discuss the Biblical text.

[Meeting 4: If we find we need another meeting we will negotiate a suitable time with the group, this meeting will take the same format as meetings 2 and 3].

Meeting 5: Meet to discuss the experience of the participants and process that was followed, fill in a final questionnaire, thanks and wrap up.

All of the meetings will take place in Somerset West and the meeting times will be negotiated with the group to find the most convenient time to accommodate the largest number of participants.

Conclusion

If you are willing to participate in the research project I would be most grateful! Please could you let me know whether you are able to participate or not? If you are able and willing to participate I will inform Rev Forster who will be in contact with you to invite you to the first meeting where he will be able to answer any questions that you have and get the process started.

Thank you for your consideration,

Rev Murcott / Rev Moses

ETHICAL CLEARANCE FORM FOR PARTICIPANTS

Radboud Universiteit

RADBOUD UNIVERSITY

CONSENT TO PARTICIPATE IN RESEARCH PROJECT

Research Topic: *Structured Interview and Focus Groups on Bible Reading and Bible Interpretation.*

You are asked to participate in a research study conducted by Dr. Dion Forster, (from the Faculty of Philosophy, Theology and Science of Religion at Radboud University). The research from this research project will form part of a PhD dissertation being completed by Dr. Dion Forster at Radboud University. You were selected as a participant in this study by the minister of your Church.

1. PURPOSE OF THE STUDY

This study aims to understand how a sampling of South African Christians read and understand the Bible. The aim is to have a number of persons from two Churches participating in the project (some from Church Street Methodist Church in Somerset West and some from Coronation Ave Methodist Church in Somerset West).

You are invited to participate in a few group discussions and a personal interview on the Biblical text. On these occasions questions will be asked of the participants in order to understand how you, and the rest of the group, understand the meaning of the passage we are reading (Matthew 18.15-35). The project is not aimed at working with trained Biblical scholars. The aim of the research is to understand how 'regular members' of these churches would read and make meaning of the Biblical text in their normal faith life.

2. PROCEDURES

If you volunteer to participate in this study, we would ask you to do the following things:

The project aims to 'kick off' towards the end of April or early in May. It is envisioned that you will have to be able to commit a total of +- 6 hours over a period of about 4 weeks.

- Meeting 1: Explain the research project, answer any questions, get the consent of the participants, have an opening conversation.
- Meeting 2: Meet with a group from your own Church to read the Biblical text and discuss it.

- Meeting 3: Meet with the larger group to read and discuss the Biblical text.
- Meeting 4: Meet with the larger group again to read and discuss the Biblical text.
- Meeting 5: Meet to discuss the experience of the participants and process that was followed, discuss the initial findings of the process, thanks and wrap up.

All of the meetings will take place in Somerset West and the meeting times will be negotiated with the group to find the most convenient time to accommodate the largest number of participants.

Before each meeting the participants will be asked to read a prescribed text from the Bible (Matthew 18.15-35). The participants will be required to participate in the group discussion, sharing their views, and understanding of the text. The discussions will be recorded using an audio recorder and transcribed for analysis at a later stage.

3. POTENTIAL RISKS AND DISCOMFORTS

The research process does not foresee any significant risks or discomfort for the participants.

Naturally, each of the participants will need to make a sacrifice of time to participate in the conversation and focus group meetings. It is also possible that the participant may experience some discomfort in engaging with the views and opinions of others around their understanding of the Biblical text. While it is highly unlikely, it is possible that there could be some conflict of values and opinions among the participants that could lead to differences of opinion and even conflict.

The facilitator will do everything within his power to accommodate time constraints and availability among the participants. The group interactions are carefully constructed and will take every precaution to avoid any possible conflict between participating members.

4. POTENTIAL BENEFITS TO SUBJECTS AND/OR TO SOCIETY

The outcome of this research will be of benefit to the two communities from which the participants come. First, the outcome of the research offers carefully considered theological reflection on the perspectives of the various participants. This theological knowledge will allow greater understanding of theological diversity among the participants. Second, there is a possibility for the participants to be personally enriched in their perspectives and views from the perspectives and insights in the broader group.

Furthermore, the research aims to make a contribution to the broader academic discourse and the academic discourse in South Africa in particular. The research data will be carefully considered, interpreted and presented in a manner that will enrich both theology and practice in the broader context and the South African context.

Finally, the primary researcher, Dr. Dion Forster, will gain the benefit of necessary data and information that can be used in the completion of his PhD research project at Radboud University. It is expected that this research will add novel theological insights to the general academic discourse, it is envisioned that both the methodology and content of the research process will be of value to academic theological scholarship.

5. PAYMENT FOR PARTICIPATION

This research is voluntary. No payment is offered to the research participants for participating in the research project.

6. CONFIDENTIALITY

Any information that is obtained in connection with this study and that can be identified with you will remain confidential and will be disclosed only with your permission or as required by law. Confidentiality will be maintained by means of the anonymizing the information gained from all participants through the use of generic naming conventions accepted in the academy (for example, Participant 1, Participant 2 etc.).

The proceedings of the conversation and focus group meetings will be recorded on a secure audio recording device. The audio recordings will be stored on a password protected and encrypted hard drive that is not connected to the internet. The original recordings will be deleted from the audio recorder upon transfer to the secure hard drive. No person or institution, other than the primary researcher (Dr. Dion Forster) will be able to access the recordings. Upon successful completion of the research project the original recordings will be deleted from the secure hard drives.

The recordings will be transcribed and anonymized by the primary researcher for purposes of analysis and interpretation. The outcome of this process will be presented in a formal academic dissertation for the degree of Doctor of Philosophy (which complies with the ethical research standards set by Radboud University). The process of anonymizing the data for use in the dissertation will ensure that the identity of the participants will not be compromised in any way. The participants will be listed in any published material using generic naming conventions accepted in the academy (for example, Participant 1, Participant 2 etc.)

7. PARTICIPATION AND WITHDRAWAL

You can choose whether to participate in this study or not. If you volunteer to participate in this study, you may withdraw at any time without consequences of any kind. You may also refuse to answer any questions you don't want to answer and still remain in the study. The investigator may withdraw you from this research if circumstances arise which warrant doing so. You may be asked to withdraw from the project if you are unable to attend / participate in the conversation or focus group meetings, or if you are involved in any behaviour that is harmful to the rights and safety of the other participants or the primary researcher. In such a case the primary researcher will not require your consent to withdraw you from participation in the research project.

8. IDENTIFICATION OF INVESTIGATOR

If you have any questions or concerns about the research, please feel free to contact:

Dr. Dion Forster
Email: dionforster@sun.ac.za
Telephone: 083#######

9. RIGHTS OF RESEARCH SUBJECTS

You may withdraw your consent at any time and discontinue participation without penalty. You are not waiving any legal claims, rights or remedies because of your participation in this research study. If you have questions regarding research ethics you can contact Margret van Beuningen (secretary Ethics Assessment Committee (EAC) of the Faculty of Arts and the Faculty of Philosophy, Theology and Religious Studies), m.vanbeuningen@let.ru.nl or 024-3615814.

SIGNATURE OF RESEARCH SUBJECT OR LEGAL REPRESENTATIVE

The information above was described to me by Dr. Dion Forster in English and I am in command of this language or it was satisfactorily translated to me. I was given the opportunity to ask questions and these questions were answered to my satisfaction.

I hereby consent voluntarily to participate in this study.

I have been given a copy of this form.

_____

Name of Subject/Participant

_____   _____

Signature of Subject   Date

SIGNATURE OF INVESTIGATOR

I declare that I explained the information given in this document to _____. She / He was encouraged and given ample time to ask me any questions. This conversation was conducted in English.

_____   _____

Signature of Investigator   Date

APPENDIX C

CONFIRMATION OF ETHICAL CLEARANCE FROM RADBOUD UNIVERSITY

Ethics Assessment Committee Humanities

Faculty of Arts and Faculty of
Philosophy, Theology and Religious
Studies

Erasmusplein1
6500 HD Nijmegen
The Netherlands

Telephone +31 (0)24 3615814

www.ru.nl/eac-humanities

dr. D.A. Forster
Radboud University
Faculty of Philosophy, Theology and Religious Studies
Erasmusplein 1
6525 HT NIJMEGEN

Our reference	Your reference	Telephone	Date
	Let/MvB15U.013372		September 16, 2015
Subject		E-mail	
ethical approval		m.vanbeuningen@let.ru.nl	

Dear Mr. Forster,

I hereby inform you that the Ethics Assessment Committee of the Faculty of Arts and the Faculty of Philosophy, Theology and Religious Studies (EAC) has evaluated the application of the research project *The (Im)possibility of forgiveness: An AQAL approach to forgiveness in a racially divided Church using an intergroup contact theory approach to reading Matthew 18.15-35 (application 4954)* on September 8, 2015 and has formulated the following advice:

This research project is approved for a period of five years. Please note that any modification to the research project that might warrant review of the ethical approval must be submitted to the EAC.

Yours Sincerely,

dr. M.J.Becker

Acting Chair of the Ethics Assessment Committee Humanities
Faculty of Arts and Faculty of Philosophy, Theology and Religious Studies

Radboud Universiteit

APPENDIX D

INTERRATER RELIABILITY CALCULATION OF COHEN'S KAPPA

The following formula for calculating Cohen's Kappa was used:

$$Kappa = \frac{(Observed\ Agreement - Expected\ Agreement)}{1 - Expected\ Agreement}$$

The interrater reliability score, calculated according to Cohen's kappa, delivered the following scores.

Interraters	Calculation of Kappa
R3 and R1	0,73
R3 and R2	0,68
R1 and R2	0,68

R3 and R1

		R3				
		0	1			
R1	0	2	1	3	13,0%	6,52%
	1	3	17	20	87,0%	43,48%
		5	18	23		
		21,7%	78,3%			

k=(Pr(a) - Pr(e)/(1-Pr(e))

Pr(a)	0,83
Pr(e)	0,35
k	0,73

0=not agreed
1=agreed

R3 and R1   Kappa = 0,73

R3 and R2

		R3				
		0	1			
R2	0	3	4	7	30,4%	15,22%
	1	1	15	16	69,6%	34,78%
		4	19	23		
		17,4%	82,6%			

k=(Pr(a) - Pr(e)/(1-Pr(e))

Pr(a)	0,78		0=not agreed
Pr(e)	0,31		1=agreed
k	0,68		

R3 and R2   0,68

R1 and R2

		R1				
		0	1			
R2	0	2	5	7	30,4%	15,22%
	1	0	16	16	69,6%	34,78%
		2	21	23		
		8,7%	91,3%			

k=(Pr(a) - Pr(e)/(1-Pr(e))

Pr(a)	0,78		0=not agreed
Pr(e)	0,33		1=agreed
k	0,68		

R1 and R2   0,68